Studies in the Economies of East and Southeast Asia

General Editor: **Peter Nolan**, Sinyi Professor of Chinese Management, Judge Institute of Management Studies, University of Cambridge, and Fellow of Jesus College, Cambridge, England; and **Malcolm Falkus**, Professor of Economic History, University of New England, Armidale, New South Wales, Australia

In the last decades of the twentieth century the small and medium-sized nations of East and Southeast Asia have begun a process of potentially enormous political and economic transformation. Explosive growth has occurred already in many parts of the region, and the more slowly growing countries are attempting to emulate this vanguard group. The impact of the region upon the world economy has increased rapidly and is likely to continue to do so in the future.

In order to understand better economic developments within this vast and diverse region, this series aims to publish books on both contemporary and historical issues. It includes works both by Western scholars and by economists from countries within the region.

Titles include:

Rajeswary Ampalavanar Brown
CHINESE BIG BUSINESS AND THE WEALTH OF ASIAN NATIONS

John Butcher and Howard Dick (*editors*)
THE RISE AND FALL OF REVENUE FARMING

Mark Cleary and Shuang Yann Wong
OIL, ECONOMIC DEVELOPMENT AND DIVERSIFICATION IN BRUNEI DARUSSALAM

Pierre van der Eng
AGRICULTURAL GROWTH IN INDONESIA

Amarjit Kaur
ECONOMIC CHANGE IN EAST MALAYSIA
Sabah and Sarawak since 1850

Amarjit Kaur and Ian Metcalfe (*editors*)
THE SHAPING OF MALAYSIA

Paul H. Kratoska (*editor*)
FOOD SUPPLIES AND THE JAPANESE OCCUPATION IN SOUTH-EAST ASIA

Ryōshin Minami, Kwan S. Kim and Malcolm Falkus (*editors*)
GROWTH, DISTRIBUTION AND POLITICAL CHANGE
Asia and the Wider World

Jonathan Pincus
CLASS, POWER AND AGRARIAN CHANGE

Rajah Rasiah
FOREIGN CAPITAL AND INDUSTRIALIZATION IN MALAYSIA

Anthony Reid (editor)
THE LAST STAND OF ASIAN AUTONOMIES
Responses to Modernity in the Diverse States of Southeast Asia and Korea,
1750–1900

Studies in the Economies of East and South-East Asia
Series Standing Order ISBN 0–333–71499–7
(outside North America only)

You can receive future titles in this series as they are published by placing a standing order.
Please contact your bookseller or, in case of difficulty, write to us at the address below with
your name and address, the title of the series and the ISBN quoted above.

Customer Services Department, Macmillan Distribution Ltd, Houndmills, Basingstoke,
Hampshire RG21 6XS, England

Chinese Big Business and the Wealth of Asian Nations

Rajeswary Ampalavanar Brown
Lecturer in Asia-Pacific History and Management
Royal Holloway, University of London

First published 2000 by
PALGRAVE
Houndmills, Basingstoke, Hampshire RG21 6XS and
175 Fifth Avenue, New York, N.Y. 10010
Companies and representatives throughout the world

PALGRAVE is the new global academic imprint of
St. Martin's Press LLC Scholarly and Reference Division and
Palgrave Publishers Ltd (formerly Macmillan Press Ltd).

ISBN 0–333–75344–5

This book is printed on paper suitable for recycling and made from fully managed and sustained forest sources.

A catalogue record for this book is available from the British Library.

Library of Congress Cataloging-in-Publication Data
Brown, Rajeswary Ampalavanar, 1943–
     Chinese big business and the wealth of Asian nations / Rajeswary Ampalavanar Brown.
     p. cm.
     Includes bibliographical references and index.
     ISBN 0–333–75344–5
     1. International business enterprises—Asia, Southeastern. 2. Corporations, Chinese—Asia, Southeastern. 3. Business networks—Asia, Southeastern. 4. Capitalists and financiers—Asia, Southeastern. 5. Chinese—Asia, Southeastern. 6. Wealth—Asia, Southeastern. 7. Asia, Southeastern—Economic conditions. I. Title.
     HD2901 .B76 2000
     338.8'8951059—dc21
                                             00–033329

10   9   8   7   6   5   4   3   2   1
09   08   07   06   05   04   03   02   01   00

Printed and bound in Great Britain by
Antony Rowe Ltd, Chippenham, Wiltshire

*With love for **Ian, Andrew** and **Ali** and in loving and precious memory of my father **Ampalavanar** and my mother* **Chellamah**

Contents

List of Tables

List of Figures

List of Abbreviations

ABM	Asian Bond Market
ADM	Asian Dollar Market
ASEAN	Association of Southeast Asian Nations
BCA	Bank of Central Asia
CDL	City Developments Ltd
CP	Charoen Pokphand
DBS	Development Bank of Singapore
FEO	Far East Organisation
F & N	Fraser & Neave
FPH	First Pacific Holdings
GDP	Gross Domestic Product
GNP	Gross National Product
HDB	Housing Development Board
HLF	Hong Leong Finance
HSBC	Hongkong and Shanghai Banking Corporation
MNE	Multinational Enterprises
MRT	Mass Rapid Transit (System)
MTR (Hong Kong)	Mass Transit Railway
NEP	New Economic Policy
NHM	Nederlandsche Handel Maatschappij (Netherlands Trading Co.)
NTT	Nippon Telegraph & Telephone
OCBC	Overseas Chinese Banking Corporation
OPH	Orchard Parade Holdings
OTTH	Orient Telecom & Technology Holdings
OUB	Overseas Union Bank
PPB	Perlis Plantations Bhd
R&D	Research and Development
TQC	Total Quality Control
UMNO	United Malay National Organisation
UOB	United Overseas Bank
USB	United Savings Bank
YHS	Yeo Hiap Seng

Acknowledgements

My family and friends have contributed to this book from beginning to end. Ian, Andrew and Ali through critical reading and staunch encouragement have earned the dedication of this book.

Professor Malcolm Falkus was an indispensable source of critical insights and advice. I am also grateful to Geoffrey Jones for all his intellectual support for many years. The other great contribution to this book was made by Andrew Brown and Sara Carneiro Soares, who assisted with the tables in the manuscript. My sisters Mages, Cheeni, Yoges, and Nir, and my brother, Jeyaratna, have supported me with their encouragement. Joy Hemmings-Lewis assisted in innumerable ways. Her wisdom and encouragement were a source of continuing strength. Friends, Ivy Lim, Tommy Lee (Singapore), Choi Chi Cheung, Cheng Yui Tat, Sun Wen Bin (Hong Kong) Wu Wei Ping (Beijing), Kullada Mead, Pannaradee and Phaisoot of Bangkok, diligently collected materials for me. I owe an enormous debt to them. They were generous with their time as well as with money, frequently collecting documents and paying for them. I am also immencely indebted to Keith Povey for his patient and skilful editorial assistance.

The project also benefited from funding by the British Academy Committee for South-East Asian Studies. The ESRC funded research trips to Asia. This financial support enabled me to cover China as well as Southeast Asia. I must also thank my Bank Manager, Peter Houghton of Lloyds Bank, Hitchin. Throughout the three years he permitted me to secure personal loans to cover research expenses.

Finally, although friends and family saved me from many errors, those remaining are entirely my own fault.

Hitchin, Hertfordshire RAJ BROWN

1
Introduction

This study is concerned with Chinese business in the Association of Southeast Asian Nations (ASEAN) countries of Malaysia, Singapore, Thailand, Indonesia and the Philippines. To identify the Chinese in the ASEAN region is not simple; many 'Chinese' are, in fact, racially mixed. Some have adopted local names, and many speak the local language rather than a Chinese dialect. In addition, there are the complications of residence and nationality. Almost all Chinese in Southeast Asia possess a Southeast Asian nationality, reflecting their country of residence, yet they also often operate from China or Hong Kong in accordance with their long-term origins. Moreover, the overseas Chinese are not a homogeneous group, but split, for example, into the Hokkien, Teochiu, Cantonese and Hakka language groups. The Chinese immigrants to Southeast Asia largely come from China's south east coast and the adjacent inland provinces of Fujian, Guangdong, Kwangsi, Hunan and Kiangsi. The majority of Chinese in Southeast Asia are the descendants of the most recent waves of migration, which began in the late nineteenth century. The major Chinese business families discussed in this volume are also descendants of the later waves of migration.

An early migration of Chinese to Southeast Asia took place in the fourteenth and fifteenth centuries and principally involved merchants seeking tribute for the Emperor. Some merchants settled in the region and married local women. The 'babas' in the Straits Settlements – Singapore, Penang, Melaka – were descendants of this early migration. The second major wave of migration took place in the late eighteenth and early nineteenth century, and mainly involved skilled artisans, miners and traders – represented in the Hakkas in the gold mines in West Borneo, the Hokkiens in the Philippines and Java, and the

Teochius in Thailand. Many of these migrants also inter-married on a large scale.

The third wave of migration – from the middle of the nineteenth century – was a migration of unskilled labour. Many went to Canada, California and Australia to work in gold mines and railway construction. Others went to Southeast Asia, working on plantations, in tin mines, in railway construction and in dock labouring. The migrants to Southeast Asia often began as temporary migrants, committing themselves to a number of short-term labour contracts, before settling permanently in the region. In time, they formed clearly defined communities in their new land, to advance their social, economic and political interests; they were predominantly urban, although some rural Chinese communities survived. Permanent settlements existed alongside the maintenance of ties with the Chinese mainland – with villages and lineages – through remittances and visits. Over time, however, and under local political pressures, the Chinese in Southeast Asia became increasingly assimilated – or if not assimilated, at least an integral component within the local political, economic and social structures. The communist take-over of China in 1949, which cut off further emigration and greatly diminished the attractions of return to the home village, encouraged greater assimilation. No longer replenished by further immigration from China, the Chinese in Southeast Asia sought greater integration with, or a more structured place within, the local societies. In many cases, this implied closer associations with local politicians and government officials.

The Chinese migrated from specific parts of China and, consequently, dialect became an important identification in Southeast Asia. In Thailand, the Teochius dominated but there were also Hakka and Hainanese. In Malaysia, one-third of the Chinese was Hokkien, although there were also significant communities of Cantonese and Hakkas. In Singapore, Indonesia, and the Philippines, Hokkiens were the major dialect group.

The numerical importance of the Chinese in the Southeast Asian countries is almost impossible to define because of the extensive assimilation. The Chinese perhaps form around 3 per cent of the total population of Indonesia. The Chinese in Indonesia are divided into two groups, the assimilated pernakans and the unassimilated, Chinese-speaking, *totok*.

The major Chinese capitalists in Indonesia come from a variety of backgrounds. Liem Sioe Liong (Sudono Salim), who became powerful through his links with Soeharto, is a *totok* Hokchia from Fuqing.

Prajogo Pangetsu is a *totok* Hakka, while William Soerayadjaya (Tjia Kian Liong) is a *pernakan* Christian. In Malaysia, which has seen very limited assimilation, the Chinese now form just over 30 per cent of the population. In the Philippines and, in particular, Thailand, where the Chinese are highly assimilated, it makes little sense to put a figure on the percentage of the population that is 'Chinese'.

Across Southeast Asia, the economic power of the Chinese far outstrips their numbers. In Indonesia, Chinese business accounts for 73 per cent of the market capitalisation of all listed companies. In addition, the Chinese have major holdings in government and foreign companies operating in Indonesia. In the Philippines, Chinese corporations account for 50 per cent of the market capitalisation of listed companies, in Malaysia, 60 per cent, in Singapore, 81 per cent, and in Thailand, 90 per cent.[1] The use of the market capitalisation of listed companies as a measure of the economic power of the Chinese in Southeast Asia is not without its difficulties. Firstly, the listing of a company is simply a device to secure additional capital, and therefore may not reflect the economic importance of the company. Secondly, Chinese economic activities are extremely diverse – ranging from itinerant trading in far-flung provinces to corporate dealing in the commercial powerhouses of Asia, Europe and the United States. Not all these activities will be caught by stock market listings. The Chinese commercial 'community' is fractured by family, lineage, dialect, regional and political considerations, making it dangerous to speak of the collective economic power of the Chinese in the Asia-Pacific region.

Much of the existing literature on Chinese business has emphasised Chinese culture and ethnicity as the core elements in entrepreneurial success. Attention is directed towards the family, the dialect group and the Confucian value system.[2] With respect to the latter, the orthodox view is that social trust, the social obligations that bind family and lineage, is strengthened by Confucian belief and that this is the bedrock of commercial networking. Confucianism, it is argued, also places loyalty to the state and bureaucracy above personal interest; it therefore explains the close relationship between the Chinese capitalist and the state's functionaries. This approach ignores the relationship between culture and physical environment, and the ways in which institutions are embedded not only in culture but also in their historical experiences and the economic changes wrought by history.

There is a wide secondary literature that is relevant to the question of Chinese business in Southeast Asia and how it was organised. The transactions cost theory originating from Coase seeks to demonstrate that transaction costs in the market (which include discovering relevant prices and arranging contracts for market transaction) could lead to firms internalising costs through the vertical and horizontal integration of their functions or through exploiting networks.[3] Use of the transaction cost theory by historians of Chinese business needs refinement and adjustment; in particular, there should be emphasis on how Chinese firms integrate through networking not just through vertical integration.

Theories on entrepreneurship are also relevant to this study. Casson, for example, sees entrepreneurs as extraordinary innovators, and argues that the amount and quality of entrepreneurship differs between countries for complex social, economic and ideological reasons.[4] We need to construct a specific theory of entrepreneurship that will help us to understand why such risk-taking entrepreneurs abound in Chinese society, whether in Southeast Asia or China itself. The culture of total risk, symbolised in the 'Hong' of the nineteenth century, was perhaps particularly influential and enduring.[5]

Chandler's thinking on business organisation should also be considered when analysing the Chinese firm.[6] In *Strategy and Structure,* Chandler argues that the success of a business depends upon the organisational form of the firm. The multi-divisional structure has a corporate headquarters and a number of product or geographical divisions. The headquarters determine long-term strategies for the entire firm, and allocate and monitor resources. Chandler's corporate structures and management hierarchies have serious limitations for the Chinese family firm because the personality of the patriarch has a dominant influence that often undermines any form of corporate hierarchy. The role of government and foreign investment are also central to understanding the evolution of Chinese business. The development of Chinese companies in Southeast Asia are rooted in the region, making the thematic structure of this book, which analyses company development in the context of the one core industry in which they are located, more valuable than simply constructing a business biography of each large company. The historical context helps refine and devise a more sophisticated understanding of the growth, responses, and attitudes of these big Chinese business groups.

The emphasis on economic and business institutions brings us to the contributions of the institutional economists. Within the institutional fold, Yoshihara, Robison, and MacIntyre, among others, emphasise one trait in Chinese entrepreneurs – their close relationship with the state.[7]

Even revisionists like McVey reinterpreted and advanced Chinese entrepreneurs as the main promoters of economic potential in Southeast Asia, but still significantly assisted by the state and the influx of foreign capital.[8] McVey sees linkages to rural communities and rural investments, allowing more diverse political–economic relations than simply ties with central government.

Yoshihara and Robison saw Chinese capitalists in Southeast Asia as rent-seekers, a capitalist class dependent on the state and foreign capital. McVey rejected this scepticism and traced the evolution of the Chinese entrepreneur from 'pariah to paragon', with indigenous actors evolving from 'parasites to promoters' and the state from 'incubus to incubator'. McVey's dramatic theoretical shift led her to pronounce that the bureaucratic state in Southeast Asia was now able to exploit foreign direct investment and Chinese entrepreneurs to accelerate economic growth. McVey perceived rapidly expanding private enterprise and the growing provincial middle class as introducing local pressures on the bureaucratic apparatus to develop a more pervasive capitalism. The new 'economic miracle' of the 1980s and 1990s was assembled by these various actors, which McVey celebrated as a source of strength. Chinese business is thus described by McVey as a product of diverse domestic economies and a reflection of capital and labour advantages, and also a product of international economic changes, in particular involving Japan and the complex of political relations in Southeast Asia since the late 1960s.

This study takes the debate on Chinese business a step further, showing that while Chinese capitalists were a large factor in Southeast Asia's economic success, their institutional make-up bore the seeds of economic collapse. The organisational fault line was where family and business overlapped; the heavy reliance on the family was fatal in some cases. Above all, it was the Chinese attitude to finance that lay at the heart of the problem. Capital was pursued at the expense of risk appraisal. The guarantees provided by the state and foreign multinationals encouraged further recklessness, with bankruptcy apparently holding only a vague meaning. Fraud arose from the lack of distinction between family and business resources, and the resources of the state. The failure to invest in long-term innovation and technologies increased instability and indifference to the need for competitive behaviour. Restructuring was often undertaken to strengthen the hold of the family rather than in response to market changes and innovation. Such institutional aspects of capitalist growth determined survival. The 1997 financial crisis has forced a stringent reappraisal. New competitors, more considered forms of financial accumulation, transparency in business dealings, and the introduction of non-family members into executive and controlling positions will assist in forming the basis of a successful future.

This book attempts to locate Chinese business growth in its institutional structures, exploring that growth through an examination of specific industrial and commercial sectors – banking, textiles, land dealing, telecommunications and food manufacturing. Chinese business growth is considered in its institutional context – the relationship of Chinese firms (as intermediaries) with other capitalist groups. Chinese business is also placed in the context of the extraordinary economic transition of the Asia-Pacific region in the decades since 1945.

The major institution within Chinese business has been the family. The family was the source of funds, contacts and managers. The primacy of the family has been maintained in recent decades, despite rapid diversification and international expansion. In many cases, the Chinese firm had no distinct existence outside the family. The founder–patriarch usually dominated for as long as he lived. The structure of Chinese business did not radically alter, largely because of family domination. Over time, there was greater use of professional managers, yet equity, control and decision-making remained within the family. While adapting to economic and political pressures and opportunities to create more sophisticated business structures, the family's control remained undiluted. The core of the business remained the family, even as minority equity and peripheral control fell to outsiders – indigenous political and military élites and professional managers. Through interlocking share ownership and interlocking directorates, family control held, even as the business expanded and diversified. Expansion also came through joint ventures with foreign capital, particularly in capital-intensive sectors, again without threatening the family's dominant position.

Wong Sui-Lun has suggested that the life cycle of the Chinese firm has four phases – emergent, centralised, segmented and disintegrative.[9] The first two phases cover the growth of the firm, the third and fourth cover the death of the founding patriarch, the division of the inheritance, and then decline. The practice of equal inheritance and the widespread existence of polygamy resulted in a splintering of the family assets. An important example of the ways in which the long-term survival of a corporation can come under threat as a result of the divisions of inheritance was provided by the death of Chin Sophonpanich of the Bangkok Bank in 1988. A bitter dispute between seven heirs was brought to an end only when Chatri Sophonpanich clambered to the top of the pile.[10] Chinese inheritance can be further complicated by local law. Oei Tiong Ham in Indonesia attempted to pass on his business to his sons, cutting out his daughters, but this was not permitted under Dutch colonial law, and he was forced to relocate to Singapore, where English law permitted him to ignore his female offspring.

From the fourteenth century, Chinese capitalism in Southeast Asia was shaped by local conditions. In the earliest period, the vigour of Chinese traders arose from the fact that Southeast Asia's rulers favoured foreign over local merchants because the latter might pose a political threat. The Chinese came to command the region's commercial centres, while indigenous traders were relegated to the hinterland. At the same time, the major local trading communities – Malays, Bugis, Javanese and Filipino – flourished until the mid-seventeenth century. A. J. Reid has identified a seventeenth-century crisis in Southeast Asia arising from a contraction in world trade.[11] The crisis, and the first major intrusions of Western commerce into the region, strengthened the commercial position of the Chinese, for they reinvented themselves as intermediaries for an expanding commerce with the West. This period saw the spectacular emergence of Chinese capitalism in Southeast Asia.

During the age of high colonialism in Southeast Asia, the Chinese became crucial for the collection of state revenues in their position as revenue farmers across the region. Here, the Chinese occupied an ambiguous position, as they balanced their own pursuit of wealth with the need to satisfy the colonial state's demand for revenues. The ambiguity was oft repeated – for the Chinese in Southeast Asia, autonomy and dependence continually co-exist. The seventeenth-century crisis also produced an important divide, in that it eroded the strength and networks of the indigenous trading communities. Henceforth, the *pribumi* and *bumiputera* (indigenous people) felt threatened by the Chinese presence. That fear has continued to determine the relative positions of Chinese and indigenous capitalism in the region through to the present.

From the mid-nineteenth century, Southeast Asia emerged as a major primary exporting region, producing rice, teak, tin, rubber, petroleum and a host of other commodities. To a large degree, alien commercial communities, European, Chinese, Indian and Japanese, commanded this growth. Indigenous capitalists were largely excluded. Growth slowed during the inter-war depression and reversed during the Second

World War, but was then strongly resumed. In the pre-war period, growth was driven by the expansion of agricultural production and trade.

The economic reconstruction of Southeast Asia after 1945 involved attempts to indigenise wealth and reduce foreign influence. For example, there was clear discrimination in the state's economic management in Indonesia and Malaysia against the Chinese, and in Burma against the Indians. But the truth was that rapid economic growth and structural transformation relied heavily on the Chinese capitalist. This was the case even where the state emerged as a major economic player, for often the state was forced to seek alliances with Chinese economic power. State corporations – either public utilities or industrial enterprises – commonly involved Chinese sub-contractors. The attempts to exclude western – previously colonial – capital also greatly increased the opportunities for the Chinese. Chinese businessmen were central to economic reconstruction after 1945, the early attempts at import-substitution industrialisation, and to the export-led industrialisation from the 1960s. Even when there was sharp discrimination against the Chinese, as in Indonesia in the mid-1960s, the victim was more often the little trader than the tycoon. Paradoxically, the Chinese rode on the back of strident economic nationalism.

The alliances between the state and Chinese capitalists were secured through licensing arrangements, tariff protection, exchange controls and the provision of subsidised credit. Competition was eschewed and oligopoly favoured. Even in Singapore, oligopolistic state capital was dominant, at least until the privatisation of utilities and corporations in the 1990s. However, privatisation also strengthened the commercial and economic power of Chinese capital, as it was the major purchaser of sold-off state interests.

The macroeconomic growth of Southeast Asia is important in giving a context to the history of the development of Chinese capitalism in the region. Agricultural growth, industrialisation, levels of foreign direct investment, technology and competition affected the organisational forms of Chinese business and its partners. In the late 1930s, agricultural output accounted for more than half the national product in the major countries of Southeast Asia – Thailand and Indonesia. By 1960 the agricultural share of Gross Domestic Product (GDP) in Southeast Asia declined, and by 1988 the agricultural share was less than a quarter in Thailand, Indonesia, Malaysia and the Philippines. The share of manufacturing in GDP in Malaysia rose from 9 per cent in 1965 to 32 per cent in 1990, in Indonesia, from 8 per cent to 20 per cent, and in Thailand, from 14 per cent to 26 per cent. The manufacturing sector accounted for 69 per cent of total export value in Thailand in 1989.[12] With the heavy influx of foreign capital from the 1970s, the expansion of manufacturing output came as much from capital investment as improvements in total factor productivity.

The second important feature of the Southeast Asian economy was the changing level of foreign direct investment in industry. Foreign direct investment from USA and Japan grew at an average rate of 21 per cent per annum between 1970 and 1982, and accelerated further after 1986, reflecting increased intra-regional trade and the intra-regional division of labour pursued by foreign multinationals. The portfolio element of foreign investment increased dramatically after 1989, exacerbating the pockets of instability in the Southeast Asian region. Japan peaked as the major capital supplier in Southeast Asia in 1989 and declined sharply from 1992 onwards. These developments led to rising GDP in the four major ASEAN countries, where from the base year 1960 the index of real per capita GDP rose from 119 in 1970 to 232 in 1985.[13] The 1990s saw a slight contraction in growth, when Indonesia had the rate of growth of real GDP decline from 9 per cent in 1990 to 5 per cent in 1997. Thailand fell from a growth of 11.7 per cent (1990) to minus 0.4 per cent in 1997.[14]

Foreign economic interests were powerful in Southeast Asia despite the rise of the state–Chinese axis. The United States was particularly important in Indonesia, the Philippines and Thailand. Between 1970 and 1975, Thailand received US$650 million in economic aid, US$1 billion in military assistance and US$1 billion for operating costs.[15] American aid to Indonesia came after the political crisis of the mid-1960s, which saw the eclipse of the communists. In all three countries, there were also major inflows of American private investment.[16]

Japan was also crucial, particularly from the 1970s, when the restructuring of Japanese industry led to the relocation of manufacturing to Southeast Asia. Japanese ties with local Chinese capitalists went back to the 1930s, had been greatly strengthened during the years of Japan's occupation of the region, and were maintained from the late 1940s through to the early 1960s during the years of Western decolonisation. European and Middle Eastern investors were also important after the oil crisis of the early 1970s; a number of alliances were struck between Chinese capitalists and Arab oil partners eager to invest in a rapidly expanding Southeast Asia.

The heavy influx of foreign capital was closely tied in with the relocation of manufacturing, notably in electronics, car assembly and textiles, from the industrial cores of Japan, the United States, and Europe to Southeast Asia. This was a process encouraged by the imposition of trade restrictions on Japan, Hong Kong, Korea and Taiwan, and involved the integration of the capital-intensive manufacturing sectors of the industrial cores with labour-intensive production within Southeast Asia. The industrial centres in Southeast Asia were highly concentrated – in Singapore, around Bangkok and along the west coast of peninsular Malaysia.

The final feature of Southeast Asia's economic transformation that should be noted is that it has involved a major extension of the region's business reach to the rest of Asia, and in particular into China. Between 1981 and 1995, trade between China and Southeast Asia increased ten-fold. At the same time, Chinese corporations in Southeast Asia began to invest heavily in China, notably in light manufacturing, property development and in infrastructure construction.

This volume is concerned with the problems of long-term growth and business cycles, focusing on a region of the world that has seen the most spectacular growth in recent decades and now a humbling collapse. I have approached the important issues of development in Southeast Asia by focusing on the growth and weaknesses of the region's capitalists, most importantly the Chinese capitalists who are usually seen as the driving force behind economic change.

This book seeks to explain the impressive growth and collapse of Southeast Asia by using a number of case-studies of Chinese corporations in various economic sectors. The central concern of development economists has been trade policies and macro-economic performance. Often micro-economic structures – of business groups – allow a much sharper analysis of growth. Firm-level studies offer a more precise view of resource (mis)allocation.

The emphasis on the private sector in economic growth has been vindicated by the Asian currency crisis of 1997, which was a private sector collapse caused by excessive investment – much of it unproductive – financed through offshore banks and multinationals. Study of the microeconomic changes within Chinese corporations located at the core of their industry exposes the deeper, institutional and technological sources of growth in a way in which theoretical or empirical economists are unable to achieve. Critical features of endogenous growth are identified, making possible an evaluation of the relative contribution of different influences and institutions attracting and using investment to promote accelerated growth.

In addition, the study of Chinese corporate development makes it possible to assess the historically determined nature of growth. Seventeenth-century Chinese merchants, linked to the mercantilist state in Southeast Asia, created state trading and state monopolies: their present-day equivalents are the huge business structures of Indonesia and Thailand, linked to state development and policies. It is easy to trace the evolution of the Chinese as wealth creators. Chinese capitalists respond to opportunities, act under constraints, and take advantage of the state, foreign capital and trading networks.

The ability of Chinese capital to drive economic change is heavily influenced by the form of corporate organisation, corporate governance, the ability to create and manage joint ventures, and relations with the state. Thus when the Southeast Asian economies – for example Singapore or Indonesia – mimic trends toward rapid industrialisation and rapid economic growth, entrepreneurial attitudes and responses are critical. These agents react to market information, creating a 'group selection mechanism' which shapes growth.[17]

Detailed study of the Chinese firm also provides a crucial insight into, for example, the impact of Japan on the Southeast Asian economies. Levels of Japanese foreign investment and technological imports differ from country to country in Southeast Asia. These differences are often explained in terms of the transfer from Japan to Southeast Asia of the less capital-intensive manufacturing processes. By focusing on the Chinese firm – the joint venture partner of the Japanese multinational – it soon becomes clear that it was often capital-intensive processes that were being relocated. That focus also shows that Japanese plants overseas frequently produce not for the Japanese market but for the Western world.

As a last example of the value of this approach, it is commonly argued that 'research spillovers' and research and development (R&D) are determined by endogenous factors, such as education, institutions and intellectual infrastructure. However, I would propose that in the case of Southeast Asia, the technology issue is further complicated by the oligopolistic nature of Chinese business and its institutional linkages with the state. Continuous innovation should be driven by competition, with the state and capitalists acting merely as catalyst. The government's role in maintaining the cartel structure of Chinese business and in absorbing risk distorts the processes of innovation.

The dependency school of the 1960s identified the causes of underdevelopment in the forces of imperialism and international business.

The experience of Southeast Asia since the 1960s – perhaps in particular in the crisis of the late 1990s – would suggest that the culprits are domestic, not foreign.

Methodology

Despite the fact that Chinese businesses in Southeast Asia are principally conglomerates, this study is organised thematically, using different industrial and commercial sectors as themes. Each corporation is discussed within a particular industry. There are various reasons for the adoption of this approach, rather than organising the book around biographies of each company. First, a thematic approach can help in understanding broader economic changes and the company's responses to these developments. For example, the study of Charoen Pokphand (CP) in the telecommunications sector illuminates Chinese business attitudes to technology transfer. Without this industrial location, the study would simply present Chinese businessmen as mimics, imitating each other by moving into any sector that offers opportunities. The more complex responses would be concealed within the rather simple pragmatic accumulation of entrepreneurial opportunities. The difference between a Kirzner type of entrepreneur and the occasional Schumpeterian entrepreneurial forays of some Chinese businessmen will not be clear in a prosaic listing of company activities without an industrial focus. Kirzner's view is that entrepreneurs are alert to opportunities and possess an ability to exploit such possibilities. Such entrepreneurship is often associated with a state of disequilibrium, and exploitation of these opportunities is part of the process towards equilibrium. Inevitably such entrepreneurs possess confidence, almost a kind of hubris when exploiting these opportunities. From a different perspective Schumpeter's entrepreneur is highly innovative and thereby disturbs the world through innovation rather than by concentrating on exploiting the existing situation. In addition Schumpeter believed that corporate growth achieved through innovation would ultimately make the entrepreneur obsolescent. Kirzner in contrast believed that large corporations would attract entrepreneurs and afford them greater scope for their skills, their alertness and confidence.[18]

An analysis of industrial changes also helps in understanding the changes in the organisation and financial structures of these corporations. The diffusion of manufacturing technology, processes, and products are then easily related to the internal changes within the corporation. This affords crucial insights into the changing nature of international competition and relations with foreign multinationals.

Since the interaction between the external environment and the internal structure of the Chinese corporation is complex, the chronology may appear chaotic. There are periods or phases of intense activity in one sector, followed by sluggish periods, making strictly chronological analysis unfeasible. For example, Robert Kuok moved from primary production in sugar to higher value added interests in transportation and the hotel industry, which involved a geographical dispersal. The regional focus thus shifts, with economic and geographical expansion. The constantly changing, dynamic nature of the growth means that the discussion cannot be strictly linear or geographically static. The developments in the region in the 1980s and 1990s are hyper-charged. Therefore the choice of company and country studied in this volume may at times appear *ad hoc*, although the size and importance of a company are consistently used as criteria for inclusion.

A sample of large Chinese corporations was selected for detailed analysis. The sample includes firms that were noted for their size, industrial importance and geographical distribution. However, there was also a need to prioritise industrial importance over geographical distribution. The choice of corporations was also determined by the availability of reasonably accurate balance sheets and other data. The following rule was adopted: only companies whose accounts were audited by reputable international accounting firms, like Price Waterhouse Coopers and Ernst and Young, were selected. When the accounts were prepared by other companies, like Jaiyos (Bangkok), then complementary accounts for these companies were sought and checked before using them. This was because of personal and family ties between Thai accounting firms and large Thai corporations.

Secondly, a serious effort was also made to collect and cross check the accounts of subsidiaries, as well as study the consolidated balance sheets of the business groups. In addition, balance sheets and profit and loss accounts for each company in a group were collected from the domestic registrar of companies, as well as from other registrars of companies abroad. For example, in the case of (CP) of Thailand, data was collected from Beijing, Shanghai, Hong Kong, Bangkok, Jakarta, New York and Taipei. This variety of business sources could provide not only verification but also substantial and valuable empirical sources.

Thirdly, the study was constructed around commercial and industrial themes, which meant that further detailed study of official and unofficial records was undertaken. The corporate business data was therefore placed in the context of reliable qualitative material, which could reveal glaring inaccuracies and discrepancies. The use of registrar of companies' files, stock exchange documents, government records, and, more significantly, bank records – clearing banks as well as merchant and investment banks – all contributed to a clearer understanding and appraisal of the performance of Chinese companies. The archives of Lloyds Bank, Midland Bank (which hold the Hongkong and Shanghai Bank (HSBC) records), the Siam Commercial Bank and the Bangkok Bank were all researched. In addition, Western merchant banks and investment and securities firms produced detailed records. All this material could be employed as a useful tool for cross checking and authenticating data.

The use of industrial and commercial sectors as themes meant that when analysing two companies in one industrial/commercial area, the falsification of records could be detected through a broad comparison with the other firm. Furthermore, the macro-economic changes in that sector would help verify the truth of the fluctuations in the business data. The micro-economic and macro-economic data were matched and compared throughout the study. For example, the activities of Kwek Leng Beng (CDL – City Developments Limited) and Ng Teng Fong (Sino-Land) in land and property development were studied together to tease out common phases of growth and check the accuracy of the data. The use of government information was also essential in this process of verification. The most used instrument for verification was bank data. Bank data included detailed information on loans, assets, and share prices. In addition, economists employed by banks often provided detailed reports on Chinese corporations, particularly before acquisitions or mergers were transacted, or for the issue of bonds, as well as for attaining large syndicated offshore loans. Ministries of finance, trade and industry throughout Asia provided reports that were used to correlate or dismiss data.

Few historians have forensic accounting skills, but a series of checks on both balance sheet finance and off balance sheet finance was undertaken. Firstly, care was taken in analysing a corporation's acquisitions and disposals, which some Chinese corporations used as a source of earnings. Secondly, off balance sheet financing, often undertaken through subsidiaries located in foreign countries, was complicated by joint venture arrangements. These were frequently omitted from the consolidated balance sheets. Such anomalies were considered when preparing the statistical material. Thirdly, the financial liberalisation of

Southeast Asia also meant increased foreign currency borrowing. Chinese corporations often financed large projects through foreign currency borrowing and used this to assume large debts that did not appear in the balance sheets. These borrowings had to be traced through bank archives, government records and newspaper reports, in order that the net debt of a company could be checked.

Fourthly, if there were significant swings in borrowing or cash in hand, they were examined in detail. Liabilities outside the normal types of borrowing, such as bonds and syndicated loans, were separated from bank overdrafts. Changes in working capital were also traced.

Fifthly, a close examination was made of any switching of assets between categories, for example of development properties being transferred to investment. Sixthly, the company records covered a minimum period of 10 years; some were from 15 to 20 years. Notes on accounting policies were examined for that period. These often held clues as to how the firm calculated depreciation changes, the market value of shares and profit margins, which often highlighted serious discrepancies. Share price manipulation was often achieved through dubious accounting. Thus share price information was included in evaluating the performance. The restructuring of companies was a strategy used when Chinese companies faced difficulties or needed capital for growth. This restructuring was also studied in relation to the business data from the balance sheets and profit and loss accounts, which could be used to detect the transfer of assets between subsidiaries.

This study was undertaken two years before the crisis. The companies studied happened to be the major survivors, which indicates that they possessed a level of prudence. The companies studied here were carefully selected for the reliability of the data on them, a trait that is further indicated by the fact that they were the survivors of the crisis. For example, Astra fared better than Salim: the appointment of A. L. Vrijberg as Astra's accountant helped to ensure greater transparency, although even under this regime, Edward Soeryadjaya (son of the founder of Astra, William Soeryadjaya) was able to use company resources to invest unwisely in property and stock markets. The indivisibility of the family and the firm remained a major flaw. The banking aspects of Salim have been examined here to illustrate this weakness.

In the case of Finance One, a major Thai financial group, a researcher working in the headquarters was employed. The researcher concluded that the general consensus suggested that although fraud occurred through leakage of funds, the most important feature was the constant revaluation of assets to exaggerate their value in order to raise offshore loans using overvalued assets as collateral. There was, therefore, a detectable logic in misrepresentation; but to brand all Chinese corporations as indulging in fake accounting is not only inaccurate but also sensationalist. CP could indulge in creative accounting just as Unilever could; but there is little logic or rationale for always practising fake accounting. Most Chinese corporations could avoid paying taxes almost with impunity and they could borrow with ease – even after the crisis, funds are still flowing in. Misleading accounting was unnecessary for certain Chinese corporations given the advantages they secured from the Southeast Asian state and from their relationships with foreign partners.

2
Chinese Business Organisation: Institutional Choice and Contingency

Family ownership has dominated the Chinese firm since the early nineteenth century. The founding family maintains ownership and control, investing equity and management in the main company and its affiliated firms. In this chapter the changes in the organisation of Chinese businesses are examined against the backdrop of the continued primacy of the family.

The role of the family is not unique to Chinese enterprise. Family domination in business has survived in most Asian and European countries; the complexity and diversity of family ownership needs to be emphasised. Family businesses are common in Europe, although nationalisation in France and Britain after 1945 disturbed this pattern. European family firms were successful in heavy industry, as with the Krupp, Siemens, Michelin, Pirelli and Peugeot corporations. In spite of nationalisation, succession crises and financial difficulties, family control persisted. Fiat Auto is still the preserve of the Agnelli brothers.

In the Chinese firm, family control has been consistent. Partners were secured from similar lineage and kinship; friends, bureaucrats and politicians were limited to non-executive, non-ownership categories. The main parent company often expanded and diversified into related and unrelated industries, including primary production, manufacturing, finance, insurance; it responded to opportunities while absorbing wholly owned subsidiaries and affiliated companies into a large diversified conglomerate, held by a holding company or a core parent company. In some of the affiliated companies, the parent company held substantial equity, in others the stake was only in the form of meagre ownership, or it was simply a joint venture. The main company and its subsidiaries and affiliated and associate companies came to be connected by multiple links, not just equity. The connections included providing managers,

17

loans, and credit, acting as guarantors and commissioning agents, selling goods and services to each other, and managing processing and manufacturing, shipping, and insurance. The management of a large multinational was highly concentrated, involving the patriarch and his sons or close relatives and lineage members. The overriding authority remained with the founder–patriarch. Managerial hierarchies did emerge from the early 1970s but largely in overseas operations rather than in the parent company. The subsidiaries and affiliated companies, which often arose to exploit new products and new markets, were sustained by multiple networks and joint ventures with foreign capital. In effect the overall organisation relied more on the diverse activities and networks linking family and lineage than on rigorous internalisation. These networks provided such firms with core information, enabling them to diversify in scale and scope. In essence they were acting like venture capitalists.

The existing theories of the firm and competition, including those of Coase, Williamson, Alchian, Chandler and Porter, provide critical perspectives for analysing the organisational structure of Chinese firms. Coase, in a pioneering article in 1937,[1] argued that firms and markets represent alternative methods of organising production. The market is a costly and inefficient arena for certain transactions that could be achieved within the firm at a lower cost. Coase explained the primary cause of growth of large enterprise in terms of his transactions cost theory. Williamson's emphasis on human and environmental conditions in determining costs is useful in identifying the historical sequences in the evolution of Chinese business in Southeast Asia.[2] The sequence of decisions and strategies that confer flexibility on the Chinese business structure deserve to be emphasised, as indicated by Williamson's theory. Chinese entrepreneurs adopt strategies that have proved successful and abandon others. The interrelationship between business structure and the historical sequence of decisions made by the firm is emphasised throughout this book. Williamson's bounded rationality and opportunities concepts are more useful than the perfect rationality in the market and profit maximisation hypotheses.

In some respects, the Chinese entrepreneur corresponds to Alchian's 'maximising agent in economic theory who could adapt to new circumstances', except that, unlike Alchian's agent, this agent is selected not by the market but by the state.[3] North also identifies the institutions that provide opportunities for the agent and institutions that determine both production and transaction costs. Changes in these institutions are historically determined – actors have limited competence in relation to the complex environment they confront. This uncertainty is reduced for Chinese capitalists through liaisons with the state and foreign capital. The risks that often prevail through unlimited expansion come from the indiscriminate use of capital. Finance is at the centre of these risks and liabilities.[4] Chandler's research on large enterprises stresses structure, organisation and the strategy of management.[5] He argues that large enterprises can be efficiently coordinated only by managerial hierarchies. While Chandler emphasises the importance of managerial capabilities in the creation of international competitiveness, for Porter the environment surrounding the firm, factors such as demand conditions, existence of related industries, corporate rivalry determine success or failure.[6]

In the period 1830–1918, Chinese family companies operated wider and wider networks through the creation of syndicates, principally in revenue farming. The intra-regional financing of revenue farming in tin, opium and gambling produced influential Chinese syndicates that came together to pool capital, labour, management and political ties. Loke Yew was part of a wealthy and powerful Chinese syndicate comprising the Loke brothers (no relation to Loke Yew), Chan Sow Lin (manager of the Selangor general farm), San Ah Peng (Pahang farm), Zhang Bhi Shih (Sumatra) and Foo Choo Choon (Perak tin mining).[7] Similarly, the Khaws used Chinese, Chettiars and Australian associates in Singapore, Penang, Bangkok, Tasmania and Sydney to finance their tin mining in Southeast Asia.[8]

Although the family remained the cornerstone of Chinese business, there were changes in the inter-war period, when some firms moved towards incorporating joint stock capital within the company. The Overseas Chinese Banking Corporation had partners and professional managers from the mid-1930s.[9] The accelerated economic growth of the Asian economy from the early 1960s, accompanied by crucial changes in international production, processing and marketing, transformed the role of the Chinese entrepreneur in Asia. Western and Japanese multinationals, eager to exploit cheap labour and the natural resources of Southeast Asia by sub-contracting, identified the Chinese as central to their interests. The major infrastructural developments of this period initiated by the state also created opportunities for Chinese capitalists, thereby forging their close relationship with the state, indigenous merchants and foreign multinationals.

Another response of Chinese business to this wealth of opportunity was to expand through mergers, acquisitions and joint ventures with the state and foreign groups and to indulge in a variety of contractual and licensing arrangements. This increasingly obviated the need for a more vigilant attitude towards technological assimilation and globalization strategies. Chinese entrepreneurs could achieve the first through joint ventures with foreign multinationals and the second through Chinese networks. Despite a more complex interaction between the various geographical, product and functional interests of the Chinese conglomerate, there was a persistent failure to create specialist divisions in marketing, international operations and R&D.

The expansion forced the Chinese multinational to delegate some operational decision-making and increase the responsibility of on-site management. At the same time, centralised decision-making and the control of vital strategic concerns remained with family members. A balance was needed between the centralised structure and the maintenance of a more flexible response to market and new technology. Various sectors of these firms felt the need for coherent local and global strategies to achieve success in subcontracting functions, as well as in marketing, co-ordinating investment, technology, training and innovation within the company.

Since 1945 Chinese business has had to restructure, respond to rapid economic growth in the region and confront the rise of aggressive state and indigenous capital, as well as competition from foreign multinationals. A more complicated business structure was an inevitable development. The core of the business remained with the family, but surrounding layers of equity were held by competing Chinese groups, as well as by state élites, indigenous businessmen and foreign multinationals, often through joint ventures. In fact the prolongation of family control was often achieved by such links with the state and foreign capital.

Despite the complex shareholding patterns that developed between the core company and the subsidiaries at home and abroad, centralised ownership and decision-making remained with the patriarch and his sons. The Chinese also exploited the holding company structure to pioneer this rapid diversification, developing new interests and increasing the scope of operations with a profusion of separate companies. From the 1960s, when Chinese companies sought to exploit the stock markets of Asia, the United States and Australia, publicly listed companies within the group were either held together through majority equity holdings by the family and its network or separately through a holding company.

The use of the holding company structure to balance conflicting interests is shown in the case of the Hong Leong Group. The Kweks established Hong Leong in Singapore in 1941. They moved from trading in the 1940s to plantation investments in the 1950s and to manufacturing in the late 1950s. They diversified into real estate and property development in the 1960s and expanded into finance and heavy infrastructural activities in the 1970s. Although they became a public-listed company in 1982, many of their component companies remained privately owned. Figures 2.1 and 2.2 show the complicated shareholding patterns that existed between parent company and its subsidiaries. Hong Leong (Malaysia) had three publicly listed companies: Hong Leong Credit, Hong Leong Industries and Hume Industries. These had interests in other listed companies: OYL Industries, Nanyang Press, Bedford, Malaysian Pacific Industries, Hong Leong Bank and Zalik Berhad. In addition, Hong Leong owned 200 other companies, with an annual revenue in 1993 of M$3.3 billion (US$1.3 billion).[10]

As well as diversifying its products, Hong Leong expanded from Singapore into Malaya from 1941, and into Hong Kong, China, Australia, the United States and the United Kingdom between 1968 and 1996. By the mid-1980s, Hong Leong had 91 subsidiaries in Singapore and 73 in Malaysia, all held together by family ownership through an intricate holding company structure. In co-ordinating and managing such a diverse enterprise, the holding company was essential. There may be not one but several holding companies, integrating separate product, regional or specialist divisions. For example, Hong Leong Company (Malaysia) was a privately held investment company registered in Kuala Lumpur, in which the Quek family of Malaysia held 46.7 per cent equity (1993) and their cousins the Kweks of Singapore held a further significant proportion.[11] The Kweks (Singapore) had a separate holding company (HLIH) whose 30 shareholders belong to these two families. A third holding company is Hong Leong Industries (Malaysia), which coordinates the manufacturing and heavy industry sectors of the group throughout Asia. The fourth holding company, Guoco Group (Hong Kong), controls the banking and financial activities of the conglomerate, supervising firms in Asia, Australia, the United Kingdom and the United States. See Figure 2.1.

The reasons for this organisational structure are mixed. For the Chinese, diversification provided revenues, reduced risks and opened new markets and sectors. The holding company was a pragmatic device to direct the operations of the separate companies, both regionally and functionally. In a Western firm, the group is consolidated externally through the holding company and internally through product organisation. The holding company, which is owned by the parent company, coordinates different subsidiaries through separate hierarchies of

22

Figure 2.1   Hong Leong Group, Malaysia, 1994

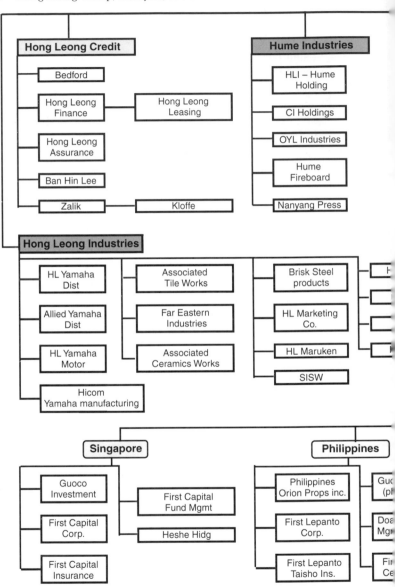

Source: *Malaysian Business*, 1 March, 1994, p. 10.

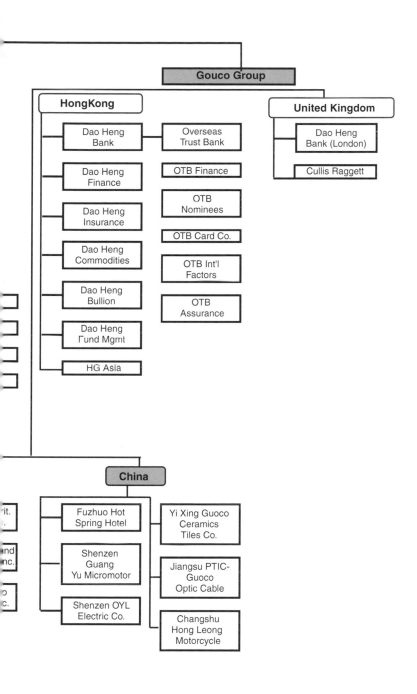

24

Figure 2.2   Hong Leong Group, Singapore, 1990

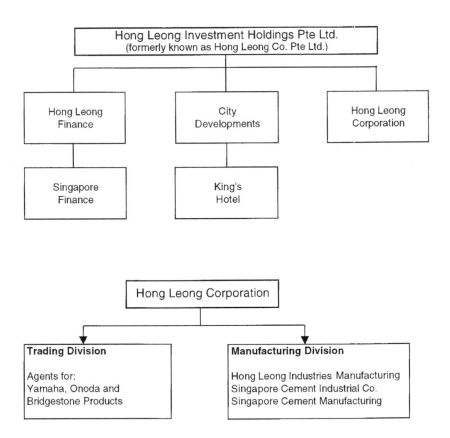

Source: Annual Report, Hong Leong Group, 1993.

control and ownership. Holding companies such as Royal Dutch/Shell and Nestlé expect their operating companies to function with considerable autonomy. Chinese holding companies have interlocking ownership and management ties. The founder's authority permeates the entire corporation through the control of investment, personnel, finance, decisions on product development, market expansion and R&D, producing a tangled web of control. Japanese multinationals refrain from the use of holding companies. They have evolved from trading companies and have developed product/function specialist companies and a multitude of related divisions linked to the core trading companies. In 1991, Hitachi had 688 subsidiaries, Mitsui had 513 and Matsushita had 340.[12] These affiliated and associated companies produce related products and supply component parts, services and finance. Financial management was critical in making this pluralism coherent. Each Japanese conglomerate had a bank-insurance company that provided financial services. The trading firm within the group co-ordinated international manoeuvres and initiated production ventures overseas, often on a joint basis. When they expanded, Japanese firms often separated sales operations from product divisions. This functional split was reproduced internationally; Hitachi had product divisions, marketing divisions and R&D. These divisions maintained cross-hierarchy organisational arrangements, which provided some cohesion between the units. Although the headquarters retained overall control over investment, personnel, finance and product development, individual units had operational autonomy

The expansion and diversification of Japanese companies was on the basis of well-developed technology, as seen with Hitachi in electronics. Diversification was often used by Chinese companies to cover problems in product quality. Furthermore, globalisation had serious pitfalls, as Jack Chia saw in Australia in the 1980s and Yeo Hiap Seng in the United States in the 1990s, demonstrating that organisational forms developed in one corporate culture cannot necessarily be transferred to another with the same effectiveness.

Japanese multinationals, having dispensed with the holding company structure, bonded with a plethora of related companies (*keiretsu*) and created a high degree of specialisation, with specialists in the product, the market, finance and banking, trading and business overseas. Horizontal networks also developed and the long-term mutual transactions between independent firms sustained Japanese multi-assembly operations overseas, particularly in the automobile and electronics industries.[13] Chinese business organisations and their networking systems are fluid and loose. Decision-making is highly centralised, with little power-sharing. The Chinese system has a distinct institutional mix, determined by the local economic environment and state policies. Chinese organisational structure is a product of its location in a highly fluid and rapidly growing set of economies.

A highly diverse corporation as Hong Leong is still controlled by a small cadre of family members drawn from Singapore and Malaysia. A brief analysis of the methods used to raise capital and finance expansion will show how capital markets in Asia, Australia and the United States and the state in Southeast Asia were used to fund dramatic growth. Hong Leong's accelerated expansion from the 1960s was often accomplished through takeovers, mergers and joint ventures with the state and foreign multinationals. In 1982, Hong Leong purchased the Dao Heng Bank in Hong Kong to integrate its financial initiatives, as well as to exploit its relationship with the Kuwait Investment Office, a shareholder in the bank, and tap into capital in the Middle East and Britain. The bid for MUI Bank in the 1990s was motivated by the latter's large cash reserves as well as its property assets and by the need to incorporate a bank in Malaysia.[14] Hong Leong paid US$370 million to Khoo Kay Peng for MUI Bank and US$250 million for MUI Finance in 1993.[15] Immediately after acquisition, MUI Bank was changed to Hong Leong Bank, listed on the stock exchange and raised US$700 million. Hong Leong Credit and the Quek family held 61 per cent equity, with *bumiputeras* holding 5.3 per cent and the Hongkong and Shanghai Bank, Chase Manhattan and Citicorp holding 15 per cent in total.[16]

The subsidiary, Hong Leong Finance (Malaysia), also increased its capitalisation from US$4 million to US$6 million in 1983 by using shares in a *bumiputera* enterprise, Beraya Sdn. Bhd.[17] Hong Leong effectively manipulated the New Economic Policy and incorporated *bumiputera* capital into the group.[18] Hong Leong Finance (Singapore) also raised its capital from US$35 million to US$80 million in 1982 by tapping into the burgeoning capital market in Singapore.[19]

The division of companies into smaller units, which gained pace in the 1980s, was an effective device for raising capital from capital markets (often through recurring share issues) and for denoting increased cross-shareholdings between companies in the group. The group also used shares of one company in the group to secure new finance. All this was achieved despite the ubiquity of the extended family, with tight blocks of equity, ownership and management vested in individual constituent parts of the family. The investment holding companies helped embrace these separate units and initiatives. In Singapore, three new investment firms were active in 1984: Kwek Hong Png Investment, Kwek Hong Hai Investment and Hong Leong Investment Holdings. This introduced a new layer of private investment companies alert to predatory moves by other Chinese capitalists. The Chinese competed with each other because they duplicated each other's interests and activities. While public listing was sought to secure increased funds, the distinction between public and private ownership was blurred through frequent company restructuring.

Even in the case of Shinawatra in Thailand, which operated in the capital-intensive industries of electronics and telecommunications, the family structure remained undisturbed. A privately held company, Shinawatra Holding had 50 per cent equity in the publicly listed company, Shinawatra Computer and Communications. Shinawatra Computer and Communications in turn had 60 per cent equity in the publicly listed company, Shinawatra Satellite, 58 per cent in Advanced Information Services, 55 per cent in International Broadcasting Corporation and 100 per cent in Shinawatra International, a private company. A range of associated companies was held by each of the publicly listed companies; these associated, affiliated and publicly listed companies all revealed Shinawatra family links through directors' equity and managers (see Figure 2.3).[20]

Ownership and control by the family persisted in the Chinese firm. Centralised decision-making and heavy reliance on one dominant executive meant that information was vested in individuals rather than exploited as an organisational resource. From the 1970s, activities rapidly spread, incorporation was instituted and some decentralisation through non-family management was introduced, but the highest echelons of management remained within the family. The biggest changes were in the creation of divisions, with budget and planning becoming dominant. The accounting system was upgraded and regular reports were produced. These changes in part arose from the fact that the non-family shareholders, stock exchanges and banks needed information. Effectively combining centralised decision-making with functional divisions and geographical dispersal was a key problem. Chinese companies needed greater power-sharing, with independent and dynamic managers responsible for areas like marketing and technology. Comparative advantage and the complementarity of separate units and subsidiaries had to be emphasised. Integration could only be achieved by a corporate team that had to be informed about the capital and budgets available,

Figure 2.3   Capital ownership structure of the Shinawatra Group, 1993

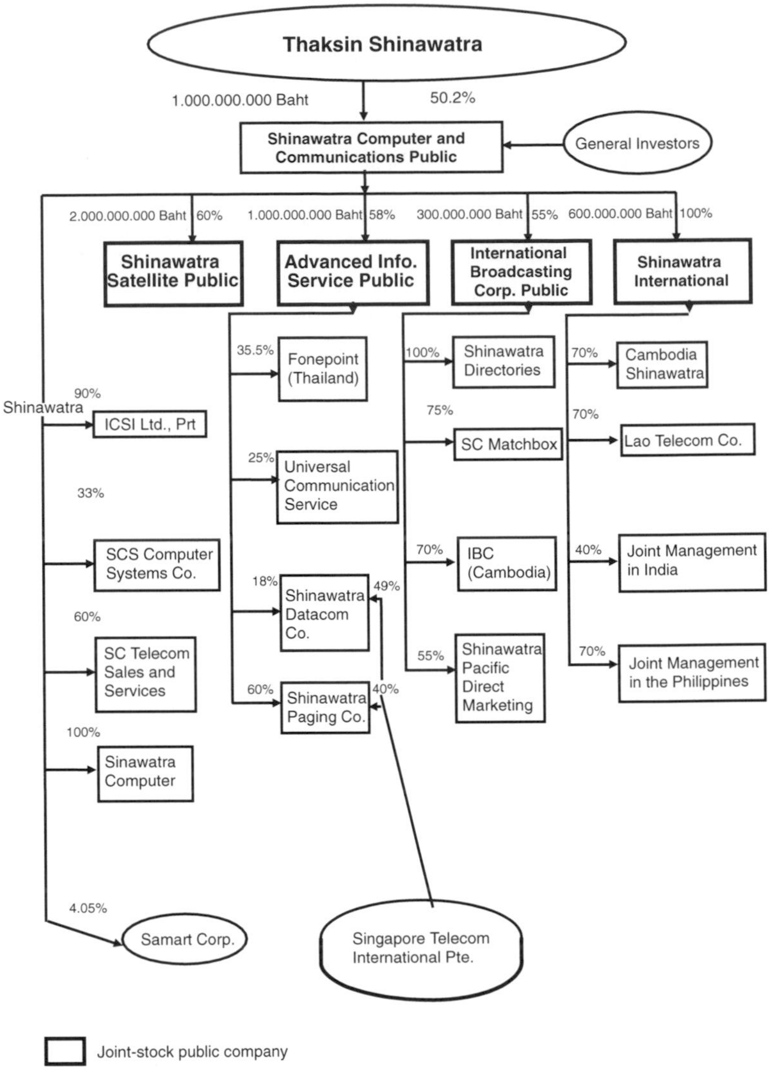

```
                    ┌─────────────────────────────────────┐
                    │         Thaksin Shinawatra          │
                    └─────────────────────────────────────┘
            1.000.000.000 Baht              50.2%
                            │
                ┌───────────────────────────┐        ┌──────────────────┐
                │ Shinawatra Computer and   │◄───────│ General Investors │
                │ Communications Public     │        └──────────────────┘
                └───────────────────────────┘

  2.000.000.000 Baht │60%   1.000.000.000 Baht│58%   300.000.000 Baht│55%   600.000.000 Baht│100%

   ┌──────────────┐   ┌──────────────┐   ┌────────────────┐   ┌──────────────┐
   │  Shinawatra  │   │ Advanced Info.│   │ International   │   │  Shinawatra  │
   │Satellite Public│ │Service Public │   │ Broadcasting   │   │ International │
   └──────────────┘   └──────────────┘   │ Corp. Public   │   └──────────────┘
                                         └────────────────┘
```

International
Broadcasting
Corp. Public

| 35.5% | Fonepoint (Thailand) | 100% | Shinawatra Directories | 70% | Cambodia Shinawatra |

90%
Shinawatra
ICSI Ltd., Prt   75%   70%
                                                  SC Matchbox   Lao Telecom Co.
33%   25%   Universal
                     Communication
                     Service

SCS Computer   70%   IBC   40%   Joint Management
Systems Co.   18%   (Cambodia)   in India
                     Shinawatra   49%
60%   Datacom
                     Co.
SC Telecom   55%   Shinawatra   70%   Joint Management
Sales and   60%   Pacific   in the Philippines
Services   Shinawatra   40%   Direct
100%   Paging Co.   Marketing
Sinawatra
Computer

4.05%

Samart Corp.   Singapore Telecom
                      International Pte.

☐   Joint-stock public company

Sources: Annual Reports 1990–1993 Shinawatra Computer and Communications Co. Ltd; Akira Suehiro, 'The Shinawatra Group Thailand's Telecommunications Industry and the Newly Rising Zaibatsu', *Asia Economies* (Japanese), 36, 2, 1995, p. 4.

sales projections, manufacturing input–output and production diversification strategies. Chinese companies needed to delegate information to teams and team managers in order to access, plan and implement programmes, yet even in the case of CP, the family still dominated its technology-intensive firms.

The centralisation of the business structure around the patriarch had serious implications for succession within the Chinese business family. The Teo family lost control of Malayan Credit in 1992 to Cycles and Carriage and Hotels Properties because of family disputes. The Yeo family also faced difficulties after the death of Yeo Thian In in 1985. These tensions were exacerbated in 1993 following losses in the United States.[21] In 1988, the Bangkok Bank Group faced a crisis with the death of Chin Sophonpanich that was finally resolved by the accession of Chatri Sophonpanich. The financial speculations of one family member could imperil an entire conglomerate. In 1993 the financial activities of Edward Soeryadjaya left P. T. Astra International (with assets of US$4 billion) facing bankruptcy; it was rescued by Toyota and Barito Pacific (Projogo Pangestu).[22]

Rapid economic growth since the 1970s has triggered predatory action among Chinese capitalists. A prominent example was Yeo Hiap Seng. The absence of a regulated and sophisticated capital market, as well as the aggressive tactics of Chinese capitalists, caused the difficulties experienced by Yeo Hiap Seng in the early 1990s when it became a target for take-over. Yeo Hiap Seng Holdings was established in 1969 to retain family control over the publicly listed company. The paid up capital was split between six families. The holding company held 40 per cent equity in the Singapore company and 35 per cent in the Malaysian company. The death of Yeo Thian In, followed by failures in the United States, placed an enormous strain on this family firm, attracting the interests of would-be buyers like Quek Leng Chan and Ng Teng Fong between 1993 and 1995 and resulting in Ng's successful takeover of the company in September 1995. Yeo Hiap Seng was still highly profitable when this hostile take-over occurred. Yeo Hiap Seng's paid-up capital between 1989 and 1994 rose from S$80 million to S$142 million, turnover rose from S$248.3 million to S$266.5 million and gross profits increased from S$7.1 million in 1990 to S$10.7 million by 1993. In 1994, profits from China alone were S$13.44 million.[23] In spite of this, the family lost control of the firm. The aggressive strategies favoured by Chinese capitalists proved highly successful for Computer Associates in the United States. Between the mid-1970s and the mid-1990s, Charles Wang has absorbed 60 computer software companies and their technologies to become the third largest software firm after Microsoft and Oracle, with an annual revenue of US$ 3 billion.[24]

In conclusion, the Chinese firm's organisational structure and the reasons for its survival cannot be explained by existing theories of the firm and of competition, including those of Coase, Chandler and Porter. The situation is more complex. Chinese enterprises are shaped by family politics and their relationships with the state and political élites. The rapidly growing economies of Asia and in particular the internationalisation of production by Western and Japanese multinationals concentrated in the region, have also determined the form of Chinese capitalism. Traditional market relationships and their influence on the companies' organisation and growth have dovetailed with the activities of both foreign multinationals and the state and bureaucracy. While Chinese companies transformed the method of financing this rapid expansion, patterns of ownership and control remained almost unchanged. Before 1945, Chinese firms relied on retained earnings and profits for more than 60 per cent of their total finance, with bank loans accounting for a further third. After 1960, stocks accounted for a third of the total finance and dependence on retained earnings fell to less than 40 per cent.[25] Despite this fundamental change in company financing, ownership and control by the founding family remained essentially undisturbed throughout this period. Chapter 3 will examine in greater detail the external institutions that assist or hinder Chinese business development.

3
Dancing with Wolves: Chinese Business and Outsiders

Chinese business in Asia has always flourished as a result of interactions with outside agents: Western traders and financiers, Chettiar moneylenders, the indigenous states, hybrid Southeast Asian trading groups and Asian merchants like the Japanese and Gujeratis. This chapter aims to describe the main features of these relationships and their consequences for Chinese capitalism.

From the eighteenth century and even earlier, the traditional role of the Chinese businessman has been that of middleman, active in wholesale, intermediate and retail trades, collecting produce from indigenous producers for the European agency houses and Japanese *sogo shoshas* (Japanese trading companies). The Chinese, with their well-established trading and financial networks throughout Asia, reached deep into the hinterland, extracting produce for exchange at the ports of Southeast Asia. The Chinese middleman and entrepreneur was crucial to indigenous export production from the early nineteenth century, creating a market through advance payments and the exchange of Western and Japanese consumer goods with the cultivator. The Chinese stimulated rice production, pepper and gambier cultivation and from 1910 encouraged the development of rubber smallholdings among Southeast Asian producers. Chinese peddlers in remote villages in west and southeast Kalimantan bartered with Dayaks. Only gradually did European and Japanese businesses pursue direct internal trade with the peasantry. Throughout the nineteenth century, European and Japanese trading and commercial interests stood at the periphery, focusing on the final shipment of the region's commodity exports and dependent on Chinese networks for the internal distribution of manufactured consumer goods.

The Chinese trader bound the peasantry through the provision of credit and consumer goods. In Malaysia and Sumatra, Chinese middlemen procured smallholder rubber for American Firestone, as well as for large Chinese rubber barons such as Tan Kah-Kee, Chin Seng Chan and Lee Kong Chian. In southern Sumatra, the Chinese faced competition from Minangkabau and Arab traders, in Kalimantan, from Arab, Bugis and Malay traders and in Sulawesi, from the Bugis and Madurese. In Thailand, Indochina and Malaysia, the Chinese stood at the centre of the rice milling trade. Mills were strategically placed to collect, store, mill and ship the processed rice. Chinese rice networks reached into the interior. Thai villagers, in particular women traders travelling down the canals, sold their produce to Chinese dealers/moneylenders. Through the provision of advances to Thai and Vietnamese rice farmers, Chinese businessmen controlled purchases, milling, transport and the export trade. In 1932, 73 out of 75 rice mills in Cholon were Chinese owned.[1] The rice was principally exported to other parts of Asia and, along with the flow of remittances from Chinese labourers in Southeast Asia to their home villages in south China, they intensified intra-regional economic cohesion. Before 1920, these rice and remittance networks coincided with revenue farm networks. Khaw Sim Bee and Kim Seng Lee, revenue farmers in the Siam peninsula and the Malay States from 1880 to 1913, were examples of this. Southeast Asian rice millers revealed dialect concentration: Teochius dominated the rice trade in Thailand, Hokkiens in northern Malaya and Singapore and Hakkas and Teochius in Indochina.

In the Philippines, the Spanish monopolised the international galleon trade and permitted the Chinese to penetrate the interior. The Chinese became the middlemen in the sugar industry in Negros, providing credit and marketing the produce. Chinese entrepreneurs were important in the financing and export of tobacco and the distribution of manufactured textiles from Western agency houses in Manila and Iloilo. Western and Japanese companies and Chettiars retained profits from Chinese firms and financed the growth and diversification of Chinese traders. The easy credit arrangements with foreign financiers often led the Chinese to over extend themselves; Chinese traders' bankruptcies were high between 1819–1939. Between 1919 and 1939 the NHM (Nederlandsche Handel Maatschappij, Netherlands Trading Company) faced a higher percentage of bankruptcies with Chinese clients than with European clients. Chinese clients constituted around 65–70 per cent of NHM's total bankruptcies while the Europeans accounted for only 16 per cent of bankruptcies. The Great Depression bucked this tendency, causing the European total to rise to 34 per cent[2] while the Chinese rate of bankruptcies remained at 70 per cent. This reveals an important facet of Chinese business relationships with Westerners and Chettiars – a tendency to speculate, over-extend and borrow excessively, thereby incurring a high level of risk. The Chinese trader was often negligent in the use of strict financial accounting and company structures to guard against unnecessary risk.

European banks were prominent in providing retail and wholesale finance to Chinese traders and financiers in the dramatic expansion of commodity production in the nineteenth and twentieth centuries. Of the HSBC business in Singapore, 40 per cent was with the Chinese in the 1920s, rising to 60 per cent in the 1930s.[3] European banks financed the production and distribution of crops, short-term lending often gave way to the provision of long-term credit, using intermediaries, such as the compradors to carry the risk. A comprador was usually a prominent Chinese capitalist with a wide range of contacts, particularly in his own community and who had to appraise the credit worthiness of potential customers. With the rapid growth of international trade, Western banks became more involved in the provision of foreign exchange. Bank compradors also recruited local bank staff and were responsible for their work. Although a comprador received a monthly salary, his main source of income was the commission on the business he attracted. A comprador had to provide security to protect a bank against the misuse of its funds: a cash sum was provided as deposit to guarantee against the misappropriation of funds and property guarantees were also supplied. Guarantors from within the community and from Chettiars were also required. Western banks also had dealings with Chinese banking connected to specialised remittance houses, since the latter required foreign exchange. Compradors provided vital information on production and marketing; they knew about large capitalists' loans, impending investments and changing business conditions.

From the inter-war period lending became available to small and medium-size enterprises from compradors, Chinese merchants and Chettiars, who were all seen as responsible lenders. The relationship with Western banks was essential for the establishment of financial networks by the Chinese and Chettiars. The international networking between Western banks, Chinese compradors, Chinese banks and influential Chinese businessmen was integral to the commercial and financial development of the Asian economy. Chinese banks used the HSBC or the Javasche Bank to secure a high proportion of their working capital during periods of boom, as well as to tide them over during trade crises. Through the Chinese banks, the Western banks extended credit to native peasants and aristocratic élites. These Chinese links connected metropolitan capital with the hinterland of Southeast Asia. The relationship between Western and Chinese finance precluded credit scarcity in the region; this was because of the competition, as well as the inter-dependence, of the two lenders.

The Chettiars, as suggested above, were the major financiers for the Chinese. The Chettiars of South India operated money-lending networks throughout Asia. The relationship between the Chettiars and the Chinese sheds light on the Chinese commercial community and its relationship with outsiders. The relationship addresses the problem of whether the Chinese were autonomous capitalists or a dependent trading and financial group; whether large Chinese family firms and partnerships could sustain themselves with internal banking and insurance activities, or were dependent on assistance from Western banks and Chettiars. Smaller Chinese traders were excluded from these diverse external financial sources and were more dependent on the capital provided by internal sources. The Chettiars were prepared to lend long, often on light security. While financing large Chinese rice millers in Saigon and the rice traders of Siam, the Chettiars were also actively involved with the rubber smallholders in Malaya and Indonesia and urban retailers throughout the region.

The most famous case of Chettiar involvement with the Chinese was that of the Khaw family of Penang and southern Siam. The Khaw business empire included revenue farms throughout Asia, primary production and retail and international trading interests in Southeast Asia. Chettiar credit for this group focused on four areas. The first was Eastern Shipping, in which A. M. K. Raman Chetty was a large shareholder; the remaining investors were drawn from the immediate family and powerful Chinese affiliates, including Lim Cheng Teik and Lim Eow Hoy. The shares of Eastern Shipping were listed on the Australian stock market and that capital was used to create new tin mining companies with major Australian shareholders. The Khaws used Chettiar finance to preserve some degree of control and autonomy in these joint ventures with Australian mining interests. The second area of Chettiar involvement was in the redistribution of Chettiar loans by the Khaws to small Chinese traders, miners and rubber producers in south Siam, who had little access to local banks such as the Siam Commercial Bank and the Chartered Bank. The credit facilities provided by the Chettiars were a particularly vital form of assistance during the slump of 1919–21. Thirdly, the Khaws also acted as intermediaries for the Chinese rubber entrepreneurs who were expanding from Malaya into southern Siam in the inter-war decades. The expansion of Tan Kah-Kee and Chan Hock Sun into rubber and coconut production in southern Siam was assisted by Chettiar finance, as Western bank operations there were limited. This intra-Asian expansion of production, trade, merchant activity and retailing was therefore sustained in part through Chettiar moneylenders in Southeast Asia.

The relationship between Chinese businesses and Chettiars reveals major structural changes in how Chinese merchants financed their activities in Southeast Asia from the mid-nineteenth century through to 1941. In the nineteenth century, although the Chinese tapped into Chettiar capital networks, they had various alternative forms of finance. Barter persisted as one form of financing the trade in tin, rice and tobacco. Chinese firms like Chong Moh and Company in the Straits Settlements would import Chinese cargoes and exchange them for rice, tin and coconuts through contracts and pre-arranged credit. Similarly, Western agency houses would exchange manufactured goods for Southeast Asian primary produce through barter with Chinese middlemen.

The explosion of Chinese, Western and Japanese trading networks in the last decade of the nineteenth century demanded new forms of credit. Large Chinese capitalists had revenue farming activities to fuel the expansion, as well as finance from Western banks and Chettiars, thereby alienating smaller Chinese traders who became increasingly dependent on Chettiars to finance their trade. The formation of Chinese banks in the late nineteenth century did not lessen the difficulties for the small Chinese trader. There were distinct intra-communal dialect and kin divisions that acted as barriers to access to capital. Chinese banks were formed along dialect divisions and often catered to those divisions. The Chinese compradors of Western banks also discriminated in favour of their own kin and language group. Before 1935, Chinese banks were not broad-based credit networks on a national or international scale. They had to maintain a highly liquid position because of the fluctuating fortunes of rubber and tin, resulting in higher rates of interest than those imposed by Chettiars. The Chinese banks were undercapitalised and overextended, making them eager to draw deposits, rather than act as lenders. Thus Chinese financial networks in Southeast Asia, while attracting circulating credit, were predisposed to finance the major Chinese rice and commodity traders and not all sections of the community. The more sophisticated business of discounting bills of exchange or promissory notes was left to Chettiars and Western banks. The Chettiars' acceptance of business was crucial for Chinese traders and middlemen in rubber, pepper and gambier.

The relationship between Chinese and Chettiar capitalists had important implications. Chettiars channelled capital into Chinese networks from Western sources, as well as from South Asia. Chettiars in South Asia and Burma received substantial deposits from caste members as well as Burmese, Marwaris and even Chinese and from this they lent to small and large Chinese firms. The use of promissory notes and credit issues facilitated the easy and rapid financing of trade in the region. The acceptance of these promissory notes was sufficient for Western banks to guarantee the transaction, since Chettiar lending was highly regulated by the caste group. Western banks were dependent on such vetting and were influenced by the Chettiar rate of interest.

The intra-Asian financial networks of Chinese and Chettiars enabled the evolution and spread of separate but parallel capital grids, channelling Western as well as Asian, capital; a single Western capital source did not dominate as it did in Latin America and Africa in this period[4]. Links between Western capitalism, Chettiars, Chinese and Japanese, helped sustain competition. Intra-Asian capital could maintain its autonomy, but interaction was to the advantage of most groups in Asia.

Intra-Asian integration was further achieved through the links between Chinese and Japanese. Chinese relations with the Japanese in the intra-Asian economy go back to the sixteenth century, when Japan sought teak, sugar, hides and sapanwood. Chinese traders dominated the triangular trade between Nagasaki, the Chinese ports and the ports of Southeast Asia from 1651 to 1724. Only after 1720 did the Dutch attempt to marginalise the Chinese. Even in the Sakoku period from 1767, Chinese traders were essential as middlemen, used by the Japanese to overcome their self-imposed restrictions. The Chinese needed Japanese copper, while the latter wanted Chinese silk products and Southeast Asian raw materials.

With the spread of European rule, the Chinese also established allegiances with the Spanish, Dutch, British and French trading houses and colonial state élites. A complex network of often interdependent Chinese, Indian and European capitalist classes was established by the early nineteenth century. The growth of the rubber industry in the inter-war decades intensified the link between Japanese and Chinese business. Chinese rubber entrepreneurs, such as Lee Kong Chian, Heah Joo Seang and Lim Lean Teng, were assisted by their relations with the Japanese. International rubber restriction in the inter-war years led to the dispersal of production to evade quotas. In this trans-regional rubber production, the Chinese rubber trader needed Japanese finance. In the 1920s and 1930s, Japanese shipping rapidly expanded as a direct result of increased rubber exports to the United States and Japan. Japanese *sogo shoshas* like Nomura and Mitsui also provided additional finance for rubber manufacturers. Japanese capital thus enabled the Chinese to redirect rubber exports to the growing market in the United States, rather than concentrate on trade within Asia and also increased their forward linkages into manufacturing.

The Chinese relationship with the Japanese since 1945 has been even more pervasive and important. Liaisons with Chinese merchants assisted the Japanese move into local production and retailing in Southeast Asia and the rest of the Pacific Rim. Two case studies will illustrate the relationship. First, in retailing, the Wing On Department Store, which had been established in 1907, restructured and formed an amalgamated venture with the Japanese retailing group Seiyu in 1989, with the latter acquiring a 40 per cent stake in Wing On Department Store. The capital base rose from HK$12.3 million in 1988 to HK$170.1 million in 1989 and by 1990 its dramatic expansion produced a turnover of HK$1.9 billion, with retail outlets in Hong Kong, Singapore and China. This expansion was based on the combined benefits of Seiyu's product development and retailing networks and Wing On's strong property base, insurance and warehousing.[5] A wider retailing network was established with Family Mart (a Seiyu subsidiary), Panvest Group (Taiwan), CP Group (Thailand), Lion Group (Malaysia), Hero Group and Pasaraya Group (Indonesia) and Gem (United States). This case clearly demonstrates how internationalisation and product development were assisted by the formation of a joint venture with the Japanese.

A second example of the relationship between Japanese and Chinese business is found in the development of P. T. Astra since 1969. Astra's interests are numerous: the automobile industry, both in assembly and component production with Toyota, Honda and others; heavy equipment assembly and component production with Komatsu; and office equipment with Fuji Xerox. Astra expanded through the acquisition of sole agencies, buying out existing companies, the establishment of new companies, mergers or joint ventures through licensing and other contractual agreements. Between 1976 and 1995, Astra's share of the Indonesian market for 4-wheel vehicles rose from 35 per cent to 55 per cent.[6] Cooperation with Japanese business led to expansion in heavy capital-intensive industries and in acquisition of production technology, the maintenance of quality control methods, the modernisation of financial management and the development of a precise corporate philosophy. On the other hand, it is clear that Astra resisted the absorption of Japanese corporate attitudes, with the emphasis on technology and corporate structures and philosophy driven by innovation.

The relationship of the state with Chinese business has been a central subject of scholarship in recent decades. From pre-colonial times to the present, Chinese commercial groups, from traders, merchants, revenue farmers to industrialists, were in defined relationships to the traditional courts, to the colonial state and to the state and foreign multinationals in the post-independence era. Each relationship was built on the conduct of regional and international trade, in raising capital, in pooling labour from southern China and within Southeast Asia and in the international mobility of substantial capital and investment. In all this, the relationship of Chinese firms with outsiders was critical for the accumulation of capital and the search for markets and technologies. There is continuity in the roles assumed in the relationships with outsiders. In the sixteenth to the eighteenth centuries, Chinese traders of Batavia collected tolls, revenue and produce for the Dutch East India Company and private traders. In the nineteenth and twentieth centuries, they acted as middlemen for the Cultivation System in Java and in revenue farming throughout Asia, opening up the hinterland. To In of Mataram secured revenues for Sultan Mangkabumi and similarly, Oei Tiong Ham and Be Biaw Tjoan assisted the Dutch colonial authorities, as did Liem Soei Liong for Soeharto in more recent times. The Chinese assisted sections of the aristocracy in increasing the state's revenues through increased commodity production and the taxation of services such as gambling and prostitution.

The Chinese position remained stable despite considerable variation in systems of government, ranging from the interventionist model of the Dutch in the East Indies to the *laissez-faire* British in Malaya, Singapore and Burma and the French vision of a state dedicated to a mixed economy of public and private enterprise. The Chinese were always important private agents. With their broad and extended networks, the Chinese were, until the 1930s, also assisted by the openness of the Southeast Asian economies. In the face of increasing protectionism, economic nationalism and anti-Chinese legislation in the 1930s, the Chinese still acquired important positions in state-sponsored economic initiatives and joint partnerships with the state. Then, with the rise of Japanese capital, the Chinese again obtained a clear advantage through their alliances with the Japanese *sogo shoshas*.

After 1945 some countries – Burma in the 1950s and Vietnam in the 1970s and 1980s – expelled the Chinese and other minority capitalists.

Malaysia and Indonesia sought to curtail their activities, while Thailand attempted to assimilate them further. Chinese dominance continued despite such constraints. Foreign multinationals employed local Chinese as contractors in their direct investments. The need to attract foreign investment and promote development set limits on economic nationalism, particularly in the late 1970s and early 1980s. At that time industrial initiatives were dictated by the direct invest-ment motives of Japanese, Korean, Taiwanese and Western transna-tionals, with Chinese and native businessmen as crucial promoters, assisted by the paternalism of the state apparatus.

The relationship between Chinese merchants and the state has been interpreted by many scholars as showing the dependence of Chinese cap-italism on Southeast Asian élites. Richard Robison, Chatthip Nartsupha and Kunio Yoshihara saw Chinese capitalists as rent-seekers.[7] The impor-tant elements of state power and control were the tax-farming monopo-lies, trade privileges and protection and the state's control of labour. Only the intra-Asian connections of Chinese capital could overcome this dependence on authoritarian regimes. Any failure of Chinese businesses to take on independent, innovative roles in economic activities was attributed to this dependence on the authoritarian state. This view per-meates much of the writing on pre-colonial, colonial and post-colonial Southeast Asia, except for those of Ruth McVey. McVey in 1992 rejected this cynical view of the Chinese and saw benefits in the Chinese relation-ship with the Southeast Asian state, arguing that the state together with the native provincial élites and Chinese capitalists were responsible for a more pervasive capitalist growth.[8]

In alliances between Chinese capital and the state and foreign multi-nationals, there are important variations between the Philippines, Thailand, Indonesia and Malaysia. In the Philippines, Chinese relations with the state and the foreign multinationals were affected by the com-petition of long-established, vibrant Filipino capitalists. The Elizalde, Soriano and Ayala families were prominent from the mid-nineteenth century and only briefly declined under the Marcos regime. The Chinese, who since Spanish rule had built their wealth on sugar and real estate, were now joined by a new Chinese rich: J. Gokongwei, Henry Sy, Alfonso Yucheng and Lucio Tan. The new wealth was stimu-lated by the burgeoning Chinese networks in Asia and the accelerated inflow of Western and East Asian investments in the export processing zones, finance, real estate and tourism. But competition from Filipino capital was constant. The Philippines was the only Southeast Asian country where there was a strong indigenous business contender in the form of the indigenised Spanish Filipinos, who had also traditionally benefited from the establishment's support. The Chinese in Indonesia and Thailand confronted a weak local bourgeoisie. Indonesian *pribumi* (indigenous) capitalists assisted in extending state patronage to the Chinese, not in restricting it. Nationalisation of European enterprise in the mid-1950s further assisted the Chinese role in industrialisation.

Finally the growing interdependence of the Asian economy, through increased intra-Asian trade and investment and the rapid inflows of American and European investment, were mediated through Hong Kong, Singapore and Bangkok.[9] Here Chinese networks were sought to locate production in areas of comparative advantage, such as cheap labour in Indonesia and Thailand and hi-tech and finance in Singapore and Hong Kong. The transfer of technology from Japan and later Korea and Taiwan, to Southeast Asia in the 1960s was effectively exploited by Chinese networks. Joint ventures with Western and East Asian multinationals were common in textiles, cement, automobiles and electronics. In the last two sectors, the assistance of state capital was a priority. P. T. Astra's involvement in heavy equipment began in 1969 with Allis Chalmers as the partner, but in 1972 Astra switched to Komatsu. Indonesia became the largest market in Southeast Asia for Komatsu heavy equipment in 1988, acquiring 52 per cent of the market, compared with 35 per cent for Caterpillar.[10] From the 1970s the Indonesian Government invested in highways, forest clearance and dam construction: 90 per cent of its contracts were with United Tractors, a subsidiary of P. T. Astra. In 1979, logging accounted for 55 per cent of the sales output of United Tractors, which was the sole agent for Komatsu. From the late 1980s United Tractors diversified into mining exploration and resource exploitation. The rapid growth and diversification from 1972 occurred partly because foreign multinationals were forced by the Indonesian Government to choose local partners; Chinese businesses were identified as the immediate choice, along with the state and *pribumi* alliances. In 1986, with export-oriented industrialisation policies now being implemented by the Government, P. T. Astra International began manufacturing components for Honda. When private enterprise was stressed, accompanied by large inflows of direct foreign investment, P. T. Astra rose as a contractor for the government, the army and foreign multinationals.

The relationship with the state and foreign companies had two important implications. First, it led to an over-extended, unwieldy enterprise structure, highly speculative and risk prone, because firms could shift risk to the foreign partner or to the state. Secondly, the acquisition of core technology remained peripheral to the Chinese firm. A multi-layered subcontracting relationship was conducive to information access but not to the assimilation and internalisation of competence in technology. Japanese technology transfer is closely welded to particular management skills and know-how and can be transferred only alongside the transfer of management skills rooted in the new technologies. The lack of research and development divisions in Chinese firms produces difficulties in the transfer of non-standard technologies.

Two examples will illustrate the predicament surrounding the acceptance of technological development. One example is Shinawatra, which from the early twentieth century had been engaged in silk weaving in northern Thailand, but from 1983 was an important computer and telecommunications corporation, supplying computer services to Thai railways, academics and government departments. With its links to IBM, NASA and the Thai state, Shinawatra moved into satellite communications, cable television and mobile phone networks. This was achieved through diversifying into foreign markets in the Philippines, Cambodia, India and China from 1991 and by forming joint ventures with AT & T, NEC, Erricsson and BT. Shinawatra and CP have major broadcasting and telecommunications companies in Asia, with interlocking shareholdings and links with large foreign multinational and state partners in the countries in which they are located. In this way a large Thai multinational has emerged in a hi-tech industry but one with no technological base. R&D is provided by the foreign multinational. In other words, Chinese companies seek markets in technology but still neglect innovation, concentrating on the transfer of commercial skills. Would the telecommunications networks of Shinawatra and CP be able to compete with the networks of foreign as well as indigenous state enterprises (such as Singapore Telecom) in Southeast Asia in the 1990s? Here the product-cycle theory has been overtaken by the comparative-cost theory, imposed on a close liaison with the state. Shinawatra is not responsible for the life cycle of the product but simply for the partial transmission of the technology. Shinawatra subcontracts the installation and management of switchboards and circuits to AT & T, while CP does the same with Nynex.

The second example of the problem of technological development involves Loh Kim Teow in Penang. Loh Kim Teow progressed from dealing in computer hardware to producing computer hardware for IBM, Acer and Siemens in the 1980s. Some technology was transferred from the electronics industry to automobiles and telecommunications, where disk drives were supplied to Proton Saga and Malaysian Telecom. However, this moving technology frontier has been peripheral to the internal technological improvements within the Chinese firm. Research and development divisions are limited to imitation and to acquiring new technologies through partnerships. Consideration of changes in quality, technological linkages, long-term product development and flexibility of technology assimilation is absent from the decisions made by Chinese multinationals. The issue of technology is crucial because long-term competitiveness is dependent on innovative skills and the creation of technological clusters. Chinese ascendancy in recent decades has been assisted by the flow of information and favourable policy changes, such as the state's reduction of barriers to trade and investment and through privatisation initiatives since the late 1980s. For long-term development, technology is critical to maintaining competitive edge.

In Malaysia, the rise of Vincent Tan, Ting Pek Khing and Quek Leong Chan was based on developments in infrastructure and the privatisation of public utilities. Hong Leong's links with UMNO(United Malay National Organisation) from 1989 have led to Hume Industries securing contracts for the North–South Highway. Vincent Tan, active in sewerage and telecommunications industries, has, within a decade, acquired assets of M$1.7 billion and Quek has assets of M$2.1 billion, built up over three decades. The success of both was achieved through state patronage and privatisation policies.[11]

In summary, the cultural embeddedness of Chinese capitalism is a product of historical cultural factors. Chinese capitalism in Southeast Asia, despite its heterogeneity, is not competitive. The accumulative, predatory tendencies of Chinese capitalism should not be mistaken for competitiveness. The Chinese links with the state, indigenous merchants, local élites and native technocrats, have varied from co-opting élites onto the boards of Chinese companies, to raising equity from indigenous sources, government capital, to operating joint ventures with the state and with foreign multinationals and seeking technological alliances with foreign multinationals. The state has ranged from patron to partner, from investor to executor. The Chinese entrepreneur, meanwhile, has to re-address these links and achieve autonomy based on technical competence and financial rigour if long-term growth is to be secured.

4
Socialising Capital in Indonesia: P. T. Astra in an Age of Financial Abundance

The development of the company P. T. Astra since 1966 mirrors the economic changes in Indonesia, in particular the shift in emphasis from agriculture to manufacturing. The Indonesian government's push into heavy industry since the 1970s and the move into the automobile and electronic industries were encouraged by strong domestic demand and increasing protectionism. Manufacturing in Indonesia became more capital-intensive and the growth of Astra Graphia, the electronics arm of the company, reflected this trend. Export-oriented manufacturing, which replaced import substitution, produced an export boom from 1980 to the mid-1990s. The sudden rush of foreign investors into manufacturing did not result in the dominance of foreign-owned firms; Chinese and state-owned firms dominated. Domestic firms were also strong in finance. A few large corporations emerged, such as Astra. The monopolistic concentration was further assisted by the state's protectionist policies in trade and manufacturing. Astra's exploitation of abundant finance, available as a result of financial liberalisation in Indonesia and the subsequent inflow of direct foreign investment, are vital in explaining the company's extraordinary development. The financial crisis of 1997 dramatically exposed this dependence on abundant finance in propelling growth.

The state and Astra

The relationship between Chinese business and the state has dominated recent academic work on the Southeast Asian economy. From pre-colonial times to the present, Chinese commercial groups – from trader, merchant, revenue farmer, to industrialist – were defined by their relationships with the traditional courts and the colonial state during the pre-independence era, and the state and foreign multi-nationals following independence. From the early nineteenth century until the 1990s each relationship developed in the context of regional and international trade. Key features of this changing economic context were the raising of capital, the recruitment of labour from southern China and within Southeast Asia and the international mobility of capital investment into various commodities, industries and services. Historically, there has been considerable continuity in the roles adopted by Chinese capitalists. From the sixteenth to the eighteenth century, Chinese traders at Batavia collected tolls, revenue and produce for the Dutch East India Company and private traders. In the nineteenth and twentieth centuries, they acted as middlemen for the Cultivation System in Java and by revenue farming throughout Asia, they opened up the hinterland. The relationship between Liem Soei Liong and Soeharto in more recent times follows that pattern.

To clarify and explain the diversity and impact of the relationships developed by Chinese businesses, we need an empirical example. The primary aim here is to study the growth of P. T. Astra in Indonesia and explore how a large Chinese conglomerate adapted to achieve scale and scope through the exploitation of the state apparatus and the liberalisation of the region's financial systems.

The Astra group was originally established as a commodity trading company in 1957 by William Soeryadjaya (also known as Tjia Kian Liong) and his brother. Under Sukarno, Astra succeeded in securing government contracts for the import and supply of construction materials. However, it was under the Soeharto regime that Astra sustained rapid expansion. Although Astra's phase of prodigious growth co-incided with the increasing power and paternalism of the Soeharto regime (1970–97), the critical issue here is not only the direct relationship between Astra and the government but also the responsiveness of the group to changes in state policy, institutions and the economic environment.

Astra was assisted by Soeharto's regime in various ways. Special licences and contracts to produce goods were provided. Astra also had access to state finance, and an advantageous exchange rate was arranged, allowing Astra to borrow US dollars at an artificially low rate. Overall, Astra operated in a highly protected environment, in which there was very little competition.

The ability of the state to govern capital is in part determined by the institutional and organisational structure of private capital, which in Indonesia is mainly Chinese capital. Thus while the Soeryadjaya

Figure 4.1 Structure of the Astra Group

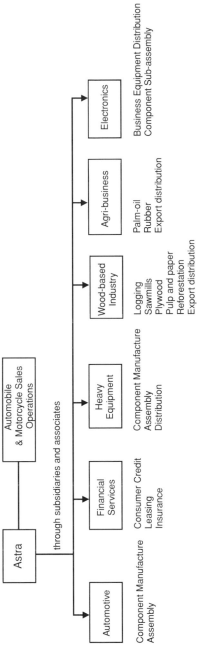

Source: Annual Reports of P. T. Astra International, 1987–1994.

family was rarely identified as part of the Soeharto clique, much of Astra's growth could not have occurred without the benign acquiescence, if not outright support, of the Indonesian establishment. After the political and economic ravages of the 1960s, Soeharto faced a formidable task in wooing investment to Indonesia, reducing inflation and promoting growth. This meant attracting Chinese capital, which had fled to Singapore and Hong Kong in the early 1960s. Eventually, the surge in oil prices from 1973 catapulted a core group of Chinese and *pribumi* (indigenous) capitalists to wealth and prominence. This produced important joint ventures between the Chinese and both Japanese and American multinationals. The growth in the 1970s also saw the replacement of market forms of regulation with regulation at Soeharto's personal discretion. Undeniably, the imposition of the compulsory use of local partners for foreign investors, control by the state of all contracts for infrastructural projects, lucrative initiatives in oil and mineral extraction and the state's control over credit, benefited the large Chinese corporations, who faced no competition from foreign or indigenous capital. The indigenous entrepreneurial class formed during the colonial period was small and had declined after independence. The nationalisation of Dutch enterprises in 1957 had created large state organisations from which the Chinese benefited as the important contractors.

Table 4.1 shows the process of the creation and nurturing of capitalists by the state and the dominance of large Chinese groups that emerged around the late 1960s. In 1993, the top seven conglomerates in Indonesia belonged to the Chinese and to the President's children. Only four *pribumi* firms were among the top 25 corporations and two of these were owned by the President's children. Most of these 25 corporations had risen since the late 1960s by identifying economic opportunities and understanding the bureaucracy and patronage culture of Soeharto. These business groups were highly concentrated monopolies, sustained by a collusive rather than a transformative state. Indonesia, unlike Japan, did not possess the networks of industrial organisations, such as the *keiretsu* and *kigyo shudan,* which could curb rent-seeking activities and guarantee greater competition. State connections to private capital without these kinds of protective institutions rendered the economy unstable and lacking industrial vitality. This in part explains the turbulence of 1997.

Government investment remained high throughout the Soeharto period. Between 1969 and 1975 and 1986 and 1991, direct foreign investment accounted for only 2.0 to 3.5 per cent of total investment

Table 4.1 Major business conglomerates in Indonesia, 1993, identified by racial origin

Conglomerate	Principal owner[a]	Principal activities	Turnover (Rp b)	Ranking (by turnover)		No. of companies, 1993
				1993	1987[b]	
Salim	Liem Sioe Liong	Cement, finance, autos, agro-industry	18,000	1	1	450
Astra	Prasetia Mulya group, and public shareholders	Autos, estates	5,890	2	2	205
Lippo	Mochtar Riady	Finance	4,750	3	4	78
Sinar Mas	Eka Tjipta Widjaya	Agro-industry, pulp and paper, finance	4,200	4	3	150
Gudang Garam	Rachman Halim	Kretek (clove) cigarettes	3,600	5	5	6
Bob Hasan	Bob Hasan, Sigit Harjojudanto	Timber, estates	3,400	6	12	92
Barito Pacific	Prajogo Pangestu	Timber	3,050	7	26	92
Bimantara [*Pribumi*]	Bambang Trihatmodjo [President's son]	Trade, real estate, chemicals	3,000	8	13	134

Table 4.1 Major business conglomerates in Indonesia, 1993, identified by racial origin – *continued*

Conglomerate	Principal owner[a]	Principal activities	Turnover (Rp b)	Ranking (by turnover) 1993	Ranking (by turnover) 1987[b]	No. of companies, 1993
Argo Manunggal	The Ning King	Textiles	2,940	9	15	54
Dharmala	Soehargo Gondokusumo	Agro-industry, real estate	2,530	10	14	151
Djarum	Budi and Michael Hartono	Kretek (clove) cigarettes	2,360	11	6	25
Ongko	Kaharuddin Ongko	Real estate, finance	2,100	12	11	59
Panin	Mu'min Ali Gunawan	Finance	2,080	13	10	43
Rodamas	Tan Siong Kie	Chemicals	2,000	14	18	41
Surya Raya	Soeryadjaya	Property, estates, trade	1,980	15	n.a.	242
Jan Darmadi	Jan Darmadi	Real estate	1,940	16	9	60
CCM/Berca	Murdaya Widyawimarta Poo	Electronics, electricity	1,800	17	n.a.	32
Humpus [*pribumi*]	Hutomo Mandala Putra [President's children]	Oil, trade, chemicals	1,750	18	23	11

Table 4.1 Major business conglomerates in Indonesia, 1993, identified by racial origin – *continued*

Conglomerate	Principal owner[a]	Principal activities	Turnover (Rp b)	Ranking (by turnover) 1993	Ranking (by turnover) 1987[b]	No. of companies 1993
Gadjah Tunggal	Sjamsul Nursalim	Tyres, finance, real estate	1,650	19	24	49
Raja Garuda Mas	Sukanto Tanoto	Pulp and, rayon, finance	1,590	20	34	66
Gemala	Wanandi	Chemicals, automobiles	1,550	21	7	78
Pembangunan Jaya	several	Real estate	1,390	22	n.a.	57
Metropolitan	several	Real estate	1,200	23	n.a.	57
Soedarpo [*Pribumi*]	Soedarpo Sastrosatomo	Shipping, trade, pharmaceuticals	1,200	25	16	35
Tahija [*Pribumi*]	Julius Tahija	Finance	1,200	23	n.a.	39

Notes:

[a] In some cases owned by the family of this individual. All are Chinese owned, except for the *pribumi*-owned category.

[b] n.a. indicates that the conglomerate was not ranked in the top 40 in 1987.

Sources: Warta Ekonomi, 24 April 1994, and earlier listings in this magazine, as cited in Hal Hill, *The Indonesian Economy since 1966*, Cambridge, Cambridge University Press, 1996, p. 111.

in Indonesia, compared with 29.4 per cent in Singapore, 9.7 per cent in Malaysia and 6.3 per cent in Thailand. Indeed all external sources of finance accounted for only 13 per cent of total investment in the period 1969–90. The remainder came from the Indonesian government (oil revenues) and from private domestic sources. Foreign private capital inflows in the form of long-term loans were substantial for the years 1990–92, mostly borrowings by Indonesian corporations. See Table 4.2. The privatisation of major state enterprises in the 1990s did not weaken Soeharto's influence. By 1990, total private sector investment comprised 9.6 per cent of GDP, or 46 per cent of total investment. Recent estimates of the total value of state enterprises indicate that in 1992–93, they were 230.3 trillion rupiah, or 90 per cent of GDP in 1992.[1]

Government and private investment remained dominant, despite a drop in the 1980s following a decline in oil prices, which stabilised in the 1990s. The World Bank, in a 1993 report, classified Indonesia as an investment-driven economy, unlike Japan, Korea, Hong Kong, Taiwan and Thailand, where growth in the 1980s and 1990s was attributed mainly to increases in productivity.[2] All this attests to the importance of the state power vested in Soeharto and the groups close to him. State patronage has existed through much of Indonesian history, but the combination of Soeharto's political and economic power and the decline of talented technocrats, eroded the autonomous basis of the state since the 1980s. These changes also took place in an age of financial abundance and rapid economic growth in Asia. At this time, zonal capitalism, which wove parts of Indonesia, Malaysia, Singapore

Table 4.2   Indonesia: cumulative value of investment flows, 1969–90 ($US billion)

Foreign flows	1969–75	1976–82	1983–90
Direct foreign investment	1.96	2.17	3.52
Portfolio investment	0	0.64	0.26
Official capital inflows	6.28	15.21	17.64
Other capital inflows	–2.94	–0.96	5.87
Development budget (specific projects)	17.92	65.43	64.52
Total investment (GDP)	40.38	126.78	203.92

Sources: IMF, *International Financial Statistics Yearbook*, 1992, pp. 410–11; *Indonesian Financial Statistics*, various years.

and Thailand into zones of capital-intensive manufacturing, too emerged. Riau Johor and parts of Singapore became the focus of massive foreign direct investment. Rather than weakening state power, this strengthened it, because of the foreign and Chinese capital networks. Although large corporations were the main driving-force of this regional integration, a hierarchy of capital came into existence – a hierarchy supported by the Indonesian state and foreign and private capital, each responding to the rapidly changing international economy. By the 1990s, Soeharto was insulated from the technocrats, resulting in a more centralised and coercive power.

William Soeryadjaya's close ties with Professor Sumitro Djojohadikusumo, the Trade Minister and with Pertamina (the National Oil Corporation), helped secure government contracts for building roads, steel bridges and irrigation dams, for the supply of automobiles and in technology projects. Since 1974 the state has been a partner in the creation of large oligopolies in public works, banking and in import substitution industries that involved William Soeryadjaya, Salim and Bob Hassan. These cartels prospered (not least in cloves and plastics) under the protection of the state's licensing and import barriers, but they also remained highly vulnerable.

The Indonesian government had a pivotal role in corporate development. As capital became socialised, its forms were changed in a period when the economy and society were being deregulated. The powerful state often swamped the immaturity of the state's regulatory framework, whose actions could be thwarted by highly mobile capital, whether Chinese or *pribumi*. Consequently, large corporations enjoyed a considerable measure of autonomy, while sharing wealth and risk with the state and foreign multinationals.

Growth and diversification through joint ventures

This section focuses on the role of joint ventures in Astra's spectacular growth since 1970. Astra specialised in the capital-intensive sectors of automobiles and heavy engineering and was largely confined to Indonesia. Astra also possessed managerial hierarchies that manipulated the burgeoning capital markets of Asia to finance dramatic corporate growth over three decades. The importance of each of these factors in Astra's growth has been the source of some debate. This chapter argues that the Astra example vindicates Porter rather than Chandler. Porter's emphasis on favourable finance and industrial clusters in automobile assembly, heavy engineering and electronics to explain growth, is more effective in Astra's case. Chandler stresses the importance of management hierarchies, in particular the diffusion of control in preference to centralised family power. In the case of Astra, structure and strategy were merely reinforcing factors in the achievement of growth.

William Soeryadjaya founded Astra in 1957 as an exporter of primary produce. The company moved into the automobile industry in the mid-1960s as an importer for the Indonesian state and later into joint ventures with Toyota and General Motors, importing as well as assembling cars and trucks (see Figure 4.3.) By 1970, Astra was the sole agent and distributor for Toyota, Daihatsu, Peugeot, Honda and Komatsu,[3] which involved the manufacture of component parts and body accessories, as well as assembling cars, trucks and motor cycles. In the 1980s, Astra moved into the building of chassis frames, brakes and engines. Much of this production was for the domestic market although some was for export.

Astra's development coincided with changes in corporate structure and governance. Although retaining core family ownership, the company adopted a divisional structure. The first division was the automobile sector, which had four holding companies: Toyota Group, Astra Mobil, Honda Motor Cycle Group and Components Group. These four holding companies in turn controlled diverse automobile firms (see Figure 4.2). The growth of this sector was impressive. By 1982, Astra was dominant in jeep sales in Indonesia, accounting for 70 per cent of total sales. In 1988, Astra's locally assembled Toyota and Daihatsu vehicles accounted for 45 per cent of total car sales in Indonesia. In the same year, car and truck production contributed 74 per cent of Astra's total revenues, rising to 80 per cent in 1994.[4] The components segment of this group also achieved spectacular growth – 34.3 per cent per annum in the 1990s. In 1992, Astra's sales revenue was 1,080 billion rupiah, its total assets were 695 billion rupiah, its fixed assets were 298 billion rupiah, and net profit 42.5 billion rupiah.[5] Astra was ranked second in corporate output and value in Indonesia in 1993, behind the Salim Corporation.

Astra's second sector was heavy equipment manufacture and leasing. Until the early 1970s, this sector mainly worked in joint ventures with Allis Chalmers (USA). In 1972, Komatsu (Japan) replaced Allis Chalmers as Astra's partner. The heavy equipment sector supplied equipment for mining, shipbuilding, industry, construction and agriculture. The main company was P. T. United Tractors and its affiliated firms, P. T. Tractor Nusantara and P. T. Komatsu. United Tractors was the most successful firm in the Astra Group. Between 1973 and 1980 it achieved a growth of

39 per cent per annum, falling to 19 per cent in 1980 to 1986 but rising to 36 per cent from 1988 to 1990 (see Table 4.3).[6] Astra's close involvement with the state and in particular with the Soeharto family, is evident in this sector. Since the 1970s the Indonesian government had invested in highways, forest clearance and dam construction and 90 per cent of its contracts were with United Tractors. In 1979 logging accounted for 55 per cent of the sales of United Tractors, which was the sole agent for Komatsu.[7] In 1988, Indonesia became the largest market in Southeast Asia for Komatsu heavy equipment, acquiring 52 per cent of the market, compared with Caterpillar's 35 per cent.[8] From the late 1980s, United Tractors diversified into mining exploration and resource exploitation. United Tractors' rapid growth and diversification since 1972 was partly achieved because foreign multinationals were forced by the Indonesian government to choose local partners: Chinese firms were an immediate choice, along with the state and *pribumi* interests. In 1986, with the government pursuing export-oriented industrialisation, P. T. Astra International began manufacturing components for Honda. Thus when the state sought to encourage private enterprise and inflows of foreign direct investment, P. T. Astra was well positioned as a contractor to the government, the army and the foreign multinationals.[9]

Astra's third division concentrated on forestry and wood-based industries, including logging, timber processing, pulp and paper products. Indonesia's timber industry rose at the phenomenal rate of 35 per cent per annum from 1966 to 1970, only declining after 1980. The value of timber exports had, by 1970, exceeded that of all cash crops

Table 4.3   P. T. United Tractors

Year	Capital (rupiah million)	Revenue (rupiah million)	Net profit (rupiah million)	Dividend (rupiah per share)	Earnings per share (rupiah)
1987		212,400	4,600		
1988		304,600	11,060		
1989	20,300	403,360	20,280		
1990	23,000	517,180	35,080		
1992	34,500	600,250	26,988	230.00	196.00
1993	34,500	857,188	35,718	150.00	259.00
1994	138,000	1,250,906	46,040	110.00	334.00
1995	138,000	1,608,680	58,528	130.00	424.00
1996	138,000	1,979,743	73,426	160.00	532.00

Sources: SP.T United Tractors, Annual Reports, 1987–1992. See also *Asian Company Handbook 1997*, Tokyo, Toyo Keizai Inc., p. 396.

Figure 4.2 P. T. Astra International's Seven Divisions and the Main Affiliated Compar

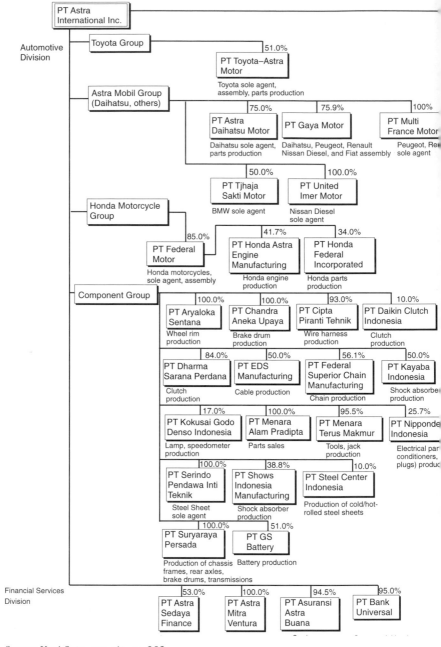

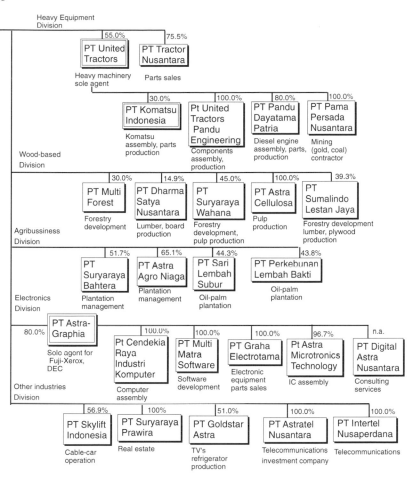

Heavy Equipment Division

55.0% PT United Tractors — Heavy machinery sole agent

75.5% PT Tractor Nusantara — Parts sales

30.0% PT Komatsu Indonesia — Komatsu assembly, parts production

100.0% Pt United Tractors Pandu Engineering — Components assembly, production

80.0% PT Pandu Dayatama Patria — Diesel engine assembly, parts, production

100.0% PT Pama Persada Nusantara — Mining (gold, coal) contractor

Wood-based Division

30.0% PT Multi Forest — Forestry development

14.9% PT Dharma Satya Nusantara — Lumber, board production

45.0% PT Suryaraya Wahana — Forestry development, pulp production

100.0% PT Astra Cellulosa — Pulp production

39.3% PT Sumalindo Lestan Jaya — Forestry development lumber, plywood production

Agribussiness Division

51.7% PT Suryaraya Bahtera — Plantation management

65.1% PT Astra Agro Niaga — Plantation management

44.3% PT Sari Lembah Subur — Oil-palm plantation

43.8% PT Perkebunan Lembah Bakti — Oil-palm plantation

Electronics Division

80.0% PT Astra-Graphia — Solo agent for Fuji-Xerox, DEC

100.0% Pt Cendekia Raya Industri Komputer — Computer assembly

100.0% PT Multi Matra Software — Software development

100.0% PT Graha Electrotama — Electronic equipment parts sales

96.7% Pt Astra Microtronics Technology — IC assembly

n.a. PT Digital Astra Nusantara — Consulting services

Other industries Division

56.9% PT Skylift Indonesia — Cable-car operation

100% PT Suryaraya Prawira — Real estate

51.0% PT Goldstar Astra — TV's refrigerator production

100.0% PT Astratel Nusantara — Telecommunications investment company

100.0% PT Intertel Nusaperdana — Telecommunications

☐ Joint venture, or some relationship, with foreign capital   ☐ Listed company

Figure 4.3 Astra: the automobile sector

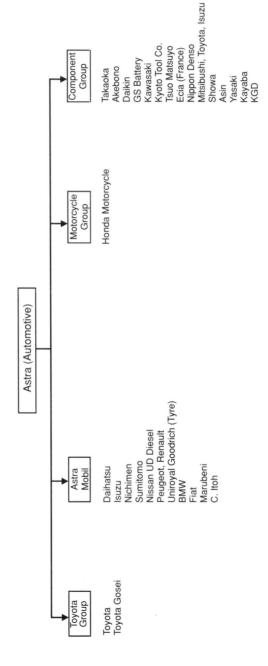

Astra (Automotive)			
Toyota Group	Astra Mobil	Motorcycle Group	Component Group
Toyota	Daihatsu	Honda Motorcycle	Takaoka
Toyota Gosei	Isuzu		Akebono
	Nichimen		Daikin
	Sumitomo		GS Battery
	Nissan UD Diesel		Kawasaki
	Peugeot, Renault		Kyoto Tool Co.
	Uniroyal Goodrich (Tyre)		Tsuo Matsuyo
	BMW		Ecia (France)
	Fiat		Nippon Denso
	Marubeni		Mitsibushi, Toyota, Isuzu
	C. Itoh		Showa
			Asin
			Yasaki
			Kayaba
			KGD

Source: Annual Reports of P. T. Astra International, 1987–1994.

except rubber. Plywood production grew from 0 per cent to 10 per cent per annum between 1975 and 1990. Timber grew from 3 per cent to 10 per cent per annum between 1970 and 1990. Similarly, logging achieved higher, although fluctuating, growth rates of 25–30 per cent per annum in the same decades. P. T. Astra participated in this growth, ranking twelfth in wood-related exports from Indonesia. It also had a lucrative joint venture in logging with Barito Pacific Timber, Indonesia's 'timber king'. The wood-based division of Astra saw an increase in turnover from US$5.4 million in 1981 to US$95.6 million in 1991, the sharpest rise being between 1988 and 1991.[10] The investment flows into that sector rose from US$5.5 million in 1981 to US$54.9 million in 1991.[11]

P. T. Astra's fourth division was electronics, produced for both the automobile division, which absorbed more than 80 per cent of electronic output and heavy industry, which absorbed another 13 per cent. The retail electrical and agricultural units absorbed the remainder. P. T. Astra Graphia (established in 1976) dominated the distribution of photocopiers and office equipment, including the distribution of computers for US, Japanese, Hong Kong and Korean firms. P. T. Astra Graphia wholly owned four subsidiaries in personal computers, software, electrical components, micro-technology and satellite communications. Astra Graphia had concentrated on Japanese products until 1983 when it moved into American and Korean products. Prior to 1980, Astra Graphia concentrated on the distribution of electronic machinery and software, moving into assembly operations for the Fuji Xerox Company. In 1990 Astra Graphia began the assembly of semi-conductors for Singapore companies and in 1991 it undertook the production of circuit boards for South Korea's Lucky Goldstar. The assembling and export of integrated circuit boards led to its location on Batam Island for production targeted at markets in Asia, Europe and the US.

Astra achieved its competitiveness in the electronics business principally as a contractor for the Indonesian government, Pertamina and foreign multinationals. In 1983, it moved into joint ventures and strategic alliances with Korean, American, Japanese, European and Singaporean multinationals. In 1991 Astra's net sales of electronic instruments were valued at 141.2 billion rupiah, with government and oil companies accounting for 45 per cent of this turnover.[12]

Astra Graphia diversified into the information and telecommunications industries. In the 1980s Astra Graphia had access to Digital's information systems and between 1983 and 1986 its turnover of digital products rose to US$3 million and by 1991 to US$25 million.[13] IBM had a 50 per cent share of Indonesia's electronics market in the late 1980s and early 1990s. Astra Graphia had, through its joint ventures, achieved a niche market share of 18 per cent. Astra Graphia's links with Digital were critical in carving out this share. From the late 1980s, its links with Lucky Goldstar enabled it to diversify, widening its range from expensive to cheaper lines. Astra Graphia's connections with French Telecommunication further assisted this penetration. All this activity implied an increased inflow of foreign direct investment, particularly from Samsung and Lucky Goldstar of Korea in the 1990s.

Astra Graphia's volume of sales rose from 4.5 billion rupiah in 1976 to 99.7 billion in 1989, to 123.4 billion in 1990 and to 141.2 billion in 1991. The sharpest increase was in 1989, when it registered 84.6 billion rupiah, almost double the sales of 1987 (45.7 billion rupiah). This spectacular growth in the late 1980s led to Astra Graphia being listed on Jakarta's Stock Exchange in November 1989, with a share issue of 3.07 million shares at 8,550 rupiah each. Despite this phenomenal success, Astra Graphia contributed only 2.86 per cent of P. T. Astra's sales and 3.52 per cent of P. T. Astra's profits in 1990–91.[14] The Astra Group continued to concentrate on the heavy machinery sector.

Astra's fifth division was agriculture. Although Astra had its origins in primary production, its agricultural sector was insignificant until the mid-1990s, accounting for only 3.6 per cent of the Group's net sales in 1991. Although the percentage share of agriculture in total sales was higher than that for Astra Graphia, the latter had a higher revenue yield. P. T. Multi-Agro Corporation was established in 1973 to invest in coconut, cassava, oil palm and rubber plantations in Java and Sumatra. The accelerated growth of these interests reflected the growth of Astra as a whole.

The parent company, P. T. Astra International, grew from one firm in 1957 to 125 firms in 1995 (see Figure 4.2 and Table 4.5 for growth indicators). Phenomenal growth and diversification were achieved without sacrificing family ownership, until 1992. Exclusive ownership was vested in the founding family until 1988, when Astra was restructured into divisions with managerial hierarchies: 10 per cent of equity was then held by blood-related managers, although the majority shareholding (75 per cent) still remained within the family. In 1989, the International Finance Company (IFC), an affiliated investment company of the World Bank, was co-opted into Astra through a 5 per cent shareholding. In 1990 the Astra Corporation was listed but the majority shareholding (77 per cent) still remained with the family. The Summa Bank crisis in 1992, caused by foreign exchange speculation in

Table 4.4.   P. T. Astra International Management

Board of Commissioners
[largely family members]

William Soeryadjaya, President; Benjamin Soeryadjaya, Vice-President;
Edward Soeryadjaya; Joyce Soeryadjaya; Judith Soeryadjaya; Mohammed Tahir;
Marseno Wirjosaputro; Soeharto Sigit and Torstein Stephansen.

Board of Directors

Theodore Permadi Rachmat (nephew), President;
Adhi Mulja, Vice-President;
Edwin Soeryadjaya, Vice-President;
Benny Subianto, Vice-President;
Subagio Wirjoatmodjo; Rudyanto Hardjanto; Himawan Surya; Budi
Setiadharma; Rine Mariani Sumarno: Soewandi; Danny Walla and Michael
Ruslim.

the Summa Bank, owned by the family's Multivest Company, drastically reduced the family's ownership to 10 per cent. Indonesian state financial institutions, *pribumi* capitalists and foreign firms shared the rest. Barito Pacific, Napan, Salim, Sinar Mas, government banks' pension funds, Toyota, IFC and Astra's managers and employees emerged as the shareholders of Astra International.[15]

Structure and management

There were three important factors in this achievement of growth without depletion of family ownership. The first factor was the close liaison with the Indonesian establishment, discussed earlier. The second factor was the organisation of the company, its management structure and operations. The third factor was the multiple methods of financing expansion from the mid-1980s.

The liaisons between Astra and the state and foreign multinationals have already been discussed. How Astra sought to consolidate its success through organisational restructuring and management now needs to be analysed. Astra International separated ownership from management in a restructuring of the company in 1970.[16] This division was unusual for a Chinese company. William Soeryadjaya's wife held 60 per cent of the equity and his children held 40 per cent, but only *pribumi* professionals and blood-relatives, not the family, held managerial positions. In 1988 the managers were allowed to acquire up to 5 per cent equity in the corporation. The family constituted the Board of Commissioners, while the Board of Directors comprised *pribumi* friends and company managers. In 1991, only the son, Edwin Soeryadjaya was on the Board of Directors, as Vice-President (see Table 4.4). This separation of ownership from management and the creation of managerial hierarchies that co-existed within a more centralised decision-making structure, was unique for a Chinese family firm. The divisional system of management coincided with divisions in production, finance and marketing.

The reasons for this change are not fully evident. Possibly the need for rigorous company accounting and the appointment of A. L. Vrijberg as chief accountant persuaded the company to move closer to a multi-division structure. The system was not rigidly Chandlerian, in other words, control was not fully diffused through a professional management hierarchy. There were aspects of the organisation that were irrevocably Chinese in their retention of family involvement. The specialist corporate team, the lynchpin managers responsible for specific functions in production, marketing and technology, still existed. The specialist teams fed information on capital and budgets, sales, manufacturing input and output and production diversification strategies, to teams and team managers who assisted them in planning and implementing programmes, an unusual practice for Chinese firms. The separation of function between the Board of Commissioners (largely family members) and the Board of Directors (pre-eminent Indonesian

Table 4.5   P. T. Astra International

Year	Capital (rupiah million)	Total assets (rupiah million)	Sales (rupiah million)	Net profit (rupiah million)	Dividend (rupiah per share)	Earnings (rupiah per share)
1987	25,000	124,800	1,103,000	20,100		
1988	25,000	251,200	1,210,000	14,400		
1989	60,600	519,400	1,741,000	81,000		
1990	242,198	3,248,115	4,309,276	175,000		
1991		4,589,385	4,933,457	210,000		
1992			4,462,703	81,490	100.00	336.00
1993			5,887,076	132,372	225.00	137.00
1994	1,162,550		8,885,825	279,004	80.00	247.00
1995	1,162,550	15,617,034	11,668,756	370,932	80.00	319.00
1996	1,162,550	16,732,823	12,284,331	469,447	120.00	404.00

Sources: P. T. Astra International, Annual Reports, 1987–1995. See also *Asian Company Handbook 1997*, Tokyo, Toyo Keizai Inc, p. 350.

technocrats) also created a distinctive management hierarchy. One important distinction should be noted. The heavy reliance on one dominant executive in each division meant that information was vested in individuals rather than exploited as an organisational resource. This often led to an overlap of control between family members and favourite technocrat executives. The problem of integrating the centralised decision-making with functional divisions and product diversification also remained. Without necessarily advocating the Chandlerian prescription for corporate growth, the need for appropriate structures in a rent seeking socio-economy should be stressed.

The specialised control and coordination of activities was assisted by the introduction of quality control circles from 1983 in production, sales, accounting, planning, R&D and human resources, which also incorporated joint-venture partners. The vertical relationship between each of the divisions of the corporation and its affiliated companies developed through the exchange of information, personnel, technology and finance. The TQC (total quality control) introduced in the mid-1970s through agreements with Toyota further assisted growth and diversification. For example, company-wide supervision of quality, sales, accounting, planning and the development of human resources through training and education was made possible. These quality control units facilitated regular meetings of divisional managers and affiliated companies' personnel and streamlined planning and future strategies. Liaisons with the Japanese also nurtured a corporate philosophy of teamwork, excellence and national pride. Corporate culture, with the creation of professional managers and the integration of finance, human resource management and information systems, increased the overall efficiency of the corporation. The introduction of specialist managers was another important aspect of Astra's modern structure. Benny Subianto was one such specialist manager in heavy machinery, while Subagio Wirjoatmodjo controlled financial services. Annual meetings of the group, together with monthly division meetings and an emphasis on training and education, assisted Astra's corporate growth and productivity.

In spite of Astra's management hierarchies, divisional structures and total quality control circles, the centralisation of decision-making remained entrenched. A few executive managers, such as B. A. Suriadjaya, H. A. Widjaja, D. A. Gandaatmadja, Marseno Wirjosaputro and Benny Subianto, dominated. With no clear-cut division between information-processing, decision-making and implementation, strategic corporate decisions were made unilaterally by top management without exchanges of information or opinions across the various levels of the hierarchy. Astra was a centralised multi-divisional corporation, characterised by head office involvement in operating decisions. Such a structure, if it over-diversifies, increases operating risks. Astra's competitive strength principally lies in its responsiveness to changes in demand and the fact that joint-venture partners and the state share the risks. In traditional management hierarchies, as in American multinationals, operational tasks and the coordination of decision-making are usually rigidly separated. In Astra, the simplified information system is interwoven with multi-layered subcontracting relationships. The use of multiple subsidiaries in any one sector is pervasive; there is no integration of information through one major subsidiary.

Astra flourishes in a subcontracting culture, as in the automobile industry with its multi-vendor system, where multiple satellite firms supply various parts of the core company.[17] Thus P. T. Aryaloka Sentana concentrated on wheel rim production, while P. T. Suryaraya produced chassis frames and other components. Within these subsidiaries, smaller companies such as Inti Ganda Perdana produced rear axles and propeller shafts and P. T. Gemala Kempa Daya produced other components. There were more than 21 minor firms supplying Astra's Components Group in 1995. (See Figures 4.1 and 4.2 for an illustration of multiple firms, subsidiaries and holding companies in the Astra Group.) This can be inefficient, but the advantages lay in securing diverse financial sources, that is, in overcoming credit constraints. Astra, like most Chinese businesses, had a horizontal information system because of its joint-venture alliances, which facilitated technological accumulation for their several firms. American Multinational Enterprises (MNEs), with rigorous hierarchical structuring, had hierarchical information access and consequently much of the information could be acquired within the internal structure. The only decentralising pressure on American MNEs was market competition. Astra's internal information system defied hierarchy. Astra has been sustained by joint ventures, a sub-contracting culture where a variety of firms supply intermediate goods and market finished products and share technology as well as risk. In these relationships it is difficult to see how Astra allocated cash flows between these separate units; the internal capital market would be impossible to operate without constant intervention from headquarters. In brief, Astra again supports Porter rather than Chandler. Industrial clusters (in automobiles, heavy engineering, electronics) and abundant finance, rather than structure and strategy, explain Astra's success.

Financial accumulation

Indonesia's economic and financial liberalisation of October 1988 introduced new financial instruments that increased the importance of global finance in Indonesian corporate development. Private banks could now deal in a wide selection of financial instruments, including derivatives, as well as employ sophisticated loan formulae, such as multi-currency revolving credit, often authorised by syndicates of foreign banks. There was also increasing participation in the stock exchange. Listings on the Jakarta Stock Exchange rose from one company in 1977 to 218 in 1994, the largest increase taking place between 1988 and 1994. Capitalisation on the stock exchange rose from 2.7 billion rupiah in 1977 to 482 billion rupiah in 1988 and to 104 trillion rupiah in 1994.[18] All this occurred without the introduction of rigorous regulation or accounting procedures. Between 1990 and 1993, mismanagement, manipulation and fraud on the Jakarta Stock Exchange resulted in company failures. Risk was also increased by the acquisition of securities loans in addition to traditional bank loans during the 1980s and 1990s. When rejected by one source, corporations moved to another. This took place when banks had yet to develop the ability to handle major changes in securities markets. The use of bonds to secure long-term capital and of commercial bills to prop up short-term bank loans and venture capital funds increased from 1988. Bonds provided start-up funds in the form of equity, as well as securing convertible bonds for large corporations. Venture capital companies could list in any sector and became popular in the 1990s. It was a highly risky form of capital participation because accounting procedures were not well established.

P. T. Astra used diverse methods to finance its impressive growth. The creation of banks and finance companies was one method used, but it was not the most significant. Leasing, fund management and other financial instruments were used to tap into capital markets to overcome the constraints imposed by the state and by competitors both from outside and within the Chinese community.

The initial impetus for financial development in the 1980s came from the need for consumer finance, largely for purchases of motor vehicles. This remained important and by 1990 credit finance amounted to 890 billion rupiah.[19] The second factor was that Astra's leasing contracts, particularly in financing heavy equipment leases, amounted to 177 billion rupiah by December 1990.[20] Total lease contract values in Indonesia rose from 680 million rupiah in 1975 to

436 billion rupiah in 1984, 1,761 billion rupiah in 1988 and to 7,800 billion rupiah in 1994. Seventy per cent came from abroad.[21] Leasing became an excellent method of raising new funds for investment. A lease contract granted the use of real estate, equipment or another fiscal asset to raise capital. This was particularly useful for foreign and Chinese companies seeking to finance through capital assets. It attracted less burdensome taxes and provided a convenient tool for overcoming government credit ceilings. The major subsidiary here was P. T. Surya Artha Nusantara. Finance was also secured through factoring facilities provided by an Astra subsidiary, P. T. Artha Sedaya Finance (PTASF). Artha Sedaya Finance had, by 1992, acquired transactions to the value of 63.5 billion rupiah and assets of 37.5 billion rupiah. PTASF was also the main financial company involved in consumer financing. Insurance was a fourth important financial interest. P. T. Astra had three major insurance subsidiaries: P. T. Asuransi, Jiwa Astra and P. T. Buana Jasa Pertama.

Astra also moved into the securities business. In addition to acquiring in January 1990 a 10 per cent equity interest in P. T. Nomura Indonesia as part of a joint venture with Nomura Securities and several local partners, Astra had, by July 1990, established its own securities firm dealing in securities brokerage, trading, underwriting and corporate financial operations. In 1992 Astra securities earned a revenue of 994.5 billion rupiah.[22] The sixth form of financial development taken up by Astra was in the form of banking. Astra had four small banks: P. T. Indo Commercial Bank, Bank Malbor, Bank Umum Bantu and P. T. Summa International. Astra's banking interests remained small and often unstable: Summa Bank collapsed in 1992. The Summa Bank was created from an existing bank in 1988 and expanded dramatically between December 1988 and June 1990. The bank was used to finance the family's real estate speculation. The failure of Summa Bank in 1991–92, when it was finally liquidated, was due to a decline in property values and to Edwin's foreign exchange speculations. The bank's losses in June 1991 were 591 billion rupiah. By 1992, its non-performing loans were valued at 1.5 trillion rupiah (US$720 million).[23] By 1994 Summa Bank still owed US$650 million to Bapindo, the state development bank.[24] Although Summa Bank was not listed, its failure still affected Astra's stock market valuation. Astra's major shareholder was the Soeryadjaya family. The family sold its shareholding in Astra International to pay off the bank's debts.

In addition to the financial institutions established by P. T. Astra, there were other important sources of finance for large Chinese conglomerates. Between 1968 and 1989 the government, through Bank Indonesia, was heavily involved in subsidised credit. The Investment Credit Programme financed infrastructural growth through private contracts and P. T. Astra emerged as the largest borrower. Astra's links with the military and regional and local government élites assisted it in securing credit.[25]

State-controlled banks accounted for 80 per cent of the Indonesian banking system and remained dominant even after bank deregulation and privatisation in 1988. Government credit for Astra remained substantial throughout. The decade of the oil boom, from 1973 to 1982, led the government to use oil revenues to finance economic development with the assistance of Chinese capitalists like Soeryadjaya. In this period, Chinese capitalists were thus financing manufacturing and trading activities by using state-aided finance and offshore banks.

When the state deregulated banking in 1988, because of the fall in oil revenues, the Chinese asserted their dominance in private banking. Between 1983 and 1994 private Chinese banks grew from 11 per cent to 44 per cent of total private banking; this was part of an overall increase in privatised banking.[26] Chinese banks, which, when subject to loan ceilings prior to June 1983, often competed for offshore loans and deposits in Hong Kong, Singapore and USA, now established their own private banks in Indonesia. Astra contributed to this by taking over existing banks as well as founding new ones. Chinese private banks had, between 1988 and 1990, increased their total assets by 220 per cent.[27]

The assets of three of the Chinese private banks, including Salim's Bank Central Asia, increased by 600 per cent.[28] Privatisation particularly helped the Chinese who were close to the Soeharto family. Even before the 1980s, interventionist policies in industry and agriculture had led Chinese conglomerates to tap into official sources. Thus both the regulated and de-regulated economic structures assisted P. T. Astra. These varied tactics and strategies of financing were effective because Chinese capitalists, like William Soeryadjaya, acted as financial intermediaries and innovators in a period of financial transformation and heavy foreign direct investment.

Astra would also use other devices to tap credit. For example, Astra would cover a debt by creating a new credit note that was discounted at a local domestic bank. Astra would use the credit note to pay the first debt and then secure from a joint venture partner long-term credit to expand production facilities via a promissory note, which was used to finance yet another project. Ultimately the state bank would guarantee all the credit notes. Another device was to use banks in Singapore and Hong Kong to guarantee credit for imports, this being guaranteed either by the corporation or by an Indonesian government institution.[29]

The result was an increase in borrowing from both domestic and foreign sources, even after the failure of Summa Bank. The funds, secured at lower cost and long term, were channelled between subsidiaries, affiliated companies and associate companies in the group. Astra's growth was often driven by cheap and easy credit, as well as by the opportunities created by a rapidly developing region. The rise of venture capital, leasing and factoring initiatives further secured growth.

Large Chinese conglomerates like Astra established leasing companies to provide forms of financing outside the loan ceilings. Leasing companies could raise new funds for domestic and joint-venture business in Indonesia. These specialist-leasing companies increased from one in 1973 to 83 in 1988. Between 1988 and 1994 these gave way to multi-financing leasing firms, rising to 193 by 1994.[30]

P. T. Surya Artha Nusantara Finance, which provided lease financing mainly of heavy equipment for construction and wood based industries, had, by December 1990, acquired a lease portfolio of 177 billion rupiah. Factoring was another capital source. The rise of factoring companies, particularly after 1990, led to this sector recording assets of 63.5 billion rupiah and total assets of 37.5 billion rupiah for the three years 1990 to 1992.[31]

Another crucial source of finance was loans secured from offshore banks. In Indonesia, the open capital account made it relatively easy for both borrowers and lenders to conduct business offshore. Leasing activity was not subject to credit or entry restrictions. Loans through joint ventures provided one channel of credit. In 1976 Astra had raised a syndicated loan of US$28 million to finance the assembly, distribution and importation of Honda motorcycles. William Soeryadjaya siphoned off the loan to finance real estate development, which later failed.[32] The abuse of funds persisted, despite the organisational restructuring by the Dutch accountant, A. L. Vrijberg. In 1981, Astra raised US$25 million through a floating rate loan on Singapore's Asian Dollar Market. This was followed, in June 1989, by a loan in Hong Kong of US$100 million, through Barclays Bank in Hong Kong. In 1989 Astra used a Euro Note to raise US$25 million and later that year borrowed US$70 million under an arrangement with Chase Manhattan.[33] (See Table 4.6.)

Table 4.6 Fund procurements by the Astra Group, 1974–93

No.	Year	Procured by	Method	Source	Amount
1	1974	PT Astra International Inc.	Short-term loan	Jakarta branches of US banks	Rp 2.69 billion
2	1981	PT Astra International Inc.	FRN	Singapore: ADM	US$25 million
3	1983	PT United Tractors	Syndicated loan	Singapore: ADM	US$45 million
4	1988	PT Astra International Inc.	Syndicated loan	West Germany	DM 50 million
5	1988	PT Astra International Inc.	Bonds	Jakarta stock market	Rp 60 billion
6	1989	PT Astra International Inc.	NIF	Hong Kong	US$100 million
7	1989	PT Astra International Inc.	RUF	Indonesia	Rp 40 billion
8	1989	PT Astra Graphia	Stock listing	Jakarta stock market	Rp 26.3 billion
9	1989	PT United Tractors	Stock listing	Jakarta stock market	Rp 59.6 billion
10	1989	PT Astra International Inc.	Disposal of shareholdings + loans	IFC	US$37.5 million
11	1990	PT Astra International Inc.	Stock listing	Jakarta stock market	Rp 446 billion
12	1990	PT Astra International Inc.	Syndicated loan	Tokyo offshore market	US$50 million
13	1990	PT Astra International Inc.	Syndicated loan	Indonesia	Rp 140 billion
14	1990	PT Raharja Sedaya Finance	Syndicated loan	Hong Kong	US$75 million
15	1991	PT Astra International Inc.	Convertible bonds	Jakarta stock market	Rp 50 billion

Table 4.6 Fund procurements by the Astra Group, 1974–93 – *continued*

No.	Year	Procured by	Method	Source	Amount
16	1991	PT Astra International Inc.	Convertible bonds	Luxembourg stock market	US$125 million
17	1992	PT Astra Sedaya Finance	Syndicated loan	Indonesia	Rp 50 billion
18	1992	PT Astra Sedaya Finance	Disposal of shareholding + convertible bonds	GECC	US$49 million
19	1993	PT Mitracorp Pacificnusantara	Convertible bonds	Consolidated Resources Ltd[a]	US$21 million

Notes
[a]Singapore-based multinational investment company
FRN: Floating rate note;
GECC: General Electric-affiliated investment company;
IFC: World Bank affiliated investment company;
NIF: Note issuance facility;
RUF: Revolving underwriting facility.
Source: Yuri Sato, 'The Astra Group: A Pioneer of Management Modernization in Indonesia' *The Developing Economies*, 34, 3, 1996, pp. 266.

In 1989, a one-year revolving credit facility involving 19 international banks and international finance companies was set up to help Astra repay mounting debts and improve its products in its automobile and electronics sectors. In April 1990, 25 financial institutions, including Bank International Indonesia, syndicated a loan of US$22 million for Astra Credit Card as its working capital. Another US$50 million was secured through Barclays for the same purpose.[34]

Bond issue was another method used by Astra to acquire credit. (See Table 4.6.) Issuing bonds on foreign markets was employed from 1981, although only in 1988 did Astra issue bonds both on domestic and international markets. In 1988, the Jakarta Stock Market was tapped by Astra for 60 billion rupiah. In March 1991, Astra issued a Eurobond for US$1 billion with a 15-year maturity, guaranteed by Morgan Stanley International. In the same year, Astra raised US$125 million on the Luxembourg Stock Exchange and 50 billion rupiah from Jakarta. In 1993, Astra secured convertible bonds from Consolidated Resources Ltd Singapore for US$21 million.[35]

A continuous source of funds came from joint-venture partners. In July 1989, International Finance Corporation (IFC), an affiliated investment company of the World Bank, took a 6.6 per cent equity in Astra, channelling loans and equity for US$37.5 million to the automobile sector and plantations. Much of the IFC loan was devoted to the upgrading of production facilities for light commercial vehicles and motorcycles. Joint ventures were crucial in the search for capital. In 1986 Astra's links with Bank Indonesia's pension fund led to the creation of its major finance company, P. T. Astra Swadharma Bakti Sedaya Finance. The Indonesian state banks' pension funds were used to stabilise the capital base of the Astra Credit Card Company and expand its automation services. By 1992, General Electric (USA) had equity participation in P. T. Astra Sedaya Finance, which enabled Astra to exploit General Electric's capital and technology resources. General Electric also had shareholdings in the Astra Credit Card Company.

A further source was the creation of finance companies within the group. From 1982, Astra created finance companies to handle the consumer finance arising from its automobile activities. In 1989 the Astra Credit Card Company was the largest finance company in Indonesia. In 1991, it had finance liabilities of 890 billion rupiah and assets of 643.5 billion rupiah.[36] By 1990, there were six finance companies in the group and by 1991, it had attracted government and foreign capital partners.

In the 1990s Astra diversified into securities through P. T. Adipura Sumber Sedaya Finance. It also held 10 per cent interest in

P. T. Nomura Indonesia, a joint venture with Nomura Securities. These subsidiaries were involved in securities brokerage, trading, underwriting and other corporate financial operations. By 1992 the revenue of Astra securities reached 944.5 billion rupiah, revealing how lucrative a business this was.[37]

Another major source of funds for Astra remained equity, particularly from the Jakarta Stock Exchange. Prior to the 1980s, Astra relied heavily on bank credit (both onshore and offshore) and in particular on government-subsidised credit and loans through joint ventures. The capital market had been critical since the 1980s. The expansion of the Jakarta and Surabaya stock exchanges in the 1980s led Astra to list some of its companies. Astra's restructuring in the 1980s was intended to transfer the burden of financing to the separate subsidiary companies rather than concentrate capital sourcing in the group's holding company, P. T. Astra International. Consequently the high performing subsidiary companies were listed. United Tractors was listed on the Jakarta Stock Exchange in June 1989 and Astra Graphia in September 1989, followed by the parent company, Astra International in February 1990. After Astra was listed on the stock exchange, the family still had a 76.4 per cent interest, while the International Financial Corporation (a part of the World Bank) had 5.4 per cent equity.

During restructuring, the total capital raised was 423 billion rupiah.[38] Most was employed in the repayment of company debts, while 20 per cent was used for Astra's expansion into the American automobile components industry. The use of listing as a means of reducing very high debt ratios at relatively low cost and simultaneously expanding and diversifying was common practice for large Chinese corporations. The proportion of company funds derived from banks, both domestic and offshore, remained high.

The listing of Astra International was unique for Chinese business. Chinese capitalists generally listed capital-intensive subsidiaries but never compromised on the family ownership of the holding company. In fact multiple holding companies were created within Chinese conglomerates to transfer funds between individual firms in the group while retaining control of the holding company. By 1992, Astra had lost its founding family because of the Summa Bank crisis and the conglomerate was transferred to other Chinese and *pribumi* capitalists, Toyota and Indonesian state institutions. Despite this change, by 1993, Astra's stock was the most active in trading values on the Jakarta Stock Exchange and the second in market capitalisation in Indonesia – at 3,875 billion rupiah, 5.6 per cent of total market capitalisation. Only Barito Pacific Timber exceeded Astra, with 8,960 billion rupiah, 12.96 per cent of market capitalisation.[39]

Capital flowed from one company to another within the group, frequently with little transparency in accounting procedures. After the listing of Astra International in 1990 and with the restructuring of the relationship between Astra and its subsidiaries and the introduction of sophisticated information systems and more rigorously audited accounts, such capital transfers were more simply detected. The continuous restructuring from the 1970s and the separation of the Board of Directors from the Board of Commissioners, also allowed for greater financial and managerial rigour and control. By 1992, there were four financial divisions: (1) International Banking and Investment; (2) Domestic Finance and Local Capital Market; (3) Budget Division; and (4) Financial headquarters with specialists in finance and production. In spite of this sophisticated divisional system, centralisation in decision-making persisted.

As a mechanism for financing Chinese conglomerates, networking is difficult to explore. Close family and business connections persisted between Astra and other dominant capitalists in Indonesia but their significance should not be over emphasised. Chinese companies did hold equity in other Chinese corporations and this external shareholding created conflict as well as cooperation. Chinese corporate raiding was a growing feature in Southeast Asia in the 1980s and 1990s. The variety of linkages and modes of operation among the Chinese should be stressed rather than the influence of Chinese networks with the state on Chinese business performance. The Chinese business network was not simply cooperative; it was formed out of complex relations, which were not always benign. The common notion that the cooperation created by Chinese business networks as the reason for the success of Chinese capitalism is profoundly misleading. In fact, Southeast Asian states rather than Chinese networks supplied most of the knowledge and information that assisted the success of Chinese capitalists. The importance of this relationship with the state is indicated in the failure of Chinese capitalism to expand into markets outside Southeast Asia, particularly the US. The reason for this failure was not a lack of Chinese business networks in the US, but a different relationship with the state. Collective ability within Chinese firms undoubtedly rested on access to knowledge and information and here networks and links with the state are paramount. This explains why Chinese expansion was located in Asia. When the Chinese entered Australia, USA, or Europe, they faced new threats, found no patrons and so success eluded them. The competencies of Chinese businesses were built on region-specific experiences and not on product advantages, such as quality and brands, or on costs, including that of labour.

The weaknesses in Chinese business methods became clear during the financial crisis of 1997, when Astra faced debts of US$2 billion, largely incurred since 1996. Foreign currency debts in 1996 had been US$900 million. Astra's major creditors were Fuji Bank, Chase Manhattan and Sumitomo Bank. In addition, Astra had debts of US$265 million in local currency, run up as a consequence of Astra's strategy of competing with the Timor car project of Soeharto's son. Astra's automobile division saw sales slump by 80 per cent in 1998.[40] Astra sold off part of its shareholding in the automobile and motorcycle divisions to Isuzu and Honda in order to reschedule its debts. In the heavy equipment division, United Tractors experienced an even greater decline in sales and only the assistance of Komatsu saved it from bankruptcy. Astra sold off its electronics subsidiaries and raised US$70 million in November 1998. The remaining 30 companies were restructured by focusing on three categories – automobiles, heavy equipment and commodities. Astra sought to freeze interest payments (Indonesia's interest rates rose to 50 per cent in 1998) and to stagger repayments of its debt, it also asked creditors to forgo 70 per cent of the debt but this was resisted.[41] Indonesia's bankruptcy laws were so inadequate that creditors relied on persuasion rather than force. All these measures still did not prevent the sale of Astra to a foreign company. The Indonesian Bank Restructuring Agency (IBRA) owned 40 per cent of Astra by 1999, but sold the company to a consortium led by Singapore's Cycle and Carriage Corporation for US$506 million in March 2000. The Singapore concern, with interests in motor vehicle distribution and property development in Singapore, Malaysia, Australia, New Zealand, Thailand and Vietnam, was now poised for expansion into Indonesia.

Conclusion

The foregoing analysis of Astra's growth has major implications for the study of Chinese business structure. First, it is important to determine the form the business takes, its powers and the institutions in which it is embedded. Astra adhered to a hierarchical functional model and was still burdened with debt, fraudulent speculation and the loss of family ownership. This suggests that despite responding to domestic and international economic changes by a unique and sophisticated operation of ownership and control, Astra was still caught in an institutional warp. Most modern Chinese conglomerates tend towards mimicry and converge on similar structures and strategies. In the late nineteenth and early twentieth century, Khaw Sim Bee, like many of his contemporary Chinese capitalists, presided over a diverse business empire involved in revenue farming, tin extraction, rubber production, international trade and shipping. His empire had disappeared by 1920. As he diversified to exploit opportunities, he lost the core competence and became inefficient and unwieldy. Alternatively, this diversification was a reflection of Chinese institutional isomorphism – where the life cycle is dictated by attitudes to risk, speculation, unfettered growth, patron–client ties, the economic/political environment and historical legacies. Or was growth and successful diversification into new products, new regions and new technologies, based on a hubris that made these capitalists wildly over-optimistic about their ability to manage all kinds of business and diversify too far? Certainly long-term survival eluded many. Facile generalisations should be avoided, but it can be safely argued that Astra's financial base was over-extended, risk-taking too pervasive and that credit abundance distorted managerial options and specialisation.

5
The Food and Drink Industry: Structure and Performance

This chapter examines Chinese entrepreneurial initiatives in the food and drink industry through an analysis of organisational structure, strategies for expansion, links to the state and relationships with foreign multinationals and ethnic networks. The food industry demonstrates how certain characteristics of Chinese business in Southeast Asia determined the success or failure of the companies, particularly when it came to international expansion. The role of state support, the dominance of the family and the weaknesses of family structure, and the intensely predatorial nature of Chinese capitalism, all shaped the Chinese food and drink industry.

Chinese capitalists have been important in both commodity production and the food industries of Southeast Asia since the middle of the nineteenth century. Early commodity producers such as Oei Tiong Ham in sugar and Zhang Bhi Shih in rice and sugar were successful until the depression of the 1930s. The specific local Chinese market and ethnic networks served as financial and marketing channels. Milling rice and sugar, maintaining shipping firms and distributing manufactured food products, the Chinese capitalists succeeded in an industry characterised by high volume and comparatively low profit margins.

After 1945, Chinese industrialists developed similar economic and political strategies; they operated well-integrated enterprises in close liaison with the Southeast Asian state. The food and drink industry in Southeast Asia comprises both small and large companies, expanding their activities with the rapid economic growth of the region since the 1970s. Chinese firms moved away from primary raw materials, like rice production, to the manufacture and processing of food products; as this happened, the issue of brand became increasingly important for the success of a company. Each firm possessed a number of divisions, such as confectionery, snacks, biscuits, frozen and fresh chicken, shrimps or seafood. The multiplicity of products frequently developed as a consequence of the integration of commodity production with the manufacture of finished foods. Innovation in products and the increasing use of technology further encouraged this form of growth, despite the fact that the commitment of Chinese firms to R&D remained low in comparison with Japanese and American firms. The innovation of Chinese companies was in the control and extraction of raw materials. Minor changes in food quality were instituted but the firms rarely undertook basic research on new products or improved processes.

The broad spectrum of interests created various organisational structures, influencing not only production but also the precise forms of contractual and joint venture relations. The different organisational structures often determined success or failure when it came to adapting to different economic environments, both at home and abroad. The ability to plan, implement, monitor and adjust behaviour is essential if economies of scale are to be achieved in such a highly competitive industry as food and drink. The inability to identify risk in an uncertain foreign market could undermine global ambitions. As we will see, Yeo Hiap Seng's takeover of Chun King in California in 1989 is a case in point.

Mapping strategies of diversification and multinationality

The fortunes of Chinese business in the food and drink industry can be traced through Yeo Hiap Seng (YHS), to illustrate the pressures towards internationalisation and the dangers of such development given the particular structures used by Chinese capitalists.

YHS possessed a successful brand name, popular for Chinese sauces, canned food and Asian herbal drinks. YHS remained a food and drink specialist and sought only limited diversification into related industries, such as poultry and mussel farms, and into supermarket food retailing. Yeo retained its market share through its brand name, as well as innovative products and packaging in response to changing market conditions. Markets in Singapore and Malaysia were limited and YHS needed to move abroad to develop. The objective was not simply to enlarge market share through globalisation but also to establish production facilities abroad, acquire foreign food specialists and enter into joint-venture arrangements. The strategy involved identifying and capturing market niches and acquiring new productive processes, including new technology. This

would introduce differentiation in products, new marketing channels and new managerial resources.

Internationalisation entailed high costs, declining profits, mounting
legal barriers and organisational changes for YHS. The company's structure evolved through long periods of stability, punctuated by relatively
short bursts of revolutionary change, such as its move into California
in 1989. The phase of international expansion, beginning in the early
1980s, coincided with increasing family friction and organisational
rigidities that threatened the firm with disintegration.[1] The entry into
California to secure a food market among distinct ethnic and cultural
groups was risky. The YHS brand name had little value in California:
joint-venture arrangements would have been safer. Instead, YHS held
fully-owned subsidiaries in a situation where it lacked knowledge and
experience; and access to financial resources was difficult, expensive
and risky because of foreign exchange fluctuations.

There are four major arguments arising from this case study. Firstly,
the integration of global initiative with organisational reform is essential. The desire of YHS to capture locational advantages in the United
States was not matched by the organisational and managerial competence to operate there. Secondly, success depended on local managerial
know-how and marketing networks. The company possessed neither of
these, and production management alone was not enough. Marketing
skills and financial management were critical. Alan Yeo's inclination
was that his Singapore partner, Temasek Holdings, would deal with
these problems.[2] Thirdly, Chinese family business is vulnerable to divisions, particularly when profits decline. Family rivalries attract the possibility of Chinese corporate take-over. Chinese families and networks
can be divisive and adversarial rather than cooperative, and the potential volatility of Chinese family management is abundantly clear from
the example of the YHS.

The fourth important point arising from the YHS example is the
relationship between food production facilities and property investment. Food and drink firms often have investments in highly lucrative real estate, that is hotels and distribution chains. Food and drink
companies in an industry with low profit margins, failing to secure
economies of scale abroad and facing severe competition at home,
can become victims of take-overs. The corporate raider's calculations
of profit are based on the value of real estate. Yeo had factories on
lucrative land in Singapore, Hong Kong and Malaysia, which
attracted property developers like Ng Teng Fong and Quek Leng

Chan. Increased dissension within the founding family coincided with losses in the parent company. The company was ripe for take-over manipulations by 1992.

The founder of YHS was Yeo Keng Lian, who established a factory producing soy sauce in 1901 in Guangzhou. Following the civil war in China, the company moved to Hong Kong in 1930. Facing competition from the Amoy Canning Corporation, the company transferred to Singapore in 1938. As a result of involvement in food and beverages, it faced few difficulties during the Japanese Occupation. In the 1950s, it expanded into Malaysia. The main factories in Singapore produced 130 different sauces and 100 different canned foods. By the mid-1960s, it had expanded into fruit drinks and the canning of curries and processed meat and seafood, partly to supply the armed forces of Malaysia and Singapore. The 1980s saw further changes in product innovation and diversification with the acquisition of 7-Up in 1987. YHS was responsible for its production and retailing. This was followed in 1988 by the establishment of mussel farms and the aqua-culture of prawns, as well as increases in the variety of fruit juices produced. This phase of product innovation coincided with rapid regional growth, and expansion into Hong Kong, China, USA and Canada. The 1980s witnessed uninterrupted growth but recurring losses in certain constituent firms in the group. When Ng Teng Fong acquired YHS(Singapore) in 1994, restructuring led to a separation of YHS Foods and Beverages from its property interests. This separation of the food and property divisions in turn led to the alliance of YHS Food and Beverages with Danone, the French food company, in 1998. Danone took 12.45 per cent of the equity in YHS (Singapore). The property interests were increasingly absorbed by Ng Teng Fong's's listed company, Orchard Parade Holdings.

YHS (Singapore) was the parent company, while YHS (Malaysia) was the major subsidiary. YHS (Malaysia) was registered in 1959 as a trading company but was converted into a publicly listed company in 1970, manufacturing beverages and canned foods. In 1975, the four subsidiaries in Malaysia were restructured to form an autonomous group. This was in response to the constraints on foreign ownership imposed by the New Economic Policy. The Yeo family retained 40 per cent of total equity. Lembaga Tabung Angkatan Tentera (LTAT) held 11 per cent equity. Smaller shares were held by other Malaysian institutional investors, such as the Employees' Provident Fund and Permodal Nasional Bhd. The restructuring was followed by expansion into the rearing of livestock and the processing of meat. YHS then ventured into retailing in 1987.

YHS (Malaysia)'s impressive profits were derived partly from its drinks sector where it held franchises for Schweppes, Pepsi and 7-Up (see Table 5.1 for the performance of YHS (Malaysia)). The franchise for Tuborg Beer produced a loss and it was disposed of in 1987. The firm's own non-carbonated drinks, including soybean milk and chrysanthemum tea, were popular as health drinks, as well as offering choice and variety. YHS (Malaysia) concentrated on its factories in Sabah, Sarawak and Melaka, where costs were lower than in Kuala Lumpur. YHS (Malaysia) also manufactured canned foods, drinks, sauces and instant noodles for the Singapore company. YHS (Malaysia) produced packaging for foreign multinationals, processed palm oil and also manufactured products related to these primary commodities. YHS (Malaysia) saw impressive growth in the 1980s, expanding into northern and eastern Malaysia, and integrating its bottling operations as well as its distribution and retailing. The turnover of YHS (Malaysia) rose from M\$55.9 million in 1978 to M\$114.04 million in 1982, M\$122.8 million in 1986, and M\$262 million in 1990. The company made many acquisitions in the 1990s; it had acquired *Poultry World* in 1988, and this was followed by coconut plantations in Sarawak in 1992, a grain producer in 1993 and a noodle manufacturer in Hong Kong in 1994. Diversification into investment and securities in 1994 marked a radical departure. These acquisitions inevitably produced a decline in profits, to \$14.85 million in 1994.

Within YHS (Malaysia) too there was increased instability accruing from share manipulation between 1992 and 1994, prior to the takeover of YHS (Singapore). Rumours of an impending take-over by Idris Hydraulic fuelled speculation in YHS (Malaysia) shares in September 1994. Trading in shares had to be suspended temporarily. YHS (Malaysia) recovered, retained its autonomy, and rumours of a sale proved false. The Yeo family still retains a 35 per cent shareholding, an ownership not relinquished despite increased *bumiputera* participation. YHS ambitions in China have increased with joint venture arrangements with the Success Foods Company of China.

The takeover of YHS (Singapore) from the Yeo family occurred principally because of family feuds and conspiracies among the Chinese business network. YHS (Singapore) recorded impressive rates of growth in the 1970s and early 1980s but by 1984 the company had suffered a reversal because of losses in property purchases by a Hong Kong subsidiary, while its bottling activities there faced stiff competition from other bottlers in the colony.

Table 5.1 Yeo Hiap Seng (YHS) (Malaysia) Berhad (RM 000)

Year	Gross profit	Net profit	Balance carried forward	Issued and paid-up capital	Reserves	Total current assets	Fixed assets	Net assets	Turnover
1976	1,686	738		9,000		12,660			31,812
1977	5,059	3,054		9,000		14,750			43,558
1978	8,851	6,516		18,000		22,930			55,895
1979	10,463	6,373		21,850		31,890			81,416
1980	8,053	5,120		21,850		41,500			100,263
1981	4,603	2,650		43,700		65,090			119,803
1982	5,647	2,886		43,700		45,910			114,048
1983	6,491	2,823		43,700	26,090	46,230			129,850
1984	3,953	2,153		43,700	25,620	45,870			128,141
1985	5,207	1,714		43,700	25,210	45,920			154,990
1986	5,432	3,243		43,700	26,883	44,010	56,758		122,830
1987	11,340	5,835	14,171	43,700	30,096	58,735	61,881	15,079	161,882
1988	11,334	7,217	18,135	43,700	34,560	71,018		19,379	207,161
1989	12,191	9,127	23,922	43,700	40,850	78,070			229,898
1990	13,541	10,377	23,213	83,800	61,696	116,997		60,354	261,920
1991	17,220	12,356	29,122	83,800	68,605	122,943		57,497	283,065
1992	22,911	16,428	35,539	83,800	77,021	138,931	111,463	53,370	334,232
1993	18,097	14,524	41,147	83,800	82,620	128,944	121,391	49,465	342,541
1994	20,170	14,855	47,019	83,800	88,501	147,757	122,930	48,125	370,238

Sources: YHS (Malaysia), Annual Reports, Balance Sheets and Profit and Loss Accounts, 1975–95.

YHS (Singapore)'s gross profits rose from S$6.9million in 1977 to S$13.4million in 1988, but fell to S$7.2m in 1990, before rising again to S$10.8 million in 1993 and S$13.0 million in 1996 (see Table 5.2 on YHS (Singapore)). This trend was remarkable in view of adverse developments in the USA in 1994, with losses of $2.1million in 1994. The group's turnover in 1968 was S$15 million, rising to S$267 million in 1993.[3] The profits were mainly the result of its operations in Singapore; global expansion met with mixed results. YHS expanded as a trading concern into Hong Kong, Canada and the USA in 1982. In 1989, YHS acquired Chun King, America's second largest ethnic food manufacturer. YHS successfully moved into Indonesia in April 1984. In Indonesia YHS produced sauces with McCormick and canned food and non-carbonated drinks with the Salim Corporation. The same year, 1984, YHS initiated the production of sauces in the Philippines and in Mauritius. Also in 1984, YHS secured a contract with Sharwood to produce oriental food sauces for the UK market.[4] YHS's investment in the Guangzhou food industry was successful.[5] Another sector that achieved remarkable success for YHS was its drinks franchise. By 1995, the Pepsi franchise accounted for a quarter of YHS's turnover in Singapore; in that year, Pepsi franchise alone provided S$207 million. YHS also held franchises for Mirinda, Budweiser and Canada Dry.

Multinationals coveted its knowledge of prices as well as the potential regional market for new products. Its bottling operations in Singapore and Hong Kong became larger, assisted by these multi-franchise connections. Pepsi and other major beverage groups needed YHS because of the cumbersome distribution system in Asia, where small coffee shops as well as large restaurants and hotels were important clients. The ability to supply information about customers and to monitor the disparate distribution channels necessitated links with intermediaries like YHS.

The Pepsi franchise accounted for a quarter of YHS turnover in 1994, $261 million, falling to $207 million in 1995. Pepsi held joint ventures with YHS in Thailand and China, while the latter used Pepsi to improve its image and compete with its main local competitor in beverages, Fraser and Neave (F&N). F&N had a highly profitable subsidiary, Malayan Breweries, which contributed 70 per cent of its profits. F&N held a significant share of the drinks market in Singapore and Malaysia, and almost a monopoly in Papua New Guinea. Competition with F&N increased when the latter began encroaching on YHS's specialist foods and drinks lines. F&N started manufacturing fresh noodles and increasing its range of beverages to include soybean milk and

Table 5.2 Yeo Hiap Seng (YHS), Ltd (Singapore) (S$ 000)

Year	Gross profit	Net profit	Share capital	Reserves	Total current assets	Fixed assets	Turnover	Earnings per share (S$)
1971	1,320	768	7,150					
1972	1,444	773	7,150				19,090	10.8
1973	2,110	1,011	9,295				24,960	10.9
1974	3,430	2,130	9,295				38,520	22.9
1975	3,751	2,255	9,295				25,240	24.5
1976	4,998	2,961	15,492	8,792			31,725	19.1
1977	6,970	4,120	15,492	11,590			39,478	27.5
1978	9,910	6,858	15,492	11,091			51,514	40.3
1979	9,649	6,037	25,819	18,278			55,600	23.4
1980	10,329	6,692	25,819	22,085			69,630	26.7
1981	11,497	7,550	25,819	67,398			95,777	
1982	13,092	8,460	77,458	56,949			145,798	
1983	12,857	7,263	77,458	63,095			151,595	
1984	4,229	1,043	77,458	61,772			136,653	
1985	2,489	1,878	77,458	62,080			175,585	
1986	11,966	7,661	77,458				154,780	
1987	14,342	9,107	77,458				185,070	
1988	13,443	9,387	80,008	106,975	163,266	131,919	214,249	11.8
1989	13,393	7,636	80,018	105,987	171,356	188,832	248,363	9.54
1990	7,169	1,924	80,027	99,908	126,574	230,685	304,404	2.4
1991	3,655	-1,409	80,027	90,530	140,296	202,012	341,221	-1.58
1992	12,861	7,279	120,041	99,217	150,700	148,850	265,704	6.27
1993	10,749	7,278	120,042	94,315	175,800	184,087	266,552	6.06

Sources: YHS, (Singapore), Annual Reports, Balance Sheets and Profit and Loss Accounts, 1970–94.

chrysanthemum tea, thereby trimming YHS's profits. In the 1980s, F&N was recording net profits three times that of YHS. By 1993, the gap had increased to 12 times. (See Tables 5.3a and 5.3b for a perspective on the company's competitors in Malaysia and Singapore in the 1990s.)

The drinks sector demanded innovation both in production and in the establishment of a vending-machine network. Much of the company's innovation was in production. From the introduction of the Wink range of carbonated soft drinks containing real fruit juices to the adoption of new forms of packaging, YHS was responsive to competition. It even attempted to centralise production in Malaysia and Singapore and to export to Hong Kong, Australia, and the Pacific Rim countries but was still faced with increasing competition in Singapore and Malaysia, as seen in Table 5.3a.

To cope with this growing competition, YHS was coaxed into globalisation. Since F&N had carved out markets in Vietnam, Cambodia,

Table 5.3a   The four largest listed food firms in Malaysia, December 1990 (RM 000)

Company	Paid-up capital	Turnover	Profit pre-tax	Profit post-tax
Nestle (M)	234.5	968.6	106.0	65.0
YHS (M)	83.8	262.0	13.6	10.4
Cold Storage (M)	82.3	208.0	–2.3	–2.3
Dutch Baby Milk Industry (M) Bhd	16.0	206.4	7.8	4.7

Source: Malaysian Business, 16–30 June 1991

Table 5.3b   Performance of listed food and beverage groups in Singapore, 1993 (S$ 000)

Company	Turnover	Operating profit	Profit margin (%)
Good Man Fielder Asia	399.9	27.3	6.80
Provision Suppliers Corp.	138.8	8.4	6.10
QAF	264.4	20.2	7.60
Cerebos	510.6	113.2	22.20
F&N	1,465.7	188.8	12.90
YHS	266.6	1.6	0.60

Source: Straits Times, 15 June 1994.

West Asia and the Middle East from 1988, YHS pushed towards China, Canada and the USA.[6] The strategy of aggressive growth in Canada and the USA from the late 1980s was fraught with problems. In the USA, it established subsidiaries in addition to seeking mergers and acquisitions. Banly Foods in California was acquired in April 1989 with a factory in San Jose. As noted earlier, in 1986 YHS had teamed up with McCormick to distribute sauces under the name 'Yang'. This was followed by the purchase of Chun King Foods in 1989.

Jeno Paulucci, an Italian-American, had set up Chun King in 1945. Chun King had been bought by R. Nabisco, who, in 1988, during the YHS negotiations, were engaged in stripping the assets of the company, in addition to imposing substantial management fees on it. When YHS purchased Chun King with Temasek Holdings for US$52 million, it was a denuded, debt-ridden company, despite being the second largest producer of canned Asian food in the USA. In 1988, Chun King had sales revenue of US$40 million and a profit of US$4 million. Two under-utilised North American factories and an ill-defined supermarket shelf space weakened the company. R. Nabisco had also sold off the frozen food division. Chun King, therefore, was an attenuated enterprise in the rather restrictive speciality of ethnic foods. The motive in acquiring the company was to exploit Chun King's ethnic distribution networks in California and New York. Its lack of research on ethnic foods and regulations in California made the firm vulnerable in a difficult and highly competitive small sector. American legal constraints on food sourcing and manufacture meant that it could not dump its low cost products from Malaysia/Singapore in the American market.

Initially, after its purchase in 1988, Chun King increased its sales revenue by US$1 million. After that, sales revenue declined. By 1994, Chun King's total losses amounted to S$30.6 million.[7] Earnings from Singapore and Malaysia propped up the North American firms, reducing payments to shareholders and causing divisions within the family. YHS was finally forced to sell Chun King and its firms in China, although losses in China were small and the companies could have survived. Increasing dissension within the family and the executive management of YHS forced the sale of its Chinese subsidiaries. The Canadian subsidiary, Pacific Fruit Concentrate, also faced losses but Yeo found no buyers. The dismal performance of YHS in North America clearly shows the difficulties of penetrating heterogeneous markets. YHS had carved out niche markets in Singapore in the 1960s and 1970s, the markets which F&N had ignored. The segmented markets that succeeded for YHS in Southeast Asia could not be duplicated elsewhere. In the USA, its ambitions were in the food division, not in drinks. Its herbal drinks were designed for Southeast Asians not Asian Americans. The suspicion remains that in acquiring failing, asset-denuded firms in the USA, YHS had not done its research. The American food industry is closely regulated, and YHS lacked the skills to operate in that market. The support of the Singapore state through Temasek Holdings seems to have bred complacency. The global initiatives eventually began to undermine the success of YHS in Singapore. In 1991, YHS (Singapore) recorded a loss of S$1.49 million. There was a temporary reprieve in 1993, with a profit of S$7.28 million, but this was followed in 1994 with a loss of S$2.13 million.[8]

The move into the USA and Canada, and the consequent huge losses there, had two important repercussions for the parent company. The first effect was that market research and product development for the local enterprise had been halted. This lack of innovation was in contrast to the 1970s and 1980s, when the company's introduction of new packaging and new products was conspicuous. The second repercussion was that the losses led to low staff morale, and in particular introduced serious dissension within the family and members of the executive board. Alan Yeo had tightly controlled YHS, with most senior positions still held by family members. Michael Yeo, the deputy chairman, had served in YHS (Malaysia) and YHS (USA). Ben Yeo, Charles Yeo and two other siblings were also connected to the management. Apart from Ben and Michael, Alan kept the other relatives out of power, exacerbating suspicions between the two sections of the Yeo family, one group under the leadership of Alan and the other under Charles and Ben.[9] Alan's view was that the second- and third-generation Yeos lacked business acumen. Another source of difficulty was that YHS Holdings possessed a 38.9 per cent stake in YHS, the parent company. There were six family units which held shares in YHS Holdings, and which had to exercise authority as a unified group and arrive at unanimous decisions. The concentration of ownership and decision-making in YHS Holdings was the main source of division and friction between family members from the late 1980s. This was particularly evident in the years 1992 to 1994 when the group suffered serious losses. Partners were sought to rejuvenate the company, which unleashed further suspicion and factionalism.

Charles and Ben Yeo formed opposing cliques to Alan Yeo, the Chairman. Alan then sought, in early 1994, to dissolve YHS Holdings, which was too rigid in structure and a serious obstacle to effective management. Alan Yeo's aim was to distribute this shareholding within the holding company to the parent company, YHS (Singapore). Alan Yeo failed; suspicions surrounding him were insurmountable, largely because he had expanded into the USA and this venture was the reason for the fall in dividends. The family also resented Alan's autocratic management style and feared the succession of his son Timothy. Inflexibility in ownership, control and decision-making in YHS Holdings aggravated these animosities.[10] Before this, in August 1992, a restructuring of YHS had introduced non-family members to executive positions in finance, information technology and marketing. This forced Michael and Ben, and other opposing relatives to step down.

The attempt to dissolve YHS Holdings, the only remaining area of family control, was resisted vehemently. Each of the factions now sought outside partners to salvage the firm. In April 1994, Alan invited Wing Tai to purchase 40 per cent of the equity of YHS.[11] The other family members opposed this and they immediately began a determined campaign to oust Alan Yeo. The family infighting opened the way for advances by Quek Leng Chan of Hong Leong (Malaysia) and Ng Teng Fong of Far East Organisation (Singapore) to purchase YHS shares, manipulate the warring factions and take over the company.

At the heart of this family dispute and the advances of outsiders was the company's highly lucrative property portfolio. The Bukit Timah land (a factory site where the value of the land had considerably appreciated) was being redesignated as suitable for private residential construction, increasing its then value of S$172 million several-fold and inflaming family greed and divisiveness.

The situation was ripe for corporate raider Quek, who had engaged in an intensive purchase of YHS shares.[12] Quek had spent S$30 million acquiring a 5.5 per cent stake, while Ng Teng Fong was also rapidly buying shares from disgruntled family members. By March 1995, Quek had raised his holding to 20 per cent, while Ng Teng Fong held 21 per cent.[13] Within the next fortnight, Ng Teng Fong had gained 25 per cent of the equity. Quek then arranged a buy out by a consortium including the government linked Sembawang Corporation, Haw Par Brothers International (the tiger balm manufacturers), and Salim. Quek himself now possessed 43 per cent of the total equity, amid suspicions that Alan's shares were being filtered through to Quek. In spite of this, Ng Teng Fong succeeded in his take-over and Quek was forced to withdraw. Quek sold his shares at an inflated price, reaping profits of S$50 million; his share price was exorbitant and the assets of YHS did not justify the price. Ng Teng Fong faced a massive debt; his property company, Orchard Parade Holdings, borrowed S$537.04 million in

June 1995 to sustain the take-over. The high debt–equity ratio was an inevitable consequence of the share buying Ng Teng Fong had indulged in for two years. This alone cost him S$1 billion. YHS properties in Bukit Timah and Dunearn Road could not justify this intense, take-over bid. The only gain was unremitting publicity and the thrill of a stock market ride.

YHS was restructured in September 1995. There was separation of its property interests from food and drink manufacturing. New products were introduced and expansion into China became a priority in 1996, with Robert Ng (Ng Teng Fong's son), as Chairman. Aggressive expansion was pursued in Guangzhou, Xiamen and Shanghai, as well as in Thailand and Indonesia. Although it recorded profits of S$9.1 million for 1995–96, the depreciation of the Dunearn Road property resulted in a decline in net profits. The crisis in 1997 accentuated the depreciation in land values, and Ng Teng Fong was sustained largely by his exploitation of state land development initiatives in Singapore and China.

The case study of Yeo Hiap Seng demonstrates the importance of brand in the success of a food company. Expansion into the US, where the brand was not recognised and food production was controlled by bureaucratic restrictions, weakened YHS. Vulnerability created by the tensions of family-ownership and the attractions of the real estate associated with old factory sites, meant that the time was ripe for take-over by competing Chinese businesses. The recurring themes in Chinese business determined the fate of YHS; the problems arising from inflexible family control, the distorting locational advantages of government support and the eagerness of rival Chinese enterprises to take-over, all took their toll on YHS in the 1990s.

'Open sesame': national hegemony and international diversification

This section will focus on CP of Thailand. The case of CP demonstrates how the protection of the state, which created an oligopoly for CP's core poultry interest, strengthened the company when it came to international expansion and diversification. CP's other strength was its ability to introduce technical innovation in its poultry production. CP, therefore, benefited from one typical factor of Chinese business in Southeast Asia, state support, and from the less typical factor of technical innovation.

CP began as a seed importer in 1921, importing seeds from China. In the 1930s, CP started to import fertilisers from Bayer in Germany, and in the 1950s it integrated animal feed production with the breeding of poultry and pigs in north-east Thailand. Much of this integration was achieved through joint ventures with Arbor Acres (USA), who supplied feed and fast-breeding chicks. Further expansion took place in the 1970s, into food retailing and the manufacture of non-food products with Makro (a retailing group), and into restaurants with Kentucky Fried Chicken. This phase of rapid growth coincided with the establishment of feed mills, broiler chicken breeder facilities, pig rearing and the aquaculture of prawns. To achieve economies of scale, international expansion followed into Indonesia (1972), China (1983), Philippines and the USA (1975), Malaysia (1977), Taiwan (1972) and Turkey (1983). In 1979, CP had 80 affiliated companies, 15,000 employees, and a sales revenue of US$500 million. By 1993, it had 200 affiliated companies, 70,000 employees, and a sales revenue of US$5 billion. Diversification into various sectors of agribusiness was largely achieved through the selective breeding of high quality chicks secured from Arbor Acres of Connecticut, USA. CP remained under the control of one dominant family, the Chearavanont, and the head of the firm was Dhanin Chearavanont.

In 1986, CP moved into prawn farming. Farmers were supplied with prawn larvae and prawn feed, and CP then bought the mature prawns and processed them for export to Japan, the USA and Europe. Thailand's earnings from prawn exports were US$1 billion in 1993, for which CP was largely responsible. Success in agribusiness was due in part to the fact that Arbor Acres provided high quality stock for breeding chickens, Mitsubishi Corporation assisted in the breeding of tiger prawns and Dekalb Agriresearch provided quality strains of maize seeds for CP's animal feed production. CP took advantage of the scientific advances in food production, especially the advances made by Arbor Acres in chicken breeding. The technological advances appealed to CP because they were cheap and simple to introduce, and did not require costly long-term research and development.

To assess CP and its core interest in agribusiness, we need to analyse the structure of the group, the organisational changes that took place in the 1970s and 1980s and the sources of the finance for its rapid expansion. While YHS experienced declining market shares in the food and drink industry, both in domestic and foreign markets, CP achieved increased market share in its core product of feed meal and animal rearing, both in Thailand and abroad.

There were nine divisions within the CP conglomerate, with 60, often autonomous, firms within the separate sectors. The separate divisions included agribusiness, real estate, telecommunications, petro-chemicals, automobiles, metal manufacture and engineering, and retailing. The divisions were vertically separate with their own sub-sidiaries, each linked through a holding company that coordinated finance and investment funds. The interlinkages between the separate companies were highly complex. Cross-shareholding was only one of the bonds between CP, its subsidiaries, and associate companies. CP held 33 per cent equity in CP Feedmill, 2 per cent in CPNE, 10 per cent in Bangkok Agro-Industrial Products Ltd and 29 per cent in Bangkok Produce Merchandising Ltd. CP (Thailand) held 43 per cent equity in Central Proteinaprima, which in turn held 55 per cent equity in CP (Indonesia). CP Feedmill held 57 per cent equity in CPNE and a 60 per cent holding in Bangkok Agro-Industrial. Interlocking share-holding resulted in the Chearavanant family holding an enmeshed, tight control over the company.

The multiple holding companies provided the core structure in this labyrinthine organisational and equity system. CP Feedmill, the premier company in agribusiness, also acted as a holding company for the firms in Thailand. CP (Hong Kong), formed in 1973, CP Investments Co (Cayman Islands), and CP Finance Investment Ltd (British Virgin Islands) all acted as holding companies. CP (Hong Kong), which owned 70 per cent of Ek Chor Motorcycles in China, was a specialist investment group for CP in China. Through this complicated organisational struc-ture, funds could be transferred between companies, real costs and profits could be disguised and tax burdens reduced.

CP Feedmill (1967), CPNE, Bangkok Agro-Industrial Products, and Bangkok Produce Merchandising were the main components of CP's agribusiness in Thailand. CP Feedmill was established to undertake the production and distribution of animal feed, the rearing of chickens and pigs and the aquaculture of prawns and fresh water fish. CP was listed on the Thai stock exchange in 1987, and by 1994 it controlled 40 per cent of the feed meal market in Thailand and was the fourth largest feed meal producer in the world. In 1993 it produced 768,000 tons of animal feed.[14] CP's animal feed division used modern technology and machinery, for example, introducing cooling systems in the mass pro-duction of poultry. CP also expanded into the processing of meat.

In aquaculture, CP captured 75 per cent of Thai prawn production through the introduction of scientific practices with the help of Mitsubishi. In 1992, CP Feedmill had a production of 163,000 tons of prawn, a daily export of 50 tons to Japan, the USA, and Europe. (See Table 5.4a for performance of CP Feedmill, 1989–96.) CP also

Table 5.4a Development of Charoen Pokphand (CP) Feedmill plc, 1989–96 (million baht)

Year	Total assets	Current assets	Issued and paid-up capital	Total revenues	Earnings per share (baht)	Net profit
1989					2.82	
1990	6,963.68	1,519.00	1,200.00	11,476.70	5.51	685.00
1991	8,016.61	1,970.95	1,200.00	16,326.20	8.08	907.53
1992	9,712.17	2,651.02	1,200.00	18,681.47	10.53	1,151.39
1993	9,705.81	1,891.10	1,200.00	18,768.52	10.74	1,201.50
1994	11,269.59	2,602.08	1,200.00	21,169.57	11.88	1,364.31
1995	15,487.25	5,185.00	1,200.00		11.72	1,249.06
1996			1,200.00		11.93	1,357.86

Sources: Annual Reports 1992, 1994; Report by Securities One (21/3/97); Moody's Global Company Data Report, 1997; News Story 28/3/97, translated by the *Nation Review*.

sought to capture an expanding share of the market in India, China and Cambodia, concentrating on prawn feed production and the breeding of fresh water fish and prawns. By 1994 CPF had 19.2 per cent of the Indian market in aquaculture, while in Indonesia it held an 18 per cent share in prawn aquaculture.[15]

CP's success in agribusiness built on its vertical integration, by which it produced the feed, bred the chickens, produced drugs and vaccines for the animals, raised them to maturity, slaughtered them and processed the meat. CP also achieved backward integration, becoming involved with the growing of wheat and corn for feed. Integration allowed it to fix prices. Pricing power was further facilitated through size. CPF owned only 5 out of 38 feedmills in Thailand in 1981 and yet was responsible for 50 per cent of total production. By 1994 CP was responsible for 90 per cent of total production.[16]

The second factor in CP's success in agribusiness lay in the grouping of the company's numerous activities according to specialisation. Each division retained autonomy and was supervised by technical experts and professional managers. Innovation in agribusiness was eased by this culture of expertise. Thirdly, CP had ties with powerful politicians, the army and bureaucratic élites in Thailand. The government fixed import duties on food and fertilisers, often after consultation with CP.

Fourthly, the success of CP in agribusiness has to be understood in the context of the changing dynamics of Thai provincial enterprise since the 1970s. This transformation involved what Ruth McVey calls 'the development of middling nodes of urban life', an intermediate business and capitalist transformation occurring in the provinces, particularly in the north-east.[17] McVey's argument shows how powerful rural politicians had connections with the mostly Bangkok-based Chinese businessmen. The links between politicians and businessmen enabled CP's agribusiness to dominate farming and undermine small local farmers. Small farmers reared the chicks supplied by CP, feeding them with chicken feed bought from CP, before selling the chickens back to CP. Economies of scale meant that working independently from CP was not viable. The collusive relationship between CP and rural politicians made CP even less avoidable. The criticism that CP destroyed the livelihood of small breeders was countered by Dhanin Chearavanant's argument that he had created new wealth in rural markets. Dhanin's oligopolistic practices increased the power of provincial barons at the expense of private rural households.

CPNE was a direct beneficiary of these profound changes in the Thai countryside. CPNE, a subsidiary that was involved in animal feed production and distribution, was based in north-east Thailand (see Table 5.4b). CPNE bred 16 million chickens per year and in 1973, 250 million eggs were yielded. By 1993, it had 50,000 young swine. In tiger prawn production, CPNE had a turnover value of 142.24 million baht.[18]

Another subsidiary, Bangkok Agro-Industrial Products, was established in 1977, and listed on the stock exchange in 1984 with a registered capital of 45 million baht. Bangkok Agro-Industrial Products bred poultry and swine and produced animal feed. In 1986, it increased its capital to 75 million baht and increased production in various provinces of Thailand. By 1987, Bangkok Agro-Industrial Products formed joint ventures in China in animal feed production and in the rearing of ducks.

Although CP faced serious difficulties during the crisis of 1997, its core agribusiness remained highly profitable. As the agribusiness contributed 70 per cent of the revenues of the group, it could in effect subsidise the losses in telecommunications and motorcycle manufacturing. CP's total revenues in 1998 were US$7 billion, from its operations in 20 countries. In 1997, CP's revenue was US$9 billion, an increase of 12.5 per cent on 1996.[19]

A major difficulty for CP was an enormous increase in debt. The holding company in Hong Kong was faced with the danger of defaulting – over $100 million – on one of its offshore borrowings. CP already had loans and debt issues of US$1 billion. The instability caused by debt made its share price in Hong Kong fall from HK$3.0 to HK$0.79 in April 1998.[20] In Indonesia, CP was forced to postpone debt repayments totalling US$400 million in 1998. Difficulties in China created the greatest turmoil for the company. CP had derived 30 per cent of its profits from initiatives in China. In the midst of the crisis, CP sold its 50 per cent equity in Shanghai Ek Chor Motorcycles to raise US$12.8 million. This was to finance the repayment of loans incurred in acquiring properties in Pudong in Shanghai. As part of this restructuring, CP sold Shanghai Mila Brewery to Heineken. CP also sold its Lotus retailing unit to Tesco in 1998 for US$350 million, and negotiated with foreign investors for the sale of the 7–Eleven stores, both in Thailand. In spite of CP's loss of US$400 million in 1997, incurred as a result of the foreign exchange turmoil, it retained Telecom Asia.[21] These difficulties, in particular those of CP Hong Kong, are surprising since it recorded impressive profits prior to 1996.

Protectionism and rent capitalism

Robert Kuok provides the final case study. Kuok is a good example of how the relationship between Chinese business and the state was

Table 5.4b Development of Charoen Pokphand (CP) North-Eastern Subsidiary plc, 1992–96 (million baht)

Year	Total assets	Current assets	Issued and paid-up capital	Total revenues	Earnings per share (baht)	Net profit
1992	1,503.88	389.52	300.00	2,563.42	2.96	88.86
1993	1,609.08	455.84	300.00	2,825.74	2.81	84.21
1994	1,628.26	502.42	300.00	2,965.04	3.36	100.84
1995	1,991.11	774.80	300.00	3,600.86	3.91	117.30
1996	2,257.20		300.00	4,419.20	4.25	127.60

Sources: Annual Reports, CPNE 1993, 1994, 1995; Moody's Global Company Data Reports, London, 1997.

crucial to a company's success, and how, once the company interna-
tionalised and no longer resided in a state protected environment, the
fragility of the family-dominated company structure became a serious
weakness. Confident of government support, Kuok was encouraged to
develop a high-risk approach, which further increased Kuok's vulnerability when circumstances became less favourable.

Robert Kuok's father had been active in the rice trade with
Mitsubishi during the Japanese Occupation. Kuok himself exploited
Japanese connections when he became involved with the sugar trade
in 1959, marking the beginning of Kuok's activities in commodity
trading. The links here were with Mitsui and Nissin Sugar. Kuok
imported raw cane sugar from Thailand, India, Indonesia, Cuba and
Queensland. By 1971, Kuok was responsible for 80 per cent of
Malaysia's unrefined sugar imports and for 10 per cent of the world
trade in sugar.

Robert Kuok sought to repeat this success in Indonesia. In 1974, he
expanded into Indonesian sugar, planting and refining sugar with Liem
Soei Liong (Salim Corporation). With Yance Lim (Yani Haryanto),
Kuok established Indonesia's largest sugar plantation, P. T. Gunnung
Madee, in Lampung. Soeharto's son and son-in-law were involved in
this venture. The plantation had 10,000 hectares, and met 10 per cent
of Indonesia's domestic demand by the late 1980s.[22] Kuok provided
another 30 per cent of Indonesia's sugar imports through his joint
venture with Salim. Much of this sugar was sold directly to the government's Badan Urusan Logistik Nasional (BULOG), which was established in 1967 to control the pricing and distribution of basic
commodities, rice, sugar and flour. BULOG was also a source of government credit. Like Salim, Kuok exploited the economic power of
BULOG, relations with the state, and with large Chinese capitalists in
the diaspora.

Kuok's thriving links with Salim in Indonesia led in 1991 to seven
integrated sugar centres, producing 120,000 tons of sugar, and a
$1 billion sugar refinery. This constituted the largest sugar empire in
Southeast Asia.[23] Kuok also undertook sugar and palm oil ventures with
Djojohadikusuomo, son of Professor Sumitro Djojohadikusuomo, an
important bureaucrat. Kuok's flour import and flour-milling activities
with Salim in Indonesia earned him a niche in that market. Kuok sold
flour to Salim, which was carried on Kuok's ships.[24] This amounted to
2 million tons of wheat per annum. P. T. Bogasari (Salim), formed in
1970, held the licence to mill flour for western Indonesia. A Singapore
company, P. T. Prima, which had secured a licence to mill flour for

eastern Sumatra, withdrew because of political and military corruption. Bogasari then moved in, securing the entire monopoly. Salim's ability to operate in such circumstances is mirrored by Kuok's ability to increase his share in commodity production, processing, and shipping.

Perlis Plantations Bhd (PPB) in Malaysia formed the core company in commodity production, processing, and trade (see Table 5.5 for the structure and performance of PPB). PPB was established in 1968, primarily as a holding company within the group's commodity sector. PPB soon became the core by absorbing existing commodity firms. By 1993, PPB had companies in sugar, wheat, palm oil, tin, iron ore, feed milling, trading, transportation, hotel and property, electronics and retailing. The 10 largest shareholders in PPB were either the Kuok brothers or firms in the group. *Bumiputera* shareholding, even in 1997, averaged only 18 per cent, the largest proportion being held by Lembaga Urusan dan Tabung Haji (Pilgrim Fund).

PPB, which was listed on the stock exchanges of Singapore and Malaysia in March 1972,[25] benefited from the rise in world sugar prices, in November 1974. Despite a dramatic fall in 1975, Kuok had cleared substantial profits. This had two effects; it encouraged expansion into Indonesia, and into related commodities – a phase of mergers and acquisitions in tin, iron ore, oil palm, rubber, marble slabs (Kedah Marble), bricks and equipment for oil and gas exploration.

A significant aspect of the role of the state was the New Economic Policy (NEP) in Malaysia in the 1970s, which enabled Kuok to diversify, encouraging, in turn, internationalisation. The NEP entailed economic restructuring and redistribution to the benefit of indigenous Malays. The nationalisation that followed worked to the advantage of Chinese businessmen in Malaysia because it favoured them, as indigenised foreigners, over international competitors. The NEP could have threatened Kuok's interests but in fact provided him with oligopolistic advantages in commodity trading, and secured niches in property and hotels. Much of the expansion into other commodities was achieved through equity participation and contracts with the Malaysian Government. In Perlis and Kedah, the concentration was in sugar and property, while in Johor the focus was on flour milling. This established the base for Kuok's growth. The close liaisons with the state in essential commodities implied an ability to fix prices as well as eliminate competition.

Malaysia remained the source of Kuok's favourable performance in commodities, whether in sugar, palm oil or flour milling. When Kuok

Table 5.5 Perlis Plantations Berhad (PPB) (RM 000)

Year	Turnover	Gross profit	Net profit	Balance carried forward	Issued share capital	Reserves	Total assets	Shareholders' funds	Net current assets/liabilities
1986	349,085	76,697	13,305	101,717	137,621	54,052		293,390	68,743
1987	415,323	67,745	49,745	142,947	137,621	100,383		380,951	59,165
1988[a]	1,589,494	169,564	102,206	217,568	183,984	233,419	1,345,241	634,971	57,691
1989	2,003,973	156,667	121,797	310,844	245,312	182,684	1,663,782	738,840	−26,862
1990	2,564,164	204,043	135,171	414,391	245,312	192,372	2,209,360	852,075	106,028
1991	2,927,484	209,847	137,007	502,231	245,312	216,388	2,826,039	963,931	−38,310
1992	3,329,113	235,857	172,325	634,289	294,374	969,695	2,536,662	1,898,358	157,237

Note:
[a]These figures are for a 15-month period.
Sources: Perlis Plantation Bhd (Registrar of Companies, Kuala Lumpur), Balance Sheets, Profit and Loss Accounts, Financial Summaries and Consolidated Statement, 1986–93.

formed a joint venture with the French commodities' trader Sucden in 1987, he enjoyed none of these oligopolistic advantages and faced serious difficulties. The joint-venture enterprise SKI Sucden Kuok International (SKI), with Kuok having 30 per cent equity and Sucden 70 per cent, had, in 1989, exported 1.8 million ton of sugar from Cuba to Russia. But, by 1991 prices fell by half and SKI had to endure a loss of US$100 million. Kuok absorbed a third of the losses. These losses were mitigated by the fact that Kuok's ties with Sucden led to the acquisition of a stake in Chile's sugar trade in 1990. Despite these difficulties, SKI had revenues of US$560.4 million in 1990.[26] This is reflected in the impressive performance of Malayan Sugar Manufacturing Company Bhd (see Table 5.6).

PPB was responsible for 70 per cent of Malaysia's sugar refining capacity, and for 45 per cent of the Malaysian flour market in the period 1970–90.[27] The government provided Kuok with contracts to import and refine sugar, maintaining fixed prices for three years. The Malaysian Government procured wheat for Federal Flour Mills at fixed prices (see Table 5.7 for performance of this company). Price fixing was reinforced through government measures to maintain retail prices of flour and sugar. PPB profited from this efficient and stable commodity position, strengthened by the acquisition of land from the Perlis, Kedah and Johor Governments at highly favourable rates. A third of the cane sugar purchased for refining was secured on the open market. This provided the possibility of speculation on commodity futures. The stable source of high quality sugar gained through purchasing agreements with the state provided a steady income, without undermining Kuok's commodity speculation in the more risky international sugar trade of Latin America and Europe. Kuok balanced his links with the Perlis, Kedah and Johor states, with Tate and Lyle, and Mitsui and Sucden. Tan Sri Geh Ik Cheong, Chairman of PPB was also head of the Development and Commercial Bank of Malaysia thereby providing more secure sources of finance. (See Table 5.8 for performance of separate divisions within the group.)

The Kuok group's performance was variable. From the end of 1985, its shipping and property sector made losses of S$5 million. The property market in Singapore collapsed in 1983–84. This affected Kuok's listed companies, where he had raised loans charged against land and property assets. Although Kuok's business empire was valued at US$1.5 billion in these years, serious difficulties remained. These difficulties did not deter Kuok from expanding into the Philippines using the Manila stock market. He purchased Manila

Table 5.6 Malayan Sugar Manufacturing Company Berhad (RM 000)

Year	Turnover	Gross profit	Net profit	Balance carried forward	Issued share capital	Shareholders' funds	Current assets
1986	318,688	67,266	26,782	34,619	36,360	73,127	98,623
1987	367,052	60,592	46,761	57,403	36,360	142,331	82,678
1988ᵃ	468,414	107,589	74,167	100,118	36,360	185,257	100,705
1989	472,091	80,077	81,184	145,093	36,360	230,949	129,330
1990	549,827	105,194	81,137	185,271	36,360	271,908	210,181
1991	526,066	78,406	68,899	213,471	36,360	300,904	106,230
1992	530,902	106,481	102,599	259,208	36,360	320,130	149,025
1993	512,766	110,856	119,256	325,140	36,360	396,126	257,702
1994	591,526	90,414	73,708	345,094	36,360	403,865	336,894
1995	596,771	105,116	86,656	385,946	36,360	444,327	316,798

Note:
ᵃ The figures for this year (1988) are for 15 months.
Sources: Malayan Sugar Manufacturing Company Berhad (Registrar of Companies Kuala Lumpur), Consolidated Balance Sheets and Profit and Loss Accounts, 1984–96.

Table 5.7 Federal Flour Mills Berhad (RM 000)

Year	Turnover	Gross profit	Net profit	Balance carried forward	Earnings per share (ringgit)	Share capital	Reserves	Total assets	Current assets
1986	513,017	42,677	26,913	45,896	0.40	85,000	92,635		158,363
1987	628,122	47,340	34,900	63,835	0.40	85,000	121,606		168,629
1988	968,690	48,822	40,447	86,626	0.48	85,000	154,630	477,659	269,412
1989	1,286,679	53,450	44,365	118,581	0.37	119,000	156,981	674,337	424,137
1990	1,707,393	62,655	59,762	135,712	0.35	119,000	206,564	904,020	607,507
1991	1,993,141	84,260	75,017	181,102	0.47	178,500	272,607	1,230,610	859,141
1992	2,254,484	93,833	82,199	211,564	0.36	178,500	334,925	912,628	555,012
1993	2,284,734	102,479	83,708	277,198	0.48	178,500	407,904		616,547
1994	3,298,824	166,122	133,306	344,056	0.74	178,500	518,523		838,841

Sources: Federal Flour Mills Bhd, 1985–95 (Registrar of Companies Kuala Lumpur), Consolidated Profit and Loss Accounts, Consolidated Balance Sheets, Financial Summaries.

Table 5.8 Performance of the Kouk Group (RM 000)

Year	1992	1993	1995	1996
Food	2,739,115	2,987,170	5,778,810	5,585,351
Hotels	102,184	67,020	85,089	83,142
Shipping	44,391	44,154	28,028	23,231
Commodity trading	1,219,471	1,297,119	3,448,468	2,525,909
Plantation and mining	298,030	332,287	227,210	215,025
Property, entertainment and retailing	166,306	182,645	224,804	178,950
Others	69,097	95,876	228,074	313,418

Sources: Derived from Kuok Group's Annual Reports, 1991–97.

Properties, using Philippine Central Bank debt equity swap facilities, for US$15 million. In January 1990, Kuok Properties was floated in the Philippines, valued at US$35 million, but share prices fell, and it depreciated in value to US$9.1 million within a year.[28] Kuok's response was to increase the capitalisation of Shangri-La Properties through a share issue of US$44.6 million in Manila to complete the development. The repeated exploitation of the stock market was achieved through partnerships with San Miguel. Kuok's financial precariousness was even more evident in China, where the China World Trade Centre's costs of US$480 million were met through large syndicated loans. Repayment by Kuok of this debt was rescheduled over 30 years.

Intricate interlocking shareholdings secured the Kuok family's dominance. The 10 largest shareholders in Federal Flour Mills Bhd, established in December 1962 and listed in November 1970, were Perlis Plantations Bhd (48 per cent), Kuok Bros (14 per cent), Lembaga Urusan Tabung Haji (10 per cent), Amanah Rakyat (10 per cent), Lembaga Tabung, Angkatan Tentera (0.92 per cent). This interlocking shareholding ensured that the family retained 52 per cent, while *bumiputera* shareholding was only 20 per cent.[29] The widespread practice of distributing shares between various subsidiaries in the Kuok Group ensured that the family dominated while conceding limited shareholding to *bumiputera* (indigenous Malay) interests. The *bumiputera* holding itself was distributed between institutional shareholders and a few powerful Malay families. This sharing was critical for Kuok's business. Preferential state policies, state contracts, and a share in state initiatives were secured through this patronage.

The organisational structure of the Kuok Group is rather complicated, consisting of private, family-owned concerns and publicly listed companies. The group pursued a highly intricate strategy of listing and delisting companies, particularly in the years 1983 to 1992. The aims were rather ambiguous. Raising capital was a clear objective but this was often linked to devices to retain family ownership, while conceding to the NEP in Malaysia or to the state in China. The distinctive trait of all the listed firms was that they were capital intensive (MISC, SCMP, Pacific Carriers) or in highly protected commodity industries (PPB, Federal Flour Mills) where government partnerships were critical.[30] Even with listed companies, dominant family ownership was retained in two ways. Firstly, a trading company linked to the listed company would be a fully family-owned unit. For example, in the Perlis Plantations Bhd and Federal Flour Mills group, there were two distinct family-owned trading companies – Paisir Gudang Edible Oils and Kuok Oils and Grains Singapore. Secondly, there was the practice of delisting briefly for apparently random motives, as with PPB in 1992, or for serious financial reasons, as with PPB Oil Palms in August 1997.

The separate, publicly listed companies form a broad base, while lucrative assets are reserved for private holding companies. Ownership in public and private companies rests with relatives, trusts, and offshore shell companies, scattered in Panama, Vanuatu, and Liberia. The identification of listed companies was complicated through the use of offshore shell companies and nominee companies. The dominance of the family in publicly listed companies was achieved through the limited issue of public shares, even though the Hong Kong government did attempt to raise this restriction and break the stranglehold of the dominant family. Second, the cooperation of major Hong Kong families also meant that these firms could remain within the élite group which exercised a stranglehold on the Hong Kong property market. Thus Kuok, Li Ka Shing, Sun Hung Kai Properties and Lee Shau Kee, dominated property in China and Hong Kong.

Thus links with the state and the exploitation of Chinese networks ensured the survival of Chinese family enterprises, irrespective of whether they were in labour intensive industries or in capital intensive sectors. Competition was not a determining factor in the survival of Chinese family enterprises.

At the heart of the Kuok enterprise is a penchant for speculative activities. Speculation was to prove Kuok's Achilles heel in the 1997 crisis. Kuok set up Pool Heng Securities in Hong Kong in January 1986 with a paid up capital of HK$2 million. In June 1986 its name was changed to Kerry Securities. The aim was to issue debentures, and purchase stocks and other securities on property and other assets. By June 1987, capitalisation was raised to HK$10 million, by November 1993 to HK$30 million, and by May 1994 to HK$80 million. In 1996, Kerry Securities failed as a regional brokerage company and ceased operations with the closure of five overseas offices.[31]

Kuok's shares fell dramatically in October 1997. Shangri-La shares fell from HK$12.70 in July 1997 to HK$5.00 in October, resulting in a loss of HK$4.62 billion. Kerry Properties shares fell from HK$21.10 in August to HK$13.60 on 28 October 1997, incurring a loss of HK$4.5 billion. These difficulties coincided with changes in management. Working in the shadow of the patriarch, Robert Kuok, posed serious problems for his sons. While turnover between 1989 and 1997 had increased fourfold, the economic crisis of 1997 and the group's management crisis were threatening the conglomerate. The commodities sector, however, provided increased profits and success. Beau Kuok (son of Robert) became chairman of Shangri-La Asia in September 1997, while Edward took over Kerry Properties.

The Kuok group is a clear illustration of the achievement of Chinese business success through links with the state and foreign multinationals. This is in contrast to YHS, who enjoyed little advantage from either the state or from foreign multinationals. For Kuok, oligopolistic niches in sugar and flour milling provided a secure capital base for diversification into property investment and the hotel industry. Perak Plantations Berhad (PPB) and Federal Flour Mills (FFM) accounted for two-fifths of the total assets of the group in 1993.[32] Fluctuating performances in non-commodity operations contrasted with stable profits secured from commodity production and trade. Despite the indifferent performance of the hotel and tourism sector, Kuok expanded here, assisted by access to capital markets throughout Asia. Throughout the expansion, Malaysia remained the core of his conglomerate. The majority of Kuok's operations – in sugar, flour milling, feed meal production, hotel and tourism and manufacturing – were located in Malaysia. Kuok's interests in Hong Kong were focused principally on China, targeting Chinese markets for palm oil and sugar, as well as carving out positions in finance, property development and retailing.

Conclusion: dimensions of family inflexibility and state capitalist fraternity

This chapter, through three case-studies, has explored the complex combination of efficiency and strategic factors that determine success or failure. Yeo Hiap Seng's disastrous take-over of Chun King foods showed that differences in culture, legal structures and the absence of marketing networks in a foreign location could undermine any creditable growth and performance.

Links with the state were critical. This is apparent from the studies of both CP and Kuok in agribusiness and in commodity production. Improved performance, increasing size and heterogeneity of production could be assured through links with the state. CP and Kuok possessed clear oligopolistic advantages in commodity production and trade aided by the state.

The impact of organisational characteristics on growth and performance is rather complicated. All three conglomerates had numerous affiliates and partly owned subsidiaries. These separate units did not possess financial or structural autonomy. Yeo Hiap Seng Holding Company enabled a family enterprise to expand and diversify, but inflexibility within the holding company led to rapid disintegration and loss of family ownership and control. Delegation and decentralisation remained limited, with the result that the rigid traditions of patriarchal decision-making finally brought about collapse. The controlling block of family members in the Kuok group was also ultimately prejudicial to growth. In 1997 the group faced serious losses in its financial and securities operations in Hong Kong and China and intra-family competiton was in part responsible for this precarious situation. A recurrent theme in Chinese business is that adjustments in industrial and organisational structures are not often accompanied by the introduction of flexible ownership and delegated decision making.

6
The Textile Industry in Southeast Asia: Structure, Growth and Concentration

Chinese textile firms in Southeast Asia were highly integrated companies that included both labour intensive and capital intensive sectors. The large, dominant firms, which integrated both textile and clothing manufacturing, existed practically as cartels because of their size and the protection they were afforded. The textile industry is interesting because it sheds light on the role of Japanese business in the economic development of Southeast Asia since 1945. In the case of textiles, it will be shown that the relationship with Japan was far more complex than the conventional assumption that Japan was the leader which determined economic development in the region. The transfer of technological innovation from Japan was often incomplete and ambiguous, and the importance of interaction with other economic players like the US and Europe indicates that Japan's position in Southeast Asia should be re-examined.

This analysis of the patterns of growth in the textile industry in Southeast Asia will test five main hypotheses. First, whether the Southeast Asian textile industry, nestling within the orbit of Japan's industrialisation, confirms the 'flying geese' pattern of late but rapid industrialisation. The 'flying geese' pattern of development is one in which the early Asian industrializer (Japan) later transferred its labour intensive industries to Southeast Asia and China as it moved into capital intensive production. The 'flying geese' pattern assumes the interdependence of the Asian economy, with Japan at the centre of intra-Asian linkages and trade exchange. Akamatsu Kaname has suggested that each country's cotton industry has a prescribed life cycle.[1] In time, the development of the industry is slowed by competition from low-wage producers able to produce similar goods more cheaply with the use of transferred technology. With the rapid diffusion of industrial technology and improved communications, the product cycle is shortened. Thus Thailand and the other Asian nations in the embrace of Japanese industrialisation, were beneficiaries of the short- ened product cycle. Japan, faced with rising costs and declining com- petitiveness, restructured and located parts of its textile manufacturing to Southeast Asia from the mid-1960s. This had a crucial impact on technological and corporate organisational transfers to Southeast Asia. The region formed critical elements of the 'flying geese' pattern of economic development, in which countries at different stages of devel- opment would grow together by constantly up-grading within the international division of labour. The 'flying geese' pattern meant that Southeast Asia achieved the transition from the manufacture of cotton yarns and cotton fabrics to the production of synthetic yarns and fabrics within two decades, from the 1960s to the 1980s. This 'catching up' theory needs to be investigated through detailed case studies of textile companies throughout Southeast Asia.

This introduces the second theme, an appraisal of organisational changes within textile firms since 1945. Why did the integration of the different segments of textile and garment manufacture and the consid- erable degree of competition in the industry produce large monopolis- tic textile firms in Thailand and, to a lesser or greater degree, in the Philippines and Indonesia? The pressures on Southeast Asian textile firms to adapt to developments in the Japanese textile industry, as well as to respond to new sources of competition in the international textile trade, produced various structures and strategies within these organisa- tions. While Thai textile firms underwent a dramatic integration of the different segments of the industry – spinning, weaving, dyeing, print- ing and garment manufacture – textile firms in the Philippines and Indonesia were more fragmented. In the Philippines and Indonesia, small weaving firms co-existed with larger textile conglomerates. The links between these separate firms were less stable and less entrenched. In Japan too, there was little internal coalescence; rather there were separate spinning, weaving and garment manufacturing firms. Vertical integration of spinning, weaving and the manufacture of cotton yarns and synthetic yarns within large corporations is of critical importance to competitive strength.

Such integration is also a consequence of foreign direct investment, as well as the presence of differentiated products and technologies in a textile sector that bestows cost advantages through centralisation. The textile industry in Thailand in the 1970s and 1980s consisted of highly integrated firms like Saha Union and Sukree-Thai Blanket Group. There were subsidiaries in spinning and weaving, as well as backward integration into raw cotton production. The trend towards integration coincided with industrial concentrations within the separate sectors of textiles and garment manufacture. In 1978, a quarter of the spinning activities in Thailand were vested in just three large firms, while in weaving, these same three firms accounted for 14 per cent of the total. By 1990, Sukree's share of spinning had risen to more than a third of the total in Thailand.[2] Indonesia had the lowest concentration, with the top three textile companies accounting for only 13 per cent of the spinning sector and 6 per cent of the weaving sector in 1978.[3] In Malaysia, a third of the spinning sector was held by three firms, while in weaving, almost half was allocated to three large firms. In the Philippines, a fifth of the spinning sector was in the hands of the three largest firms, which also accounted for a quarter of weaving output. This concentration is in stark contrast to Japan where, in weaving, the top three firms were responsible for only 6 per cent of total capacity.[4]

Even in 1990, the Japanese textile industry was characterised by a diverse, mixed firm structure, with small as well as large integrated concerns. Toray (Mitsui), Mitsubishi Rayon (Mitsubishi), Toho Rayon, Nisshin Spinning of Fuyo and Teijin (Sanwa), remained the leading textile specialists within the *kigyo-shudan* framework of the *zaibatsus*.[5] Cooperation between large textile groups and small specialist firms was constant, through contracts, supplies, and finance. An important issue is how far vertical integration and the internalisation of activities within the large Thai textile corporations was nurtured by Japanese and Western investment seeking stable joint venture partners, in particular in those Thai enterprises with close links to politicians. The parallel transition from import substitution to export expansion, and the integration into the related chemical and electronics industries, were driven by links to Japanese multinationals and the Thai state. This is the third important issue – the relationship of these large textile firms to the state and to foreign multinationals.

The fourth point is the relationship of these textile and garment companies to each other. Here we can see that Southeast Asia's competitive advantage arose not simply from the changing industrial structure of Japan from the 1960s but also from local entrepreneurs exploiting intra-Asian links, in particular Chinese networks responding to the changes created by Japan's position in the international textile trade.

The fifth point is that the constantly changing textile industry introduced regular changes in technology. This process allows us to explore

Chinese attitudes to technology and technology absorption. The ASEAN countries had reached half the output levels of Korea and Taiwan, and a third of Hong Kong's spinning sector, by 1981.[6] In garments, accelerated growth occurred in the 1980s. Among the 15 leading world exporters of textiles in 1993, Indonesia accounted for 2.3 per cent; in 1980, it had accounted for 0.1 per cent of world's exports. Indonesian textile exports rose by 37 per cent between 1980 and 1993.[7] Indonesian garments accounted for 2.6 per cent of world exports of clothing in 1993, up from 0.2 per cent in 1980.

Thailand also took an increasing share of world garment exports: 0.7 per cent in 1980 to 3.1 per cent in 1993, with an average annual percentage increase of 24 per cent. Between 1961 and 1971, an era of particularly rapid growth in the textile industry, Thailand's industry grew 5.8 times, and Indonesia's four times. Meanwhile, the Philippines stagnated.[8] Between 1968 and 1977, the ASEAN countries increased their share of world exports of cotton yarns and fabrics from 1 per cent to 4 per cent. The main part of this increase was located in Thailand and Malaysia. In man-made yarns and fabrics, ASEAN's share of world exports rose from 0.2 per cent to 1.1 per cent between 1968 and 1977. To maintain such expansion, imports of synthetic fibres from Japan rose six-fold, from US$29 million in 1968 to US$173 million in 1977. Japan exported filament fabrics to Southeast Asia and Taiwan, which produced garments for export to the USA and the European Union. ASEAN firms were particularly competitive in the production of mixed polyester cotton fabrics and in garment exports. ASEAN exports in the 1970s to the USA and the EU increased from 1 per cent to 2.5 per cent of those trading blocs' imports. In fabrics the increase was from 3 per cent to 10 per cent and in garments exports to these areas rose from 1 per cent to 4 per cent.[9]

The growth of synthetic fibres underpinned ASEAN's international competitiveness. The transition from import substitution to export oriented industrialisation was bound up with the production and export of synthetic fibres in the 1970s. Southeast Asia achieved the transition from cotton yarns, cotton fabrics, and cotton garments to synthetic yarns and fabrics within two decades, a 'catching-up' fostered by a division of labour between Japan, Korea, Taiwan and Southeast Asia. The upgrading of technology and differentiation of product were secured through liaisons with the state and foreign multinationals. The division of labour in the textile industries of the Asia-Pacific region was dictated not simply by comparative advantages in labour costs and technical capabilities but also, from 1970, by international trade constraints imposed on Japan, Hong Kong and Taiwan. The phenomenal leap in the inflow of investment and technology in the 1970s and 1980s into ASEAN's textile industries was, to a degree, precipitated by the 'quota-hopping' tactics of Japan and the others. The ASEAN four (Thailand, Malaysia, Indonesia and the Philippines) absorbed a foreign direct investment of US$13 billion in 1988 (three times that of 1987) and approximately US$17 billion in 1989. Japan contributed half of that total.[10]

This intra-Asian division created networks of economic activity and intra-firm and intra-industry transactions, with textiles being integrated into electronics and chemical industries, as design, garment manufacture and the production of synthetic fibres encouraged important links. Thailand's textile groups, Saha Union and Sukree, were integrated with Japanese firms to form supply chains. When Thailand experienced wage increases and a contracting labour supply, Saha Union and Sukree moved to new locations in Vietnam, China, Bangladesh, Latin America and even the USA. Such spatial restructuring of production created instant multinationals out of large domestic textile corporations. Supply chains and networks were integrated through labour cost and price advantages, with investment and technology flowing through these exchanges. Joint venture liaisons provided information, research and development collaboration, and an accumulation of knowledge, all of which facilitated efficient production and marketing. Southeast Asian textile groups, in joint ventures with Japanese, American, and European textile firms, tapped into new inventions and hi-technology products. There was a dual support structure, a complex mixture of Japanese subcontracting, (with specialist manufacturers assisting in and financing the production of high quality goods and sharing risks) and the state (providing incentives for securing higher productivity and restructuring in response to world competition).

Japanese investment accounted for 63 per cent of total investment in the ASEAN textile industry between 1951 and 1978. Toray and Teijin's overseas investments in 1976 were 83.6 billion yen, half of the overseas investment by synthetic fibre companies in Southeast Asia.[11] In the 1980s, Hong Kong increased its investment in textiles in Malaysia, Singapore, Indonesia and Thailand.[12] There was a nineteen-fold increase of foreign direct investment from Hong Kong into Indonesia between 1984 and 1992, when it accounted for 57 per cent of total foreign textile investment in Indonesia.[13]

A minority of large textile corporations often dominated these late-comers to textile industrialisation in Southeast Asia. This was particularly the case in Thailand, the Philippines, Malaysia and Singapore.[14]

The state was crucial in providing financial support and tariff protection for the local textile industry. Governments throughout Southeast Asia erected tariffs to encourage local manufacture. In Thailand, tariff rates on capital goods imports were reduced from the late 1950s, implying high rates on consumer imports and low rates on capital goods and components. Moreover, tariff holidays were offered to encourage import-substitution industrialisation. Finally, a differentiated tariff structure, with higher rates on finished goods and lower rates on parts and components, was intended to woo multinationals to establish production in Thailand, first to supply the domestic market and later to produce for export. Local textile firms sought joint ventures with foreign partners inside the tariff wall. Foreign capital, which was attracted by cost advantages as well as the absence of trade and exchange controls, sought local partners to gain access to local knowledge and local marketing networks in capital intensive industries producing for export, as well as for the domestic market. In 1969, foreign direct investment from Japan into Thailand was 404 million baht, while that from the USA was 476 million baht. Between 1969 and 1980, Japanese investment into Thailand averaged 523 million baht annually, that of the USA, 494 million baht. The value of Thailand's trade with Japan increased between 1960 and 1972, with import volumes rising from 26 per cent to 37 per cent and exports to Japan rising from 8 per cent to 21 per cent. With Japanese companies locating subsidiaries in Southeast Asia following the revaluation of the yen in 1985, their capital commitments rose further. The registered capital of Japanese firms in Thailand rose from 2,836 million baht in 1986 to 38,755 million baht in 1991.[15]

Throughout the years 1971–95, growth in Thailand was concentrated in four large textile companies. In fact, the share of small-scale producers fell from 50 per cent in 1961 to 16 per cent in 1979.[16] Much of this small-scale production was for the domestic market; the export sector remained the preserve of the big four and foreign multinationals.

The study now focuses on the background to this increasing concentration, the vertical integration within single corporations of the various segments of the textile industry. The internalisation of processes and products within single large corporations and the emergence of monopolistic concentration in the industry were outstanding features of the sector in this period.[17] Small or medium sized local firms co-existed but were a rapidly shrinking segment in the capital-intensive textile sector.

The majority of the large textile companies in Southeast Asia belonged to the Chinese. Although Indians were active in Indonesian textile production and in certain segments of the Philippine textile industry, and were crucial in textile marketing throughout Southeast Asia, the Chinese were pre-eminent in the industry.

How did these Chinese textile firms in Thailand and other parts of Southeast Asia become so large, and how did they secure economies of scale and scope without sacrificing family ownership and control, and without introducing strict managerial hierarchies? The international trade barriers on textiles, erected from the late 1960s, were of vital assistance. Growth was limited during the import substitution phase of the 1950s and 1960s, and only export-oriented industrialisation from the 1970s produced spectacular growth. Chinese firms faced serious competition in the import substitution period from Japanese textile firms based in Thailand, which were later curbed by government measures in the period of export promotion. Thai domestic textile manufacturers possessed less of a competitive advantage in the 1950s and 1960s in cotton textiles. The transition to higher technology and intensive man-made fibres from the early 1970s provided the competitive edge. The ratio of cotton fabrics to man-made fabrics in Thai domestic textile production shifted sharply, from 90:10 in 1968 to 56:44 in 1978.[18] The transition from natural to artificial fibres in Southeast Asia since the late 1960s also coincided with the growing Japanese crisis in artificial textile production between 1960 and 1965, which made overseas investment imperative to maintain the scale of production. The oil-crisis of 1973 accelerated this trend. The expansion of the garment industry in Hong Kong, Taiwan and Southeast Asia provided a further impulse. Another striking feature is how 'first mover' advantages for domestic textile firms were rarely eroded by new competition. Buttressed by state incentives and assistance and by foreign multinationals' technology and finance, the big textiles firms maintained a relentless expansion into the various segments of the textile industry, responding to the demands of 'quota hoppers' in Japan, Hong Kong and Taiwan in the 1970s and 1980s.[19]

The vertical integration of production in textiles provides the core of this analysis. The growth of textile firms in Thailand since the late 1960s had its origins in the growth of bureaucratic capital in the 1950s. Under the state-promoted economic growth of Sarit from 1958 to 1963, Chinese capitalists established textile syndicates. These were monopolistic companies involved in the production, distribution, and marketing of textiles with major Chinese businessmen, the Thai military, and politicians. The Sukree, or Thai Blanket Group (Sukree Photiratanankul), had had good relations with the Thai military since 1949, having been the sole supplier of textile products to government and military enterprises. The Thai Blanket Company was established in 1959 with the son-in-law of General Thanom Kittikajorn, Chamnan Phenjati, to supply blankets to the Thai military. Sukree's other company, Thai Cotton Mill, managed the military's spinning activities. By 1986, the group had 26 subsidiaries in textiles and garments, with its registered capital rising from 8 million baht in 1960 to 580 million baht in 1972, and to 3,513 million baht in 1986. By 1995 Sukree had two major subsidiaries, Thai Melon Polyester (paid up capital, 1.3 billion baht) and Thai Iryo, a garment producer (paid up capital, 42 million baht), which still retained valuable links to the Thai state and military. (See Tables 6.1 and 6.2 on Thai Iryo and Thai Melon Polyester.)

The vertical integration into spinning, weaving, bleaching, dyeing, and printing by a few large firms within a decade in Thailand is particularly striking. In 1978, integrated firms owned 83.4 per cent of the total spinning machinery and 37.4 per cent of the total weaving machinery.[20] From Figure 6.4 on integrated firms it is clear that spinning firms in Thailand were more intensely integrated than those in Malaysia and Indonesia and particularly more than in Korea. Sukree alone, in 1983, owned 21 per cent of spinning machinery and 5 per cent of looms; by 1986 its share of spinning machines had risen to 25 per cent.[21] In 1983, Saha Union and Sukree controlled 32 per cent of spinning in Thailand. Sukree, Saha Union and Luckytex had internalised all the major processes in the industry. Sukree had two spinning firms, three spinning-weaving firms, two dyeing and bleaching units and one garment manufacturer. Luckytex, since 1960, had firms producing cotton yarn, cotton fabrics, bleaching, dyeing and printing fabrics, as well as spinning and weaving. Diversification accelerated in 1972, when Toray Industrial Corporation of Japan took over Luckytex in a joint venture with Textile Alliance of Japan. By 1980, Luckytex was one of the largest textile firms in Thailand.

The reasons for this vertical integration and the increasing monopolistic concentration within the industry need to be explored. In 1978–81, the three largest Thai textile firms owned 49 per cent of the spindles in the country. Production by small-scale firms declined, by volume, from 50 per cent in 1961 to 16 per cent in 1979. These small-

Table 6.1 Thai Iryo Co. Ltd (baht 000)

Year	Sales	Total revenue	Cost of goods sold	Total expenses	Gross profit	Net profit	EPS ordinary (baht)	Total cash dividend
1987	662,016	690,005	585,078	672,093	17,912	11,394	27.3	8,400
1988	714,693	737,741	629,850	711,029	26,712	18,984	45.2	16,800
1989	843,017	929,768	724,551	828,590	101,178	71,165	169.44	16,800
1990	912,058	951,185	814,199	928,841	22,334	15,863	3.78	27,300
1991	652,064	696,356	584,083	681,076	15,280	11,528	1.66	6,958
1992	693,936	800,841	648,390	792,977	7,863	6,437	0.93	6,958
1993	569,903	604,506	560,537	648,057	-43,551	-43,551	-6.26	3,479
1994	636,010	662,745	632,865	806,618	-14,873	-143,873	20.68	
1995	462,959	498,725	454,746	573,855	-75,130	-130,742	-18.79	

Year	Cash and deposits at bank	Deposits and prepayments	Total current assets	Total investments and loans	Total assets	Bank overdrafts and loans from bank	Total current liabilities	Total liabilities
1987	17,036	580	293,061	66,639	394,446	205,914	256,861	258,464
1988	11,824	415	291,301	80,894	418,526	193,305	278,758	280,361
1989	78,835	377	476,930	60,161	607,351	293,583	413,217	414,820
1990	134,647	824	574,910	131,917	785,338	366,676	455,412	467,015
1991	45,414	542	436,450	255,699	763,035	361,567	431,627	443,230
1992	156,463	157	515,822	273,997	857,826	422,174	531,940	538,543
1993	32,637	126	403,456	275,666	735,710	312,792	456,854	463,457
1994	23,622	99	332,596	258,850	644,794	361,851	526,503	531,503
1995	12,019	89	251,410	208,554	956,825	373,721	520,844	525,844

Table 6.1 Thai Iryo Co. Ltd (baht 000) – *continued*

Year	Authorised capital	Issued and paid-up capital	Total shareholders' equity	Total liabilities and shareholders' capital
1987	42,000	42,000	135,981	394,446
1988	42,000	42,000	138,166	418,526
1989	42,000	42,000	192,531	607,351
1990	42,000	42,000	318,323	785,338
1991	69,576	69,576	319,805	763,035
1992	69,576	69,576	319,284	857,826
1993	69,576	69,576	272,254	735,710
1994	69,576	69,576	113,292	644,794
1995	69,576	69,576	430,981	956,825

Sources: Thai Iryo, Profit and Loss Accounts and Annual Balance Sheets, 1986–96.

Table 6.2 Thai Melon Polyester Co. Ltd (baht 000)

Year	Sales	Total revenue	Cost of goods sold	Total expenses	Gross profit	Net profit	EPS ordinary (baht)	Total cash dividend
1988	1,451,789	1,467,988	1,268,902	1,404,082	63,906	63,906	79.88	
1989	1,504,767	1,583,111	1,463,443	1,580,405	2,706	2,706	3.38	
1990	1,516,032	1,767,248	1,188,641	1,611,708	155,540	95,798	1.59	24,711
1991	2,101,599	2,170,386	1,665,851	1,973,618	196,768	142,069	1.64	
1992	1,552,225	1,624,200	1,279,665	1,484,252	139,948	95,427	1.02	67,500
1993	1,553,770	1,597,839	1,506,743	1,735,664	-137,825	-137,825	1.25	55,000
1994	1,924,864	2,000,787	1,661,782	1,896,529	104,259	104,259	0.82	
1995	2,589,197	2,723,193	2,273,283	2,654,191	69,001	45,651	0.31	

Year	Cash and deposit at bank	Total current assets	Total investment and loans	Total assets	Bank overdrafts and loan from bank	Total current liabilities	Total liabilities	Authorised capital
1988	13,943	1,090,821		2,082,664	931,382	1,251,922	1,602,387	400,000
1989	13,162	1,408,248		2,837,319	1,539,415	1,819,341	2,151,449	400,000
1990	5,847	1,366,604	50,341	3,387,705	1,160,043	1,525,431	2,536,365	900,000
1991	224,982	1,710,875	50,341	3,751,766	1,151,439	1,592,732	2,632,725	900,000
1992	331,008	1,633,993	54,888	4,944,589	845,156	1,561,049	2,290,328	1,100,000
1993	393,759	1,466,608	73,342	5,232,373	1,297,725	2,001,611	2,770,936	1,100,000
1994	29,459	1,352,667	52,341	6,307,811	1,562,437	2,375,716	3,522,116	1,320,000
1995	118,819	2,509,733	52,341	8,968,727	2,497,616	4,033,980	5,917,381	2,000,000

Table 6.2 Thai Melon Polyester Co. Ltd (baht 000) – *continued*

Year	Issued and paid-up capital	Total shareholders' equity	Total liabilities and shareholders' capital
1988	400,000	480,277	2,082,664
1989	400,000	685,870	2,837,319
1990	774,368	851,340	3,387,705
1991	900,000	1,119,041	3,751,766
1992	1,100,000	2,654,262	4,944,589
1993	1,100,000	2,461,437	5,232,373
1994	1,320,000	2,785,695	6,307,811
1995	1,540,000	3,051,346	8,968,727

Sources: Thai Melon Polyester, Profit and Loss Accounts and Balance Sheets, 1987–96. (Ministry of Commerce, Bangkok).

scale firms were largely involved in weaving. Sukree emerged as one of the world's largest garment producers by 1987.[22]

The reasons for this level of vertical integration and monopolistic integration are fairly clear. First of all, both Sukree (since 1949) and Saha Union (since 1961) had close relations with the Thai state and the military, and were identifiable textile powers both for East Asian and Western producers seeking new locations and new joint venture partners.

The second reason for the vertical and monopolistic integration of textiles is that textile manufacturing thrives in clusters – of cotton yarn and fabrics, chemicals, dyes, synthetic fibres, computerised assisted design and the manufacture of garments. Such clustering was essential to maintain stability in the supply of inputs as well as to maintain quality. ASEAN firms, as they expanded through an export-led strategy, were assisted by such integration in maintaining quality, and by the presence of foreign joint venture partners in the integrated enterprises. Quality competitiveness in grey fabrics (60 per cent of fabric exports in 1974 were greys), less in processed fabrics where the Japanese were major players, was supported by delivery effectiveness and access to information networks and new markets.[23] Japan, which had a tradition of production through networks of large and small producers, was, from 1967, encouraging small firms to amalgamate into larger groups. Unfettered competition was recognised to be destructive, particularly in an era of international quotas and trade constraints.[24]

The creation of such clusters was encouraged by the volume and pace of Japanese foreign direct investment into Southeast Asia. Thailand was an important cluster for Japan, and ranked third in terms of Japanese foreign direct investment in textiles in 1974, following Taiwan and Korea. By 1988, Japanese foreign direct investment in textiles in Asia accounted for 52 per cent of total Japanese foreign direct investment. The Japanese provided the capital, technology, and commercial expertise,[25] while the domestic textile firm controlled the financial apparatus. Management was frequently shared by the two companies. The Japanese strategy of offshore processing was critical for the creation of large, integrated textile corporations, particularly in Thailand. With the assistance of government, the large textile groups squeezed out foreign competitors, and in fact used the foreign competitors to mould an integrated organisation in the domestic economy. Sukree had joint venture partners in Shikibo, Nomura Trading, and Rhone-Poulenc (the largest French chemical firm, which provided 10 per cent of its equity capital in 1972).[26] Research and development spending was negligible in Thai–Chinese textile firms because technology was acquired from Japan, Korea, Europe and Taiwan (in that order of importance). R&D expenditure was just 0.85 per cent of sales revenue in 1990, which is low in comparison with that of the Japanese research and development expenditure in Thai textiles of 1.76 per cent.[27] Thai–Chinese firms were also dependent on the Japanese for upgrading technology and worker skills. The Japanese were constantly upgrading to more profitable products and seeking less restrictive markets, making research and development acquisition more difficult. From 1981, Shikibo and Nomura Trading reduced their equity in Sukree from 16.7 per cent (in 1972) to 5.7 per cent, although other Japanese companies increased their equity in Sukree from 2.6 per cent in 1972 to 7.4 per cent in 1981.[28] These changes in equity reflect the changes in the relationships between the Thai companies and their foreign venture partners.

Japanese integrated manufacturing in the dyeing and processing of textiles did produce quality efficiency but in most textile sectors productivity was achieved through the use of machinery. This technology-induced productivity, where the condition of equipment became a critical factor in efficiency rather than labour costs, propelled Thai and even Malaysian textile firms (such as Pen Textiles) towards greater integration, and thus economies of scale and scope, more stable procurements and advantages in marketing and information networks. However, frequent friction with joint venture partners meant that technological assimilation remained incomplete. For example, Sukree had tempestuous relations with its partners. In 1973, Sukree's American partner withdrew; Rhone Poulenc took its place and established Thai Melon Polyester, a highly successful enterprise. In 1982, Rhone Poulenc withdrew because of Sukree's irregular transfer of sales revenues and profits between affiliates. The level of antagonism is indicated by the fact that a death threat was issued to French engineers at the plant. Bangkok Bank bought out the French shares and distributed them to Sukree. Questions over financial probity had surfaced in 1959, when Shikiba and Nomura Trading had asked for capitalisation shares, but Sukree insisted on reinvesting profits in plant expansion. Continuing doubts led to a reduction in Japanese equity from 46 per cent in 1968 to 6 per cent in 1981.[29]

By 1981, the group's registered capital had risen to 1,687 million baht, in joint ventures with Toyo Menka, Rhone Poulenc and Kanebo. The share of foreign capital had fallen to 25 per cent. However, with internal transfers of foreign equity between subsidiaries rising from

12 per cent in 1972 to 21 per cent in 1981, the actual ratio of foreign capital to total capital in the group rose.

The important conclusion here is that overseas investors increased rather than reduced the hierarchical nature of corporate organisations in textiles, as they strengthened organisations rather than weakened them, and assisted in perpetuating rather than denuding family ownership. Core textile firms remained within the family, while certain subsidiaries were listed on the stock exchange. Retained profits were used by the large family firms to supplement income derived from the foreign multinationals, the state, and domestic and offshore banks. The centralised control of Chinese textile firms was a reflection of weak collective commitments beyond the core family. Trust is highly personalised and limits the degree to which coordination and control are delegated. The Chinese capitalists, because of their personalised authority, possessed low collective commitment, and market relations were often conducted on the basis of the personal connections of the patriarch, which could not survive his demise. This deficiency was often compensated for by relations with foreign multinationals and the indigenous state, which were critical in acquiring complex technologies, generous funding and assistance in seeking new markets.[30]

The third factor promoting vertical integration is the strength of the firms' relationships with financial institutions. Such relationships, advanced in the Japanese 'Main Bank' literature, prevailed in textile groups in Thailand.[31] These were long-term relationships and had a risk-sharing character. Banks in these textile clusters often held equity in firms in the group. Although the banks had access to capital markets across Asia, reciprocal shareholdings between large corporations and dominant private banks were common. The Bangkok Bank's links to Sukree were through holding equity in the group: 0.2 per cent in 1972 rising to 3.0 per cent in 1981. Bangkok Bank held 4.2 per cent of Saha Union equity in 1995. In 1977, Bangkok Bank had assisted in the restructuring of Saha Union following the recession and integrated textile production with the manufacture of garments. In the 1980s, Saha Union attempted to introduce managerial hierarchies by co-opting influential Thai bureaucrats. Dr Amnuay Virawan of the Ministry of Finance, NESDB (National Economic and Social Development Board) and of Bangkok Bank, joined Saha Union as an Executive Manager. Dr Amnuay Virawan had earlier been instrumental in the purchase of shares in a Japanese joint venture partner of Saha Union, and in arranging Mitsui's loans to the company. When Saha Union expanded into China in the 1990s, Bangkok Bank followed as a partner, investing in China with Chinese state companies. In 1986–87, Bangkok Bank loans to Saha Union tripled to assist the growth and diversification of the group.[32]

The fourth major factor propelling firms towards integration and increasing concentration was rising wage costs. The earlier competitiveness of ASEAN textile firms was derived from low labour costs. In 1979, labour costs in textiles in Thailand were one-third of the labour costs in Japan. Rates were still lower in South Korea.[33] By 1985, this advantage was steadily eroding, particularly in spinning and weaving, where rates in Thailand, Malaysian and the Philippines had almost doubled. Only Indonesian labour costs remained low, although they had increased.

Declining competitiveness in labour costs and the increasing disparities in competitiveness in the different segments of textile exports from the ASEAN countries forcefully showed that success would come through amalgamating the different sectors of the industry. ASEAN countries were facing stiff competition from South Korea and Taiwan in cotton yarns and man-made yarns from the second half of the 1970s. From the 1980s, their competitiveness remained in garments and man-made staple fabrics but not in man-made filament fabrics and man-made staple yarns.[34] The integrated production system assisted them in retaining this lead.[35] Integration, while achieving economies of scale and maintaining quality, was also critical in establishing information and marketing networks.

The garment industry is labour-intensive. Labour costs soared in the 1990s, when average wages in Bangkok rose by 5–8 per cent per annum.[36] Wages in Indonesia and China were less than in Thailand. Although wages outside Bangkok were 23 per cent lower and there were tax concessions from the Board of Investment, the lack of adequate transport and telecommunications infrastructures was a serious inhibiting factor. The solution was to integrate, and cross-subsidise low performing sectors with higher performing ones.[37]

By 1994 wage costs were uncompetitive. The solution was to upgrade technology and improve productivity, but also to move into producing for designer labels such as Liz Claiborne, Polo, Banana Republic, Gap, Nino Cerruti, Daniel Hechter and Saks Fifth Avenue. The other path was to locate in China, Vietnam and Laos. Laos faced no quota restrictions on exports.[38]

The fifth major factor assisting vertical integration was the fact that forward and backward integration was not impeded by competition from Western or Indian textile merchants. In the period 1910–41,

European firms such as Berli Jucker, Diethelm and Louis Leonowens, together with Japanese *sogo shoshas*, and Indian traders, competed with the Chinese in Thailand's textile trade. From 1961, some Indian traders and a few Japanese survived but the European textile traders retreated. The Indian traders remained as wholesale importers, exporters and limited retailers. This trading sector was highly competitive and not concentrated, in contrast to the manufacture of textiles. Suehiro, in a survey in 1981, found 1,300 wholesalers, importers, and exporters registered in Bangkok between 1961 and 1962.[39]

Saha Union was established in 1961 as a joint venture with a Japanese firm to produce metal zips. In 1964, Saha Union expanded into the import business and only in 1971 did it move into spinning and weaving in a joint venture with Kanebo Textiles. In the 1970s and 1980s, accelerated growth took place when influential technocrats/bankers were brought in, such as Dr Amnuay Virawan and Anand Panyarachun. Dr Amnuay Virawan was chief executive of Bangkok Bank. Anand Panyarachun, briefly left the company to become prime minister in 1991, but returned to undertake a major restructuring when Saha Union diversified into the power industry in Thailand and China. Saha Union was a highly diversified conglomerate with interests in textiles, energy, construction, finance and securities, and trading. Saha Union invested in power projects in Shanghai, Guangzhou, and Songjiang in joint ventures with Japanese multinationals, Singapore state enterprises and the Chinese State Enterprise Board. The Bangkok Bank was a major financier. Although Saha Union was a highly diversified conglomerate, it had an integrated textile sector, which included spinning, weaving, knitting, dyeing and the printing of yarns and textile accessories. The company had plants for cotton ginning as well as garment manufacturing, producing for Van Heusen (UK), Wolsey (UK) and Grand Slam (USA). Table 6.3 clearly indicates the rising profits and increasing capitalisation of Saha Union. The impressive growth did not result in the erosion of family ownership and control. Saha Union is owned by the Darakanonda family. Even after being listed in June 1975, Saha Union remained a family firm. In 1996, the family possessed 30 per cent of the controlling stake in equity with Bangkok Bank as the next major shareholder with 4 per cent. Managerial hierarchies were maintained, with four manufacturing divisions, each with its own managing director. Executives were professionals, not family members. Family members were directors and technological personnel, often with engineering qualifications.

Table 6.3 Saha Union Corporation (baht 000)

Year	Sales	Total revenue	Cost of goods sold	Total expenses	Gross profit	Net profit	EPS ordinary (baht)	Total cash dividend
1987	6,125,796	6,322,544	5,750,948	5,997,477	325,067	226,466	31.06	60,000
1988	7,381,368	7,656,812	6,932,429	7,191,822	464,990	353,894	36.93	112,500
1989	9,448,255	9,962,782	8,907,219	9,219,763	743,019	542,119	30.98	150,000
1990	11,578,876	12,171,850	10,910,573	11,357,667	814,183	605,922	30.3	300,000
1991	11,366,881	12,111,988	10,842,570	11,374,717	737,271	552,530	2.37	360,000
1992	11,521,334	12,320,931	10,815,176	11,405,947	914,984	744,218	2.98	375,000
1993	10,577,272	11,181,977	9,698,880	10,402,166	779,810	642,982	2.57	433,701
1994	11,329,307	11,926,037	10,497,354	11,106,339	819,698	653,201	2.21	448,571
1995	12,643,481	13,497,022	11,769,828	12,549,906	947,116	788,384	2.63	

Year	Cash and deposits at bank	Deposits and prepayment	Total current assets	Total investments and loans	Total assets	Bank overdrafts and loans from bank	Long-term loans	Total current liabilities	Total liabilities
1987	4,791	152,175	2,083,311	756,100	2,956,463	781,106		1,743,798	1,743,798
1988	4,021		2,605,452	900,599	3,801,670	782,775		2,097,611	2,097,611
1989	163,157	192,712	4,908,827	1,680,014	7,009,621	1,116,554		2,913,443	2,913,443
1990	138,288	179,461	5,408,994	1,845,663	8,155,857	1,339,056		3,753,757	3,753,757
1991	144,084	159,234	5,521,417	2,241,000	9,416,784	717,132	997,227	2,824,926	3,822,153
1992	133,602	166,618	5,541,559	2,579,674	9,827,125	1,089,576	782,296	3,080,981	3,863,277
1993	140,646	126,471	5,616,171	2,951,291	10,214,668	1,287,764	911,797	3,129,743	4,041,540
1994	70,218	143,084	8,037,523	3,559,954	13,444,027	1,172,328	1,925,734	3,068,094	4,993,828
1995	39,659	115,746	8,233,553	4,004,014	14,049,140	1,480,557	2,498,179	3,266,246	5,764,425

Table 6.3 Saha Union Corporation (baht 000) – *continued*

Year	Authorised capital	Issued and paid-up capital	Total shareholders' equity	Total liabilities and shareholders' capital
1987	750,000	750,000	1,212,665	2,956,463
1988	1,000,000	1,000,000	1,704,059	3,801,670
1989	3,000,000	2,000,000	4,096,178	7,009,621
1990	3,000,000	2,000,000	4,402,100	8,155,857
1991		2,500,000	5,594,630	9,416,784
1992	3,000,000	2,500,000	5,963,848	9,827,125
1993	3,000,000	2,500,000	6,173,128	10,214,668
1994	3,000,000	3,000,000	8,450,199	13,444,027
1995	3,000,000	3,000,000	8,284,715	14,049,140

Sources: Saha Union Corporation, Profit and Loss Accounts and Balance Sheets, 1986–96.

Sukree was more tightly controlled by the family patriarch, Sukree Photiranakul. Although his relations with the Thai army and politicians were central to his success, he had a more tempestuous relationship with Thai bureaucrats.[40] His conflicts with the Board of Investment between 1981 and 1987 over his expansionary strategies became legendary. Land investments made possible Sukree Photiranakul's expansion during periods of recession, as in the mid-1980s. By 1986, Sukree was the second largest industrial group in Thailand; Siam Cement was the largest. In the 1990s, it invested in the petrochemical sector of the textile industry and also expanded into China. The two important subsidiaries in the group are Thai Iryo and Thai Melon Polyester. Thai Iryo was established in 1972, listed in 1981, as a manufacturer of garments for the USA, the UK, and West Germany (see Table 6.1 and Figure 6.1 for performance indicators). Thai Melon Polyester was established in 1972 and listed in 1993 (see Figure 6.2). Thai Melon Polyester manufactured artificial polyester yarn, including staple yarn, flat filament yarn, textured yarn and pre-orientated yarn, and exported a major part of its production. Thai Melon Polyester imported raw materials from Mexico, Canada and Saudi Arabia and sold approximately 94 per cent of its finished textiles, in contrast to its yarn, in the domestic market. Thai Melon Polyester has joint venture

Figure 6.1   Thai Iryo Co. Ltd: performance indicators

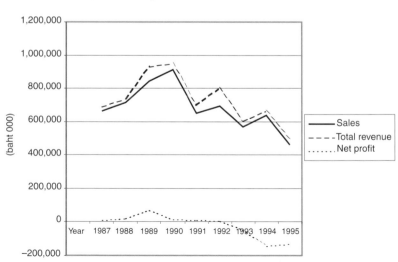

Sources: Thai Iryo Profit and Loss Accounts and Annual Balance Sheets, 1986–96.

Figure 6.2   Thai Melon Polyester Co. Ltd: performance indicators

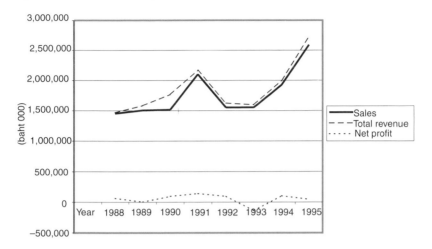

Sources: Thai Melon Polyester, Profit and Loss Accounts and Balance Sheets, 1986–96.

arrangements with Mexican and Canadian firms to produce garments for export.

The Thai garment industry also saw steady growth. Ready-made garments, which in 1959 had accounted for 10 per cent of total exports, accounted for 25 per cent in 1989, and employed more than half a million workers, principally female. By 1992, garments were the largest Thai export, with Japanese and Taiwanese investment predominating in the industry.[41] The Asian crisis of 1997 did affect Saha Union, particularly its subsidiary, Union Energy, which had a number of power projects in China. Sukree had also endured serious foreign currency difficulties in early 1997 in Thailand as well as through its regional expansion (see Figure 6.3 for performance indicators). Thai Iryo recorded substantial losses throughout the 1990s while Thai Melon Polyester endured losses in 1993 but recovered swiftly. The scale of these difficulties, however, was small compared to that of other industrial groups such as Siam Cement.

Integration, concentration and limited success

The textile industry in the Philippines also had integrated firms, integration being most marked in the period 1967–84.[42] The integrated

Figure 6.3   Saha Union Corporation: performance indicators

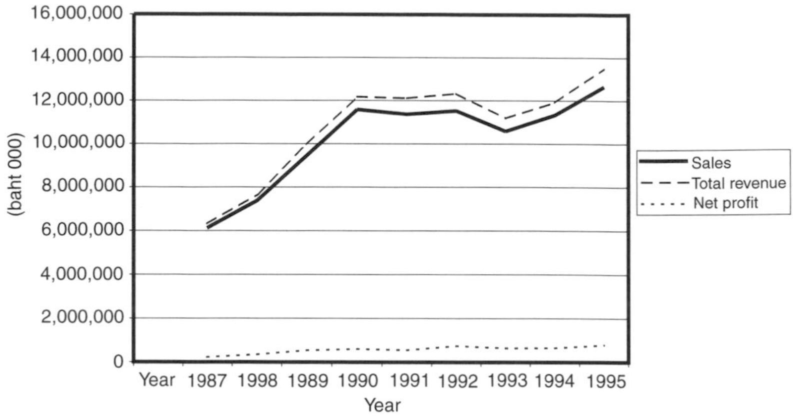

Sources: Saha Union Corporation, Profit and Loss Accounts and Balance Sheets, 1986–96.

textile firms accounted for 30 per cent of total textile employment between 1967 and 1984. Concentration was also an important aspect of the Philippines textile industry. In 1977, the four largest textile groups held 61 per cent of the total assets of the industry, accounted for 44 per cent of total employment in the textile sector and were responsible for 49 per cent of total sales.[43]

The creation of large integrated firms, accompanied by concentration by a few, was a direct result of government policies and import-substitution industrialisation. Import substitution began in 1949, when import controls and foreign exchange restrictions encouraged the emergence of monopolies in the industry. Protectionism was maintained in the Philippines for too long, in contrast to Thailand where it was limited to the period from 1959 to 1970 and was highly selective in the products protected. The textile industry had access to state funds, with foreign exchange allocations for imports of machinery and raw materials. The industry grew rapidly, and by the mid-1960s there was excess production for the domestic market. The long-term use of protectionism in the Philippines distorted performance, increased imports of components for manufacturing, reduced foreign participation, reduced the assimilation of technology and limited exposure to new management skills and critical marketing networks. Then, after February 1970, following the devaluation of the peso, an export strategy was promoted. Under the Export Incentives Act of 1970, export-processing zones were created and state credit was made available for the import of capital goods. These measures started a period of significant growth in yarn and fabric manufacture between 1978 and 1984. Textile exports, which had averaged a 6.4 per cent increase per annum between 1963 and 1969, now increased by 31 per cent per annum by 1978. Foreign exchange earnings from the export of fibre, yarn and fabrics rose from US$25.9 million per annum in 1971–77 to $37.2 million in 1978–84.[44] However the Philippines despite an earlier start in textile production lagged behind Thailand in textile exports throughout this period.[45]

The integration of activities within single corporations and the carving out of large market shares by a few was an inevitable consequence of the dominance of business by some Chinese and Filipino families. Foreign competition was diminished by state protectionism. Yoshihara's survey of business groups in the Philippines in 1985 revealed that out of 34 textile firms, 17 belonged to Chinese, 12 to Filipinos and foreigners owned five firms.[46] The low number of foreign firms meant insufficient capital, inadequate technology and less competition. This had serious implications for the Philippines in 'catching up' in the industry and in the transition from cotton to synthetic fibres. In Thailand, Japanese capital, technology and management expertise were critical for advances, particularly into synthetic fibres. In 1975, half of the investment in Thai textiles was from Japan. Out of 23 companies, in cotton–polyester spinning 13 had Japanese involvement. Of the nine polyester–rayon spinning firms and eight polyester––rayon weaving firms, ten were dominated by the Japanese. The Thai state and the affiliation with Japanese multinationals assisted the growth of the industry in Thailand, as well as producing vertically integrated, increasingly monopolistic textile groups. In the Philippines, integration and concentration were achieved through state incentives and protectionist policies, not through affiliation with foreign capital. While vertical integration improved productivity in Thailand, in the Philippines integration bred inefficiency. Productivity per spindle was higher for integrated spinners than non-integrated spinners. Total asset expenditure was higher in integrated firms, although capital productivity was lower.[47]

The Japanese influence was central to Thailand's assimilation of technology. Automation was faster in synthetic fibre production, assisting Thailand's 'catching up' in textiles, while the Philippines concentrated on cotton textiles and was slow in moving into artificial fibres.

Thailand was moving more rapidly through the stages of textile production, and moving to higher and more profitable stages in the product cycle. This explains the differences in performance, in spite of firms in both Thailand and the Philippines being integrated and monopolistic. The Philippines saw a slow expansion from 1949 to 1972 then began to decline. In contrast, Thailand's growth between 1950 and 1962 concentrated on cotton based products and catered for the domestic market. In this period, technology was derived from Europe. The second phase, expansion from 1963 to 1966, was marked by Japanese investment in local spinning and weaving companies. The third phase, 1967 to 1972, saw the growth of synthetic fibre production and export-led industrialisation. The export strategy was boosted by government incentives. Firms that exported at least 65 per cent of their output were exempted from duties on raw materials imports. Between 1975 and 1984, Thailand's textile exports rose by 28 per cent.

In addition, the Philippines, as an early industrialiser in the region, faced a similar situation to that of the United Kingdom – obsolete machinery. While Thailand's high export growth was related to its high factor productivity, the Philippines' poor export performance was linked to low factor productivity.[48]

The Philippines should have had a competitive edge in garments, a sector of the industry that had had an early start in the 1950s but, even here, decline was swift. The garments sector grew in the 1970s, particularly between 1975 and 1980, but declined after 1982. Output increased briefly in 1986, although growth was less than in the 1970s. Between 1972 and 1988, the share of manufacturing employment located in the garments sector increased fourfold. Growth was sluggish because of the divide between textile operations and the garments sector. Garment production was targeted at overseas markets, although exports from Singapore, Thailand, and even Indonesia exceeded those of the Philippines in 1985.[49] In the garment division, firms were small. These small-scale firms mushroomed in the 1970s and 1980s. Between 1972 and 1978 there was an increase in the number of small firms of 158 per cent, and an increase of 257 per cent between 1983 and 1985,. A few large firms such as Gokongwei, did dominate the sector from the mid-1980s. Gokongwei's main textile companies – Litton Mills, Robitex, and Westpoint Mills – produced yarn and knitted and woven fabrics from the early 1970s. Gokongwei's garments company, Brittania, produced for export to Japan and the US. In the 1980s and 1990s, Gokongwei's diversification into telecommunications, banking, food manufacturing, and real estate threatened its textile interests.

Telecommunications and real estate were the profitable cores in the family group.[50]

The co-existence of integrated and non-integrated firms

The following case-study of Indonesia reaches the same conclusion. Large, vertically integrated textile enterprises have a natural advantage in attracting support from the state and from foreign multinationals. Following the Pacific War, the Indonesian government was active in reviving the textile industry. The textile mills of the Dutch were nationalised and new mills were established. The number of spindles rose from 59,000 to 178,000 between 1957 and 1964.[51] In the same period, large spinning mills were constructed and the number of power looms rose by 60 per cent. However, the striking fact is that the number of handlooms increased by 116 per cent between 1960 and 1965. The Sukarno regime's emphasis on self-sufficiency and its control of cotton imports and the distribution of textiles and yarns, meant the persistence of traditional methods of weaving alongside a sluggish modern sector. The government also dominated spinning and weaving through state enterprises. Private enterprises were dependent on yarn from the state, to which they also sold the finished product. A small group of indigenous producers and traders grew, sustained by the state. The quality of the textiles declined, while inflation, which rose to 600 per cent per annum by 1966, destroyed competition.

The restructuring of the economy carried out by Soeharto in the late 1960s was decisive in introducing a new corps of textile producers and traders. Although trade protection was retained, business*men* identified by the state were now profiting from it. Banking was liberalised, and credit was targeted for imports of raw materials and capital goods. The export-oriented strategy encouraged large domestic businesses with foreign investment to specialise in higher value-added products, in other words those that provided more profit; for example, making garments produced more profit than the actual manufacture of textiles. Large firms co-existed with small firms. However, political interference made the fortunes of big business.

The majority of textile and garment companies were small, with few economies of scale. Between 1966 and 1981, 76 per cent of the weaving sector remained small (mills with less than 50 power looms). Only seven companies had 400 or more looms.[52] The large weavers were Chinese with sufficient capital reserves. The small weavers, largely indigenous, could not adjust to the production of synthetic fibres because they lacked capital and technology. Although linkages between large and small producers were encouraged, the Indonesian textile industry was characterised by fragmentation and division. The small producer, spinner and weaver, was disadvantaged, both through the period of state enterprises, 1949–66, and in the New Order after 1967. By 1988, with the rise and dominance of private enterprise, the small firm languished, while the large firm became more vertically integrated with the help of foreign investment. In 1988, of all Indonesian textile firms, 68.1 per cent remained private, 24.8 per cent were in foreign hands, and 7.1 per cent were state enterprises. In the garment sector, private enterprises accounted for 98 per cent of the total, state enterprises were a mere 0.2 per cent, and foreign firms accounted for 1.8 per cent[53]

The Indonesian textile industry experienced impressive growth, with exports of textiles rising from 0.1 per cent of world exports in 1980 to 2.3 per cent in 1993. The average annual percentage increase between 1980 and 1993 was 37 per cent, while the share of textiles in Indonesian exports rose from 0.2 per cent in 1980 to 7.2 per cent in 1993. In garments, Indonesia had 2.6 per cent of world exports, having risen from 0.2 per cent in 1980. This was equal to a 9.5 per cent share in Indonesian exports in 1993, having risen from 0.4 per cent in 1980.[54]

This growth was, in small measure, attributable to the inflow of foreign investment into Indonesian textiles. Between 1967 and 1989, 80 per cent of foreign direct investment into this sector was derived from Japan; Europe and the USA contributed only 1 per cent of the foreign direct investment in textiles.[55] However, foreign direct investment was still very limited. Most of the investment (96 per cent in the mid-1980s) was derived from domestic sources. In the 1990s, this changed, with increased investment from Hong Kong, Taiwan, the USA and Europe.

The factors responsible for the emergence of large vertically integrated firms were numerous. The major textile firms included Texmaco Jaya, established in November 1970 and listed in March 1994. Texmaco Jaya was an integrated company with units in weaving, spinning, the knitting of yarn, design, and dyeing, finishing and printing fabrics. Texmaco Jaya also produced traditional batik in East Timor. Texmaco Jaya had foreign partners from South India, Holland and Hong Kong. Polysindo Eka Perkasa, its subsidiary, which was established in 1984 and listed in 1991, had Japanese and American partners. Polysindo Eka Perkasa was also integrated into spinning, weaving, chemical production and synthetic fibres. Polysindo Eka Perkasa's fabric interests accounted for 56 per cent of total textile production, in yarn 28 per cent, of total yarn produced in Indonesia in December 1995. Polysindo Eka Perkasa's part-owner, Marimuthu Srinivasan, was from South India, indicating that Indians did retain a niche in textiles in Southeast Asia.

Another large vertically integrated textile company, the ninth largest in Indonesia, was Argo Manunggal, whose owner, The Ning King, had 54 subsidiaries in different segments of the industry. Astra International and Salim also had sizeable investments in textiles in the period after 1970. Government measures often acted in favour of the large enterprise. Besides providing finance through state owned banks, the state also encouraged foreign multinationals to participate with large domestic textile groups (often Chinese) in the manufacture of capital-intensive synthetic fibres.[56] Large domestic textile firms were involved in dye production with P. T. Hoechst Ciligon Kimia in West Java and with P. T. Chandra Sari, which was partly owned by Ciba Geigy. P. T. Hoechst Ciligon Kimia received American investment of US\$27.2 million in 1985.

The state distorted the textile industry in favour of large enterprises.[57] Besides encouraging foreign capital to align itself with large business in Indonesia, many of its fiscal, trade and financial incentives benefited the large textile conglomerate. The government allowed exemption from import duties on raw materials and equipment for the first two years and tax amnesties for the domestic investor. These incentives applied to new factories, to extensions, as well as to machinery. Companies were also allowed to carry forward losses in the first six years of operation, and permitted generous depreciation allowances. The net effect, as Hal Hill argues, was to reduce the cost of capital relative to that of labour, and support the capital-intensive segments of the textile industry. The over valued rupiah also stimulated capital-intensive, large, vertically integrated firms. Capital-intensive groups had advantages from cheaper imports. There were few links between large and small firms. The large Indonesian Chinese textile firm attracted 'quota hoppers' from Hong Kong and Taiwan. Finally, the large vertically integrated firm was more able to overcome the difficulties of a fragmented, geographically dispersed domestic market than the small weaver and garment producer. Garment producers were generally small and concentrated in Jakarta, parts of West Java, and, to a lesser extent, in East Java. Even here, large enterprises emerged after 1976. Between 1980 and 1992, the size of the garment industry grew by 3,000 per cent.[58] In 1980, garment exports from Indonesia were US$97 million, rising in 1992 to US$3,189 million. These small garment producers were dependent on large and medium firms for supplies of fabrics, as well as for distribution networks. The large Chinese firm, vertically integrated and possessing horizontal linkages with suppliers, foreign multinationals, the bureaucracy and the state, and regional and state co-operative firms, achieved increased market share. The links between Indonesian distributors, suppliers and producers were not efficient or competitive. Inefficiencies in supplies and dependence on imports for inputs weakened the small weaver and garment producer. Large firms provided crucial inputs for the small producer and increased the latter's dependence and vulnerability.

The textile industry in Malaysia had similar features to the industries in Thailand, Indonesia and the Philippines. There was an initial development of the industry under import substitution policies of the 1960s, succeeded in the early 1970s by export led growth. Textile exports contributed 8.4 per cent of total output in 1970, rising to 13.5 per cent of total output in 1987. The organisational structure in textiles remained large, although less vertically integrated than in Thailand, because of a dependence on imported yarn and fabrics. The large textile firms were frequently located in the export processing zones of Penang and Johor, and had crucial links with Hong Kong and Japanese textile specialists. Foreign ownership dominated, and the firms were oligopolistic in production. Only in the expansion of the 1990s did local competition surface.[59]

Foreign multinationals in both textiles and garments relocated to Malaysia to evade the quota restraints of the Multi-Fibre Arrangement (MFA) in the 1980s.[60] In 1989, foreign investment was 77 per cent of total investment in Malaysian garments, mostly from East Asian companies avoiding quota constraints. There were undoubtedly other attractions in relocating production to Malaysia, including free trade zones with tariff and tax exemptions, and abundant cheap labour, cleared of unionisation. Labour productivity was low, however; in 1984, it was two-thirds that of Korea and half that of Hong Kong, principally because of lack of training.[61] The Malaysian textile industry catered for the lower end of the market, principally in the US. There were less textile imports into other Southeast Asian countries. Technology and components are acquired through Japan but finished products are exported to the US and to Western Europe, exploding the myth of an intra-Asian basin of industrialisation and trade, at least in textiles. This question will be examined more closely later in this chapter.

Malaysian textile firms, which were frequently part of a large conglomerate, began locating production in lower wage countries such as Puerto Rico and Bangladesh. Vincent Tan used labour-intensive textiles and capital-intensive telecommunications to continue his 'rent seeking' activities in Bangladesh. This was globalising without upgrading. The transfer of production overseas before achieving domestic maturity and technical expertise exposes the hollowness of parts of Southeast Asia's industrialisation. In the primary textiles sector, the production of a variety of high quality fabrics is essential, together with increased capabilities in grading, marking and design. Market information is also crucial. Technology transfer was limited, even in textile firms. Key technical and managerial posts were held by Japanese and Hong Kong personnel. There was increased technology transfer in the labour-intensive garment industry, such as computer-aided design. Large, foreign dominated textile firms in Malaysia relied on imports of high quality intermediate goods, thus undermining vertical integration. Above all, the education and training of a multi-skilled labour force is paramount. After two decades of foreign domination, the Malaysian textile industry saw replacement by cheaper Indonesian and South Asian workers in Malaysia or movement of the production abroad. The following description of Pen Group, the largest textile corporation in Malaysia, demonstrates these points.

The Pen Group in Penang is composed of five large textile subsidiaries owned by Toray of Japan. The Pen Group was initially controlled by a Hong Kong firm, Textile Alliance, with some Malaysian equity. Hong Kong capital, which had dominated Malaysian textiles in the 1970s, was replaced by the Japanese in the mid-1980s, although Hong Kong companies retained their interests in knitting, garments, but also in consumer electronics. Pen Group exploited the advantages of production in the free trade zones, which were dominated by foreign capital. In 1987, foreign capital accounted for 97.8 per cent of the paid up capital of textile firms in the free trade zones, a total of M$213.0 million.[62] Eleven local firms contributed only 2.2 per cent of the total paid up capital in 1987. This changed in the 1990s with increased local participation.

Conclusion

This chapter has examined the methods by which Chinese textile firms in Southeast Asia constructed fully integrated textile companies, absorbing and consolidating capital-intensive sectors in spinning and in synthetic fibres with labour-intensive weaving and garment divisions. The internalisation of different products and manufacturing processes within a single textile group conflicts with the 'flying geese' pattern of Japan's industrial restructuring, which implied the transfer of labour-intensive manufacturing to Southeast Asia.

Saha Union and Sukree had contrasting styles of management; Sukree was dominated by the founding father Sukree Photiratanakul, while Saha Union attempted to introduce a limited form of managerial hierarchy by bringing in influential technocrats such as Anand Panyarachun. Despite the differences in approach, both firms pursued an identical internalisation of a broad spectrum of textile products, technology, and processes. (See Figure 6.4 for the vertical integration of Sukree.)

The growth and diversification of the Southeast Asian textile industry, particularly in Thailand, was not simply a direct result of Japanese industrial restructuring, in the 'flying geese' model of development. The idea that Japan was at the head of technology transfer and intricate trade linkages in the Asia-Pacific region is also misleading (see Tables 6.4 and 6.5).[63] The reduction in joint-venture liaisons and the equity held by Japanese textile specialists in major Thai textile corporations from the early 1980s is evidence of a rather ambivalent relationship. Sukree constantly swapped and changed foreign partners, as did textile groups in Indonesia.

The horizontal division of labour evolved slowly (see Table 6.5). The transition from labour-intensive to capital-intensive systems was not straightforward. ASEAN countries did not rigorously follow the move from exporting a comparative advantage in cheap labour to capital-intensive structures. The interplay of generous inflows of foreign direct

Table 6.4   Market penetration ratios for imports from ASEAN of textiles and garments into industrialised countries, in percentages

	1970			1985		
	EEC	USA and Canada	Japan	EEC	USA and Canada	Japan
Clothing	0.01	0.2	0.03	0.8	1.57	0.12
Textiles	0.01	0.04	0.03	0.46	0.24	0.37

Sources: U. Hiemenz, 'Expansion of ASEAN–EC Trade in Manufactures: Pertinent Issues and Recent Development', *The Developing Economies*, Vol. 26, No. 4, 1988, cited in Wolfgang Hillebrand, *Shaping Competitive Advantages Conceptual Framework and the Korean Approach*, London, Frank Cass, 1996, p. 54.

Figure 6.4 Vertical integration in the production process: the Sukree Group, 1993

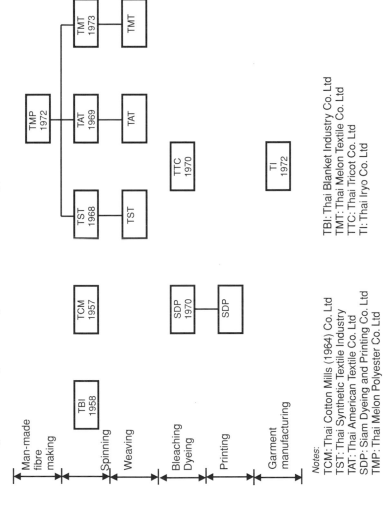

Notes:
TCM: Thai Cotton Mills (1964) Co. Ltd
TST: Thai Synthetic Textile Industry
TAT: Thai American Textile Co. Ltd
SDP: Siam Dyeing and Printing Co. Ltd
TMP: Thai Melon Polyester Co. Ltd

TBI: Thai Blanket Industry Co. Ltd
TMT: Thai Melon Textile Co. Ltd
TTC: Thai Tricot Co. Ltd
TI: Thai Iryo Co. Ltd

Source: Sukree Ltd (Thailand), Annual Report 1993.

Table 6.5   Index of the horizontal division of labour between Japan and ASEAN

	Consumer non-durables		Consumer durables		Capital goods	
	1980	1986	1980	1986	1980	1986
Thailand	0.13	0.27	0.04	0.14	0	0.03
Indonesia	0.27	0.27	0.04	0.15	0.03	0
Philippines	0.31	0.19	0.18	0.16	0.04	0.02
Malaysia	0.09	0.19	0.13	0.19	0.06	0.09
Singapore	0.09	0.11	0.25	0.2	0.14	0.16

Note:
The Index is calculated as 1 minus the ratio of the absolute value of the difference between bilateral exports and imports to the two-way trade for each category of goods.
Source: H. C. de Bettignies, 'Japan – NIE's Strategic Independence in the Pacific Basin', in M. Kulessa (ed.), *The Newly Industrializing Economies of Asia, Prospects of Cooperation*, London, 1990, p. 13; cited in Hillebrand, 1996, p. 59.

investment, the existence of a powerful state, and dominant diasporic Chinese capitalists, and rapid changes in world trade including the institution of quotas meant that major countries in ASEAN did not conform to a stages of growth model. Southeast Asia often shot through several stages of growth within a brief period. Labour and capital-intensive structures in textiles and garments co-existed.

ASEAN did not conform to the Japanese pattern of industrialisation. Even the poorer countries of ASEAN, such as the Philippines and Indonesia, often had more capital-intensive sectors than higher income countries such as Malaysia and Thailand. In the Philippines, capital-intensive sectors such as spinning and manufacturing synthetic fibres accounted for 10 per cent of total textile production, 16 per cent in Indonesia, but 10 per cent in Thailand and 8 per cent in Malaysia in the 1980s.[64]

The individual ASEAN countries also did not follow a clear path from import-substitution industrialisation to export-oriented industrialisation. In 1975, Indonesia, which had 99 per cent self-sufficiency in garments, spinning and dyeing, also had a low export ratio of 0.9 per cent to 0.4 per cent. Thailand and Singapore had higher export ratios in spite of being less self-sufficient. The Philippines too had a higher export ratio of 37.8 per cent in garments. Local political and economic factors need to be stressed.[65]

Industrial relocation did not necessarily imply speedy technology transfer between Japan and the textile firms of ASEAN. The costs, different economic environments, levels of technical expertise, and technological infrastructures, as well as variations in management of plant and equipment, produced substantially different results. The transfers through joint-venture liaisons varied greatly. The channels of technology acquisition were also very diverse. On rare occasions, R&D was internalised within the firms, supplied by the state or joint-venture partner; elsewhere there was outright purchase of capital goods or technology transfer through licensing arrangements. The local firm's absorptive capacity would also determine the mechanism of technology acquisition.

The experience of Sukree and Saha Union suggests that diffusion of technologies occurred but that constant upgrading was still achieved through joint-venture partners. The constant swapping of joint-venture partners by Sukree in the 1980s and 1990s suggest a vacuum in technological innovation filled by different joint-venture partners at different stages of development.

The discussion of individual countries has shown that it is not the comparative advantage of cheap labour that secures success but a combination of organisational structure, relations with the state and foreign multinationals (particularly financial and technological linkages), and international trade restrictions. Oligopolistic concentrations by the three large textile firms in Thailand assisted the achievement of impressive growth and performance. The three main firms also pursued a strategy of broadening the industrial base through capital-and technology-intensive textile sections alongside labour-intensive garment manufacture. Such a development benefited from the imposition of international quotas that restrained earlier developers like Japan and Hong Kong, and passed the baton to Thailand, Indonesia, Singapore and Malaysia. Imitation led to the narrowing of the technological gap and aided the development of export potential. Micro-efficiency was provided by the vertically integrated structure of these textile firms. The organisational framework and levels of concentration gave competitive advantages and ensured the firms responded quickly to the opportunities presented by quotas in the international textile trade.

Organisational structure affected the level of technological assimilation and provided financial capabilities easily identified by the state and foreign multinationals. The large vertically integrated group was able to act strategically on the basis of information procured from the state, multinational companies, or ethnic Chinese networks. An irrepressible market position was achieved, which was assisted by close ties with banks and financial institutions, as was the case with Saha Union and Bangkok Bank. However, while this worked in Thailand, it could not be reproduced in the Philippines, where the economic and political environment was different. The organisational structure in Thailand was a by-product of fundamental change in the organisation of the textile industry, the relocation of Japanese firms, shorter product cycles, rapidly changing market situations, international quotas, and the relocation of the production of branded and designer goods to Southeast Asia.

The complexity of the development of the textile industry needs to be stressed, instead of the 'flying geese' model of industrial development. The internalisation and vertical integration of textile companies meant that outsourcing by Japanese companies was less pervasive than is generally perceived. Japanese multinationals acted in joint ventures, as well as operating as fully owned companies in Southeast Asia. In garments and in certain textile products, sub-contracting and outsourcing may be common, but overall, the amount of production for inputs market was less than orthodoxy has suggested. Sukree, Saha Union, and many others achieved competence in the 1960s and 1970s with expanding world trade, and with technology and finance from the state and from Japan and Europe. These were used to achieve economies of scale, argues Hillebrand, and to secure flexible manufacturing and design, which in turn produced further economies of scale to expel competitors, both local and foreign. Even when products were highly differentiated, economies of scale appeared critical for competition. This supports Lazonick's thesis that vertically integrated multifibre textile groups like Courtaulds are able to improve quality.[66]

Family businesses like Sukree and Saha Union internalised and yet competed; they are split into strategic units but remain hierarchical in terms of management and authority. The argument that the Japanese textile industry achieved competitiveness through the *kereitsu* and *kigyo shudan* – vertical and horizontal linkages – also needs revision. Although diverse structures characterised Japan's textile industry, product diversification was at the heart of its competitiveness. Southeast Asian entrepreneurs substituted family, technocrats, politicians and strategic foreign multinationals for the long-term clustering and institutionalisation used by Japanese companies. Innovations in textiles occurred in clusters. Southeast Asian entrepreneurs purchased these innovations. Chinese entrepreneurs in Southeast Asia integrated the joint ventures into their own global ambitions; it was not only the Japanese and Western multinationals that integrated Southeast Asian firms into their outsourcing global initiatives. The Southeast Asian firms used the Japanese and Westerners to launch their own international ventures. ASEAN textile groups, when losing competitiveness from cheap factors of production, relocated themselves in China, Vietnam, Puerto Rico and even the US; this was globalisation of markets and globalisation of output, rather than simply the search for cheaper inputs.

Organisational structure, abundant finance, and access to technology and appropriate production processes can reduce labour costs, making them no longer critical. Instead, differentiated products, changing markets, flexible methods of manufacturing, different locations of manufacturing, and widening prospects for technological leapfrogging, confirm that organisational structure and strategy are more crucial than labour costs. Chinese entrepreneurs in Southeast Asia were successful in exploiting cheap, disciplined labour. But the state and foreign multinationals were crucial in providing technical knowledge and management skills to adapt, upgrade, and continually search for new niche markets. Structure and sequencing were at the heart of their success.

7
Eyes Wide Shut: Chinese Attitudes to Technology and Innovation

As a technology-intensive industry, the telecommunications sector demonstrates how Chinese companies responded to and absorbed technological innovation. As has been the case throughout this study, the relationship between the Southeast Asian state and Chinese business is crucial. The state assisted technology transfer, enabling businesses to bypass the development of a technological infrastructure, resulting in rapid expansion on inadequate foundations.

The aim of this chapter is to analyse the growth patterns of Chinese telecommunications companies in Southeast Asia, principally in Thailand. The emphasis will be on the mechanisms by which telecommunications companies acquired technical skills and penetrated global markets. The two main case studies, CP and Shinawatra, are Sino-Thai companies. Salim (Indonesia), Gokongwei group (Philippines), and Singapore Telecoms also achieved remarkable success in the industry. However, CP and Shinawatra provide perhaps the clearest examples of rapid growth, built upon liaisons with the state and with foreign multinationals, in an industry that used standardised technology. Sino-Thai telecommunications firms were strictly private firms, while in Malaysia, Singapore and Indonesia, the state held considerable equity in telecommunications firms. The active role and frequent direct intervention of the state distort Chinese entrepreneurial activities. Therefore this chapter will focus on Thailand. The privatisation of public utilities such as telecommunications, provides an insight into the responsiveness of Chinese business to economic developments, not just in Southeast Asia but also in the growing market of China.

The telecommunications industry in Southeast Asia has witnessed phenomenal growth in the last two decades, involving developments in industrial infrastructure as well as advances in information technology.

The advances include the construction of main-line networks, cellular phones, electronic mail, satellite and cable television, and trunk radio, as well as the manufacture of components with limited research and development inputs. By 1994, the world's fastest growing telephone networks were in Thailand, the Philippines, Indonesia, China, Vietnam, Laos and Pakistan.[1] Of the 30 million fixed line networks installed throughout the world in 1994, two-thirds were in Asia. Of the Asian total, more than a quarter was in China. Including mobile subscribers, 16 per cent of the world's total of new lines was located in Asia in 1994. China achieved 20 per cent growth in mobile network expansion, and 57 per cent in terrestrial growth between 1986 and 1994.[2] This impressive growth was a consequence of Asia's economic success, the rapid inflows of foreign investment and the increased activities of foreign multinationals.

Before 1980, most of the telephone networks in Thailand were designed and set up by Japanese and European firms for the Thai state. NEC and Nippon Telegraph and Telephone (NTT) were responsible for the Bangkok area, while Ericsson developed the provincial networks. Long-distance networks were the responsibility of Fujitsu and Toshiba. The equipment purchased and installed was provided by these multinationals.

The Chatichai government in Thailand of 1988–90, like the majority of Asian governments, saw economic liberalisation and the privatisation of public utilities, like telecommunications, as critical for economic growth. Privatisation of telecommunications was part of the state's ambition to acquire advanced information technology. The privatisation and liberalisation of the industry drew large Chinese corporations into the sector. Sensitivities over national security and access to privileged information made the authorities favour domestic corporations over foreign multinationals. Local entrepreneurs with powerful state connections were preferred to foreign telecommunications specialists. Tables 7.1a and 7.2 show how Thai companies were favoured over telecommunications specialists in the award of concessions.[3]

There are seven main issues to be considered in this chapter. The first point is that Sino-Thai involvement and performance in telecommunications was clearly dependent on state patronage. The state was critical for Sino-Thai firms in securing concessions, in raising finance and in promoting their global ambitions in the 1990s. The second issue is that Sino-Thai firms were further advanced by their connections with foreign telecommunications specialists. Related to this, the extent to which technology was trans-

Table 7.1a   Thailand: comparison of revenue-sharing proposals for the
3-million-line telephone project

1-million-line project in rural provincial areas

Bidder	CP	Ericsson	Toyomenka	Alcatel
Investment (million baht)	52,311.00	26,530.54	40,300.00	35,024.00
Concession years	28	24	30	15
Revenue sharing (%)	6	51	5	56
TOT[a] Income: 15 years	29,196.18	47,015.88	5,596.77	30,106.38
Income: 20 years	41,970.48	75,626.88	7,806.77	
Income: 24 years	58,610.28	101,376.78	10,016.77	
Income: 28 years	68,802.78		11,342.77	

2-million-line project in the Bangkok metropolitan area

Bidder	CP	Mitsui	Ericsson	Alcatel
Investment (million baht)	96,951.00	33,174.00	53,755.48	55,612.00
Concession years	28	20	24	15
Revenue sharing (%)	6	15	20	51
Income: 15 years	17,936.58	16,826.10	21,104.00	38,155.55
Income: 20 years	38,959.08	25,404.90	41,510.40	
Income: 24 years	54,556.98		51,713.60	
Income: 28 years	66,371.88			

Note: [a]TOT = Telephone Organisation of Thailand.
Source: Compiled from TOT documents, cited in Sakkarin Niyomsilpa, 'The Political Economy of Telecommunications Liberalization in Thailand', PhD thesis, Australian National University, 1995, p. 252.

ferred through these connections also requires examination. The third issue is how far financial liberalisation in the region from the late 1980s led to diverse forms of financing by 'immature' telecommunications firms, including Telecom Asia (CP) and Shinawatra. The fourth issue is to consider the argument that the government's distribution of concessions and revenue estimates distorted prices and demand, and encouraged the segmentation of telecommunications products such as television services, paging and satellites. The fifth task is to examine how the Sino-Thai telecommunications firms went regional, for example Shinawatra in Laos and Cambodia,

Table 7.1b   Changes in telecommunications business in Thailand, 1969–93

Item	1969	1980	1988	1990	1992	1993
Telephone (1000 circuits)						
Capital area	74	315	947	1,126	1,354	1,572
Other area	33	108	439	559	812	920
Total	**108**	**423**	**1,386**	**1,685**	**2,166**	**2,493**
Long-distance phones		4,210	54,010	61,729	122,758	
International phones			11,090	25,510	40,210	
Mobile phones			17,600	74,700	273,200	414,000

Source: Tara Siam Business Information Ltd, *Thai Telecommunications Industry*, 1993/94, Bangkok, 1995, pp. 259–64.

Telecom Asia in India, China, Vietnam and Hong Kong. Sixth, attention will be given to the ways in which structural organisation affected the different phases of growth in the industry, and in particular rapid product diversification – the construction of telephone networks, expansion into the mass media and entertainment and the development of internet provision. The impact of product diversification and organisational restructuring on management structures and decision-making within these firms needs to be analysed. These issues will be explored through an examination of CP's subsidiaries in telecommunications, Telecom Asia, Orient Telecom, and Technology Holdings Ltd (OTTH) and Shinawatra. The main focus will be on CP, whose growth in the telecommunications industry was particularly impressive between 1993 and 1996.

The material in this chapter will be used to challenge Chandler's views on markets and technology dynamics. Chandler argued that technology has a far greater influence in determining the size and degree of concentration in an industry than the quality of entrepreneurship, the availability of capital, and state policies.[4] Contradicting this view, Thai telecommunications firms joined with the state and with foreign capital to create a major industry. Access to technology and to markets was secured through political and social processes, which enabled newcomers to enter and dominate regional markets. Technology development required institutional structures, which included university research facilities and other clusters of innovation. If the state, as the purchaser of technology, disturbs its evolution, creation and choice in the advance of technology are aborted.

Table 7.2 Thailand: concessions to private firms in the telecommunications industry, 1986–93

Projects	Granted by	concessionaire (operator)	Year	Period (in years)	Government share (%)
	CAT[a]	Pacific Telesis	1986	10	33% of gross revenue
	TOT[b]	Shinawatra Paging (Shinawatra Group)	1989	15	25–40% of gross revenue
Paging services	TOT	Percom Service	1989	15	25–40% of gross revenue
	TOT	Hutchison Telecommunications	1990	15	25–46% of gross revenue
	TOT	Worldpage (UCOM Group)	1993	15	41% of gross revenue (minimum 1.5 billion baht)
	PTD[c]	Samart Telecoms (Samart Group)	1988	15	5% of gross revenue
	PTD	Compunet (BKK Group)	1988	15	5% of gross revenue
Data communications through satellite	TOT	Shinawatra Datacom (Shinawatra Group)	1989	10	15–20% of gross revenue
	TOT	Acumen (Jasmine Group)	1991	15	17–25% of gross revenue
	CAT	Thai Skycom	1992	15	23.5% of gross revenue (minimum 0.8 billion bath
	TOT	Advanced Info (Shinawatra Group)	1990	20	15–30% of gross revenue (minimum 13.1 billion baht)
Cellular mobile Phone	CAT	Total Access Communications (UCOM Group)	1990	15	12–25% of gross revenue (minimum 9 billion baht)
	TOT	Fonepoint (Shinawatra, CP, Shinawatra, CP, UCOM)	1990	10	15% of gross revenue
Telephones Bangkok	TOT	Telecom Asia (CP Group)	1991	25	16% of gross revenue
Telephones Countryside)	TOT	Thai Telephone and Telecommunications	1992	25	43% of gross revenue

Table 7.2 Thailand: concessions to private firms in the telecommunications industry, 1986–93 – *continued*

Projects	Granted by	concessionaire (operator)	Year	Period (in years)	Government share (%)
Satellite	MOTC[d]	Shinawatra Satellite (Shinawatra Group)	1991	30	minimum 1,415 million baht
Trunked radio phones	CAT	United Communication (UCOM Group)	1992	15	9–16% of service charge
	TOT	Radiophone (CP, Jasmine Groups)	1992	15	25–28% of gross revenue
Videotext	TOT	Technology (CP Group)	1993	15	15–25% of gross revenue

Note: [a] CAT = Communications Authority of Thailand; [b] TOT = Telephone Organisation of Thailand; [c] PTD = Postal and Telegram Department; [d] MOTC = Ministry of Transportation and Communications.

Sources: Tara Siam Information Ltd, *Thai Telecommunications Industry, 1993/94*, Bangkok, 1995; *The Nation Review*, 1 March 1993; *Prachachat Thurakit*, 16–18, 1992.

The state in the Southeast Asian telecommunications sector contains both the dynamic of the market and the genesis of regulatory control. State intervention and the distribution of resources and opportunities to favourites distorts technology development; it may provide quick returns but it will adversely affect the linear growth of technology. Whatever competition there is, exists only between the advanced telecommunications firms, largely the Western multinationals, which respond by becoming more powerful, both through technology advances and through organisational and operational changes.

The privatisation of telecommunications, which allowed the entry of domestic firms into the industry, increased the monopoly power of large private Chinese corporations. Privatisation, in the end, simply secured the ascent of Chinese business, principally oligopolies, despite the argument that privatisation would reduce government involvement and expenditure, increase competition, improve efficiency and widen ownership.

CP, originally a chicken feed company as seen in Chapter 5 of this book, was not only able to enter the Thai telecommunications industry in 1989 but also to invest throughout Southeast Asia, Taiwan, India and China by 1994. In Thailand, CP was supported by contracts with the military and politicians. In 1990, the 3 million-line telephone network for Bangkok and the rural areas was awarded to CP. Five groups, including Ericcson, NEC and Alcatel also bid for these concessions, promising higher revenues for the state and more advantageous terms. But CP was offered the contract, a decision that a World Bank Report of 1991 criticised as encouraging an unfair oligopoly (see Table 7.1a).[5] Although the criticism led the Thai Prime Minister Anand to reduce the concession to 2 million lines, CP still retained highly advantageous terms with respect to revenues, equipment upgrading and management. The participation of Jasmine, Loxley and Ital Thai in the provision of the remaining 1 million lines did little to introduce competition. Shinawatra won the concessions for cellular phones, paging, data communication services and contracts for television and satellite communications.

The ability of CP and Shinawatra to dominate the telecommunications industry went beyond their relationship with the state. CP's relationship with Nynex (USA) was critical in a capital- and technology-intensive industry. In the 1980s, Nynex sought partners in global expansion. CP was identified as a valuable partner because of its close relations with Asian establishments. Nynex was also attracted by CP's market and regional knowledge. CP maintained joint-venture arrangements with

Nynex throughout India, the Philippines and Vietnam in fixed-line construction, cellular phones, satellite transmission, undersea fibre optics and cable transmission, as well as in interactive television, software, video and the manufacture of equipment. CP expanded, with FLAG, an important fibre optic cable network, into Asia and Europe. CP relied heavily on Nynex for technology, design, quality control and the supervision of contractors. Nynex retained operating control, in spite of its minority shareholding of less than a fifth of total shares. CP assumed the management of state links, secured contracts and provided the finance. Increasing foreign investment was accumulated by CP for telecommunications projects in Asia, rising from US$2.7 billion in 1989 to US$34.0 billion in 1993. CP and Nynex rotated managers, with Thai managers acquiring advanced technical competence. The preservation of ownership and control by CP persisted, in spite of its dependence on the state and foreign multinationals.

The following analysis of Telecom Asia, Telecom Holdings, and OTTH, all subsidiaries of CP, will assist in tracing the organisational and institutional changes in the industry. Telecom Asia was established in November 1990 with a paid up capital of 1 billion baht, rising in 1992 to 22 billion baht (US$1 billion). This increased to US$4 billion in 1994 (see table 7.5). The Chearavanont family held 22 per cent of the total equity, while its investment company, OTTH, held another 22 per cent, and Nynex had 15 per cent (valued at US$1.3 billion) in 1994.[6] The share value fluctuated greatly. Telecom Asia shares, issued at 55 baht in November 1993 rose to 150 baht in December 1993, but lost more than half their value in 1994. By 1997 they registered at 43 baht.[7]

The second subsidiary, Telecom Holdings, was established in 1991 with 5 billion baht, rising to 10 billion baht in 1997.[8] Nynex possessed an equity stake of 18.5 per cent in the company. The third subsidiary, (OTTH), was established in October 1992 through the restructuring of Chia Tai, CP's holding company in Hong Kong. Nynex absorbed 23 per cent of equity (US$180 million) in OTTH. Much of the original capital was derived from sales of property in Hong Kong. Prior to the conversion, Chia Tai's capital in 1992 was increased from HK$100,000 (US$12,987) to HK$50 million (US$6.5 million), HK$32 million (US$4.16 million) of which was fully paid up. Chia Tai's income from its rental and restaurant business had accumulated to HK$54 million (US$7 million) by 1993. It had assets of HK$445 million (US$57.79 million).[9] Within a year of OTTH's formation through restructuring, it achieved a turnover of HK$70.4 million (US$9.14 million), with assets of HK$4.8 billion (US$ 0.623 billion).[10]

Nynex was attracted by OTTH's impressive performance. OTTH maintained its growth and performance after Nynex became a major shareholder recording assets of HK$6.8 billion (US$0.883) and net income of HK$363 million (US$46 million) in 1994[11] (see Table 7.3). OTTH acquired a large stake in power generation in China in 1994. The partnership with Shenyang City Electric Co. and N.E. China Powergroup (a state enterprise) ultimately led OTTH to abandon telecommunications and concentrate on other infrastructural projects that were less sensitive politically.[12] OTTH, however, increased its shareholding in Telecom Asia (to 22.5 per cent/US$10 billion) in 1996. This was because Telecom Asia had registered a dramatic fall in net profits – from 1,291 million baht in 1995 to a loss of 1,924 million baht in 1996, and OTTH was compensating for this huge reversal. Nynex was prompted to sell its 23 per cent stake to Dhanin and Sumet Chearavanonant. These developments triggered a fall in the share value of OTTH, despite its profits of HK$70.6 million (US$9 million) for the half year.[13]

The creation of these separate companies coincided with the emergence of a loose form of regional specialisation for CP. While OTTH concentrated on China, Japan and Hong Kong, Telecom Holding (TH) invested in Thailand, Nepal, Vietnam, the Philippines and India. This separation did not disturb the interlocking shareholding and financial linkages that served these three firms.

The important issue here is the nature of the technology in telecommunications, for this enabled non-specialists to participate in the industry. Fibre-optic transmission and digital switches allowed business and technology units to be combined. That is, Nynex could be in control of operations, while CP could manage the business. Regional compartments could exist within flexible networks.

Digital transmission not only ensured high quality but also permitted a vast differentiation of services (digital networks, transport networks and intelligence networks). Within this highly differentiated service, transmission, processing information and databases were carried, through the use of computers and computer-based skills. Fibre-optic systems have reduced the demand for skilled engineers, with computers being used in their place to test and repair. New advances in software programming made digital switches both self-diagnostic and self-repairing. Remote testing and repair of equipment was also possible. The cumulative effect of this was that CP could operate in a high technology industry with limited skills. CP and Shinawatra both gained entry into a core technology industry without the need to

Table 7.3 Development of Orient Telecom and Technology Holdings (OTTH) Ltd, 1989–95 (million HK$)

Year	1989	1990	1991	1992	1993 mid-year	1993	1994	1995
Dividends				17.02	17.02			
Reserves				223.25	4,521.84	4,993.75	4,896.18	
Deposits				43.51	85.32	51.50		
Long-term loans						867.87	695.62	
Cash and bank balances				4,937.00	4,452.00	45,334.00	40,795.00	
Bank loans and long-term loans				142.26		475.50		
Total assets	136.51	148.68		445.71	4,831.87	6,659.60	6,769.64	7,099.29
Fixed assets			392.67	13.75	25.07	1,079.06	1,107.40	
Shareholder funds/equity	119.75	122.18	254.19	275.72	4,813.13	5,380.22	5,469.54	5,544.88
Retained earnings				20.23	90.83	176.79	363.89	
Premium on share					4,265.19	4,338.78	4,338.78	
Issued and paid-up capital				32.24	202.43	209.47	209.47	
Share capital				50.00	250.00	250.00	250.00	
Revenue							515.49	625.44
Earnings per share				6.45	6.51	4.41	8.94	
Total liabilities	16.75	26.50	137.76	169.99	16.76	1,279.38	1,300.10	1,554.41
Turnover	46.68	6.08	19.50	53.91	70.40	354.05	511.92	619.97
Net profit	6.28	2.19	3.03	20.80	70.60	91.12	187.33	76.41
Net book value				13.75	25.07	1,079.06	1,107.40	1,052.53
Operating profit				23.30	48.62	121.55	229.67	
Number of directors						9	11	
Cash and cash equivalents				48.45	89.77	96.85	40.80	

Note: 1993 saw important organisational changes and these are reflected in the statistics.
Sources: Orient Telecom and Technology Holdings Ltd, (Hong Kong) and Chia Tai Co. (Hong Kong), 1988–96, Balance Sheets, Annual Reports and Minutes of Meetings.

acquire a base of entrenched skills. This is an important industrial change. Inexperienced corporations entered the market for diversified telecommunications services, uninhibited by cost or technology barriers. CP and Shinawatra were expanding into different technologies, including satellite networks, without incorporating separate R&D divisions. Indeed they were able to provide telephones, TV services, video and cable, and to launch satellites and manufacture component parts. Telecommunications permitted immature technological corporations to dominate as successful regional providers.

CP could emerge as an Asian market leader in telecommunications through its access to state finance and technology. Internalisation and assimilation of core technical competence was avoided. Indeed a multi-layered subcontracting relationship created niches in a high technology sector. This form of technology relationship based on subcontracting challenges the 'social capability' theory of Ohkawa and Rosovsky.[14] Social capabilities hinge on levels of education, training, new concepts of management, finance and legal adaptations. Telecommunications fostered new forms of technology transfer, more accurately called 'spillovers'. As Moses Abramovitz argued, 'catch up' was determined not only by the gaps in levels of technology and capital intensity but also by the scale and scope of the market, the organisational structures of corporations, and sources of finance.[15]

The stable, secure niches could soon produce vertical integration between data sources and telephone services. The economies of scale and scope led to an increasing concentration of services in the hands of large corporations. Thus different operators did not specialise in different sectors. Individual operators combined most of the segments of the network. CP, Shinawatra, and UCOM (a Thai telecommunications group) absorbed all the separate divisions of cellular phone, fixed telephone network, video production and data provision (see Table 7.4).[16] The integration created convergence between computer hardware, software entertainment information, educational services, telephone equipment, and cable and broadcast television sectors. CP faced few barriers in developing such a wide range of activities, which implied the creation of a form of shared monopoly among a few large Sino-Thai corporations.

This brings us to the issue of privatisation, which was intended to increase competition, improve efficiency, promote wider ownership, and reduce state contributions, but in practice produced private monopoly. In reality, privatisation removed competition. A 'natural monopoly' already existed in the industry. For example, one regional monopoly in local tele-

Table 7.4 Thailand: major business groups in the telecommunications industry, 1994

Group	Year established	Name of Company	Capital ownership (%)	Partners	Business activity
	1982	ICSI Limited Partnership	90		Computer services
	1983	Shinawatra Computer & Communications	50	Foreign Investors (24%)	Computer services systems integrator
	1985	International Broadcasting	55		Cable Televisions
	1986	Advanced Info Service	72	UCOM Group (4%)	Mobile phone service
Shinawatra Group	1989	Shinawatra Datacom	34	Singapore Telecom International (49%)	Data communications
	1990	Shinawatra Paging	40	Singapore (60%)	Paging services
	1991	Shinawatra Satellite	75	American International Assurance (10%)	Satellite
	1991	Shinawatra Directories	42	AT&T	Directories services
	1991	SC Matchbox	75		Advertising
	1993	Shinawatra International	100		Investment
		Telewiz Company	80	UCOM Group (20%)	
	1989	Fonepoint (Thailand) (Bangkok Feedmill)	27	Shinawatra (36%) UCOM group (27%)	Mobile phones
	1990	Telecom Asia Corp.	85	NYNEX Network Systems (15%)	Public phones (Bangkok)
CP Group	1991	Telecom Holding	100		Investment in TI
	1991	Radiophone (Telecom Holding)	60	Jasmine group (40%)	Long distance transmission
	n.a.	Com-Link (Telecom Holding)	20		Long distance railway
	1992	China's satellite (Chia Tai International)	25	China government	Satellite (1994)

Table 7.4 Thailand: major business groups in the telecommunications industry, 1994 – *continued*

Group	Year established	Name of Company	Capital ownership (%)	Partners	Business activity
CP	1993	Lines Technology (Telecom Holding)	90		Videotex
	1982	Jasmine International	93		Sale of computers
	1984	Siam Teltech			Sale of communications equipment
Jasmine Group	1988	Acumen	96		Data communications
	1991	Radiophone (Jasmine International)	40	CP group (60%)	Long distance transmissions
	1992	Thai Telephone & Telecommunication (Jasmine International)	20	Loxley Group (34%) NTT (20%); Japan	Public phones (countryside)
	1975	Samart Engineering	100		Television antennas
	1986	Samart Telecoms	60	OTC International (Australia: 40%)	Data communications
Samart Group	1988	Samart Satcom (Samart Corp.)	80	Shinawatra (20%)	Manufacture of parabolic antennas
	1989	Samart Corp.			Investment of TI
	1992	Cambodia Samart Communication	100	Cambodian Government	Mobile phones in Cambodia
	1980	United Communication Industry (UCI)	93		Import of communications equipment
UCOM Group	1989	Total Access Communication	56	CP group (10%)	
	1989	Fonepoint (Thailand)	27	CP group (27%) Shinawatra	Paging

Table 7.4 Thailand: major business groups in the telecommunications industry, 1994 – *continued*

Group	Year established	Name of Company	Capital ownership (%)	Partners	Business activity
UCOM	1991	Worldpage	100		Mobile phones
Loxley Group	1990	Thai Skycom	40	Thanayong (60%) NTT (20%) Jasmine (20%)	Data communications
Strifuengfung	1992	Thai Telephone & Telecommunication	34		Public phones (countryside)
Bangkok Bank	1996	Compunet Corp.	30 30	Cable & Wireless Plc. (40%) UK	Data communications

Sources: Tara Siam Business Information Ltd, *Thai Telecommunications Industry*, 1993/94, Bangkok 1995; Khu Khaeng, 23 February 1991; Sakkarin Niyomsilpa, 1995, pp. 104, 120, 166. See also: Akira Suehiro, 'The Shinawatra Group – Thailand's Telecommunications Industry and the Newly Rising Zaibiatsu', *Asia Economies*, 36.2, 1995, p. 4.

phone services could connect to several other regional operations without introducing competition. This in turn could be linked to long-distance telephone services. There was no technical divisibility in laying, maintaining or purchasing a network system. Vertical integration between local and long distance services could achieve horizontal integration into, for example, electronic mail or data services. Telecom Asia was not a fragmented organisation but included lucrative segments integrated through a business owned, controlled and financed by the CP group. The structure of the industry possessed monopolistic advantages. These were further intensified by state support, relations with foreign multinationals, and a networked relationship between all the large Sino-Thai telecommunications firms, CP, Shinawatra, UCOM, Jasmine and Samart (see Figure 7.1). Interacting with one another, these business groups tended to mimic each another, producing identical products and services. They converged towards similar organisational structures and strategies, often dictated by inflows of foreign direct investment and the decisions of foreign telecommunications multinationals. Rising demand in one country often stimulated demand in a neighbouring country.

In the different branches of telecommunications, all the technologies were organised into these large corporations, seeking to monopolise markets despite their diversity. They were successful because they formed separate individual oligopolies, with solid working relationships with suppliers and with access to expanding capital sources, both domestic and foreign. Social and political factors were more important for survival. CP faced the same environmental conditions as Samart and Shinawatra. Certainly there was a threshold of technological requirement, and minimum profits were necessary for survival, but the institutional isomorphism engendered by the technology and patronage-based society meant that frequently political power and legitimacy determined organisational structures, strategies and ultimately success. Chandler's argument is challenged by this situation; Chandler argues that firms are organisational entities rationally adapting to the needs of new technology and to opportunities for increased market share. The Thai telecommunications firms clearly refute this paradigm. CP's growth in telecommunications is dependent on the state, foreign capital, monopoly profits, and the standardisation of technology – on the pre-eminence of software rather than hardware technology. The state and foreign capital created a diverse yet homogenised telecommunications sector.

The Thai state assisted dominant businessmen like Dhanin Chearavanont to become active in Asian telecommunications. In

Figure 7.1 Interlocking shareholding between the Thai telecommunications firms and their foreign joint-venture partners

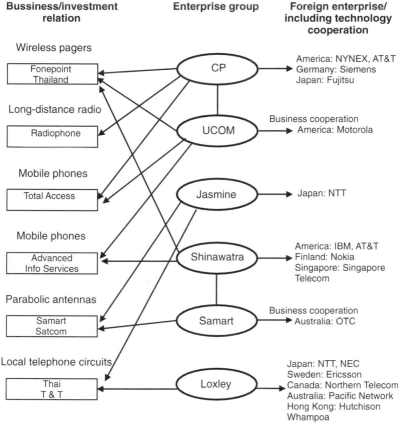

Bussiness/investment relation	Enterprise group	Foreign enterprise/ including technology cooperation

Wireless pagers

Fonepoint Thailand — CP — America: NYNEX, AT&T / Germany: Siemens / Japan: Fujitsu

Long-distance radio

Radiophone — UCOM — Business cooperation / America: Motorola

Mobile phones

Total Access — Jasmine — Japan: NTT

Mobile phones

Advanced Info Services — Shinawatra — America: IBM, AT&T / Finland: Nokia / Singapore: Singapore Telecom

Parabolic antennas

Samart Satcom — Samart — Business cooperation / Australia: OTC

Local telephone circuits

Thai T & T — Loxley — Japan: NTT, NEC / Sweden: Ericsson / Canada: Northern Telecom / Australia: Pacific Network / Hong Kong: Hutchison Whampoa

Sources: Tara Siam Business Information Ltd, Thai Telecommunications Industry, 1993/4, Bangkok 1995; *Khu Khaeng*, 23 February 1991; Sakkarin Niyomsilpa, 1995, p. 120.

Thailand, the state sought to create a modern financial and industrial nation through the development of telecommunications. The fierce desire to establish Bangkok as the financial capital of Asia required the construction of sophisticated communications. The close relations between CP and the Chatichai government in the late 1980s put the former at the centre of this drive for regional dominance. CP's regional initiatives in telecommunications and satellites in Southeast Asia and

China were a natural outcome of its successful links with the Thai state and its strategic alliances with telecommunications transnationals. International growth was not a consequence of the possession of the more advanced research and development necessary in the industry, where innovation resulted in greater cross investments of capital and technology between countries. International expansion was a result of the effectiveness of Chinese business networks and of good relationships with governments in Asia. Telecommunications and information technology, with its potential for political risk and sensitivities, needed trustworthy industrial brokers like CP. Competition was not via the market but through an allocation between domestic agents and the foreign specialist. In this, CP acted as broker in China, Indonesia, India and Indochina.[17]

How did CP finance this phenomenal growth in telecommunications? (See Tables 7.5 and 7.6 on Telcom Asia's growth and financing techniques.) The initial strategy was to finance expansion in telecommunications through the public listing of specialist firms, such as Telecom Asia. Frequent corporate restructuring and re-issue of shares stemmed from financial necessity. The listing of Telecom Asia in 1993 provided CP with the second largest market capitalisation in Thailand in that year, at US$3.52 billion. Only the Bangkok Bank exceeded this with a capital creation of US$6.1 billion. During the listing of Telecom Asia, CP acquired 70 per cent of the total capital, which, together with share premiums amounted to $5 billion.

Share issues often led to closer linkages between subsidiaries because they held equity in each of the firms in the group. The subsidiaries purchased the shares irrespective of the profitability of the companies. For example, in May 1996, OTTH acquired Telecom Asia shares of $10 million when it already held 23 per cent of the equity in Telecom Asia. This purchase of new shares was particularly notable since Telecom Asia had suffered a decline in profits of 249 per cent in 1996. Telecom Asia's profits in 1995 were 1,290,701,000 baht, but in 1996 it suffered a loss of 1, 924,119,000 baht.[18] At precisely this time OTTH was divesting its stake in Chinese telecommunications and moving into electricity generation in China, Hong Kong, Vietnam and Thailand. Nynex was also disposing of its 23 per cent stake in OTTH, having failed to expand in China.[19] These rather complicated movements suggest the possibility that CP was making internal transfers between its companies to conceal a deteriorating financial position (see Tables 7.3 and 7.5).

The technique of issuing shares and restructuring ownership within subsidiaries was used to finance critical changes in the corporation's

Table 7.5 Development of Telecom Asia Corporation plc, 1992–96 (million baht)

Year	1992	1993	1994	1995	1996
Dividends			1,532.70	2,667.20	
Reserves		−85.00	453.00	1,092.00	
Bank overdraft and loans			26.01	141.21	248.13
Long-term loans			6,250.08	18,713.53	30,305.20
Total assets	23,072.00	42,138.00	56,235.71	77,537.43	96,931.50
Shareholder funds/equity	21,715.00	34,545.00	35,183.47	36,474.17	34,550.10
Retained earnings			1,187.47	2,409.20	485.10
Premium on share	1,800.00	11,835.00	11,835.00	11,835.00	11,835.00
Issued and paid-up capital	20,000.00	22,230.00	22,230.00	22,230.00	22,230.00
Cash in hand			11,002.70	10,444.59	9,999.40
Revenue		2,018.00	4,198.00	7,166.00	
Total revenue			5,163.00	9,375.00	12,080.41
Earnings per share (baht)	−0.04	0.28	0.29	0.58	−0.87
Total liabilities	1,334.00	7,559.00	20,995.18	41,023.61	62,304.20
Net profit	−31.00	611.00	638.00	1,290.00	−1,924.00
Operating profit			1,683.50	3,947.20	
Operating revenues				4,865.00	9,855.00
Operating expenses				5,428.00	10,313.00
Operating income				−563.00	−458.00
Interest income				1,798.00	1,584.00
Interest expenses				1,846.00	3,530.00
Net income from operating activities			638.00	1,290.00	
Other income				2,713.00	641.00
Share prices			70.00		
Number of staff				3,460	

Table 7.5 Development of Telecom Asia Corporation plc, 1992–96 (million baht) – *continued*

Year	1992	1993	1994	1995	1996
Number of shareholders				11,791	
Total costs and expenses			4,557.00	8,191.72	13,948.46
Net income	−43.00	565.00	638.61	1,290.70	−1,924.12
Cash and cash equivalents		1,538.07	2,381.47	3,608.32	
Trade accounts & notes receivables			935.40	1,488.30	3,399.30
Short-term investments			7,236.10	8,925.10	5,159.90
Investment in associated companies and others			1,275.00	3,099.00	

Sources: Telecom Asia and Subsidiaries, 1992–97, Consolidated Balance Sheets, Annual Reports, and Minutes of AGMs.

activities. Telecom Holding increased its capital from 9 million baht to 11 billion baht in March 1997 to capture the market in video and cable television. Telecom Holding's subsidiary, Asia Multi-Media, also increased its capital from 50 million baht to 2.4 billion baht in March 1997 to purchase a universal cable television network.[20]

The inter-linkages were highly complex but central to growth and success. The investment companies remained fully under family ownership and control. Chia Tai International, formed in 1989 in Bermuda with a capital of HK$100,000, increased its capital to HK$250 million in 1992, before its conversion to OTTH.[21] The increase was effected through a transfer of HK$80 million from Chia Tai Hong Kong. Chia Tai was then listed on the Hong Kong Stock Market to raise more capital, bringing the total equity to HK$125 million. Three other family investment companies, registered in Liberia and Hong Kong, paid another HK$125 million to OTTH. Equity transfers removed the need for mergers between sub-sidiaries.[22] The issuing of new shares, and the creation of share swaps between the firms in the group, ensured capital increase without loss of family ownership.

Shinawatra, in contrast, faced difficulties in raising finance because of its dependence largely on capital markets. Electronics had been Shinawatra's main interest from the 1980s, providing computer hard-ware and software to the Thai government and the universities. The company had few interests in other sectors. Unlike CP, Shinawatra was unable to effect capital transfers between subsidiaries in different regions or allow one industrial sector to subsidise another. CP had profits from its chicken business to nourish a cash strapped telecom-munications sector.[23]

The second source of income for expansion in the telecommunica-tions sector was internally generated profits. CP's half-year profits of US$21.8 million in 1992, secured principally from agribusiness in Thailand, Indonesia, Turkey and China, were allocated to Telecom Asia. Shanghai Ek Chor Motorcycle also contributed 26 per cent of its 1992 profits to Telecom Asia. A major share of CP's consolidated net sales revenue of US$3.1 billion in 1992 was targeted for its telecommu-nications sector.[24]

The third major source of finance was offshore banks. The issuing of corporate bonds and syndicated loans for infrastructural projects became popular in the 1990s. In October 1992, US$1 billion in American bonds was targeted for CP's Chinese initiatives.[25] CP tapped into Japanese as well as American capital markets. In November 1993,

CP launched the Far East Fund in Japan to raise US$1 billion. This fund sought capital in Hong Kong, Tokyo and Singapore to finance phone networks in Ho Chi Minh City and Hebei province in China, as well as the APT satellite.[26] In February 1994, CP raised another $150 million through a floating rate note to fund its expansion in Vietnam.[27] This was repeated in March 1995, when another US$100 million was channelled into its projects in China.

In short, CP used diverse forms of financial instruments to sustain its position in a capital-intensive sector. From 1991, CP had dealt in American or international depositing receipts, which are certificates traded on foreign stock exchanges in lieu of shares, held on deposit at designated banks. This could raise capital in New York, exploiting CP's successful political connections in China. The use of state finance in Southeast Asia and China provided another source of funds. The state often facilitated the acquisition of funds secured from Western and Japanese banks.

In the early years, more than half of CP's working capital was borrowed from banks. In 1991 this amounted to US$33.3 billion but then fell in the next year to US$16.4 billion. The decline was a consequence of increased exploitation of the stock market and of the restructuring of subsidiaries to accumulate capital. The profits accumulated through speculation on the stock market and on real estate also provided long-term finance between 1992 and 1996.

Finance from Thai banks, however, was still significant. In 1995, Telecom Asia secured US$1billion in long-term credit from Thai banks. The repayment, in twenty instalments over ten years, was to commence only in November 1997.[28] Telecom Asia's loans of US$925 million in supplier credit could not meet its costs of US$3.2 billion to finance the initial two million lines in Bangkok. Telecom Asia was forced to borrow through Telecom Holding, which also secured 5 billion baht from Thai banks. Between 1991 and 1995, the telecommunications firms of CP depended on banks for 37 per cent of their finance, on the stock market for a further 32 per cent, while internally generated cash provided 30 per cent.[29]

The fourth source of finance remained the partners in joint ventures. Nynex had contributed US$800 million in the first year (1992). Siemens AG, Mitsui (NEC) and AT&T gave dollar- and baht-denominated credit to Telecom Asia for the purchase of equipment,[30] which amounted to 6 per cent of the total finance for constructing the 2 million lines in Bangkok.[31] Equipment costs were 68 per cent of total costs for Telecom Asia. Costs relating to land were 11 per cent, and design and other operational costs averaged 12 per cent of the total cost.

Finally, real estate investment provided another useful source of finance for Telecom Asia. Siam Fortune, a property subsidiary of CP, had substantial investments in residential, commercial and office buildings by 1993. In December 1993, Siam Fortune was restructured to raise more capital on the Bangkok Stock Exchange. A new issue of 6 billion baht was targeted for telecommunications in Southeast Asia and China. Siam Fortune also issued Euro-convertible bonds to provide further working capital. In February 1997, Siam Fortune's paid up capital of 450 million baht was used to secure loans for Telecom Asia.[32] This complex system of financing telecommunications projects was necessary because the revenue earned from telecommunications in the early years was limited. This is clearly shown in Table 7.6.

The multiple forms for financing this rapid growth had serious implications for profitability and overall performance. The impressive growth in the different sectors of telecommunications – terrestrial to satellite, and the manufacture of component parts – imposed strains on Telecom Asia's business performance. The pace of construction of tele-

Table 7.6   Telecom Asia (CP): revenues 1994–95 (million baht).

Year	1994 January–June	1995 January–June
Income from telephone services	503	1,870
Sales and services	15	913
Total turnover	518	2,783
Amortisation expenses	–201	–575
Gross margin	243	1,305
Operating administration and general expenses	–1,053	–1,676
Operating income	–810	–371
Interest income	840	932
Gain on sale of investments	0	1,270
Other incomes	117	202
Interest expenses	–230	–798
Income tax	–14	–579
Earning after tax	–98	657
Minority interest	16	–8
Net earning	–82	649
Earning per share baht/share	0.04	0.29

Sources: *Telecom Asia*, report by Securities One, Bangkok, 1996; Annual Reports, Telecom Asia, 1994–1996.

phone lines accelerated from 1995. The number of subscribers in Thailand rose from 442,000 in 1994 to 804,000 in 1995. By April 1996, Telecom Asia had installed a total of 3,556,821 lines, transferring 1,237,194 lines to the Telecommunications Authority of Thailand for maintenance.[33] The firms's growth in the cellular phone market of 30 per cent per annum since 1995 was particularly stunning, since Shinawatra, Samart and UCOM were keen competitors.

The following discussion of firm performance clearly demonstrates that growth was inconsistent, and profitability was highly unstable (see Tables 7.3, 7.5, and 7.7, on Telecom Asia, OTTH, and Shinawatra Computer and Communications Ltd). Telecom Asia's performance between 1992 and 1996 was erratic. A record profit in 1995 of 1,290 million baht was derived partly from the sale of its shares in UCOM. Moreover, abnormal profits secured in the early phase were quickly lost through rising competition. The early phase was shaped by government infrastructural demand, with little management of assets, and this was further complicated by the imprecise division of functions between the corporation and its joint-venture partners. The opening up of neighbouring markets as the company acquired competence in one country sometimes eroded profits, particularly with difficult situations abroad, as in China in 1996. While rapidly falling marginal costs might have increased profit margins at home, with the expansion of operations abroad, these were immediately lost. The cross-industry, cross-company transfers within the CP group complicated profit returns. Despite unpredictability and fluctuating profitability, Telecom Asia's commitment to product diversification and regional expansion remained strong. CP's expansion into Bangalore in India coincided with the rapid expansion of the Indian electronics industry, particularly in software production.[34] By April 1996, CP had secured fixed line and cellular phone concessions in China, and in May 1996 this was extended to include cable television, radio and film concessions.

CP's involvement in China was rather complicated. Although it had close relations with the Chinese government, CP faced difficulties there. CP and Nynex were allowed to install telephones only in Hebei and Sichuan; contracts to provide a mere 200 lines and appropriate equipment were all it achieved in Hebei. Apstar, a satellite for Chinese state television, and Apstar 2 for international subscription, were prestige projects for CP but the projects failed.[35] CP's difficulties arose in part from its over-extension in China. CP had moved into the chicken feed industry, oil refining, petrochemicals, the gas industry, transport and construction, as well as telecommunications. CP's links with the

Table 7.7 Shinawatra Computer and Communications plc and subsidiaries, 1990–1997 (million baht)

Year	1993	1994	1995	1996
Net profit	1,480.68	2,765.38	3,295.92	2,631.36
Turnover	5,062.06	7,804.96	9,528.39	7,955.13
Dividends		207.90	485.10	554.40
Bank loans		3,138.75	3,170.08	2,780.47
Long-term loans		5,813.48	7,457.33	9,590.83
Loans from financial companies		465.25	915.76	256.60
Total assets		30,398.40	39,907.20	45,339.21
Shareholder funds/ equity	3,675.21	6,508.31	8,832.84	10,356.68
Retained earnings	1,644.64	3,647.32	5,925.34	7,447.90
Premium on share capital		1,224.00	1,224.00	1,224.00
Issued & paid-up capital	693.00	1,386.00	1,386.00	1,386.00
Share capital		3,000.00	3,000.00	3,000.00
Bills receivable		6,275.69	11,361.92	3,595.13
Cash in hand & at bank	1,237.87	1,427.98	1,170.47	1,260.45
Earnings per share baht/share	21.37	21.51	23.78	18.99
Book value per share	53.03	46.96	63.73	74.72
Average return on ratio of shareholders' equity (ROE)	46.69%	54.31%	42.97%	27.42%
Average return on net assets (ROA)	29.97%	34.62%	27.78%	18.90%
Dividends: Net profits	28%	33%	32%	37%

Table 7.7 Shinawatra Computer and Communications plc and subsidiaries, 1990–1997 (million baht) – *continued*

Year	1993	1994	1995	1996
Total income		16,191.27	21,051.16	21,231.45
Total expenses		12,719.62	16,274.95	16,983.15
Total liabilities		18,192.98	24,133.30	27,117.45

Notes: **Bank Loans**
Minus short-term bank loans plus debt in trust receipts.

Long-term Loans
Minus loans from local banks
Plus loans from overseas banks
Plus joint loans from overseas banks
Plus loans from overseas companies
Minus long-term loans due within one year.

Total Assets
Total assets are different to those in the consolidated balance sheet. *Total assets* column has values that are equal to total liabilities plus shareholders' equity.

Sources: Shinawatra Group (Bangkok), 1990–1997, Balance Sheets and Annual Reports.

Chinese military and cooperation with the semi-state corporation, NORINCO, helped to sustain these technology-intensive sections, although difficulties remained. The company was over-extended financially and in acquisitions. Rent-seeking activities resulted in CP being given too many contracts, from which the company often had to withdraw during the 1997 financial crisis.[36]

CP's rival, Shinawatra, was also expanding in Southeast Asia in the 1990s. Shinawatra secured concessions for cellular phones, paging, data communication sources, as well as contracts for pay TV and as the sole provider of satellite communication throughout Southeast Asia. Control of satellite communications strengthened Shinawatra's niche in mobile services. Shinawatra absorbed developments in digital technology from Nokia to enable it to operate digital mobile telephone services. In November 1993, CP attempted to duplicate this technology and these products. UCOM, which had supplied radio communications equipment to the Thai police and army since 1956, now, in 1990, obtained a 22-year concession to manage cellular phones. Pushed by the competition, Shinawatra entered Cambodian telecommunications to spread its costs. (See Tables 7.8 and 7.9 for the growth of Shinawatra

Table 7.8 Overseas investments of Thai telecommunications groups

Business group	Project	Country
Shinawatra	Trading	USA
	Postal services, paging services	Vietnam
	TV Broadcasting, telecom services	Cambodia
	Telecom services	Laos
	Telecom services	Philippines
	Paging services	India
Jasmine	Trading	Cambodia
	Telecom services	Philippines
	Telecom services	India
	Submarine cable	Malaysia
	Trunk radio	Indonesia
	Satellite mobile telephone	SE Asia
Samart	Trading, mobile telephone	Cambodia
Telecom Asia	Basic telephone	Vietnam
	Basic telephone	China
	Telecom services	India
	Paging services	Cambodia

Sources: Far Eastern Economic Review, 7 April 1994; *Phujadkarn*, 3–4 and 15 December 1994; *Who's Who in Business & Finance*, 1:4, February 1995; *The Asian Wall Street Journal*, 28 April 1995.

Table 7.9 Affiliated enterprises of the Shinawatra Group (unit: million baht, %)

Enterprise name	Established in year	Business content	Paid-up capital	1993 Investment rate
Computer business and services				
Shinawatra Computer and Communications Public Co. Ltd	1983	Computers	693	50.2
ICSI Limited Partnership	1982	Computers	10	90
SCS Computer Systems Co. Ltd	–	Computers	45	33.3
SC Telecom Sales and Service Co. Ltd	1990	Computers	30	60
Samart Corp.	1993	Services	450	4.05
International Engineering Co. Ltd	–	Services	11	5
Information services business				
Advanced Info Service Public Co. Ltd	1986	Mobiles	780	57.7
Shinawatra Datacom Co. Ltd	1982	Services	180	18
Shinawatra Paging Co. Ltd	1990	Pagers	150	60
Fonepoint (Thailand) Co. Ltd	1991	Pagers	140	30.5
Universal Communication Service Co. Ltd	–	Information services	1	25
Broadcasting, media business				
International Broadcasting Public Co. Ltd	1985	Cable Television	360	55
Shinawatra Directories Co. Ltd	1991		500	100
SC Matchbox Co. Ltd	1991		1	75
Shinawatra Pacific Direct Marketing Co. Ltd	1993	Advertising and marketing	8	55
International Broadcasting Corp. (Cambodia) Ltd	1993	Cambodia broadcasting	US$1m	70
Satellite launching and related business				
Shinawatra Satellite Public Co. Ltd	1991	Satellite	1,750	60
Shinawatra International Co. Ltd	1993	Information and communication business	600	100

Table 7.9 Affiliated enterprises of the Shinawatra Group (unit: million baht, %) – *continued*

Enterprise name	Established in year	Business content	1993 Paid-up capital	Investment rate
Cambodia Shinawatra Co. Ltd	1993	Information and communication business	US$1m	70
Lao Shinawatra Telecom Co. Ltd	1993	Information and communication business	200	70
Citadel Group (Philippines)	1993	Information and communication business		70
Himachal (India)	1993	Information and communication business		40

Sources: Shinawatra Computer and Communications Public Co. Ltd, Annual Report, 1993 (Bangkok, 1994).

and for the overseas investments undertaken by Thai telecommunications groups.) In 1993, Shinawatra secured a 20–year contract to supply Cambodia with an international exchange and television stations.[37] The Shinawatra satellite helped to minimise infrastructural costs in Cambodia by relaying calls from a switching station in Phnom Penh rather than the traditional routes through Australia. The experience gained in Cambodia encouraged Shinawatra to expand into Laos and the Philippines. The expansion in Cambodia was undoubtedly assisted by the UN operations in that country and the elections for a new government, because Shinawatra's cellular phones and satellites were critical to this operation. Despite increasing competition, CP, Shinawatra, and UCOM avoided a price war and sought to increase profits through expansion overseas. Government purchasing policies both at home and abroad meant that internal efficiency and competitive pricing were not serious priorities. Horizontal expansion was the preferred option. Consequently, the return on capital was erratic; billing revenues arising from the increasing purchasing power of the population often provided the only stable source of profits. Global initiatives were used to disguise low performing assets and low returns on capital. In addition, moves into higher technology, such as satellite communications, overcame the construction difficulties of a fixed line infrastructure.

The analysis so far has focused on the important features of the growth of domestic telecommunications corporations in Southeast Asia, demonstrating the importance of state patronage, constructive joint-venture liaisons and the ease of securing sufficient capital to invest in the industry. Price and demand did not influence segmentation of products and markets. Cellular phone companies mounted heavy promotions focusing on price. On the other hand, the fixed line sector, which saw substantial growth in revenue per line, had no incentive to reduce tariffs on local or long-distance calls.[38] Growth was rolled out by the growing number of customers. Competition between the Sino-Thai groups did exist, particularly in urban areas, but close linkages enabled them to share in the monopoly, allowing opportunities to diversify into a range of products. Critically, there were also limited adjustments in organisational structure. Listing on stock exchanges throughout Asia did not erode family ownership. The only managerial innovation was the creation of technocrat-executives who had control of operations. A combination of American, Thai and Taiwanese engineers, computer specialists and bureaucrats were employed. Ajva Taulanada and Veeravat Kanchanadul were prominent

Thai executives in this field.[39] The bureaucrats and engineers rotated, acquiring information and technological advances rapidly, although there was still no internal training of personnel. The Chearavanont family dominated the management of CP throughout the 1990s. The board of Telecom Asia comprised four members of the Chearavanont family out of a total of nine. Non-family members were dominant in research and development and technical operations, while the family retained control of finance. In the Shinawatra group, the family also retained control over decision-making, although non-family executive managers and advisers were on the board. Figure 7.2 clearly shows this centralised management structure.

The persistence of family, state, and ethnic networks, even in a capital- and technology-intensive industry, necessitates a reappraisal of the orthodoxy on institutions and markets. Chandler, Williamson and North have treated institutions as social arrangements that exist outside markets. The cases of Sino-Thai companies like CP and Shinawatra, however, indicate that no clear distinction can be made between social and economic institutions. The linkages between state, bureaucracy and businesses meant that the market could be dictated by the capitalists. R&D-intensive industries such as telecommunications could deviate from the market because the state created the legal and institutional structures within which markets could operate, that is, political and social processes helped CP to enter and dominate the market. This process was assisted by the nature of the product, technological changes and the structure of the capital market.

CP could not have sustained its high rate of growth without the financial liberalisation of the 1990s. Financial liberalisation provided access to generous bank credit, syndicated loans from offshore banks, long-term credit from international capital markets, finance from joint venture partners, and capital from the state and even the World Bank. All the debt was denominated in US dollars. The currency crisis of 1997 affected this debt burden and CP and Shinawatra had to restructure and sell some of their telecommunications interests in China and Southeast Asia. In a preliminary restructuring in October 1999, Telecom Asia sold a 24 per cent equity stake to Kreditanstalt fur Wiederaufbau, a German bank. This deal was negotiated with 50 of its creditors with the aim of reducing its debts. The bold activities in this sector may have been special to a very particular era, which has fundamentally changed since 1997. The financial freedom before 1997 enabled Chinese businesses to indulge in economically unconnected pursuits without facing financial difficulties or competition. Now new

168

Figure 7.2 The management structure of the Shinawatra Group, 1993

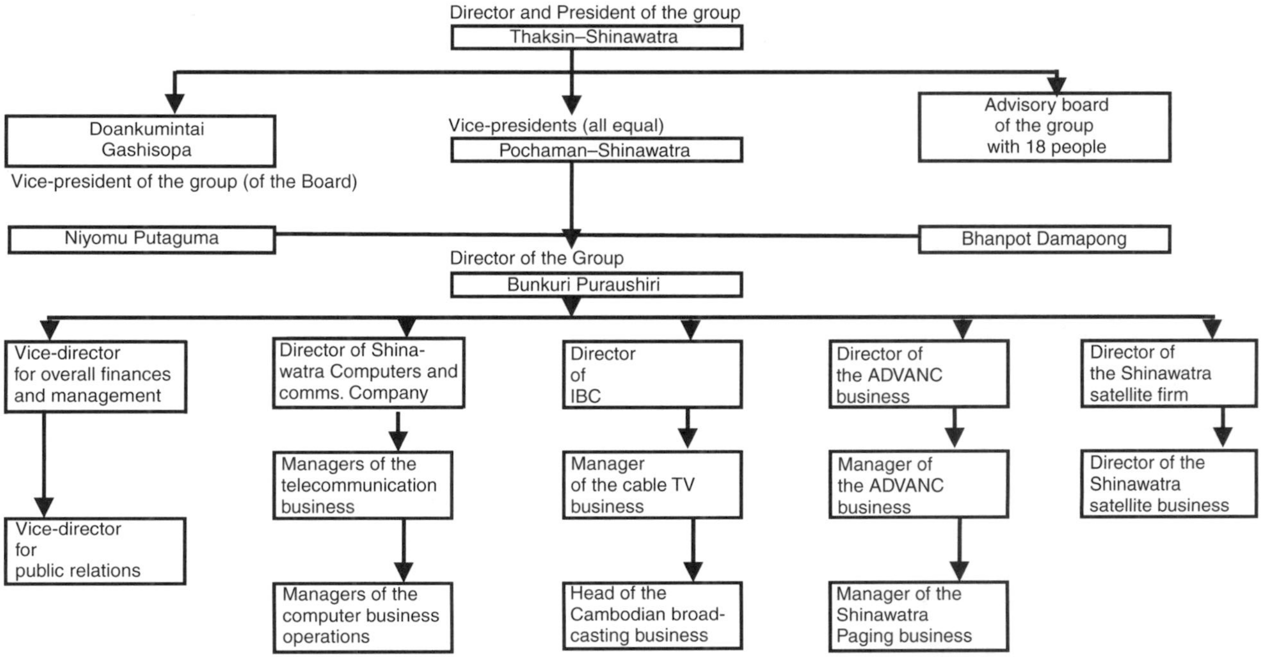

```
Director and President of the group
        Thaksin–Shinawatra
                 │
                 ├──────────────────────────────► Advisory board
                 │                                  of the group
Doankumintai                                        with 18 people
Gashisopa                                    
Vice-president of the group (of the Board)

        Vice-presidents (all equal)
           Pochaman–Shinawatra
                 │
                 ▼
Niyomu Putaguma                              Bhanpot Damapong

        Director of the Group
           Bunkuri Puraushiri
                 │
   ┌──────┬──────────┬──────────┬──────────┐
   ▼      ▼          ▼          ▼          ▼
Vice-    Director   Director   Director   Director of
director  of Shina-  of IBC    of the     the Shinawatra
for       watra               ADVANC      satellite firm
overall   Computers           business
finances  and                    │            │
and       comms.                 ▼            ▼
manage-   Company            Manager      Director of
ment         │               of the       the Shinawatra
   │         ▼               ADVANC        satellite business
   ▼      Managers of        business
Vice-     the telecom-          │
director  munication           ▼
for       business         Manager of the
public       │             Shinawatra
relations    ▼             Paging business
          Managers of
          the computer
          business
          operations

        Director
           of IBC
              │
              ▼
        Manager of
        the cable TV
        business
              │
              ▼
        Head of the
        Cambodian broad-
        casting business
```

Source: Annual report, 1993, Bangkok, 1994, pp. 30–1, Shinawatra Computer and Communications Public Ltd.

competitive regimes have emerged in Southeast Asia after the foreign multinationals intervened to salvage something from the economic devastation. Such foreign involvement will in future place constraints on the activities of companies like CP. Finally, CP's success also highlights a recurring problem. Chinese companies sought markets through technology but still neglected innovation. Enough information was taken in to meet immediate expansionary needs, but Chinese capitalists consistently failed to engage in the long-term technological learning necessary to develop a strong basis in a technology-intensive industry like telecommunications.

8
Land and Property Development: Growth Strategies, Financial Innovation and Risk

An examination of large Chinese corporations' acquisition of land and property provides an insight into the attitudes of Chinese capitalists towards speculation and risk. Investment in land and property not only offers different degrees of risk and different yields and capital values but is also inherently illiquid and inflexible. Property requires long-term commitment. An understanding of potential performance and scope for hedging risks are also necessary. Changes in the commercial or political environment over which the investor has no control can have adverse consequences for property values. The risks include changes in inflation and investment rates, changes in rent values and the yield on sales. The lack of liquidity and uncertainty can also create problems.

Property development in Asia has been influenced by the state. Chinese entrepreneurs often responded to the demands of the state's construction programmes, anticipating lucrative profits in state expansion. Chinese involvement in the property market can, therefore, provide further insight into state–capital relationships. Since the land and property market is difficult to judge, knowledge is important for transactions, which raises the question of whether Chinese networks across Asia assisted in overcoming information deficiencies. Or were Chinese networks highly competitive in property investment, competing in fragmented markets and creating separate oligopolies? This question is related to another important issue: whether the state and Chinese networks together helped to create oligopolies in the land/property sectors. The diversity of property development, with specialisation in residential, commercial, hi-tech, industrial or hotel construction, gave further scope for property cartels to emerge. With Ng Teng Fong in residential development, Kwek in commercial property, and Kuok in hotel construction, each could sustain separate and distinct monopolies in property markets throughout Asia. As discussed in the introduction, the rapidly changing economic and geographical expansion of Chinese firms in Southeast Asia means that a description of Chinese capitalism must jump between different countries, as Chinese businesses jumped. This is particularly clear when it comes to discussing the hyper-charged property market of the 1980s and 1990s.

A detailed examination of finance methods is essential in understanding Chinese involvement in property development. The changing attitude of banks towards financing land and property, the creation of finance houses within property groups, as well as financial innovations in the use of bonds and tradable property securities, illustrate the dramatic transformation in finance and property markets. Property markets cannot be seen in isolation from other markets, particularly that of finance. An analysis of property development, therefore, cannot be separated from an examination of finance. The linkage between land, property and finance illustrates attitudes to risk and risk management in Chinese business practice in Southeast Asia.

The Chinese property developer has to recognise risk and assess what profit is possible, and when the profit should be taken. The following studies of City Developments Ltd (CDL), Sino-Land, Far East Organisation (FEO), and Orchard Parade Holdings (OPH) demonstrate the extent of appraisals of risk and potential profit. CDL is a property company registered in Singapore belonging to the Kwek family. FEO and OPH are also both registered in Singapore and belong to Ng Teng Fong, whose other property firm, Sino-Land, is registered in Hong Kong. As seen throughout this volume, risk appraisal in finance – forecasting interest rate changes, inflation prospects and anticipated revenues – was often ignored by Chinese capitalists because business simply floated on great inflows of capital. The property portfolio, which included retail, industrial and commercial properties, needed careful appraisal because property value is volatile. The need to compare land and property investment with equities and gilts is critical for risk management, but both Ng and Kwek would blindly respond to opportunities rather than seriously calculate risk. Joint ventures with the state and foreign multinationals accelerated the propensity for risky investment in land and property. Absence of state or ethnic support could spell failure.

The attitude of Chinese business to debt can be partially constructed from these transactions. Chinese capitalists used land/property as collateral to purchase other assets, such as additional finance. The majority of corporate debt was secured against property. Singapore, Hong Kong and cities in China attracted property investors from Japan, Indonesia and the Middle East. Chinese entrepreneurs tapped these lucrative external sources, as well as specialist property multinationals, introducing important foreign institutional investors, and employing hi-tech advances in construction as well as innovations in financing.

Ultimately, security, status and prestige are derived from the ownership of land, bricks and mortar. In Singapore and Hong Kong this is particularly so, because land is in extremely short supply. The status and prestige of ownership led large corporations to invest in flagship buildings for the sake of corporate image. Ng Teng Fong, Raymond Kwok and Lee Shau Kee collaborated in the creation of the Central Plaza building in Wanchai in Hong Kong, the tallest office block in Asia until 1996, when Petronas Twin Towers in Kuala Lumpur was erected. The traditional importance of land ownership for lineage and ancestor worship was now being transformed into inheritance, with transferability and divisibility among kin.

The role of the state was notably evident in Singapore from the 1960s, when two-thirds of the land was held by the state and was released intermittently to tender or to be sold at auction. The process of releasing land by the state accelerated particularly from 1970 when, with the increase in population, the growth of gross national product (GNP), increases in infrastructural services – that is transport and housing programmes – land became a critical factor in growth. With considerable expansion in public housing through the Housing Development Board (HDB), the state in Singapore was the largest supplier of residential property in the 1970s and 1980s. Seventy per cent of the population occupied HDB housing. In commercial property, a sector of dramatic growth since 1968, a small number of large Chinese property firms dominated. Housing for higher income groups and expatriates also offered good prospects for investment and speculation. The Bukit Timah and Holland Road areas were prime targets, which saw the highest percentage increases in values. Here, luxury apartment prices rose by 40 per cent per annum in the early 1990s; much of the increase was attributable to speculation. Speculators were generally confined to smaller élite developments; 25 per cent of the property market was in this sector.[1] Property prices briefly fell in 1997 but recovered by the end of the year.

The increase in private élite housing in Singapore in the 1990s led to dramatic rises in price and to fevered speculation. The volatility of the private sector was not transferred to the public housing market. The government's decision that funds from the Central Provident Fund (CPF), that is pension funds, could be used for the purchase of private housing led to an increased frenzy in the property boom. The creation of industrial triangles in Johor Bharu and on Batam and the neighbouring islands further boosted the private housing sector. The consistently strong economic performance of Southeast Asia in the early 1990s and the Gulf crisis of 1992 triggered outflows of capital from the Middle East into Singapore property projects, which sustained new developments in the prime Orchard Road belt, where (CDL) was dominant. By the mid-1990s, these developments became more restrained because of rising interest rates. Construction in Singapore, however, remained highly competitive in terms of cost, being one-third of the cost of office, residential apartment, and luxury hotel construction in Tokyo, and cheaper than in Hong Kong and Sydney, despite the fact that Singapore enjoyed smaller economies of scale.[2]

The rapid expansion of Chinese property firms, such as CDL and FEO, throughout Asia has to be examined in the context of rapid economic change in the region since 1960, and its repercussions on home ownership. Accelerated economic growth corresponded with a rise in property prices between 1979 and 1984, nurtured in part by the flight of capital from Hong Kong, induced by fears over the return to China in 1997. Construction activities in Singapore expanded by 22 per cent in volume each year between 1970 and 1983, partly as a response to state housing policies, as noted above, and to the demands of tourism and industry.[3] However, the availability of abundant finance was the main trigger for this phenomenal expansion. Banks were now lending more to property companies. Innovative financial techniques also provided new methods of financing property acquisition. Increases in foreign direct and portfolio investment between 1970 and 1990 assisted the Chinese firms. By 1990, property firms in Singapore and throughout Southeast Asia were linked to domestic and foreign banks, offshore financial institutions, the stock market, and investment and unit trusts. The link between property growth and new strategies of financing also is the core theme of this chapter. It was this link that contributed to the volatility in 1987 and the financial collapse in 1997.

The connection between property and finance bought instability, particularly when oversupply led to a fall in property prices, which was further complicated by the crash of world stock markets, including Singapore's, in October 1987 following the recession of 1985–86. By 1988, the decline was slightly reversed, but revival was assured by the continuous inflow of Japanese portfolio capital into South East Asia, which intensified after the Japanese 'Big Bang' of 1992.

In tracing the growth of property firms such as CDL or Sino-Land, it is essential to identify the distinct business and property cycles. The property cycle in Singapore peaked in 1973, 1983, in the late 1980s, and again in 1994. Residential property dominated in the 1970s, in contrast to the peaks in the commercial and industrial property markets in 1981, the fall in 1986, and a further peak in 1988. CDL and other private property firms acted only as contractors for public sector housing because the state and public sector dominated residential construction. Less than 20 per cent of residential housing was in the hands of the private sector in the early 1980s.[4] This changed from the late 1980s, when the government eased restrictions on foreign investors directly owning property, and encouraged private sector housing. Japanese, Hong Kong, and Indonesian investors came in, where before they had been major investors in joint-venture private investment in housing. Foreign involvement increased still further as the yen strengthened and uncertainty about Hong Kong grew.

Much of the property growth in Singapore in the 1990s was linked to developments in Hong Kong and Japan. Between 1991 and 1994, land and property prices in Singapore rose by 98.4 per cent, in Hong Kong they rose by 81.9 per cent, while in Japan, land prices fell by almost 30 per cent.[5] Japanese land values rose from 1969, peaked in 1973, fell between 1974 and 1976, and then rose gradually up to 1990, before the dramatic fall from 1991. Japanese commercial land prices fell by 40 per cent between 1991 and 1994.[6] In the same period, land prices in Southeast Asia rose by 38 per cent. In addition to the oil price rises of 1973, the stock market difficulties of 1987–88 and other economic factors produced a property recession in Japan in the 1990s, which had serious implications, because land and property markets were closely linked to banks and financial institutions.

By January 1997, land prices across Japan had fallen for the sixth consecutive year. Land prices had depreciated by 62 per cent in the big cities since 1991, which was in stark contrast to the record growth in Japanese land prices in the 1980s. The alternating periods of boom and slump helped redirect capital towards property in Singapore, Hong Kong and China. The turning points are useful to identify. At the end of a boom, following the increasing investment in land, land prices began to fall, producing smaller profits. Decline in speculative profit led to investment capital flowing from land speculation into industrial projects. Land values then rose disproportionately because of the demand for land for industrial construction, which in turn stimulated the creation of shopping centres, residential complexes and leisure projects. In general, Singapore land values were partly protected by the state, but despite active state-intervention the deep-seated disruptions of the trade cycle were never fully masked. Speculation could still take place, particularly since land and property markets were monopolised by a few large corporations, CDL, OPH, and Development Bank of Singapore (DBS) Land. Government enforced partial demand through construction programmes but could not eliminate speculation entirely because it was driven by the economic and property boom.

That Chinese property companies in Southeast Asia were oligopolistic, carving out lucrative niches in a differentiated property sector and often operating in more than one country in Asia, should be reiterated. The following studies of CDL and Sino-Land demonstrate their rapid growth, unhindered by the volatility of land markets in the region. Growth for these firms was almost linear, not cyclical. Profits were affected by these cycles, but the growth itself was not. While the property market was immature in the 1970s (which fostered speculation), by the late 1980s and 1990s a more sophisticated response to cyclical change encouraged large, innovative projects. This also corresponded with major infrastructural developments such as the mass transit system (MTR) in Singapore, and the creation of large retail projects, including Raffles City, Republic Plaza and UOB (United Overseas Bank) Plaza, as well as the refurbishing of existing retail complexes.

The oligopolies within the industry intensified as a result of these major infrastructural developments. (See Figure 8.1 on Hong Leong's [CDL] control of Bukit Timah in Singapore in 1991.) The Singapore government's dominant role in this sector meant that construction was in the hands of just a few large private property developers. The majority of construction contracts were allocated to CDL, FEO, OPH, and DBS Land. Between 1980 and 1989, local private firms acquired 80 to 90 per cent of building contracts, 40 per cent of engineering work, and 50 to 60 per cent of mechanical and electrical work in construction.[7] In the same period, property yields rose from 4 per cent in 1980 to 8 per cent in 1985, but declined to 3 per cent in 1989. Only warehouses continued to rise, to 8 per cent.

Property barons and financial innovation

CDL owned by the Kwek Leng Beng family, is part of the Hong Leong group. CDL has hotels and properties in Singapore, New York,

Figure 8.1　Hong Leong's growing land bank in Upper Bukit Timah (Singapore)

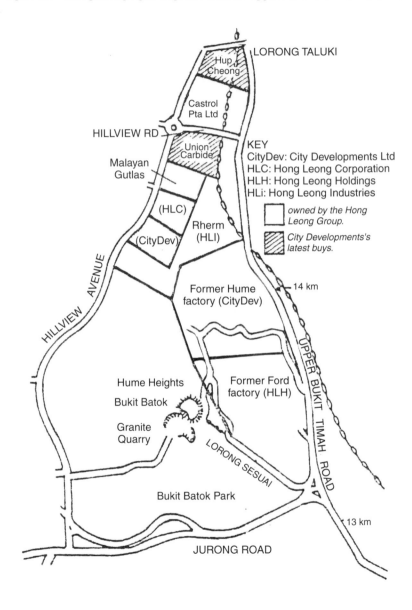

Source: Compiled from *Business Times*, 11 February 1981, *Straits Times*, 30 March 1994.

Manila, Sydney, Tapei and London, as well as in China and Malaysia (see Figure 8.2). The development of CDL mirrored the growth of the Singapore property market, in particular the activities of CDL signalled the important transition of Singapore's property market from low cost, government housing to élite housing. Unlike many of the large Chinese businesses discussed in this study, where collusive relations with the state in Southeast Asia shaped economic expansion, CDL had an ambivalent relationship with the Singapore state. CDL was not protected by the Singapore state, which encouraged the company both to be more prudent and to forge closer partnerships with companies from Japan, the Middle East and the US.

CDL, the property company of Singapore Hong Leong, was established in 1963 by Kwek Hong Png to operate in the residential, industrial and retail building sectors. By 1996, CDL dominated the listed real estate companies in Singapore. CDL's market capitalisation of US$ 6.8 billion was more than double that of its nearest rival, DBS Land. CDL, in turn, controlled CDL Hotels International, established in 1989, to expand into the hotel and tourism industries. By the end of 1996, the Kwek family controlled 56 hotels in 11 countries, including the Plaza in New York and 16 properties in the UK, Germany and France, acquired in the take-over of Copthorne Group in 1995, and 23 properties in New Zealand acquired in 1992 and 1993.[8]

CDL experienced weak growth between 1963 and 1970; its initiatives in Malaysia were less successful, and in 1970 it decided to concentrate on Singapore. In 1966, with a paid up capital of S$10 million, CDL had a loss of S$1.6m. In 1970 the situation improved with a profit of S$173,000 but, in 1971, CDL registered a loss of S$324,000 (see Table 8.1). In 1977, CDL endured a loss of S$1.45 million. These losses were serious since its liabilities, in particular bank borrowings, were substantial. The bank loans amounted to S$6.2 million in 1969, although they fell to S$3.55 million in 1970.[9] From the early 1970s, the company reduced its heavy reliance on the banks for funds by tapping into capital markets. The increasing dependence on capital markets was accompanied by aggressive take-overs of, and mergers with, existing property groups, which brought in valuable assets and increased potential for attracting new investments. Properties acquired in November 1972 cost S$206 million. At the end of 1971, CDL had accumulated losses of S$2 million.[10]

CDL made a remarkable recovery in 1972, with a net profit of $3.1 million, partly attributable to stock market speculation. The speculation was partly caused by rising land prices and a phenomenal

Figure 8.2 City Developments Ltd (CDL)

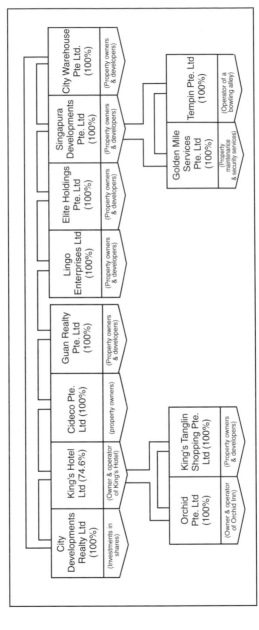

Source: City Developments Ltd, Annual Report 1994.

Table 8.1 City Developments Limited (CDL) and its subsidiary companies (Singapore $ 000).

Year	Net profit	Paid-up capital	Capital reserve	Interest in associated companies	Share premium account	Share capital and reserves	Balance carried forward	Properties	Bank loans/ overdrafts
1970	173	10,000	50			8,277	1,773		3,554
1971	-324	15,000	50			13,046	-2,004		4,237
1972	3,132	16,225	50		1,036	17,628	317	11,177	7,823
1973	1,764	18,019	50		4,181	23,520	1,270	32,769	4,891
1974	309	19,648	50		9,051	29,445	695	37,601	7,461
1975	169	19,648	50		9,051	29,613	863	41,978	3,717
1976	232	19,648			9,051	29,846	1,146	40,236	3,509
1977	-1,451	19,648			9,051	29,161	462	39,445	8,120
1978	286	24,148			13,536	37,995	311	29,267	7,155
1979	5,157	26,045			15,432	45,383	3,905	40,303	
1980	14,324	50,622			65,473	128,249	12,154	47,660	
1981	16,604	60,746			95,414	181,419	21,259	319,596	
1982	23,333	104,161			140,082	276,336	32,093	393,492	100,906
1983	19,172	133,166			215,758	382,777	33,853	578,389	200,386
1984	18,644	133,166			215,758	383,758	34,834	535,764	210,748
1985	13,205	133,166	130		215,758	384,694	35,640	556,356	256,762
1986	26,994	147,828	130		239,602	433,945	46,385	516,107	191,584
1987	23,799	184,785	1,617		304,835	542,900	51,663	588,598	78,407
1988	24,312	230,742	17,283	71,210	418,870	712,820	45,925	537,355	216,861
1989	38,531	230,743	17,238	50,233	418,882	725,421	58,558	656,466	257,194
1990	43,980	230,746	20,346	44,999	424,261	754,161	78,808	732,390	327,233
1991	51,306	230,746	27,272	48,541	424,263	788,167	105,886	814,669	468,000
1992	89,630	253,835	31,720	48,006	531,800	984,661	167,306	908,663	282,536
1993	114,797	306,741	75,148	98,099	491,255	1,110,615	237,471	909,056	197,005
1994	228,192	387,773	76,774	201,116	880,036	1,765,835	421,252	775,465	32,458

Table 8.1 City Developments Limited (CDL) and its subsidiary companies (Singapore $ 000) – continued

Year	Loan at call	Current liabilities	Fixed assets	Long-term investment	Investment properties	Cash at banks and in hand	Current assets	Turnover
1970		4,057	65		1,340,842	41	1,165	
1971		5,530	61	2,142	944,260	50	1,331	
1972		3,933	67	2,555	2,168,583	5,370	17,136	
1973	6,794	18,977	893	3,597		143	36,318	
1974	13,874	25,864	1,582	3,597		226	47,642	
1975	14,816	31,111	1,677	4,745		280	21,083	
1976	16,946	26,058	1,618	4,745		211	26,372	
1977	12,310	19,250	13,900	5,285		222	192,520	
1978		17,071	16,253	8,284		1,258	16,779	
1979	10,000	28,857	20,214	8,284		114	15,206	
1980		45,561	114,884	12,675				
1981		193,366	171,757	12,824				
1982		215,943	156,651	16,230	182,312	7,590	59,371	139,417
1983		328,954	184,701	20,690	186,442	19,330	137,852	172,398
1984		348,441	191,705	21,926	188,644	16,207	116,677	226,315
1985		357,913	187,577	25,894	215,058	16,281	67,269	198,873
1986		291,100	224,963	28,641	205,316	9,400	83,908	205,327
1987	2,368	196,561	280,244	89,599	195,030	27,735	270,733	164,645
1988		374,244	697,649	26,768		61,825	319,955	198,835
1989		599,917	1,442,855	27,191		221,047	387,205	307,479
1990		668,261	1,717,139	37,888		183,646	375,394	431,626
1991		970,856	1,830,108	38,100		1,167,420	196,564	544,311
1992		667,285	1,955,481	40,000		1,411,159	743,874	506,254
1993		884,201	2,781,341	43,778		405,121	630,322	751,787
1994		915,241	3,569,458	34,784		779,902	895,091	1,139,315

Source: CDL, Balance Sheets and Profit and Loss Accounts 1970–95.

growth in public housing and commercial property.[11] The Singapore government intervened to curb excessive speculation in CDL shares. During the period of speculative growth, CDL had acquired Goldhill Plaza, Palace Theatre, and properties in the Tampines, Telok Blangah, Bukit Timah, and Havelock and Cantonment Road areas. CDL built condominiums, which could earn a higher return. However, in 1973 CDL faced another decline in net profit, to S$1.8m, principally because of the poor performance of its manufacturing subsidiaries. Declining profits persisted into 1975, when net profits were almost half that of 1974 and revenue fell by 18 per cent.

The property slump in 1975 worsened profits, with a decline of 56 per cent. This did not deter investment in property, which totalled S$42 million for that year alone.[12] The private property sector stagnated in 1976 and 1977. Property development has to be continuous to secure economies of scale. There is a time lag depending on the speed of planning approval and the phases of construction, during which time movements in interest rates affect the costs of finance. Thus CDL expanded in both boom (1972–73) and slump (1975–77). The next year, 1978, marked a revival, stimulated by the demand for shopping complexes as well as condominium housing. CDL's largest project was City Plaza. After a loss of S$1.45 million in 1977, in 1978 CDL recorded pre-tax profits of S$910,529 and a net profit of S$286,000 (see table 8.1). The recovery was to be longterm, sustained by the expansion into shopping complexes, hotels and residential property.[13] CDL expanded into property investment as well as property development, partly to spread the risk incurred by the time lag between property development and its sale. Different investments in different properties meant that rents could be earned as well as profits made from purchase and sale. In 1980, CDL's properties for development and sale cost S$32.76 million, properties in the course of development cost S$56.96 million, and completed projects were worth S$5.23 million, meaning that 95 per cent of the capital was tied up. This had to be financed through a new share issue.[14]

Growth through acquisitions continued into the 1980s. In 1981, CDL acquired for S$63 million the large property group, Singapura Developments, which included Raffles Place, Katong Shopping Centre, the Arcade, Balmoral Point, parts of Beach Road and Clementi Road. The acquisition was secured at half price because of Singapura's difficulties.[15] To finance this acquisition, CDL introduced a rights issue and secured loans from Hong Leong Finance. CDL again increased its capital from S$50.6 million to S$60.7 million and also sold Orchard

Inn to its hotel group, Kings Hotel; the internal transfer of assets was made to raise crucial funds.[16]

The acquisitions, therefore, did not drain resources from the company. In 1982, CDL's net profits rose by 32 per cent and its property portfolio rose by S$286 million. The 1980s were marked by increased diversification into the hotel industry, reflected both in an increase in paid-up capital and an increase in profits. The slump in 1983 affected net profits, which fell from S$19.2 million in 1983 to $18.6 million in 1984. The fall in total property income and investment from S$578.3 million to S$535.7 million and a decline in current assets from S$137.8 million to S$116.7 million in the years 1983–84 reflected these difficulties. The company recovered briefly in 1987, expanding into Hong Kong in partnership with Great Eagle Company and C. Itoh, a Japanese trading company. CDL also expanded into Malaysia, Indonesia and Vietnam. Growth in Singapore in 1987 was assisted by a rise in the private housing programme. The world stock market crash of 1987 briefly arrested this profitable performance. By 1988, CDL increased its paid up capital and initiated three condominium projects for S$300 million, as the rapid growth of tourism increased the demand for shopping centres and hotel construction. The Gulf crisis caused an immediate slowdown in the property market in 1992, although it soon stimulated the market by triggering outflows of capital from the Middle East into Singapore property projects. Demand for industrial properties also increased as a result of the accelerated pace of industrialisation in Southeast Asia. There was an impressive year of growth in 1992, when share trading improved by 31 per cent and CDL expanded into Europe and New Zealand in 1993. The following years saw record profits, S$114.8 million in 1993 and S$228.2 million in 1994. Luxury residences in Jakarta were launched, while hotels in the UK and New Zealand saw their profits rise. This period of accelerated growth was partly stimulated by opportunities in capital markets, where CDL raised massive loans on favourable interest and repayment terms.[17] CDL's expansion into hotels, with the acquisition of five hotels by 1989 and 35 by 1995, was its most impressive development. In 1995, CDL bought the Plaza Hotel in New York with Saudi Prince Al Waileed for US$455 million, giving CDL a niche in the US.[18] By 1996, CDL had a property portfolio that was diverse, ranging from retail, industrial, office, leisure, and hotel and tourism assets.

CDL's regional expansion required organisational restructuring. CDL Hotels International (Hong Kong), a subsidiary, held half the properties outside Singapore, while CDL and Hong Leong International Holdings held most of the other properties abroad. The total value of these properties is difficult to estimate because assets were held by the different units within the Hong Leong Group.

The focus of this chapter is the link between property development and finance. The financial structures that underlay the growth in land and property are essential in understanding Chinese property development in Southeast Asia – that is, how far innovative financial techniques nurtured the expansion of CDL and Sino-Land's land and property interests. The construction of residential property, warehouses, factories, and office and shopping complexes had to be sustained through diverse forms of financing. The important issue of finance and its role in the growth and performance of CDL since 1963 needs to be seen from the perspective of corporate evolution. An understanding of the organisational structure of CDL, and the changes within it, will assist in identifying the financial strategies used to sustain rapid growth.

The relationship between finance and property can first of all be seen in the fact that CDL's growth from 1963 was mirrored by the increase in its financial subsidiaries; Hong Leong Finance was established in 1966, and Singapore Finance was incorporated in 1979 through an acquisition. While providing working capital for the business by attracting, savings and deposits and guaranteeing bank credit, these finance companies also provided mortgages and hire purchase facilities, and were involved in leasing activities.

The second point concerning finance is that expansion was partly assisted by the listing of new firms and the reissue of shares for existing firms. Intra-firm purchases and the distribution of new shares, as well as of property assets, guaranteed new finance for CDL's property projects. The listing of property companies to raise capital began as early as the 1980s and accelerated only with the financial liberalisation of the early 1990s. For example, in June 1980, CDL raised S$64.8 million through a rights issue, half of which was targeted to finance the acquisition and development of King's Hotel and Orchard Inn. At this stage CDL had unsecured loans exceeding S$100 million, leading the Singapore Stock Exchange to question the financial viability of the issue. CDL was not deterred by such objections. In May 1981, CDL acquired land in Bukit Timah for S$27.27 million and planned a condominium for S$44.5 million. To finance this, CDL registered another share issue, raising S$43.9 million.[19] The shareholders of Hong Leong were entitled to half the new share issue. The remaining part of the share issue was underwritten by Morgan Grenfell Asia for distribution.[20] The intra-firm distribution of new share issues assisted in debt financing without eroding ownership or control. Part of this complex relationship involved the revaluation of the assets of existing firms within the Hong Leong group. These internal transfers confuse profitability and the dividends payable to shareholders. The constant restructuring was often shrouded in secrecy and opaque accounting methods. In addition to the continuous stream of asset transfers and share issues there was the overpricing of assets when seeking public listing. In 1981, shares in Singapore Finance were priced at S$4.50, more than twice the net asset value. There was also suspicion about speculation in share prices. King's Hotel was the subject of a Singapore Stock Exchange inquiry in 1983, because of suspicion of speculation in the share price.

The third point about finance and property is that CDL had a high deb–equity ratio throughout the 1980s and 1990s. In 1985, CDL had S$256.8 million in unsecured bank loans and overdrafts and S$11.4 million in bonds, yet still sought a bond issue of S$250 million in December 1986.[21] In 1987, CDL sought two bond issues, of S$147.8 million and S$181.67 million. The corporation's turnover was equal to only half its debts in 1985–86.[22] In 1993, CDL's borrowings amounted to S$1.6 billion, including bank loans as well as bonds. Warrants were issued by CDL as part of the bonds, partly to attract investors. Issuing warrants, which is an option to purchase a particular stock at a specified price within a given period, can be speculative. If an investment's value declines, the warrant's value could also decline. The company's reputation, as well as that of the merchant bank underwriting the issue, often ensured success in acquiring such funds.

In 1994, CDL borrowed S$2,365 million, of which S$359 million was short-term debt and more than S$2,000 million was long-term. The borrowing rate was dramatically high since profits for the first six months of 1994 were only S$108.8 million – and even that was a 43 per cent rise on the profits of 1993. The pattern of huge borrowings throughout the 1980s and early 1990s was sustained principally through ties with Japanese multinationals and other portfolio equity inflows into Singapore.[23]

CDL would frequently raise funds through the issue of bonds and warrants to repay existing bank loans. In March 1993, CDL raised S$305 million through a bond issue. This helped substitute for certain bank loans, increased the period of the loan, deferred payments, and secured favourable fixed interest payments.

Another financial strategy to fund growth was the acquisition of financial institutions. Hong Leong in Malaysia was more successful in transforming itself into a finance-dominated conglomerate than Hong Leong in Singapore. The latter was persistently thwarted in its attempts to acquire a bank or a banking licence. Overlapping of finance and property activities was discouraged by the Singapore authorities. The Finance Companies Act of 1967 had legislated for the control of finance companies, including their liquidity requirements, and had placed a ban on current account business.

Since 1966, the Hong Leong Group had Hong Leong Finance (HLF), with branches in Brunei and Hong Kong. HLF was the largest finance company in Singapore in terms of assets, deposits, loans, and net profits. Hire purchase and mortgage facilities, syndicated loans, and leasing arrangements were all provided. The construction of ware-houses, factories, and residential and office complexes was also financed. Thus throughout the 1970s and 1980s, HLF secured critical finance for its associate firm, CDL.[24]

The acquisition of financial institutions increased through the 1970s and 1980s. HLF acquired Singapore Finance in 1979. Hong Leong Malaysia, which was more aggressive in creating a financial niche, acquired five banks: Dao Heng (Hong Kong) in 1982 for US$76.9 million, Hang Lung (Hong Kong) in 1989 for HK$600 million, Overseas Trust Bank (OTB) (Malaysia) in 1993 (M$1.4 billion), and Ban Hin Lee in Malaysia (1993).[25] Hong Leong (M) bought MUI Bank in 1993 for M$695m, and MUI Finance for M$405m, listing them in 1994 for M$2.6 billion. These acquisitions, restructuring and listing, imme-diately secured additional working capital for the group.

The method of funding large property programmes through institu-tions such as pension funds (notably Singapore CPF), insurance com-panies, and direct government aid also gained momentum in the 1980s and 1990s. However, from the early 1980s, banks, both domestic and foreign, were also financing property. They had to deal with the inherent illiquidity and inconsistency of property investment. Risk was enhanced by the new methods of financing, which included the issuing of stocks and debentures, which often led to high gearing ratios. High gearing is of some benefit when property values are rising ahead of interest charges but it can be dangerous when the real rate of interest is rising faster than property values. The temptation for high gearing was particularly intense in the 1990s when financial institu-tions, overseas investors and merchant banks sought to finance élite property companies such as CDL and Sino-Land. In large transactions, merchant banks acted as consultants to these property companies.

Property firms such as CDL and Sino-Land continually issued shares and property bonds. As their debts rose, the tactic was to restructure them by issuing more equity. The quality of their property assets and their location in Singapore and Hong Kong, attracted investors. The state's infrastructural programmes, such as mass transit systems, held prestige and profits for the firms and their investors. Thus Chinese property firms sought to keep majority shareholding within the family, while tapping into these new sources of finance. Family firms succeeded in raising money without diluting net asset values or earnings. What was lost in the euphoria of these investments was the influence of the minority shareholders who were in fact absorbing much of the risk. A more serious issue here is that when these companies diversified into hi-tech developments, warehouses and sophisticated leisure complexes, the need to match risks with returns was frequently lost.

The rise in securitisation in property investment, whereby merchant banks and investment houses raised capital for property companies by issuing shares in these firms, to provide more liquidity while affording the opportunity to create a portfolio of investment in different property projects, was highly risky.[26] While attracting foreign investors because of the flexibility and liquidity of such property assets – they could be redeemed under contract – the linkages were complex, and when the property bubble burst in 1997, the repercussions were felt in all sectors of the economy.

The property booms not only in Singapore but also in Hong Kong and even parts of China encouraged these firms to engage in speculative activities. Property booms in Singapore from the early 1960s and repeated in the early 1980s went in a cycle of 9–10 years, followed by a short cycle of 4–5 years from 1989.[27] These cycles were caused by a combination of government policies and abundant finance, in particular that generated by the stock market and by the merger mania of the 1980s. In the 1990s, interest rates rose, the cost of borrowing increased, property prices fell and some firms were in trouble. There was a lethal combination here of property speculation, risky although innovative financing, and state collusion.

The property collapse of 1997 was predictable in view of the dramatic development in the financing of property and the scale and pace of property development. The rapid increase in the exploitation of capital markets as well as offshore banks to finance this expansion added to the risks that were already high in property development.

This is clear even from the case study of CDL, which was a property company operating largely in the highly regulated environment of Singapore.

Ng Teng Fong and regional growth

A study of Ng Teng Fong and his property companies will illustrate the strategies for international expansion pursued by land/property companies, and crucially, how oligopolies are created and monopolistic practices survive in this sector.

Ng Teng Fong, a property developer from Singapore, established the FEO and OPH (1967), and in 1990 became the second largest landowner in Singapore, with properties in China, Malaysia, Hong Kong and Taiwan. In 1990, FEO controlled 68 per cent of OPH, which is an important developer of hotels, shopping complexes and offices in Singapore, China and Hong Kong. Ng has another property company, Sino-Land, which is a part of Hong Kong's Hang Seng index and was involved in prestigious projects such as the Chek Lap Kok airport in Hong Kong and the MTR (mass transit railway) development there. Ng purchased YHS, the food manufacturer in 1995 and that company also became involved in real estate.

Ng Teng Fong, therefore, had three major property firms. Sino-Land (Hong Kong), established in 1971 and listed in 1981, had a market capitalisation of more than US$3.3 billion in 1997. Sino-Land had become part of the Hang Seng index in February 1995. In Singapore, OPH had been established in December 1967 and was listed in 1987 (see Table 8.2 on OPH). After acquiring YHS, Ng rapidly transformed it into an aggressive property investor, as well as a food manufacturer. All four enterprises (including YHS) held a mixed land and property portfolio. Sino-Land possessed office buildings, shopping centres, warehouses, industrial structures, car parks, and residential apartments, principally in

Table 8.2 Orchard Parade Holdings (OPH) (Singapore $ million)

	Turnover	Net profit	Paid-up capital
1993	73	15	27
1994	103	31	47
1995	151	11	48
1996	401	24	103

Source: OPH, 1990–1997 Annual Reports.

Hong Kong, although after 1980 it expanded into southern China. FEO and OPH were involved in residential construction in Singapore, moving from mass public housing to élite condominiums in the 1990s. The move into quality housing was part of a new emphasis on investment in property, which would yield recurrent income, as opposed to trading profits from development projects. The emphasis on residential construction was complemented by a growing interest in hotel construction. Commercial property was less prominent in Ng's portfolio than in Kwek's, the major exception being the construction of the East Point leisure and shopping centre in 1994.

The regional division between Sino-Land in East Asia and FEO and OPH in Southeast Asia was never strictly maintained. From the mid-1980s, FEO and OPH, often in partnership with Singapore state companies, became involved in projects in China. Ng's role as a major building contractor for the state's residential housing programmes was critical for his growth. In Singapore, the state was active in planning property and infrastructural growth, and Ng emerged as influential in the state's projects in Singapore as well as abroad. Ng's ties with Lee Kuan Yew led, in 1992, to the creation of the Sino-Land – Sembawang group, a joint project to develop Shenzen airport in China.

Sino-Land's strategy of outbidding rivals to secure government and private construction contracts meant that the Singapore property market was oligopolistic; a few companies dominated the construction industry as well as hotels and tourism, which were closely linked to the building trade. In Hong Kong, Ng faced greater competition from large property firms such as Sun Hung Kai Properties of the Kwok group, and Henderson Land Development (Lee Shau Kee), as well as smaller property developers.[28]

Ng's high-priced bids for land and property was only part of his growth strategy. The second aspect of his approach was either to absorb his rivals in joint bids or to establish joint ventures with large foreign multinationals. Mitsui was a prominent partner throughout the 1990s in the development of innovative projects involving high inputs of capital and technology, such as the MRT system in Singapore and condominiums with sophisticated telecommunications, security, and shopping facilities, like the Bayshore project of 1994. This high quality residential project cost S\$260 million in its first phase, but it yielded S\$500m in pre-tax profits in 1993–94.[29]

Ng's strategy of making inflated bids at property auctions was clearly evident in the years 1992 to 1994. Ng's bid for the Robertson Quay Development, S\$16.38 million, was S\$1.39 million more than the bid made by his closest rival, Centre Point Properties. The competitive bidding unleashed a price war among the large Chinese contractors. In a tender for the Tanjong Rhu project, Hong Leong offered an inflated bid of S$33.5 million, outstripping Ng's offer of S$30.5 million. In the Bayshore project, Ng made a successful bid of S$161.2 million, defeating OUB's S$149.9 million. Similarly, Ng won the Orchard Boulevard contract because he offered almost S$10 million more than DBS Land.[30] In July 1996, FEO outbid its rivals for the development of the Novena MRT Station, with an offer of S$38.02 million, exceeding Robert Kuok by S$11 million. The contract for Scotts Tower was secured by FEO in 1996 with a bid of S$97 million, defeating DBS Land. FEO had been involved in Scotts Tower since 1960 but now sought to redevelop the site together with Cairnhill Towers to create a large, quality condominium.[31]

Between 1989 and 1993, FEO and its subsidiaries had secured 39 per cent of the total state land released in Singapore for private housing. FEO's only major competitor was CDL (see Table 8.3 for details of the construction projects of the FEO for the period 1991–98). Ng Teng Fong, Kwek Leng Beng (of CDL) and a tiny group of land/property contractors continued to keep competitors out through inflated bids at auction, particularly in the case of the quality housing schemes where Ng secured properties in Kew Drive, Woodlands, and the other élite residential areas of Singapore. The government defended Ng against critics of his emerging monopoly. The Urban Redevelopment Authority of Singapore did little to discourage Ng and Kwek in their activities.[32]

Ng and Kwek held a substantial share of the construction of private houses in 1993; FEO and OPH had around 13.5 per cent each, while CDL took 21.3 per cent. Individuals held just 11 per cent of the total. The remaining shares were held by DBS Land and the other major property companies.[33]

As a result of this concentration of ownership, houses prices rose dramatically. Prices for terraced houses increased by 49 per cent and prices for semi-detached houses and bungalows rose 68 per cent in the first six months of 1993 alone.[34] In the period 1989–93, the sale of state land for private development generated more than S$5 billion in profits for private developers such as Ng and Kwek.

The luxury, serviced apartments and properties in the Cairnhill and Peck Hay areas were close to prestigious schools, hotels and MRT stations. Many were freehold properties, thus appealing to wealthy Singaporeans. The re-zoning of areas from industrial to residential, as with Hill View and Bukit Timah, enhanced Ng's prospects in quality

Table 8.3 Construction programme of Far East Organisation

Some recently completed projects

Projects	Location	No. of units (unless stated otherwise)	Completion date
Apartments/condominiums			
Fragrant Gardens	Upper Paya Lebar Rd	37	1991
Bullion Park (Phase I)	Yio Chu Kang Rd	158	1992
Kingrove	Ang Mo Kio (Ave 1)	32	1992
Promises Gdns	Jln Lim Tai See	48	1992
Arthur Mansion	Arthur Rd	41	1993
Bullion Park (Phase II & III)	Yio Chu Kang Rd	314	1993
Emerald Park	Ganges Ave/Indus Rd	280	1993
Goldleaf Mansion	Telok Kurau Rd (Lor M)	32	1993
Kemaman Point	Jln Kemaman	89	1993
The Regalia	River Valley Rd/Close	116	1993
Villas Laguna	Upper East Coast Rd	31	1993
Ville Royale	River Valley Rd	43	1993
West Bay (Phase I)[a]	West Coast Rd/Link	127	1993
The Baycourt	Upper East Coast Rd	56	1994
West Bay (Phase II)[a]	West Bay Rd/Link	191	1994
Landed			
Bedok Ria (Phase III)	Bedok Rd	51	1991
Florida Park (Phase II)	Yio Chu Kang Rd	66	1991

Table 8.3 Construction programme of Far East Organisation – *continued*

Some recently completed projects

Projects	Location	No. of units (unless stated otherwise)	Completion date
Goldleaf Gardens	Telok Kurau Rd (Lor M)	49	1991
St. Patrick's Row	Marine Parade Rd/ Telok Kurau Rd	24	1991
Bedok Ria (Phase IV)	Bedok Rd	22	1992
Sea Breeze Terrace	Jln Angin Laut	36	1992
Blossom Gardens	Lor Gambir	10	1993
Cashew Gardens	Cashew Rd	56	1993
Gerald Park	Gerald Crescent	22	1993
Kovan Park	Kovan Rd	8	1993
Melody Villas	Yio Chu Kang Rd	52	1993
Regent Villas	Sixth Ave	46	1993
Serenity Terrace	Lor Marzuki	8	1993
Sunrise Villas (Phase IV)	Yio Chu Kang Rd	47	1993
Zephyr Park	Jln Angin Laut	49	1993
Service apartments			
Chancery Grove	Chancery Lane	33	1992
Cairnhill Tower	Cairnhill Rd	76	1993
Leonie Condotel	Leonie Hill Rd	128	1993
Leonie View	Leonie Hill	50	1993

Table 8.3 Construction programme of Far East Organisation – *continued*

	Some recently completed projects		
Projects	Location	No. of units (unless stated otherwise)	Completion date
Commercial/apartments			
Sin Ming Plaza	Sin Ming Rd/Thomson Rd	31,000 sq ft/ 102 apts	1992
Ginza Plaza	West Coast Rd	200,000 sq ft/ 40 service apts	1993
Siglap Centre	Siglap Rd/Upper East Coast	51,000 sq ft/ 13 service apts	1993
Commercial			
Lucky Chinatown	New Bridge Rd	62,000 sq ft	1992
Hotels			
Elizabeth Hotel	Mt Elizabeth	246 rooms	1993

	In the pipeline		
Projects	Location	No. of units (unless stated otherwise)	Completion date
Condominiums			
Kemaman View	Jln Kemaman	30	Early 94
Orchid Park	Yishun Ave 1	615	Early 94
Rich Mansion	BT Timah Rd	37	Mid 94
Gold Coast	Pasir Panjang Rd	67	End 94

Table 8.3 Construction programme of Far East Organisation – *continued*

Projects	Location	In the pipeline No. of units (unless stated otherwise)	Completion date
Royal Palm Mansion	Pasir Panjang Rd	23	Early 95
Serenity Park	Yio Chu Kang/Seletar Express Way	179	Early 95
Villa Margaux	Kang Shin/Ewe Boon Rd	31	Early 95
Banyan Condo	Chwee Chian Rd	104	Mid 95
Astoria Park	Lor Mydin (Kembangan MRT)	354	End 95
Bayshore Road (Phase I)	Bayshore Rd	468	End 96
Bayshore Road (Phase II)	Bayshore Rd	570	Early 97
Dover Parkview	Dover Crescent/ Dover Close East	693	End 97
Regent Park	Jln Lempeng/Clement Ave 6	276	End 97
Bukit Batok	Bt Batok East Ave 3	594	Early 98
Landed			
Mistral Park	Jln Angin Laut	46	Early 94
Palm View Row	Pasir Panjang Rd	8	Early 94
Waterford terrace	Pasir Panjang Rd	11	Early 94
Gentie Villas	Gentie Rd	71	Mid 95
Kew Drive (Phase I)	Kew Dr	114	End 97
Kew Drive (Phawe I)[a]	Kew Dr	58	End 97
Holland Grove	Holland Grove	114	Early 98

Table 8.3 Construction programme of Far East Organisation – *continued*

| Projects | In the pipeline | | |
	Location	No. of units (unless stated otherwise)	Completion date
Hougang	Yio Chu Kang Rd & Hougang Ave 2	171	Early 98
Kew Drive (Phase II)	Kew Dr	34	Early 98
Kew Drive (Phase II)[a]	Kew Dr	122	Early 98
Service apartments			
Orange Regency	Fernhill/Orange Grove Rd	16	End 94
Orchard Parksuite	Orchard Boulevard	225	Early 95
Cavenagh Lodge	Cavenagh Rd	41	End 96
Commercial/apartments			
Coronation Arcade	Coronation Rd	5 apts / 5 shops	Mid 94
Kingston Terrace	Jln Masjid	24 apts / 8 shops	Mid 94
Riverside View	Merbau Rd/Teck Guan St	20,000 sq ft / 70 apts	Mid 97
Commercial			
The Market Place (Retrofitting Project)	Bedok Rd	39,000 sq ft	Mid 94
Riverside Point	Merchant Rd	140,000 sq ft	Early 96
East point	Simei St 3	300,000 sq ft	Early 97

Table 8.3 Construction programme of Far East Organisation – *continued*

In the pipeline

Projects	Location	No. of units (unless stated otherwise)	Completion date
Hotel Albert Court[a]	Albert St	136 rooms 18,000 sq ft	End 94
Industrial Tannery House[a]	Tannery Lane	39 units	End 95

Summary

Completion	Condo (units)	Service apt units (for leasing not for sale)	Landed (units)	Apts (units)	Hotel (rooms)	Commercial (sq. ft) unless otherwise stated
1991	–	–	190	37	–	–
1992	238	33	58	102	–	93,000
1993	1,073	307	298	–	246	251,000
1994	247	–	–	–	–	–
Total	**1,558**	**340**	**546**	**139**	**246**	**344,000**

Completion	Condo (units)	Service apt units (for leasing not for sale)	Landed (units)	Apts (units)	Indust. (units)	Hotel (rooms)	Commercial (sq ft)
1994	749	16	67	29	–	136	13 shophouses[b] 57,000

Table 8.3 Construction programme of Far East Organisation – *continued*

| | | Summary | | | | | |
Completion	Condo (units)	Service apt units (for leasing not for sale)	Landed (units)	Apts (units)	Indust. (units)	Hotel (rooms)	Commercial (sq. ft) unless otherwise stated
1995	691	225	71	–	39	–	–
1996	468	41	–	–	–	–	140,000
1997	1,539	–	172	70	–	–	320,000
1998	594	–	441	–	–	–	–
Total	4,041	282	751	99	39	136	517,000

Notes:
[a] Developed by Orchard Parade Holdings (OPH). [b] Small commercial buildings.
Source: Compiled from newspapers for the respective years.

housing. Through his acquisition of YHS in 1995, Ng possessed valuable land in Bukit Timah. Kwek's dominance in the Bukit Timah area is clear from Map 1 but Ng was steadily encroaching on the area. Although FEO had completed 265 large residential construction projects since 1968, its move in the 1990s into more innovative construction, like quality condominiums and computer parks, produced impressive growth.[35]

This period also saw an increase in joint ventures with industry and an increase in initiatives in China. The need for joint ventures arose partly through the substantial capital and technology requirements of luxury building construction. In May 1996, FEO and Nissho Iwai Corporation built luxury condominiums in Simei and Tampines for S$400 million. Ng Teng Fong had had a strong base in Hong Kong property since the early 1970s but he became more aggressive in China from the late 1980s. Although expansion into China was pursued more intensely by Robert Ng (Ng Teng Fong's son) in the 1990s, Ng Teng Fong had been energetic in parts of Xiamen, Fuzhou and Guangzhou in the mid-1980s. The interest in residential development in south China, Kowloon and the New Territories in the 1990s contrasted with the earlier concentration on commercial and tourist developments in Hong Kong.

In Hong Kong and China, Sino-Land competed with powerful property networks such as the Kwok family's Sun Hung Kai Properties and Lee Shau Kee's Henderson Land. Sino-Land relied heavily on government auctions to secure land and property projects and also opted frequently for joint ventures, partly to secure access to bids and partly to share risk. The Singapore government was a close ally of Sino-Land in this respect. In the development of the Tai Kok Tsui mass transit station in the mid-1990s, Ng held a 30 per cent stake in a consortium that also included R. Kuok and DBS Land. The project's cost was HK$8 billion. Sino-Land also bid for the development of the Central and Kowloon MTR Stations for HK$110 billion.[36] These projects were highly lucrative because of the excellent location and investment potential. However, Sino-Land's investment in Chai Wan in 1996–97 for HK$20 billion proved costly; HK$11.82 billion had been disbursed on the residential complex in Chai Wan by March 1997, which was equal to half Sino-Land's market capitalisation.

The pattern of massive investment in infrastructural projects in Singapore, Hong Kong and China continued unabated because of the innovative methods of financing available to Ng and because of his support from the Singapore government. The government's

Investment Corporation of Singapore was heavily involved in large infrastructural projects in Asia. It had access to state funds, as well as to capital from the Kuwait Investment Organisation (an investment arm of the Kuwaiti authorities), the Abu Dhabi Investment Authority, and the Brunei Investment Authority. Ng was a leading venture capitalist, identifying lucrative projects for these patrons. Generous finance from offshore banks and the capital markets of Asia was also available to Ng. Through his links with the Singapore state, Ng had access to US$1 billion from the Asian Infrastructural Fund targeted at China and Hong Kong. Despite the Singapore state possessing its own property firm, DBS Land, it was keen to align itself with successful private property developers such as Ng Teng Fong, partly to encourage private enterprise in Singapore and thus reduce the image of being a state-dominated economy.

Ng's ambitious acquisitions of property continued. In November 1996, Sino-Land spent HK$12 billion on Yuen Long MTR Station. In December 1996, HK$760 million was invested in the North Point commercial area, and in January 1997, Sino-Land paid HK$2.28 billion for Tsim Sha Tsui commercial property and HK$1.9 billion for the Conrad Hotel. Although three-quarters of Sino-Land's investments were in Hong Kong (while Ng's other companies like OPH and FEO concentrated on Singapore), Sino-Land mounted an aggressive incursion into the Chinese mainland from the 1990s, particularly in southern China and Shanghai.[37]

The scale and cost of these investments made Sino-Land volatile. In 1983, there were losses of HK$111 million and in 1984, losses of $113 million (see Table 8.4). Profits returned in 1985 but truly impressive profits were recorded only after 1986. In the 1990s, however, record profits were earned. In 1995, Sino-Land had a net profit of HK$2.8 billion (see Table 8.4). Net profit in June 1996 was HK$1.1 billion, but only HK$765 million in December 1996. Some of the losses and profits arose from Robert Ng's futures trading. In 1990, Robert Ng made a catastrophic loss of HK$1 billion on futures trading.

The impressive profits arose from the high property prices created by improved infrastructure (MTR Stations) in the areas of development. Sino-Land's turnover rose from HK$156 million in 1981 to HK$1.7 billion in 1995, to HK$2.5 billion in June 1996, and to HK$1.4 billion in December 1996. Sino-Land's share capital rose from HK$342 million in 1984 to HK$2.4 billion in 1995, and to HK$3.0 billion in January 1997. The Group's fixed assets rose from HK$12 million in 1986 to HK$14 billion in 1995 and HK$ 15 billion in June 1996. However, as

Table 8.4 Sino-Land Company Ltd (in HK$ 000)

Year	Turnover	Gross profits	Dividends	Net profit	Profit for the year retained	Unappropriated profits brought forward	Earnings per share (in dollar and cents)
1980							
1980							
1981	156,238	88,538		74,499		8,226	24.80
1982	296,514	59,206		2,511		74,508	7.06
1983	479,211	164,026		-111,141		56,019	23.39
1984	54,926	182	7,000	-113,357		-55,122	0.06
1985	98,607	21,854		50,111		-168,479	7.20
1986	210,491	28,806	30,100	49,824	19,724	-116,176	7.00
1987	685,620	390,595	92,404	304,970	212,566		39.60
1988	690,539	346,703	88,462	325,228	236,766		6.10
1989	648,047	363,019	148,440	349,982	178,618		5.00
1990	1,114,110	491,540	168,251	386,202	217,951		25.60
1991	1,573,572	674,369	264,652	553,865	289,212		34.20
1992	3,671,960	1,576,939	340,346	1,164,059	823,712		62.50
1993	1,799,594	1,031,228	351,476	900,589	549,113		46.80
1994	3,655,107	1,713,857		1,476,685			66.30
1995	1,735,129	2,995,461		2,865,796			120.00

Table 8.4 Sino-Land Company Ltd (inHK$000) – continued

Year	Fixed assets	Intangible assets	Interests in associated companies	Other investments and advances	Properties under development	Current assets	Current liabilities	Net current assets/ liabilities	Medium-term bank loans
1980				561,081					
1981				910,689					
1982				893,198					
1983				785,188					
1984				787,189					
1985		12,111	719,187	816,433	126,093	159,986	214,600	−54,614	
1986	12,638	10,159	755,830	202,037	206,791	160,917	331,671	−170,754	3,500
1987	12,779	10,158	1,859,077	252,170	459,436	307,198	495,073	−187,875	187,900
1988	161,703		3,408,942	475,226	1,081,230	574,565	713,207	−138,642	621,800[b]
1989	3,511,966	6,241	3,409,107	462,893	2,605,125	800,983	1,975,425	−1,174,442	2,363,606
1990	3,629,094	4,479	3,681,994	407,583		3,826,677[c]	2,269,725	1,556,952	1,984,698
1991	4,402,023	2,718	3,572,362	377,073		4,845,578	1,741,060	3,104,518	1,795,616
1992	6,386,478	957	4,897,259	371,171		4,416,441	1,916,663	2,499,778	2,292,308
1993	8,283,893		6,101,177	442,816		5,063,966	2,658,093	2,405,873	1,880,805
1994	14,401,651		12,177,997	1,523,658		5,180,710	3,138,381	2,042,329	3,115,636
1995	14,010,128		10,368,587	1,858,443		5,030,989	2,936,422	2,094,567	3,541,633

Table 8.4 Sino-Land Company Ltd (in HK$000) – *continued*

Year	Total net assets/liabilities	Share capital	Total shareholders' funds/deficits	Share premium account and reserves
1980				
1981	1,133,681		1,133,585	
1982	1,111,105		1,111,010	
1983	995,874		995,779	
1984	878,332		878,332	
1985	926,544	700,003	900,002	342,717
1986	1,013,200	770,003	1,013,200	243,197
1987	2,217,845	770,052	2,217,845	1,447,793
1988	4,366,029	1,234,849	4,108,296	2,873,447
1989	6,199,623	1,493,247	6,199,623	4,706,376
1990	6,892,981	1,540,334	6,892,981	5,352,647
1991	8,374,545	1,838,776	8,374,545	6,535,770
1992		1,902,471	11,770,528	9,868,057
1993		1,962,584	15,294,528	13,331,943
1994		2,132,249	26,957,377	24,825,129
1995		2,448,758	24,859,198	22,410,439

Table 8.4 Sino-Land Company Ltd (HK$000) – *continued*

Year	Interests in subsidiary companies	Interests in associated overseas companies	The investments and advances to overseas companies
1985	189,793	593,021	14,442
1986	36,517	616,582	87,086
1987	1,340,739	691,895	148,877
1988	2,963,513	991,405	360,745
1989	4,685,226	1,163,923	361,873
1990	4,957,073	1,304,082	307,849
1991	6,028,756	1,314,204	307,849
1992	6,591,611	1,297,474	307,849
1993	7,335,893	1,276,687	308,149
1994	10,563,323	1,277,434	408,502
1995	9,852,717	1,275,735	684,006

Source: Sino-Land Profit and Loss Accounts and Balance Sheets, 1980–96.

the tables demonstrate, Sino-Land's liabilities were dangerously high, making Sino-Land unstable during the 1997 crisis.[38] Ng had reined in during 1990 and 1991, when he trimmed his debts and reduced his gearing to 20 per cent, but in the period 1995–96, the firm again acquired large debts, which forced Ng to reduce his equity in Sino-Land to 57.13 per cent, from 64.65 per cent in December 1996.

Despite the surge in property prices in Hong Kong, Sino-Land faced financial difficulties. In the first four months of 1997, rumours circulated about its financial position, encouraged by Ng's withdrawal from a project in Hong Kong costing US$11.82 billion. Ng lost his deposit in making this withdrawal. When US interest rates and Hong Kong mortgage rates rose simultaneously, Ng faced further difficulties. Moreover, in the years 1995–97 it was becoming increasingly difficult to attract investors to take up bond issues in property companies. In these years, property bonds in Hong Kong, as well as in Southeast Asia, were undersubscribed. Sino-Land, which had less success with a convertible bond issue for US$200 million in February 1996, in April 1997 launched a reduced issue for US$125 million, managed by Jardine Fleming and UBS. Part of the contraction in available funds was caused by increased competition for finance from large property firms in Hong Kong. Cheung Kong Property group (Li Ka Shing) had, in February 1996, sought acceptance of a convertible issue valued at HK$5.3 billion.[39]

Ng sought to contain the crisis by obtaining more properties to sustain the value of the bonds being floated, and pledged prestigious properties to raise loans. In May 1997, Sino-Land pledged its stake in Central Plaza as collateral for a loan of HK$1 billion. Central Plaza, located in Wan Chai district, was jointly owned by Ng, Raymond Kwok and Lee Shau Kee. The purpose of the convertible issue was to refinance existing bank loans. The issue was arranged by the Development Bank of Singapore and ABN-AMRO (the Dutch bank), both in Hong Kong. The rescheduling of debt and the use of properties as collateral was common in Singapore and Hong Kong. Government measures to curb speculation in land and property had led to a 40 per cent fall in prices by May 1996. Private developers had to increase property collateral, as well as raise prices, particularly for luxury residences.[40] Sino-Land, FEO and YHS all faced difficulties in completing projects because of financial deficits. The Singapore Government had allowed developers to delay completion of private homes on 50 projects, but these incurred compensation payments to buyers.

In Singapore, the worst hit companies were FEO and CDL, along with Robert Kuok's and Cheung Kok Properties. FEO's response was to raise additional finance through new bond issues for S$220 million, and to raise the prices of property by 2–3 per cent, but reduce the pace of sales. FEO also sought to tap the resources of the Singapore Government, which was providing incentives for owners to upgrade their accommodation as well as increasing the construction of lower quality condominiums.

Conclusion

The financial strategies of CDL and Sino-Land have striking similarities. For both, the transition from growth funded by bank loans to the use of capital markets was clearly evident between 1980 and 1997. Institutional investors and fund managers were attracted to these high growth economies, and increased confidence in property investment in the 1980s and early 1990s reflected their diversification of risk. The property industry showed a cycle of activity, which reflected changes in the economy as well as structural changes in financing. The influence of general investment trends and capital flows on property investment and property yields is clear from these two case studies. The internal influences on the property market – the inflexibility of investment in buildings, in the supply of stock, in sales and rent – are reinforced by the external economic factors of rapid growth, infrastructural needs and foreign portfolio and direct investment trends. The property market was inherently unstable.

Economic growth produced credit expansion and building booms. Increased demand for property creates shortages, increasing rents and prices, which provokes further construction. Demand slackens with the increased supply, and a property slump ensues, leading to collapses in rents and prices. The integration of the property market with the financial sector – that is greater bank lending as well as the involvement of stock markets, fund managers and pension agencies – creates a link that, under pressure, as in July 1997, produces market collapses in property, finance and industry. In this way, property cycles are intertwined with business cycles. This feature is reinforced by speculation, futures trading and the internationalisation of property as a tradeable asset. The diverse kinds of property development – residential complexes, shopping centres, MTR systems, hi-tech computer parks and leisure complexes, each with different capital and technology inputs – further increases the instability, since risk and costs can be evaluated only with great difficulty.

While high risk is associated with property investment abroad, the role of the Singapore state as partner in many of the investments, undertaken by CDL and Sino-Land particularly in China and Vietnam, helped to absorb the risk. The role of the state as a major promoter in the domestic property market and as a partner in overseas property initiatives is clearly evident in the activities of CDL and Sino-Land in Singapore, Hong Kong and China. In the territories discussed in this chapter, much of the land was owned by the state, making the purchase of land by private companies highly sought after and increasing the price. Property developers like Ng made exaggerated bids to acquire land. Hence, the extent of state control of land discouraged the profusion of small developers. Instead oligopolies carved up by large developers emerged, with different companies specialising in different sectors, such as commercial or luxury residential property. Unlike the industrial interests described in this book, Chinese companies like Sino-Land could specialise in property development. Chinese companies were protected by their oligopolistic carving-up of property niches in Southeast Asia and East Asia, but still became increasingly vulnerable after the financial liberalisation of the 1980s, which made larger and more long-term loans available to property developers and which led to difficulties when property prices fell.

9
Patterns of Growth and Finance in Regional Expansion: Charoen Pokphand in China

This volume has documented the accelerated economic growth of Southeast Asia over the last three decades. While Britain and many other European countries experienced an average rise of real product by 2–3 per cent a year for 1973–92, Asian growth frequently soared at over 8 per cent, particularly after 1978. China in particular saw a remarkable increase in the average annual growth rate of GDP from 7 per cent in 1976 to 9 per cent in the 1978 to 1988 period, then rising to 13 per cent in 1992, and subsequently fluctuating between 8 per cent and 9 per cent.[1] The contribution of agriculture in China to GDP increased between 1978 and 1982 from 28 per cent to 34 per cent. Thereafter a contraction in agriculture's share from 34 per cent to 24 per cent reflected a major expansion in industry and services, an increase in industrial employment from 18 per cent to 21 per cent, and in employment in services from 14 per cent to 18 per cent.[2]

An important factor in this spectacular growth and transformation has been the volume of foreign direct investment inflows into China. China witnessed a slow infiltration of foreign direct investment from 1979, with a surge between 1984 and 1986, then stabilising to a steady enlargement of the investment base throughout the 1990s. This approached US$386 million in 1982, rising to US$4 billion in 1991, US$7 billion in 1992, US$23 billion in 1993, and US$33 billion in 1994.[3] The only other recipient country to exceed this was the US.

This chapter is not concerned with appraising the impact of foreign direct investment on the Chinese economy, but with tracing the precise methods by which overseas Chinese companies, principally Southeast Asian companies, gained entry into China, and how they operated in an underdeveloped legal environment. The question arises whether these successes derived from a common language and culture or can be attributed to more complex explanations. Another issue is how overseas Chinese conglomerates distributed investments among different industries in China, and in particular, in manufacturing. A further problem is how these firms and their subsidiaries in China were organised, and what changes in corporate strategies were made as they responded to economic and political pressures throughout Asia. Also, what determined competitiveness, and in particular what shaped their research and development strategies? A detailed study of Charoen Pokphand (CP) is undertaken to provide a more dynamic view of these developments, clarifying both the pronounced changes as well as the subtle biases in its changing strategies in China between 1981 and 1997. Hopefully this case study will provide a more balanced understanding of overseas Chinese corporate growth and performance in China.

CP, which we have encountered on several occasions in this book, has been chosen to show the complexities surrounding overseas Chinese business performance in China. CP is the largest overseas Chinese investor in the mainland, with an investment of US$3 billion in 1993, rising to US$5 billion in 1995.[4] This study of CP in China might also help to explain the circumstances in which overseas Chinese businesses achieve efficient economic diversification as well as regional expansion. The Chinese market did not simply provide vast potential for heterogeneous growth but also supplied vital links with Western and Japanese multinationals, propitious liaisons readily exploited by CP to penetrate Western capital markets and research and development intensive industries throughout Asia.

CP entered the Chinese agribusiness in 1981, having developed successfully in that sector in Thailand since 1921. CP's dramatic diversification into the manufacture of motorcycles, car components and air-conditioning equipment in the mid-1980s and its forays into R&D intensive industries, including power generation, telecommunications and petroleum, revealed not simply a zeal in the search for new profits but also a coalescence of crucial political lineaments. Such an opportunistic gamble was assisted by tough managerial motivation and an understanding and trust of the Chinese authorities. Having overcome scepticism about their research and development competencies in both China and Thailand, CP was becoming ubiquitous in telecommunications projects throughout Asia, with the acquiescence of Nynex (USA), their joint-venture partner. CP's excellent relations with the Beijing government and the Shanghai municipal authorities assisted entry into the telecommunications, television and satellite, and petrochemical industries. Supported by government purchasing policies and

joint ventures with Nynex, they could then cross-invest in these industries throughout Asia, through their holding companies – Telecom
Holding, Orient Telecom and Technology Holdings, and Telecom Asia.
CP's reputation in Thailand and China was critical for its expansion
into Indochina, the Philippines and India.

A further aim of this chapter is to attempt a revision of the historio-
graphy on foreign direct investment in China, which sees Western and
Hong Kong investments as critical for Chinese economic growth since
1978. ASEAN Chinese investment is ignored; the significance of these
intra-Asian investments for China, which surpassed that of Western
and Hong Kong multinationals, has not been fully grasped.[5] ASEAN
Chinese investments were driven not simply by a search for markets
but crucially aimed to locate production in areas of cheap labour and
to gain new patrons.

The importance of intra-Asian investment for China is clear from
Tables 9.1 and 9.2. First, the changes in the sources of foreign direct
investment into China between 1979 and 1992 clearly reveal that
while Hong Kong's share rose from 58 per cent in 1979–83 to 71.5 per
cent in 1992, that of the United States dramatically declined after
1989. Singapore and Asian countries in general depicted a steady rise to
25 per cent of total investments in this period. In addition, Southeast
Asian investments in China also originated in Hong Kong, through
subsidiaries based there. More than half of overseas Chinese investment flowed through Hong Kong. Even without accounting for this
channel, in 1992, the contracted total of investment in China of the
five Southeast Asian countries exceeded that of Japan. The US and
Japan competed for second and third after Hong Kong in 1980, and
third and fourth place after Hong Kong and Taiwan in the early 1990s.[6]

The significance of these investment flows is also revealed in the
broad changes occurring as they moved from labour-intensive sectors
to capital-intensive industries. Between 1991 and 1993 the number of
American and Japanese firms located among the top 100 foreign firms
in China rose, while that of Asian Chinese firms declined, which can
be directly attributed to the Chinese Government's policy of encouraging technology intensive industries, particularly automobiles, electronics and aerospace. Despite this, of the top 100 firms, while 28 were of
Western origin, 14 were Japanese, 45 were overseas Chinese, and 13
belonged to others. While Western firms held a disproportionately
large share of sales, profits and total assets, overseas Chinese firms and
Asian firms in general produced more for the overseas market (see
Table 9.3.) The German joint venture in automobiles, Daozhang Taxi,

Table 9.1 Foreign direct investment into China from other parts of Asia (US$10,000)

	1983		1984		1985	
	No.	Value	No.	Value	No.	Value
Hong Kong and Macao	482	64,229	1,870	217,545	2,631	413,432
Japan	52	9,450	138	20,304	127	47,068
Indonesia			2	76	3	173
Malaysia			2	37	1	24
Philippines			4	210	22	4,056
Singapore	6	1,627	25	6,256	62	7,551
Thailand	5	224	9	2,328	10	1,456
Total	638	191,690	2,166	287,494	3,073	633,321

Table 9.1 Foreign direct investment into China from other parts of Asia (US$10,000)-*continued*

	1986		1987		1988	
	No.	Value	No.	Value	No.	Value
Hong Kong and Macao	1,155	177,343	1,785	236,466	4,771	416,118
Japan	94	28,282	113	38,629	237	37,060
Indonesia		150	2	118	6	205
Malaysia	2	24	6	959	9	522
Philippines	9	381	10	3,050	22	1,553
Singapore	53	14,076	53	7,984	105	13,690
Thailand	10	1,321	11	453	29	4,168
Total	1,498	333,037	2,233	431,912	5,945	619,072

Table 9.1 Foreign direct investment into China from other parts of Asia (US$10,000)-*continued*

| | 1989 | | 1990 | | 1991 | |
	No.	Value	No.	Value	No.	Value
Hong Kong and Macao	4,244	373,395	5,001	425,767	8,879	783,451
Japan	294	51,538	341	47,846	599	88,605
Indonesia	5	98	3	34	13	1,091
Malaysia	8	266	7	320	39	4,021
Philippines	12	471	18	1,078	30	1,744
Singapore	78	14,765	72	10,691	169	15,521
Thailand	30	5,679	28	4,253	52	10,827
Total	5,779	629,409	7,273	698,632	12,978	1,242,173

Table 9.1 Foreign direct investment into China from other parts of Asia (US$10,000)-*continued*

	1992		1993		1994	
	No.	Value	No.	Value	No.	Value
Hong Kong and Macao	31,892	4,269,595	50,868	7,812,860	25,527	4,901,435
Japan	1,809	332,375	3,506	570,862	3,020	596,842
Indonesia	78	12,141	149	25,708	130	28,074
Malaysia	169	20,928	442	75,855	308	61,757
Philippines	153	27,611	302	63,063	162	29,069
Singapore	742	100,727	1,751	313,960	1,443	377,798
Thailand	407	72,751	809	107,520	424	78,133
Total	48,858	6,943,873	83,595	12,327,273	47,646	9,375,610

Sources: China Foreign Economic Statistics, 1979–91, Beijing, China Statistical Information and Consultancy Service Center, 1992, pp. 317, 320, 323; *China Statistical Yearbook, 1995*, Beijing, China Statistical Publishing House, 1995, p. 555; *Almanac of China's Foreign Economic Relations and Trade 1995/96*, Hong Kong, China Resources Advertising and Exhibition, 1996, p. 765.

Table 9.2   Foreign direct investment into China from the United Kingdom and the United States (US$10,000)

	1983		1984		1985	
	No.	Value	No.	Value	No.	Value
UK	17	30,477	4	1,262	8	4,428
USA	32	47,752	62	16,518	100	115,202
	1986		**1987**		**1988**	
	No.	Value	No.	Value	No.	Value
UK	8	5,169	12	2,856	21	5,638
USA	102	54,148	104	36,148	269	38,433
	1989		**1990**		**1991**	
	No.	Value	No.	Value	No.	Value
UK	19	3,326	23	12,123	36	13,197
USA	276	64,589	357	36,568	694	55,529
	1992		**1993**		**1994**	
	No.	Value	No.	Value	No.	Value
UK	130	67,589	348	215,138	391	305,642
USA	3,265	317,085	6,750	731,006	4,223	653,693

Sources: *China Foreign Economic Statistics, 1979–91*, Beijing, China Statistical Information and Consultancy Service Center, 1992, pp. 321–25; *China Statistical Yearbook, 1995*, Beijing, China Statistical Publishing House, 1995, pp. 254–56; *Almanac of China's Foreign Economic Relations and Trade 1995/96*, Hong Kong, China Resources Advertising and Exhibition, 1996, pp. 769, 771.

recorded a sales income in 1993 of US$1815.3 million (10,529 million yuan), profits of US$159 million (924 million yuan), total assets of US$818 million (47,405 million yuan) yet its exports were valued at only US$1.41 million.[7] In stark contrast, Shanghai Dajiang (CP's feed-mill company) had exports valued at US$38.23 million. Shanghai Dajiang's sales revenue was only US$207 million (1,202 million yuan), profits of US$27 million (157 million yuan) and assets of US$247 million (1,435 million yuan).[8] Thus, in 1994, Shanghai Dajiang was targeting more than one-third of its production for export.

The pre-occupation of Western multinationals with production solely for the Chinese market was also revealed when, in 1994, the Shanghai Volkswagen Automobile Company increased its use of local

Table 9.3 Foreign ventures in China, demonstrating export-led sales, 1993

	Nationality of foreign partner	Sector	Sales (million yuan)	Profit (million yuan)	Total assets (million yuan)	Exports (US$ million)
Shanghai Dazhong Taxi	Germany	Automobiles	10,529	924	4,745	1.41
Beijing Jeep Corp	US	Automobiles	3,275	6	2,185	14.56
Shanghai Bell Telephone Equipment	Belgium	Telecommunications	2,826	1,102	3,474	16.30
Guangzhou Peugeot Motors	France	Automobiles	2,536	190	2,766	16.88
Chongqing Qingling Motor	Japan	Automobiles	2,290	470	4,600	15.00
Shenzhen Gangjia Electronics Group	Hong Kong	Electrical machinery	2,203	239	1,123	92.74
Nanhai Oils and Fats Industry	Malaysia	Food	2,000	80	800	108.00
Fujian Yongen Group	Unknown	Unknown	1,867	57	550	365.01
Huaqiang Sanyo Electric	Japan	Electrical machinery	1,865	37	594	158.26

Table 9.3 Foreign ventures in China, demonstrating export-led sales, 1993-*continued*

	Nationality of foreign partner	Sector	Sales (million yuan)	Profit (million yuan)	Total assets (million yuan)	Exports (US$ million)
Shanghai Fenghuang Bicycles	Unknown	Automobiles	1,554	169	1,640	32.51
Beijing Light Automobile	Hong Kong	Automobiles	1,513	103	1,171	32.51
Beijing Matsushita Color CRT	Japan	Electrical machinery and electronic	1,504	221	1,379	47.53
Fujian Hitachi TV	Japan	Electrical machinersy and electronics	1,441	33	356	40.38
Guangdong Jianlibao Group	Macao	Food	1,397	81	1,050	0.07
Shanghai Ciba-Geigy Chemical	Western Europe	Chemicals	1,397	194	4,271	27.43
Shenyang Jinbei Minibus Manufacturing	Hong Kong	Automobiles	1,377		1,399	

Table 9.3 Foreign ventures in China, demonstrating export-led sales, 1993 *continued*

	Nationality of foreign partner	Sector	Sales (million yuan)	Profit (million yuan)	Total assets (million yuan)	Exports (US$ million)
Shunde Huabao Electric	Hong Kong	Electrical machinery	1,776	38	1,834	4.80
Shenzhen Zhonghua Bicycle Group	Hong Kong	Automobiles	1,755	217	2,288	187.59
No. 1 Dazhong Motors	Germany	Automobiles	1,655		3,846	
Shenyang Jinbei Minibus Manufacturing	Hong Kong	Automobiles	1,377		1,399	
Jiangsu Chunlan Refrigerating Equipment	Unknown	Electrical machinery and electronics	1,352	140	386	0.86
Shanghai Mitsubishi Elevator	Japan	Electrical machinery and electronics	1,329	139	1,010	5.57
Shanghai Ek Chor Motorcycle	Thailand	Motorcycles	1,296	157	625	1.07

Table 9.3 Foreign ventures in China, demonstrating export-led sales, 1993-*continued*

	Nationality of foreign partner	Sector	Sales (million yuan)	Profit (million yuan)	Total assets (million yuan)	Exports (US$ million)
Wuyang-Honda Motors (Guangzhou)	Japan	Motorcycles	1,292	128	30	
Shanghai Dajiang Group	Thailand	Animal feed	1,202	157	1,435	38.23
Huafei Color Kinescope Systems	Netherlands	Electrical machinery	1,148	105	1,308	5.31
Beijing International Switching System	Germany	Telecommunications equipment	1,103	174	1,202	
China Tianjin Otis Elevator	US	Electrical machinery and electronics	1,084	104	353	3.97
China-Schindler Elevator	Switzerland	Electrical machinery and electronics	1,070	81	120	20.94

Table 9.3 Foreign ventures in China, demonstrating export-led sales, 1993-*continued*

	Nationality of foreign partner	Sector	Sales (million yuan)	Profit (million yuan)	Total assets (million yuan)	Exports (US$ million)
Shenzhai Saige Hitachi Color CRT	Japan	Electrical machinery and electronics	1,067	21	1,238	25.30
Shanghai Yongxin Color CRT	Hong Kong	Electrical machinery and electronics	1,064	70	1,205	

Sources: China Foreign Economic Statistical Yearbook, 1994, Beijing, China Statistical Publishing House, 1995, pp. 315–24; JETRO (Japanese Economic and Trade Research Organisation), *China Newsletter*, 119, November–December 1995, p. 16.

components to 85 per cent, had an annual production capacity of 200,000 sedan cars, and targeted principally for the Chinese domestic market.[9] The penetration of important integrated import-substitution industries was pursued with zeal by large Western multinationals. Asian Chinese firms were more flexible; they produced for both domestic and foreign markets, and focused less on their marketing strategies in China. While access to the vast Chinese market was important, because two-thirds of the products produced by overseas Chinese firms were sold in China itself, access to the Chinese market was more fundamental to Western R&D intensive firms,[10] who were attracted by low labour costs. The average cost of skilled labour was US$200 per month in Xiamen in 1990. The large economies of scale inherent in producing for the Chinese market were also extremely appealing to the Western firms.[11]

The transition by overseas Chinese in the early 1990s to both capital and research and development intensive industries was achieved through successful joint-venture arrangements with the Chinese state and foreign multinationals. A portfolio of diversified investments in power generation, telecommunications, automobiles and aerospace demonstrated the responsiveness of overseas Chinese capitalists to the Chinese State's public purchasing policies. The ability to work within a budget mechanism rather than price mechanism, and to deliver technology-intensive products through subcontracting arrangements, was also revealed by Chinese business in its expansion into China. Hong Leong joined British Petroleum in investing heavily in energy schemes in Fujian. Singapore's Keppel Corporation had been involved in Suzhou since 1993, in infrastructural developments including gas, electricity, sewage treatment plants and hi-tech industries. Thailand's M Group, in association with Sichuan Electronics, initially invested US$60 million in 1995 in developing the mobile telephone network.[12] In aerospace, Singapore joined France, Italy and the UK in June 1995 in a £1.2 billion project to build aircraft for China. CP, Shinawatra and Salim joined American and Japanese investors in transport, telecommunications and energy associated projects. Between 1988 and 1993, some 36 projects in capital-intensive sectors had major Southeast Asian Chinese participation.[13]

The overseas Chinese groups engaged in high-risk, high-return investments in individual projects, but the ratio of implementation of contracts was low when compared to Western and Japanese companies. The projects were often too speculative and were frequently abandoned. In addition, the heterogeneous investment frequently meant that the Chinese companies were dependent on Japanese or Western joint ventures, where contractual difficulties often aborted the initiatives. Finance was another serious hurdle, as well as the problem that many of these projects took years to implement because of the lack of efficient infrastructure to facilitate rapid completion. The ratio of implementation for US multinationals in China varied from 31 to 71 per cent between 1985 and 1989, declining dramatically after Tianamen Square. Thailand achieved a 60 per cent ratio in 1985, falling to 18 per cent in 1993. Overall, overseas Chinese ratios fluctuated between 23 and 56 per cent; 1988 to 1992 were peak years for the number of contracts implemented[14] (see Table 9.4). The Japanese were more cautious in investing but steady in pursuing implementation.

Another characteristic feature of overseas Chinese investment was its regional specialisation. Over 50 per cent of overseas Chinese investments were in Guangdong and Fujian provinces, the rest in Shanghai and Beijing. Only CP invested throughout China, including Mongolia, which attracted US$2.5 million in 1994.[15] American investments were confined to Guangdong, Beijing, Jiangsu and Shanghai; Japanese investments were in Liaoning province, Guangdong, Shanghai, Beijing, Jiangsu, Hainan, Fujian and Zhejiang.

The regional concentration of investment initiated structural changes in the provincial economies. Fujian's share of foreign direct investment between 1979 and 1992 rose from 0.47 per cent to 7.63 per cent of China's total foreign investment. Guangdong absorbed 31 per cent of total foreign direct investment in 1987, rising to 42 per cent in 1990, then declining to 32 per cent in 1992. After 1993, Guangdong continued to receive a third of China's total foreign direct investment. Between 1980 and 1992, Guangdong's share of total GDP rose from 5.5 per cent to 9.6 per cent; Fujian's share of industrial output in the same period rose by 12 per cent.[16] Most of the early foreign direct investment was located in light industries but this changed from 1993 with a move into electronics, telecommunications and transport. The establishment of these fast growth regions has created a buoyant intra-Asian economy embracing Southeast Asia, Hong Kong and coastal China. Growth is driven partly by overseas Chinese links with ancestral villages, as well as comparative advantages in labour supply, natural resources, markets and access to finance. Such triangles of growth have nurtured and sustained the initial internationalisation of overseas Chinese firms, while accentuating their increasing ability to move into capital-intensive niches throughout the intra-Asian economy.

Table 9.4 Ratio of implementation of contracts in China, by main countries

	1984	1984–85	1988	1988–90	1991–93	1993
USA	31.0	50.4	63.8	71.3	27.4	30.3
Europe	106.5	109.4	83.7	62.7	22.3	19.1
Germany	120.0	25.6	31.9	66.1	32.7	22.5
France	66.0	106.0	100.0	108.9	36.6	59.7
UK	161.4	296.5	81.0	38.9	12.2	11.1
Italy	79.2	108.8	281.8	84.4	42.0	42.7
Overseas Chinese	23.1	26.6	56.7	55.7	22.6	23.9
Hong Kong	23.1	27.0	59.6	57.2	22.4	23.4
Macao			23.9	32.8	19.0	20.9
Taiwan					27.0	31.5
Singapore	13.2	7.9	20.4	46.2	16.3	16.6
Thailand	60.0	34.2	15.8	19.0	17.6	21.7
Japan	66.9	80.1	186.6	117.2	43.2	44.7
South Korea					25.0	24.0
Total	30.9	36.7	60.3	57.6	23.6	24.7

Sources: See Tables 9.1 and 9.2.

ASEAN investments in China originated both from the government as well as from private entrepreneurs. Investment from Singapore was essentially from state enterprises such as the DBS, while Malaysia, Thailand and Indonesia also pursued active collaboration with private enterprise. The role of the state was useful. Through goodwill missions to China, and by carrying out pre-investment surveys, and appraising economic, technological and resource bases in the Chinese economy, governments were beneficial to private overseas Chinese enterprise. Also loans were provided by the state for Chinese investors. For example, Singapore's DBS frequently provided finance as well as consultancy services. The mix of state and private initiatives accelerated with the privatisation-phase in Asia that began in the mid-1980s. Petronas's links with Hong Leong and the connections between the Thai state and CP attest to increasing collusion between Southeast Asian states and private initiatives in China. The collaboration helped to consolidate the overseas Chinese multinationals' transition into capital intensive industries, in telecommunications, and energy and related industries. ASEAN multinationals could not reproduce such impressive performances in Europe, the United States or even Australia, being rudderless without state patronage, and being further undermined by their lack of region-specific experiences.

The emphasis of this analysis of CP in China is on the detailed production-related aspects of foreign direct investment. The questions are: how concentrated were the sectors in which they participated, what market shares were they able to carve out, and what motivated their diversification from the mid-1980s into the manufacture of motorcycles, machinery, televisions, including satellites, power generation and telecommunications? What were the sources of this heterogeneous growth? Another question about CP is: in what ways did they assimilate new production technology, marketing know-how and management expertise as a result of this growth in China? Did the dramatic expansion between 1981 and 1997 transform CP's organisational structure and management? Since most of their enterprises were through joint-venture agreements, what were the interactions between CP and its partners? In particular, in their involvement in public procurement projects, how did they adapt to changes in political, economic and legal pressures? Did CP's activities unleash pressure for greater financial liberalisation both in the banking sector and the securities market in China? An analysis of the activities of the Bangkok Bank and other ASEAN financial institutions in China would assist in showing the financial impact, because of the official constraints on the activities of overseas financial institutions in China. Another issue is whether CP's activities throughout China provided serious competition, particularly in animal and fish feed production, poultry and swine rearing, aquaculture of prawns, as well as in food retailing. Finally, how did CP finance this multitude of economic interests harnessed in less than two decades? (See Tables 9.5, 9.6 and 9.7 for details on the individual firms in the CP Group in China.)

Family ownership existed in all its companies, both in China and outside. In Shanghai Dajiang, the family held 51.5 per cent of the equity, with 48.5 per cent being held by the Chinese partner. In all the 23 subsidiaries of Shanghai Dajiang, the parent company held between 95 and 100 per cent of the equity. Family dominance was repeated in Shanghai Ek Chor Motorcycles as well as firms in the petrochemical industry, in real estate and retailing. Even in publicly listed companies, like Shanghai Ek Chor Motorcycles, the majority holdings by Dhanin and Sumet were retained.

The major investment firms active in China were also dominated by family ownership. In the 1990s, the family held 61 per cent of the equity in Charoen Pokphand Hong Kong, 65 per cent in Chia Tai International, and 22 per cent in Hong Kong Fortune.[17] Restructuring the group in 1983, following the death of the founder, Chia Ek Chiu Chearavanont, had not disturbed this concentration of family ownership of the 200 companies in the group..

The scattered firms were strategically grouped according to the type of business. Functional separation was clearly identifiable, both in product companies as well as in the parallel and related investment companies. CP Feedmill was registered in Bangkok and maintained its hegemony over the agribusiness sector throughout Asia through the provision of equity, technocrats, finance and information. Telecom Holding had a similar tenacity in CP's telecommunications growth in Asia. Despite the number of firms in the group, several were relatively autonomous, and the specialist divisions were supervised by experts. Mutual equity possession and multiple links helped to provide cohesion.

The throng of subsidiaries and affiliated companies operating in new markets, new products, and with diverse joint-venture partners, were also unified through the concentrated management vested in Dhanin and Sumet Chearavanont, who were directors in every firm in the group, despite technocrats holding executive positions. In 1994, Dhanin was director of 42 companies in Hong Kong and China alone; Sumet was director of 53.

Table 9.5 Leading firms in the CP Group in China, 1993

Company	Sector	Sales (million yuan)	Profit (million yuan)	Total assets (million yuan)	Exports (US$ million)	Sales ranking
Shanghai Ek Chor Motorcycles	Motorcycle	1,296	157	625	1.07	22
Shanghai Dajiang Group	Feed, etc.	1,202	157	1,435	38.23	24
Luoyang Northern Ek Chor Motorcycles	Motorcycle	623	83	424	2.39	60
Jilin Deda	Feed, etc.	438	34	358	14.43	95
Chia Tai Yueyang	"	414	26	324		100
Shanghai Ek Chor General Machinery	Machinery	340	45	253	0.79	117
Beijing Chia Tai Feedmill	Feed, etc.	255	14	118		155
Chengdu Chia Tai	Feed	224	22	149		173
Kaifeng Chia Tai	Feed	221		202		180
Jilin Chia Tai	Feed	203	9	823	0.42	196

Table 9.5 Leading firms in the CP Group in China, 1993-*continued*

Company	Sector	Sales (million yuan)	Profit (million yuan)	Total assets (million yuan)	Exports (US$ million)	Sales ranking
Nantong Chia Tai Livestock and Fisheries	Feed	203	4	100		199
Qingdao Chia Tai	Feed	178	4	154		232
Chia Tai Conti Shantou	Feed	158	2	51		260
Nanning Chia Tai Livestock	Feed	112		42		397

Source: China Foreign Economic Statistical Yearbook, 1994, Beijing, China Statistical Publishing House, 1995, pp. 316–24.

Table 9.6 Leading firms in the CP Group in China, 1995

	Year started	Sector	Joint venture	Production output (units or tons)	Fixed assets (HK$)	Sales income (HK$)	Employees
Shanghai Ek Chor Motorcycle	1985	Motorcycles	Yes	500,000	184,250,000	1991: 204,460,000; 1995: 2,402,470,000	4358
Kirin Jengda	1986	Mixed animal feed	Yes	200,000	67,260,000	1991: 107,990,000; 1995: 371,020,000	789
Nantong Jengda	1990	Mixed animal feed	Yes: with Hong Kong, Taiwan, China,	300,000	106,300,000	1995: 441,040,000	397
Shanghai Ek Chor Vehicle Machinery	1990	Car components	Yes	300,000	126,100,000	1991; 142,040,000; 1995; 761,540,000	1157
Chingdao Jengda	1992	Mixed animal feed	No	300,000	30,270,000	1993: 177,720,000; 1995: 313,320,000	367
Loyang North Ek Chor Motorcycle	1992	Motorcycles	Yes: with Chinese government	520,000	375,030,000	1993: 622,930,000; 1995: 1,758,960,000	4220

Table 9.6 Leading firms in the CP Group in China, 1995–*continued*

	Year started	Sector	Joint venture	Production output (units or tons)	Fixed assets (HK$)	Sales income (HK$)	Employees
Shanghai Dajiang Fishery	1993	Fish feed and animal feed	Yes	130,000	n.a	n.a	74
Yuehyang Jengda	1994	Thai jasmine rice	No	580	17,050,000	1995: 1,500,000	43
Naning Jengda Constructing Material	1993	Construction material	Yes	5,250 (concrete)	n.a.	n.a	30

Source: Unpublished report of the government's Center for Market and Trade Development, Beijing, 1990–95.

Table 9.7   Shanghai Dajiang Co.

	Sales (million yuan)	Profit (million yuan)	Total assets (million yuan)	Exports (million US$)	Earnings per share (yuan)
1991	67.16	95.00	590.94		
1992	769.50	78.85	590.94	32.15	
1993	1,202.26	157.00	1,435.00	38.23	27.4
1994	1,864.00	216.00	1,759.00		35.9
1995	2,384.00	249.00			38.3

Sources: *China Foreign Economic Statistics, 1979–1991*, Beijing, China Statistical Information and Consultancy Service Center, 1992, pp. 424–38; *China Foreign Economic Statistical Yearbook, 1994*, Beijing, China Statistical Publishing House, 1995, pp. 316–24; Report from Center for Market and Trade Development, Beijing, 1990–1995; *Asian Company Handbook 1997*, Tokyo, Toyo Keizai Inc., 1997, p. 70.

The loose structure was firmly held together by the family without managerial hierarchies. The companies expanded through joint ventures and through Chinese state and private networks. Despite the need for a firm relationship between the various geographical product and functional interests, there was little specialisation in research and development or marketing; a flexible response to both was sustained within a centralised decision-making structure. The need for various sectors to co-ordinate investment, acquire technology, training and marketing, was achieved through the appointment of high-quality technocrats from Thailand's public utilities. The technocrats successfully transplanted into their companies in China were Somphop Petaibanlue, Vice-President of Shanghai Ek Chor, Sri Manavutiveri, Bhanusak Asvaintra and Peter Francis Armour (Nynex), into its telecommunications corporation; Sunthorn Arunanondachou, senior adviser in CP investment companies; and Tongchat Hongladaromp, and Prasert Bunsumpun who assumed managerial positions at Petro Asia.

The conglomerate's most important specialisation was in Chinese agribusiness. CP moved into feedmill production in Shenzen in 1981 and soon expanded into the rearing of poultry and pigs, and in the aquaculture of prawns and fish throughout the Chinese countryside, including Mongolia. Although this sector was well occupied with state and private enterprises, CP had major advantages. CP had advanced technology in feedmilling and in broiler chicken production in Thailand, through its links with Arbor Acres, while in China its partner, Continental Grain Company of Shenzen, further added to CP expertise and performance. Since 1971, CP, through its relationship with Arbor Acres, had improved seed production and succeeded in securing superior parent stocks for chicken breeding. In 1985, CP developed techniques for breeding large black tiger prawns and eradicating diseases affecting aquaculture through a joint venture with Mitsubishi. From 1984, CP had developed hybrid types of maize in partnership with Dekalb Agresearch (US). Also through links with American chemical and pharmaceutical firms, CP assimilated specialisation in pharmaceutical products and fertilisers related to animal breeding. The integration of knowledge, assets in production, and related sectors in agribusiness, enabled CP to expand not only in Asia but also into the Middle East (see Chapter 5).

CP's second advantage in China was that many of its competitors were too inefficient to exploit the potential for mass consumption and the persistence of excess capacity in the industry. The large Chinese state enterprises lacked organisational competencies as well as technological innovation. CP's third advantage was that it had forward and backward linkages. CP's feedmill production and chicken breeding sectors were integrated forward into food retailing, both independently and through contracts with Kentucky Fried Chicken International Holdings (Pepsi Company). CP's own shopping malls provided further advantages in retailing its products. The fourth advantage was that CP's sustained growth did not only provide a significant niche in the Chinese market but also in exporting animal feed and poultry, diversification into adjacent industries, such as pharmaceutical products, for chicken breeding, and penetrating adjacent countries. By the mid-1980s, CP had agribusiness concerns in Taiwan, Indonesia, the Philippines, Malaysia and India, as well as Thailand and China.

CP emerged as the largest animal and fish feed producer and producer of broiler chickens by 1990. By November 1993, CP was involved in 40 agribusiness projects, 13 of them large initiatives held in joint-venture contracts with American multinationals and the Chinese government and regional authorities. Much of this growth was consolidated through five companies: Shanghai Dajiang, Beijing Chia Tai Feedmill, Chia Tai Conti Zhengda Feed, Nantong Zhengda Animal Poultry Aquatic Products and Nantong Chia Tai Livestock and Aquatic Products.

Shanghai Dajiang was formed in August 1985 as a joint venture with Songjiang County Feed and Livestock Company using an initial investment of US$18 million divided in shares equally between them. Shanghai Dajiang was the first agricultural venture to be listed on the Shanghai Stock Exchange.[18] The rapid growth of the company is shown in Table 9.7.

The second subsidiary, Beijing Chia Tai Feedmill, which was the largest in China and one of the earliest joint ventures in the city, was formed in October 1984, with an investment of US$10 million, and held a contract for 35 years. By July 1987, Beijing Chia Tai Feedmill produced and sold 720,000 tons of feed, accumulating revenues and fixed assets valued at 1 billion yuan and 150 million yuan in profit after paying tax of 41 million yuan. In 1992, turnover increased to 217,530,000 yuan, and a gross profit of 32,230,000 yuan and assets of 111,430,000 yuan were achieved.[19] Beijing Chia Tai Feedmill's affiliate company, Chia Tai Conti, also recorded high profits in 1991, with a sales income of 91,000,000 yuan, profits of 3,470,000 yuan and assets of 27,840,000 yuan.[20] Between 1985 and 1995, the CP group saw a steady growth in agribusiness, which amounted to 33 per cent of the overall profits of the group in China. By 1996, the agribusiness sector alone accounted for sales revenues of HK$3 billion, an income equivalent to the total revenues earned by them in China four years earlier, in 1992. CP also contributed in 1994 to the rearing of 300 million chickens out of the total of 3 billion chickens eaten in China, as well as exporting 220,000 tons of chicken. CP also became involved in forward integration into meat processing and fast-food retailing, resulting in joint ventures with Kentucky Fried Chicken.[21] CP's feedmill production in Guangdong was also successful, producing 1.55 million tons in 1994.[22]

The only serious private feedstock competitor was the Hope Group, which belonged to Liu Yong Xing. Based in Chengdu, Hope had absorbed many of the failing state grain producers in the early 1980s, and by 1992 it had an output of animal feed of 300,000 tons, and its sales were valued at 300 million yuan. In 1993, annual output rose to 2 million tons and sales value to 3.5 billion yuan. Hope also diversified into poultry breeding, consumer electronics, property and banking, having acquired the first private bank in China, Minsheng Bank.[23] Despite this impressive growth, Hope captured only 4 per cent of the Chinese feedstock market, while CP's agribusiness, in particular the feedmill units, held 33 per cent of the entire Chinese market. CP reaped the benefits of economies of scale, which enabled it to influence prices. In 1993, CP's 10 broiler farms produced 30 per cent of China's total poultry exports and its share in total poultry sales rose from 14.7 per cent in 1989 to 41.6 per cent in 1992.[24]

How CP achieved such phenomenal growth in China must now be examined. Undoubtedly one of the reasons for CP's success was the steady flow of direct investment from CP Hong Kong throughout the 1980s and 1990s. Continuous investment produced an aggregate of US$3 billion between 1990 and 1993. CP's total investments in China were estimated at US$5 billion in 1995.[25] A quarter of the investment funds was directed towards the agribusiness sector. CP's second crucial advantage was its ability to form stable and enduring relations with the state. CP had joint ventures with provincial grain bureaus in 26 provinces, and employed local officials to overcome bureaucratic barriers and exploit existing distribution channels. As Jean Oi reiterates, the use of local power was not pure rent-seeking, but increased the commercial efficiency of the local economy, with local officials sharing risk and providing market information.[26] CP soon created an integrated structure of feed-mills, broiler-breeder facilities, feed pre-mix mills, pig-raising facilities, and aquaculture of prawns, using preferential allocation and access.

The corporation's diversification into the manufacture of motorcycles and machinery in the mid-1980s was partly a response to growing economic opportunities in China and the general business euphoria experienced by investors. The opportunities and upbeat atmosphere were further stimulated by the loyalty of the Chinese authorities to the Chearavanont family; there was great trust in the managerial skills of Dhanin and his close family aides. Dhanin Chearavanont's close ties with Shanghai's mayor Xu Kuangdi assisted CP's operations in Shanghai. Shanghai Ek Chor, which was established in 1985 to produce 150cc and 250cc motorcycles designed by Honda, was CP's main source of growth in the motorcycle industry. The technology was Japanese, acquired through CP's involvement with Honda in Thailand, and adapted to China. Suzuki assisted with joint-venture contracts. In 1991, 200,000 motorcycles were produced, accounting for 15 per cent of China's total motorcycle production. The figure doubled after 1992.[27]

Shanghai Ek Chor was listed on the New York Stock Exchange in 1992. Ek Chor's growth, as seen in Table 9.8 was quite spectacular, producing half a million motorcycles each year. Between 1991 and 1994, Ek Chor's profits rose by 72 per cent, a rise that led to the sale of some of its shares, valued at US$12.1 million, to finance the group's telecom-

Table 9.8 Shanghai Ek Chor Motorcycle Co.

	Sales income (yuan)	Profit (yuan)	Total assets (yuan)	Exports (US$)
1991	704,460,000	129,900,000	403,890,000	850,000
1992		102,000,000		
1993	1,296,000,000	157,000,000	625,000,000	1,070,000
1994		172,700,000		

Sources: *China Foreign Economic Statistics, 1979–1991*, Beijing, China Statistical Information and Consultancy Center, 1992; p424 (Asian Company Handbook 1997, Tokyo, Toyo Keizai Inc., 1997, p71.)

munications expansion in Thailand. Ek Chor's asset growth was impressive, inflating the group's assets to US$1.3 billion in 1993.[28]

Luoyang Northern Ek Chor Motorcycle's growth was more remarkable. Between 1983 and 1993, the number of motorcycles produced in China rose from 406,000 in 1983 to 8 million in 1993. CP's contribution accounted for a third of this total.[29] The combination of state liaisons with Honda technology in Luoyang Motor Cycle Co. in Beijing was further accentuated through fortuitous equity sharing with Norinco (China North Industries), the largest defence conglomerate in China. The statistics in Table 9.9 clearly demonstrate Luoyang Motor Cycle's rapid growth.

Another affiliated company that performed extremely well was Beijing Ek Chor Motorcycles.

The third sector of CP's expansion into the manufacture of machinery was car components and air-conditioners for automobiles. Shanghai Ek

Table 9.9 Luoyang Northern Ek Chor Motorcycle Co.

	Sales (yuan)	Profit (yuan)	Assets (yuan)	Exports (US$10,000)
1992	257,040,000	19,830,000	229,630,000	1,930,000
1993	623,000,000	83,000,000	424,000,000	2,390,000

Sources: *China Foreign Economic Statistics, 1979–1991*, Beijing, China Statistical Publishing House 1992, p425; *China Foreign Economic Statistical Yearbook, 1994*, Beijing, China Statistical Publishing House, 1995, pp 316–24.

Table 9.10 Beijing Ek Chor Motorcycle Co. 1992

Sales (yuan)	Profits (yuan)	Assets (yuan)	Export value (US$)
622,920,000	830,100,000	423,770,000	2,390,000

Sources: *China Foreign Economic Statistics, 1979–1991*, Beijing, China Statistical Information and Consultancy Center, 1992; (China Foreign Economic Statistical Yearbook, 1994 pp. 316–24

Chor General Machinery was established in July 1990 with an investment of US$5.92 million contributed by CP and a similar amount by its partner, the Chinese state. There was a significant increase in growth in this sector. Ek Chor General Machinery had technology from Sanders (Japan), who introduced sophisticated compressor manufacturing techniques. Ek Chor General Machinery had an output of 200,000 sets of compressors, accounting for half of all air-conditioner compressors and motorcycle components manufactured in China. In 1991, Ek Chor General Machinery had a sales income of 142 million yuan, profit of 25.8 million yuan, assets of 169.4 million yuan, and an export income of US$10,000. In 1992, sales rose to 214 million yuan, profit to 33 million yuan, and assets to the value of 195 million yuan. Net profits tripled in 1991, registered a 40 per cent increase in 1992, and rose by 57 per cent in 1993.[30]

There are two further sectors in which CP had considerable interests. The first was in retailing and the second was the petrochemical industry, which included the manufacture of plastics. China opened its retail sector to foreign participation only in 1992. The growth of modern retail stores rose from 1.4 million shops in 1980 to 12.2 million in 1994, an average annual growth rate of 9 per cent. In 1994 the growth in non-food stores was double that of those specialising in food.[31]

CP was involved in the creation of large, luxurious shopping complexes, hypermarkets, warehouse clubs and department stores. Three major retail operations were established in Shanghai in 1992. By 1995 this had expanded to 14. CP's retailing in Shanghai alone attracted US$13 million between 1992 and 1995, while Beijing absorbed another US$9 million.[32] China's total retail growth between 1993 and 1995 was fuelled by investment amounting to US$39 million.[33] CP was often involved in food and non-food retailing in joint ventures with the municipal authorities of Shanghai, Shenzen and Beijing. CP marketed imported products as well as domestic manufactures. The sources of this success were fairly evident. First, China's retail sector was dominated by native companies. In Shanghai in 1994, only 30 of the 700 supermarkets were foreign-owned.[34] Within the domestic and foreign retail sector, the state dominated as the major partner, despite the increase in the private retail sector from 26 per cent in the 1980s to 70 per cent in 1994. CP's alliance with the state and municipal authorities in the major cities of China was critical to growth. Secondly, CP had crucial partners in Makro, the Dutch discount retailing corporation, and Neil Bush and Koll, the California construction and property management corporation. CP and its partners were responsible for the expansion of hypermarkets, of which CP had 55 by 1997, and Value Clubs, which were membership warehouse clubs. Although CP's agreement with Walmart collapsed in 1996, due to Walmart's insistence on control over the stores, their location and merchandising policies, this did not deter expansion.[35] Thirdly, CP had substantial real estate investments in China, which provided suitable cheap premises for supermarkets and hypermarkets. Fourthly, CP used retailing as a value-added function for its manufacturing concerns in China. CP's modern farm production was suitable for high quality retail sales, and CP's own poultry and prawn production was sufficiently large to ensure quality and reliable supplies. Although it focused on a few categories of product, the spread of frozen and fresh chicken and packaged foods was able to break the regional rigidities of Chinese diet and cuisine, making CP's popularity highly visible. With Makro instructing it in Western wholesale and marketing techniques, CP was poised to expand wholesale marketing structures, covering food and non-food consumer goods. These hypermarket stores generated valuable revenues, while balancing the variety of goods sold and strengthening the distribution network for its agribusiness.

CP's had two different types of competitors. First, there were the large diversified retail conglomerates formed by various municipal and provincial authorities, such as the Shanghai Department Store No. 1 and Shanghai Hualian. These had the advantage of state subsidies but their management was poorly skilled, and they faced difficulties with wholesale distribution networks. The second serious competitor to CP was the Watson Supermarket chain. Like CP, all the competitors were competing for the 9 million Chinese who had sufficient incomes to participate in the modern retail revolution. The retail sector, however, was large enough to provide scope for CP to sell its chickens, its own beer (Reeb brand), its own cosmetics (La Fontaine), sales of which approximated US$1.8 million in 1994, and its own pharmaceutical products.[36]

CP's involvement in telecommunications, power generation and the petrochemical industries was in response to Chinese government pressure, to channel foreign direct investment into technology-intensive sectors. Here CP had disparate joint-venture partners, including the Thai and Chinese authorities, Mitsubishi, American multinationals and China's largest defence conglomerate, China North Industries Group.

In 1992, CP joined forces with the Thai state in an aggressive move into the petroleum industry in China. CP's ambition was to establish an integrated oil and gas enterprise involving the exploration, production, transportation and retailing of fuel, as well as the manufacture of chemicals and plastics. Petro Asia was established in 1993 with US$20 million. CP held 70 per cent of the equity with China Petro-Chemical Corporation (Sinopec), absorbing the remaining 30 per cent. CP later divested 35 per cent of its holding to the Petroleum Authority of Thailand. The bulk of the refining was undertaken in Guangdong with the assistance of Sinopec Maoming, producing 120,000 barrels of oil a day. Mitsubishi provided the technical expertise. In addition, CP managed the forward integration into the manufacture of plastics in Ningbo, with an investment of US$3 billion. A large share of this was derived from the Petroleum Authority of Thailand. Both the Thai and Chinese states were being exploited; they were attracted by CP's ability to raise capital and effectively market products in China.[37] The experience in China sustained CP's expansion into Vietnam.

CP's success was due to its rapid response to changes in demand and technologies. Organisational flexibility meant that CP could add or buy skills through joint ventures and move from one industry to another with low entry and exit costs. The institutions of the state and Chinese networks could absorb some risks and also provide financial flexibility. The point to be emphasised is that it was not simply the benefits of economies of scale that were crucial, but organisational structure and co–ordination with partners and alliances. Efficiency was derived from the reallocation of financial and technological resources. These advantages would vanish if the business environment changed drastically, as it did with the financial crisis in 1997.

The discussion so far has shown how growth was achieved through an increased market share as well as expansion into new activities. The economies of scale in CP's agribusiness frequently led to vertical integration into distribution and marketing, which in turn assisted product differentiation. In research and development sectors, CP purchased or licensed production techniques in various joint-venture contracts. Joint ventures were a common way of diversifying in product and territory. With the support of the state, joint ventures were guaranteed privileged access to capital and technology, and these institutional and transaction costs models provide a potent insight into the growth strategy of CP. At the heart of this growth, however, was finance. The plethora of activities was sustained through access to generous funds, accumulated from diverse sources.

Abundant finance fuelled CP's spectacular growth. There were five major sources of finance for the CP group in China: the incredibly high level of profits accruing to the separate companies; generous bank credit, particularly large syndicated loans from offshore banks; access to international capital markets; joint-venture finance; and large speculative profits from real estate investment.

The first method of acquiring finance was the transfer of shares and assets between subsidiaries and affiliated companies at exaggerated prices. The structure of CP's subsidiaries in China, their relations with the investment holding companies of the Group, which were located in Hong Kong, Bangkok, Jakarta, the Virgin Islands and Europe, enabled the easy transfer of assets and profits between firms. CP Hong Kong, a holding company formed in the early 1970s, owned eight subsidiaries, including 70 per cent of the equity of Ek Chor Motorcycle (New York), 43 per cent equity of PT Central Proteinaprima (Jakarta), and 25 per cent of CP Feedmill company, Bangkok. CP Pokphand Hong Kong also established an investment company in the British Virgin Islands with a registered capital of US$7.5 million. These affiliated companies provided capital for manufacturing, the purchase of raw materials, investment funds for property development and initiated joint-venture agreements with foreign multinationals to assist in funding and procuring expensive technology.

Secondly, the listing of Chinese subsidiaries on various stock exchanges raised further substantial capital. The listing of Shanghai Dajiang in Shanghai assisted the expansion of feedmill production, broiler farms and fast-food retail outlets in Shanghai and neighbouring provinces. In December 1993, Shanghai Dajiang raised 250 million yuan through the flotation of 'A & B' shares on the stock exchange. Fifty million shares at five yuan each were divided equally between 'A & B' shares. 'A' shares were issued first, and 'B' shares were issued after a time lag of 10 months. The issuing of new shares to fund growth was a recurring tactic in the 1990s. By 1992, CP Hong Kong had issued new shares on 10 different occasions either with new sale of shares or warrants providing the right to acquire shares later. The flood of new shares restrained the price of each new share. Thus CP Hong Kong's share price in 1988 was HK$1 and rose to HK$3.45 only in 1992, in spite of recording a net profit increase of 164 per cent in the same period, amounting to US$44.3 million in 1992.[38]

Ek Chor Motorcycle also issued new shares in June 1993 for US$16 million, which were acquired by CP Hong Kong. CP Hong Kong bought the existing shares of Dhanin and three other directors of CP for US$37 million in January 1993. In early 1994, CP Hong Kong sold US$150 million of 5–year floating rate notes (FRN) in Shanghai Ek Chor, and US$100 million in another 5–year FRN issue in April 1995.[39] The availability of this finance from the capital markets was sustained by the strong growth of the intra-Asian economy. Only a recession could arrest the diversification and make economic re-focusing within the group an imperative.

The third source of finance was the acquisition of syndicated loans through offshore banks, both in Asia and the West. In February 1994, CP launched an issue of US$150 million floating rate notes to finance its agribusiness in China. These were secured in Luxembourg at an interest rate of 0.9 per cent above the six-month London interbank rate, and had a five-year maturity. The issue was guaranteed by a consortium, which included Standard Chartered Asia and NatWest Markets. The use of domestic and offshore banks led CP Hong Kong to build up long-term debts of US$294.5 million and US$220 million, and short-term debts of US$119.4 million and US$140.5 million by February 1993. CP Hong Kong's paid up share capital, which was US$105.9 million, and total shareholder funds of US$672 million, led to the incurring of these large debts.[40]

Fourthly, CP's joint-venture partners were a significant source of funding. Shanghai Dajiang had the Shanghai municipal government as a partner since 1985. Chia Tai Conti (Shenzen) had Continental Grain USA, and Shenzen provincial government as associates from 1981. Shanghai Ek Chor Motorcycle had been partnered with the Shanghai government since 1984, and Fortune World Company, CP's real estate company in Pudong, had the Shanghai municipal government as a partner from 1991. Shanghai Mila Beer Company had Heineken and Shanghai authorities as associates from 1989. In petroleum, CP had Sinopec (China Petroleum Company) and the Thai Petroleum Authority. Nynex was a loyal and efficient partner of CP in telecommunications projects throughout Asia.

The fifth method of financing growth was through the speculative profits accruing from CP's real estate developments in China. The main real estate investor in this group was Hong Kong Fortune, which prior to December 1991 was Creative Investment Holdings incorporated in the Cayman Islands. Hong Kong Fortune is owned by Dhanin Chearavanont (42 per cent), Sunthgorn Arunanondchai (27 per cent), and Townson Co., which holds 31 per cent equity. Hong Kong Fortune itself held 20 per cent of Siam Fortune, and the Chearavanont family had 31.6 per cent, but in October 1993 the latter sold out their interests, and used the 2.27 billion baht (US$0.09 billion) to fund projects in China.[41]

Large parts of CP's investment in China were in property development, both for industrial and commercial purposes. CP reflected the traditional Chinese fondness for real estate investment. Before 1991, Chia Tai Company invested in Shenzen and Shanghai, but the trend accelerated from 1992. In a joint venture with Shanghai's finance and trading companies, Hong Kong Fortune developed the Pudong district of Shanghai; the initial phase cost US$90.7 million. In Shenzen, Hong Kong Fortune had invested in Honey Lake Resort Village and in Pearl River Delta,[42] and five property initiatives in Liaoning Province costing 1,580 million yuan (US$287.2 million).

In May 1993, Hong Kong Fortune was involved in more industrial estates, golf courses, resorts, office buildings and condominiums. Altogether, in May 1995, Hong Kong Fortune had 40 joint ventures in construction, worth US$4 billion in Beijing, Shanghai, Shenzen, Kunming and Zhuhai. Hong Kong Fortune's involvement in real estate gathered pace from 1993, with the issuing of bonds, debentures and securities to finance property investments. Thai Euro convertible debentures in 1993 exceeded US$3.5 billion, and this was used largely to finance the acquisition of real estate assets, which were then used by Hong Kong Fortune to finance manufacturing in China. Siam Fortune (CP's real estate firm in Bangkok) also issued 6 billion baht (US$0.2 billion) debentures in a restructuring exercise in 1994.[43] The bond issue provided long-term loans at lower rates of interest, with the option to convert to share equity. Much of Thai financial liquidity was transformed by CP in the 1990s into real estate investments in China. CP was transferring money from Thailand to China, part of the capital out flow from Thailand in the 1990s.[44]

Diversification into real estate was partly motivated by rising competition in the animal feed market, which before 1993 had accounted for more than 50 per cent of CP's interests in China. The animal feed interest declined in importance, and manufacturing and real estate interests now gained pre-eminence. By 1995, Hong Kong Fortune's major projects included luxury apartments in Pudong and Shanghai, office-building in Lujiazui Finance trade zone (US$28 million), shopping complexes in Guangzhou and Tianjin, and golf-clubs in Shenzen and Shanghai. China tightened its regulations on real estate investment from 1994 as part of its inflation controls, and in the same year the Chinese State Council imposed a new value-added tax on profits from sales of real estate. But CP was able to overcome these constraints by engaging in state-initiated development projects. Here the state co-ordinated the construction, stipulated aims of use and sale, and in effect raised the number of special economic zones funded by private entrepreneurs such as CP, which in turn led to related developments in highway construction, power-generation and telecommunications by the state, with CP as a major partner.[45]

A continuous source of finance for CP was Western and Asian banks. In China, CP had access to Chinese as well as ASEAN banks such as the Overseas Banking Corporation (OCBC), Bangkok Bank, Siam Commercial Bank, and Dao Heng Bank. These banks had permission to set up branches and agencies in parts of Shanghai, Xiamen, and Guangzhou to promote financial links between overseas Chinese and mainland China. Growth was further assisted when Bangkok Bank, through a joint venture with Sichuan Bank in 1995, was given permission to operate in the local currency.[46] CP had access to their long-term and short-term loans. Between 1993 and 1995, 30 per cent of Bangkok Bank credit was taken up in long-term loans to CP.[47] The movement of overseas Chinese capital into China reflects an important development in which Southeast Asian Chinese were acquiring information and entering into risky ventures, including insurance.

The high capital gearing that persisted among the great majority of CP firms in China, coupled with the heavy dependence on offshore borrowing, created serious instability in 1997. CP's response to the turbulence in the Asian currency market in 1997 was to increase the volume of agricultural exports; the foreign exchange earnings here contributed to its accumulated revenue of US$8 billion in 1997. However, CP was forced to sell Shanghai Ek Chor Motorcycle Company, its machinery firms, its brewing interests, as well as its stake in the Apstar satellite project. Apstar's minority stake had been held by Telecom Asia, which endured a loss of US$54 million (2 billion baht) in 1998. In addition, Telecom Asia had debts of US$1 billion (64 billion baht) in unhedged foreign currency. Kreditanstalt fur Wiederaufbau (KFW), Telecom Asia's prominent creditor, faced defaults for US$500 million. In order to settle the debt, Telecom Asia was forced to sell its paging unit, equipment distributor, and software consultancy.[48] CP's diversification into capital-intensive industries had clearly failed, despite its relationship with the state and Western multinationals, even though the latter had absorbed risks and minimised losses in the turbulent months of 1997. CP had learnt an important lesson – its core specialisation in agribusiness could withstand any crisis, while its rent seeking activities in areas like telecommunications and the motorcycle industry were likely to fail.

Conclusion

This analysis of CP's growth in all sectors has been largely positive, posing the question why did CP face difficulties in 1997–98 in the wake of the financial crisis. Two important factors contributed to the sudden unravelling of CP's success: the failure of the motorcycle interest and the Chinese telecommunications sector. The agribusiness remained profitable and in fact grew during the crisis. The corporation's loss-making interests in Chinese telecommunications, motorcycles and the retailing sector were sold during a fundamental restructuring of the group.

The growth and diversification of CP in related and unrelated industries demonstrates that diversification can affect information processing and create inefficiencies in production, management and labour productivity. The costs of this diversification were often hidden by CP's linkages with the Chinese state and foreign multinationals, as CP expanded into new, technology-intensive industries unrelated to its core business. CP's strategy was largely to appropriate control through equity and decision-making rather than through production technology and its processes. The latter it conceded to Mitsubishi, Honda and Nynex and to the Chinese state. The separation of finance and operations, innovation and training was rigid. Even in the Apstar satellite project of April 1993, a joint venture with Singapore Telecoms and a Taiwanese company, CP was adamant on equity control rather than on the management of technology and marketing. The acquisition of new expertise was not the priority; instead CP valued bloated financial resources, and an ability to manipulate the state. This was a recurrent flaw in Chinese business in Southeast Asia.

CP's economic performance in China also demonstrates that competition is indeed complex; it is dynamic, new sources of competitive advantage arise as family managers seek to maximise profits through diverse initiatives. Dhanin and Sumet constantly responded to this continuously evolving frontier of opportunities, which they managed through a careful selection of joint-venture partners from the Chinese state, private business, and Western and Japanese multinationals. They were confident they could manipulate the commercial environment, the type of diversification undertaken and acquire the necessary technology through appropriate collaboration. This was folly. The absence of product specialisation in their growth in China undermined their viability and lessened the chances of survival after 1997. The financial crisis of 1997 indicated that while Dhanin and Sumet could achieve dramatic growth by responding to new opportunities and acquire new technology through rent seeking activities, all this could collapse in a brief period of uncertainty. Unrestrained growth through diversification was a seriously flawed approach. Divestment of these diverse interests and the re-focusing on agribusiness in 1998 was an acknowledgement of the fact that product specialisation was fundamental to survival and expansion both in Thailand and China.

10
Financial Development: Expansion, Deregulation and Crisis

Finance was at the heart of Chinese business ambitions. The search for financial opportunities has tended to be the highest priority for Chinese capitalists, favoured over the pursuit of new markets, innovative technology or product specialisation. Capital accumulation was often sought without adequate risk appraisal or prudence.

In the economic crisis of 1997, the extreme vulnerability of banking in Southeast Asia was revealed. This chapter argues that there were several reasons for the vulnerability of Chinese finance. One was that the banks expanded too rapidly without becoming properly integrated. Diverse forms of finance were sought, much of it in US dollars; when the exchange rate fell, massive debts ensued. The structure of Chinese business organisations also contributed to the instability in banking. The role of the family was such that there was a tendency to allow unprofessional and risky behaviour within the family. Money was moved around into different sectors and speculated in volatile areas like property. A further reason is that the growth of Chinese banks involved diversification into new and poorly understood areas, often with the help of state patronage. The move from labour intensive to capital-intensive areas was often undertaken without the required specialisation or research. The liberalisation of finance without the introduction of sufficient regulation intensified the risk-taking character of banking from the late 1980s. One overall trend can be detected in Chinese finance; traditional banking activities were combined with more risky, speculative activities, which brought the whole system into jeopardy.

Indonesia

The instability of the Indonesian financial system is rooted in two developments in post-war banking. First, the government intervened both in determining interest rates and in allocating the resources. Secondly, developing from the first point, preferential credit distributed by the state produced powerful capitalist cliques, culminating in credit concentration and large loans being made to a minority of Chinese and *pribumi* capitalists. These capitalist groups were able to transform themselves into financial caucuses in the 1980s with the privatisation of commercial banks. In the concentration of financial and industrial power, powerful Chinese capitalists, the *pribumi*, military, and political figures received infusions of capital from foreign capitalists which accelerated from the 1980s, accentuating the close links between financial and non-financial corporations.

Corporate empires were often built around a family bank, as with the Salim Group, where Bank Central Asia was the core family bank in Indonesia, with First Pacific Holdings dominating its expansion overseas. Having established themselves in government-assisted industries such as cement and food with generous credit from state banks, these groups participated in the privatisation of commercial banking. The private banking sector was, from 1974, a major recipient of oil revenues, foreign aid, foreign direct investment, and foreign portfolio capital. The private banks were part of large Chinese and *pribumi* conglomerates; their financing could often be undertaken on the basis of abundant funds, further eroding competitive market behaviour. Access to offshore banks, as well as to more diverse and innovative sources of finance, further undermined competitiveness. Competition from foreign banks was negligible throughout this period. Foreign banks were nationalised under Sukarno, while their growth under Soeharto still was dismal.

The domination by state banking continued throughout the period from 1945. The central bank (Bank Indonesia) was an important source of credit. In the 1970s, Bank Indonesia accounted for 44 per cent of all loans from commercial banks. The five government-owned commercial banks were also an integral source of credit. The government owned insurance firms and savings banks, and through equity, controlled leasing and other non-bank financial institutions. Until 1983, the government controlled 75 per cent of all bank assets, attracted 75 per cent of funds, and was responsible for 77 per cent of total credit.[1]

Bank Indonesia operated as part of the government's monetary and credit instrument. State-owned banks tended to specialise in specific economic sectors. Bank Ekspor concentrated on the import–export trade, while Bank Dagang Negara was involved in mining, and Bank Negara Indonesia was active in manufacturing. This specialisation, accompanied by state intervention, enabled prominent Chinese and *pribumi* capitalists to carve out large shares in industrial sectors with little competition from foreign multinationals. Foreign banks acted as conduits for foreign capital. The few highly concentrated private banking cliques were assisted by the fact that if they failed, they could rely on being rescued by the state. Attempts by Indonesian bureaucrats to prohibit such 'lifeboats' were ignored by the government. The risks of such behaviour will become clear in the later discussion on the series of banking collapses in the 1980s and 1990s.[2]

As state banks channelled cheap credit to a small group of Chinese and *pribumi* élites, guaranteeing monopoly profits in new initiatives, an uncompetitive banking sector developed. Although foreign banks were allowed to operate from 1968, they were too few and were often limited to joint venture banking with Chinese and *pribumis*. The consequence of these linkages is that Chinese banking emerged as 'network' banking, sustained by the state, foreign multinationals, and by Chinese and *pribumi* capitalist groups.

The major source of funds for Chinese banks in Indonesia was from equity, rather than deposits. The majority of deposits were in state banks. Chinese banks and their clients had access to state bank deposits through patronage. The second method by which Chinese capitalists were linked to state finance was through the interbank money market established by the Soeharto government in 1974 to help banks with liquidity problems. This was boosted by a foreign exchange swap facility in 1979, to help banks attract overseas funds and avoid exchange rate risks. The foreign exchange swap facility involved an exchange of foreign currency for rupiah by a bank with Bank Indonesia at the prevailing exchange rate, and an agreement to reverse the transaction in the future but at the original exchange rate. This protected the banks against the risk of fluctuations in the exchange rate. Bank Indonesia would also buy currencies and sell to domestic entrepreneurs at no risk. The foreign exchange earnings of oil exports subsidised the foreign capital inflows sought by these private corporations. Dollar deposits accounted for nearly 30 per cent of bank funds by the end of 1974. Bank Indonesia also acted as an underwriter for export credit facilities, and its certificates were traded in the secondary market, adding another significant source of funds for major Chinese traders and bankers. This preferential credit, where the state was a major source of funds as well as the risk taker, produced bold Chinese entrepreneurs like Liem Soei Liong, Bob Hassan, and William Soeryadjaya. The subsidising of funding was highest in the period 1974–90, facilitated by the surge in oil revenues. Chinese capitalists were the major recipients, unchallenged because of bureaucratic weaknesses. Direct Central Bank loans and state preferential programmes in 1990 accounted for 48 per cent of the total credit in Indonesia.[3] Such credit was invaluable in the early 1970s, when credit ceilings were in force, as well as in the recessionary years of the mid-1980s. State banks remained the cheapest source of rupiah funds throughout because of the scale of their funding and deposits. When credit ceilings were removed in 1983, state patronage was crucial in determining who had access to the large foreign direct and portfolio capital. State funds and subsidised credit were critical for the growth of Chinese banks in the 1980s and even the 1990s.

Even after liberalisation, when the number of private banks grew threefold, and the number of state banks remained at seven, state banks continued to be the major source of large subsidised credit. Between April 1995 and April 1996, state owned banks accounted for 72 per cent of all bad debts, having risen from 21 per cent between October 1993 and December 1994. In contrast, private banks accounted for bad credit of 8.6 per cent in October 1993, falling to 5.4 per cent in 1994.[4] As for non-performing loans in 1997, three-quarters of them still came from state banks.[5] This had been a conspicuous trend in the 1990s, when 65 per cent of problem loans in 1994 were from state banks, while 22 per cent were from private banks.[6] The majority of these non-performing loans were for Soeharto's children and their allies.

The non-performing loans were a drain on the five large state banks, whose declining performance is evident from the return on their assets, 0.3 per cent in 1992, falling from 1.3 per cent in 1988.[7] The return on the assets of four private banks, Bank Central Asia, Bank Bali, Bank Duta and Bank International Indonesia, had fallen slightly to 1.3 per cent in 1992, from 1.8 per cent in 1988.[8]

Government-directed lending also produced distortions within foreign capital. Excessive political intervention in business decisions and in the formulation of infrastructural projects led to investment in unproductive and speculative activities. Large syndicated loans arranged by foreign banks meant that external debt owed to foreign banks more than doubled in Indonesia between 1990 and 1997. Short-term liabilities to foreign banks rose to 181 per cent of foreign reserves in Indonesia. Although Japanese banks faced exposure in Indonesia of 10 per cent of total loans, this is much less than their exposure to Korean banks in Korea.[9] Ten per cent of Japanese bank lending was to the private corporate sector in Indonesia. Here foreign currency borrowing was high and a large proportion was in unregistered borrowing, which is short-term and nominated in dollars, producing unstable gearing ratios for Indonesian banks and companies. When the rupiah fell in August 1997, the foreign currency borrowing of banks and corporations reached unprecedented levels. Corporate borrowing alone amounted to US$38 billion.[10] The ability of Chinese banks to lend while maintaining a sufficient loan–deposit ratio was possible only because of generous state funding. The trend of lending and preserving smaller reserve ratios accelerated in the 1990s with financial liberalisation. Forsaking prudent banking, Chinese banks were less restricted because of increased inflows of foreign capital, particularly short-term portfolio capital.

The politicisation of major investment and financial decisions raised the level of risk. When the Indonesian authorities liberalised the financial sector after 1988, lifting restrictions on the entry and operation of financial institutions, they insisted that they would not assist in the rescue of any bank and confirmed the owners' liabilities for their bank's lending. However, the connections between the state and financial groups meant that rescue by the state remained the pattern.

A final issue is bank failure. Throughout the post-war decades, Indonesian banking collapse has been a regular feature because of fraud, mismanagement, the concentration of loans on individuals, or lending to investors in the volatile property market. In 1967, 30 private banks collapsed,[11] although failures were more dramatic and frequent in the 1990s. Finally, in November 1997, the financial crises culminated in the closure of 16 small private banks and the nationalisation of larger banks. In April 1998, seven small banks were closed, while seven large ones had been taken over by the Indonesian Bank Restructuring Agency in February 1998.

The major factor behind these spectacular failures was not only fraud but also the making of loans to related firms. When Bank Summa failed in 1992, 55 per cent of its total loans were to related parties.[12] In June 1995, six banks had made loans to related firms that were more than 200 per cent of the banks' own capital, 23 banks for whom the ratio was over 100 per cent, and 42 banks had loans exceeding the

50 per cent limit on lending to linked companies.[13] These accounted for almost half of the total private banks in 1995. A second factor was that the capital–loans ratio exceeded the legal lending limit, particularly in loans to individual clients. In April 1996, 15 banks failed to meet the 8 per cent ratio while 41 banks did not comply with the legal lending limit on individual clients. Many also exceeded the limits on foreign exchange exposures.[14]

The third factor behind bank failures was exposure to the volatile foreign exchange securities and property markets. Commercial banks' exposure to property rose from 13 per cent of total lending by commercial banks in 1993 to 20 per cent in 1996, and to 25 per cent in July 1997. In addition there were loans to property-related securities, shares, bonds and derivatives. In 1990, Bank Duta lost US$420 million as a consequence of speculation. Bank Duta, whose chairman was Mohammed Hasan, was formed in 1966 and had been linked to three Soeharto foundations in the 1980s. Seventy-five per cent of equity was held by the foundation, and 25 per cent was held publicly. Bank Duta specialised in corporate finance, housing and car loans. Bank Duta collapsed and was rescued in 1990 by two Chinese friends of Soeharto, Liem Soei Liong and Prajogo Pangetsu, who contributed funds for its restructuring. A spectacular increase of 60 per cent in revenues and of 17 per cent in net profits in 1996 did not avert a collapse in 1998. In April 1998, Bank Duta was taken over by the Bank Restructuring Agency.[15]

Bank International Indonesia (BII) of the Sinar Mas Group also experienced instability and in April 1999 it was recapitalised through nationalisation.[16] The Eka Tjipta Widjaja family, who owned the second largest conglomerate in Indonesia, also owned this bank, which was established in 1959 and listed in 1989. BII had leaked finance to its industrial, commercial and real estate subsidiaries. Facing difficulties, the bank undertook a share issue to the value of 967.1 billion rupiah early in 1997, 70 per cent of which was used to recapitalise the bank. The raising of equity to increase its capital adequacy ratio increased the foreign ownership of BII to 47.4 per cent, while Sinar Mas, the family group, held 51 per cent. The bank had performed well before this, with revenues rising from 853,558 million rupiah in 1993 to 2,332,750 million in 1996. Net profits also rose, from 112,434 million rupiah to 260,410 million in the same period.[17] Their high exposure to foreign exchange contracts increased their volatility in 1997.

The assistance of foreign partners was crucial for these Chinese banks. The liberalisation from 1988 eased the restrictions on the entry of foreign banks into Indonesia and they found willing partners in Chinese and *pribumi* business elites. The practice of seeking foreign partners, in addition to the raising of capital through equity, expanded in the 1990s. In 1996, the eleven listed banks raised 1.6 trillion rupiah through new share issues. In 1997, they raised 3 trillion rupiahs.[18]

The raising of equity was necessary because the banks' lending levels exceeded their capacity to attract deposits. In this participation in derivatives, they were acting more as principals than as agents. Bank Dagang Nasional Indonesia, established in 1945 and listed in 1990, with foreign ownership of 39 per cent, increased its capital from 234,601 million rupiah in 1992 to 821,107 million rupiah in 1995, a four-fold increase. The founder of the bank, Lim Cu Kong (Sjamsul Nursalim), the tyre manufacturer, had secured growth through state funds and by borrowing from Japanese banks, the International Bank for Reconstruction and Development and the Asian Development Bank.[19] The 1997 crisis affected the bank and the conglomerate. The bank was nationalised, while Gadjah Tunggal, the tyre subsidiary in the group, resisted a partial take-over by Pirelli in 1999.[20]

The diversification of financial institutions, banks, finance houses, mutual funds, leasing and factoring companies, bonds, stock markets and offshore banks, unleashed spectacular but unregulated growth. The diverse Chinese financial corporations contained seriously unstable elements. One of these was their involvement in the capital and bond markets. Capital and bond markets were small in Indonesia but expanded in the 1990s. The number of firms listed on the Jakarta Stock Exchange grew dramatically. Between 1990 and 1992, there was a 63 per cent increase in listing.[21]

The liberalisation of 1988 assisted the growth of the capital market in two ways. First, large, well-established firms were urged to issue a portion of their shares, known as partial listing. Partial listing implied that a minority share offer was an effective device for raising funds cheaply on the stock exchange, while preserving family ownership and control. Chinese financial and non-financial corporations began setting up securities firms to undertake trading in, and the underwriting, of these shares. This was clearly open to manipulation of share prices to increase the profits of corporations.

The second impetus to the growth of the capital market was the inflow of foreign capital. International groups, such as the International Finance Corporation (an investment arm of the World Bank), began to target Indonesia as suitable for the investment of World Bank 'country funds'. By 1990, there were 16 such funds available for international investors keen on Indonesia. Foreign capital in the form of private funds had also been flowing in from Japanese, Singaporean, and Western investors since the mid-1980s. Such interest was reflected in the growth of foreign investors on the Jakarta Stock Exchange, from 10 per cent in 1989 to 30.4 per cent in 1993. In 1993, foreign investors' purchases were twice those of local investors.[22] In July 1992, the stock exchange was privatised and foreigners were allowed to buy bank shares. This, together with the establishment of an exchange in Surabaya by a group of banks, led to a phenomenal increase in Chinese joint stock banking, frequently in joint ventures with foreign firms.

Risks to investors were high because regulation was inadequate or non-existent. Indonesia lacked well-informed fund managers. The stock exchange attracted speculators, both foreign and domestic. Indonesian conglomerates with good links to the government could list their companies on the stock exchange at exaggerated prices. In December 1992, Indo Cement listed Bogasari (flour millers) for 2 trillion rupiah. The pricing and issue of these shares was not accompanied by adequate disclosure of the company's assets. Bank Duta, which failed in August 1990, had been listed in June 1990. Such cases raise the suspicion that listing was sought to avert immediate default. The privatisation programme of the 1990s replenished the resources of the Jakarta Stock Exchange with the public sale of shares in the newly converted private companies in telecommunications, electricity, steel, mining, and banks, which was interrupted by the crisis of 1997.[23] Privatisation again attracted foreigners. Low levels of income in Indonesia precluded heavy local participation in the capital market. Also, domestic investors were keen on real estate investment, in addition to bank savings. The interest in bond and equity markets did grow in the 1990s. Indonesian Chinese conglomerates, riding on the euphoric prophesies of dynamic growth in Indonesia circulated by western stockbrokers' firms and World Bank economists, now even sought listing in the US. Lippo's contacts with Clinton in his home state of Arkansas, and Salim as a protégé of Soeharto and the Bush family, listed their companies in the West, in addition to Hong Kong and China, and gained access to valuable funds.

As part of financial liberalisation, the government lifted restrictions on the creation of leasing, factoring, consumer credit, and venture capital in 1988. This had an immediate effect on Chinese conglomerates establishing finance companies. The combined assets of finance companies grew from 2 trillion rupiahs in 1988 to 20 trillion rupiahs in 1994.[24] Foreigners were attracted to leasing activities because there were no credit ceilings and they had the freedom to operate outside Jakarta. Domestic firms also became involved, carving out a share of 28 per cent in 1988, rising to 47 per cent in 1994. Consumer financing remained in the hands of domestic groups, although by 1993, foreign companies had gained nearly 41 per cent of the market through joint ventures. Factoring remained the preserve of domestic firms. Finance companies tended to borrow more from abroad than from within Indonesia, which increased their vulnerability because many were part of banks that were, in turn, part of industrial–-commercial concentrations.

In the mid-1980s, the Governor of Bank Indonesia lost power when control was transferred to the Ministries of Planning and Finance. Alongside the creation of diverse forms of credit and venture capital, the capitalists could obviate technocratic restrictions by seeking off-shore loans. The large state and private Chinese enterprises then began expanding overseas.

Salim, state and overseas finance

The following accounts of the Bank of Central Asia (BCA) and First Pacific Holdings (FPH) can be used to identify three major factors that contributed to the financial crisis of 1997. The first factor was that the links with the state and the Soeharto family complicated the regulation and supervision of financial institutions. The relationship compromised government regulations on capital adequacy ratios for banks, tighter rules for loan provisions and loans to the real estate sector. Abuses of bank funds were made possible through this dominance and control by the Liem family and Soeharto's relatives.

The second factor that contributed to the crisis was the extensive cross ownership and the interrelations between industrial firms and banks, which produced further confusion in the monitoring of debt. Large foreign capital inflows, in particular in portfolio investment, intensified the confusion. Financial liberalisation since the early 1980s had led to excessive borrowing. The links between political élites and foreign capitalists meant that Chinese capitalists could avoid important corporate governance rules on borrowing and lending. Salim sustained vast industrial and commercial interests through the continuous creation and restructuring of financial institutions both in Indonesia and abroad. In the vast avenues of capital creation in both domestic and international markets, risk was underestimated.

The third factor in the 1997 crisis revealed by the Salim example was that the economic boom from 1987 had led Chinese corporations like Salim to borrow in foreign currencies, most of it short-term and unhedged. A share of the offshore funds was invested on the stock exchange and in property markets in medium to long-term projects, but the currency depreciation of 1997 led to a collapse in asset prices, increasing the liabilities and non-performing loans of the Bank of Central Asia (BCA) and others. The BCA was finally taken over by the government in 1998.

The BCA was established in Indonesia in 1957. First Pacific Holdings was purchased in 1982 and listed in Hong Kong in 1988. The acquisitions of Hibernia Bank in 1983 and United Savings Bank in California in 1986, Wells Fargo Bank and Crocker National Bank in 1985, and Hong Nin Bank (Hong Kong) in 1987 were critical to the group's transition. From the import–export trade, the Salim group moved into manufacturing, first in import substitution industries and later in export led manufacturing, with the establishment of international manufacturing and financial concerns in Hong Kong, China, the Netherlands and the US. These financial transplants corresponded to the influx of oil revenues, foreign capital inflows (Arab, Japanese and American) from the early 1970s, and the rise of the Soeharto family business empire. Privileged access to finance both from domestic and external sources prepared the way for the emergence of concentrated, oligopolistic business groups in strategic industries in Indonesia. Liem carved out powerful shares in flour-milling, cloves, cement, steel and telecommunications, predicated on access to state credit, contracts, and foreign capital. This reinforced the explosion in the banking and financial interests of the group.

From 1957 to 1978, BCA emerged as the largest private commercial bank in Indonesia. The initial period of impressive growth was between 1974 and 1978. In 1973, BCA had no foreign exchange facilities, possessed one branch, and was ranked twenty-third among 58 private commercial banks in terms of total assets. The Indonesian oil boom catapulted the bank into a dominant position. The assets of BCA rose from 211 million rupiah in 1970 to 16,903 million rupiah in 1975, 1,542,116 million rupiah in 1987, and to 7,439,999 million in 1990.[25]

Close liaisons with the state introduced Soeharto's family as shareholders. Sigit Harjojudanto (eldest son) and Siti Hardijanti (eldest daughter) held 6 per cent and 14 per cent, respectively. Liem himself held only 8.8 per cent. The remaining 42 per cent was held by 18 shareholders, mainly foreigners. Indifference to minority shareholders was fostered by the dominance of the Liem family, the Soeharto family and their allies.[26]

Liem's links to Soeharto date from the 1940s. In the 1950s, Liem was involved in the export of primary products. From 1968, Liem held exclusive rights to import cloves for the tobacco industry. In the 1980s, with export led industrialisation, he moved into the manufacture of cement, textiles, steel, aluminium and timber, and mineral extraction. Three-quarters of the group's expansion in the 1970s and 1980s was in manufacturing. The aggressive expansion in manufacturing stimulated a parallel growth in banking.

Multinational banking and investment services were essential to maintain growth. The main argument here is that the expansion and performance of financial interests within the Salim Group were sustained by the group's pre-eminence in critical non-financial industries. The Salim Corporation diversified not from its core specialisation in commodities but rather through acquisitions, absorbing a whole range of industrial projects through government contracts and procurement policies in strategic goods such as flour, textiles, clove cigarettes, cement, steel, tyres and cords. This pattern of state-led growth created appropriate financial structures. There was horizontal and vertical integration of production and manufacturing, and integration with state-owned enterprise to maintain this oligopolistic grip. Thus financial institutions were created to tap into state capital and foreign capital sources. The varying combinations of banking and finance with the non-financial sectors of the Salim Corporation are captured in these figures. Banking contributed 27.2 per cent of net profits in 1989, rising from 10 per cent in 1975. The share declined to 13.5 per cent in 1991, rising slightly to 15.6 per cent in 1993. The relative decline of banking was due to the increased importance of new capital-intensive industries attracting foreign capital. Telecommunications, which accounted for 1.8 per cent of total profits in 1989, was responsible for 26.3 per cent of company profits in 1992. The property sector also grew, with a contribution of 11.2 per cent of net profits in 1989, rising to 19.6 per cent in 1993. Production, marketing and distribution, which accounted for 59.8 per cent in 1989, fell to 48.5 per cent in 1993.[27] Therefore, the growth stages and turning points for BCA were contingent on the fortunes of the non-financial segments within the Salim Group.

Multinational banking was also essential for Indonesian private banks, because state banks dominated the domestic financial system. To tap into foreign capital as well as channel lucrative earnings available from rising military expenditure in Indonesia in the 1980s, Liem acquired suitable financial institutions in Hong Kong, the Virgin Islands and the US to mobilise and hoard these funds. First Pacific Holdings was typical of this capital movement in the 1980s.

The international ambitions of Liem are covered in some detail in the account of First Pacific Holdings (FPH) to illustrate how international expansion increased risk for Chinese capitalists. Undercapitalised Indonesian banks and finance companies borrowed heavily and invested both at home and abroad, confident that the government would bail them out. The hazards behind that guarantee and the privileged access to funds had the most serious consequences in the 1997 crisis. Non-performing loans were the result of poor investment decisions, the collapse of the property market, the decline in exports and the current account deficit and falling reserves. Foreign capital began to flow out, creating a further squeeze on liquidity, which bankrupted financial institutions and the corporate sector.

FPH is principally an investment holding company with four divisions: banking, property (FP Davies), telecommunications (Pacific Link, Smart Communications and Indo Link), and marketing (Hagemeyer, Berli Jucker and Metro Pacific). FPH was acquired in May 1982. Originally called Shanghai Land Investment Company, FPH was incorporated in 1888 by British expatriate merchants in Shanghai investing in land and real estate in China and Hong Kong. Chinese investors bought FPH in 1949. Liem bought and listed FPII on the Hong Kong stock exchange in 1983 for HK$1.25 billion, 14 times its original equity. FPH underwent radical restructuring in 1988 with separate listings in Hong Kong and Bermuda, and became an investment company, trading in land, mortgages, equity, currency, bonds and securities, as well as developing banking. The directors of FPH were family members, Chinese and *pribumi*, as well as business associates and Filipino, American and British bankers and managers.

FPH's largest interest was in banking, with Hibernia Bank and United Savings Bank (USB) in California, and First Pacific Bank (Hong Nin Bank) in Hong Kong. USB was acquired in March 1986, having been established in 1974 in San Francisco as a bank catering for the large Asian population. USB had moved into property development and mortgage lending, but this was risky, and the bank failed in 1986, just prior to its take-over. USB expanded rapidly in its first year after take-over, with a 24 per cent increase in total assets, from US$641 million to US$792 million in 1987. With increased capital in 1988, USB expanded into southern California. FPH had already acquired another bank in San Francisco in 1983 – the Hibernia Bank. After acquiring Wells Fargo

Bank and Crocker National Bank in 1986, Salim was involved in corporate finance as well as trade finance in the United States. The Hibernia Bank expanded into Hong Kong in 1987, where FPH had acquired Hong Nin Bank, and renamed it First Pacific Bank. This was to mobilise capital in East Asia, and to specialise in mortgage lending as well as trade financing.

The growth of FPH was impressive (see table 10.1). But by 1993, it had undergone another important restructuring, transferring Hibernia Bank to a unit within FPH. The reasons for this restructuring – transferring firms, swapping equities and assets between separate units within the group – is clouded in mystery. In the same year, 1993, family members, including Antony Salim, and other Indonesian partners left the FPH board. Manuel Panglinan, a Filipino executive, rose to the top and FPH strengthened through product diversification, rather than focusing on its major core financial interests. The more flexible joint ownership and joint management with Liem in overall control had survived until the mid-1980s. Then the directors' own interests conflicted with those of the board, leading to important restructuring. In contrast, the core Salim family group in Indonesia tightened control and ownership – with Liem, his second and third sons, together with professional managers, the board of directors and 11 divisions, each with a committee, deciding on strategy, and sub-division committees deciding on day-to-day operations. This pyramid controlled 400 companies. In short there was a centralised ownership – management, with delegation of operations and policy to divisional managers. Domestic and overseas operations could be managed through this system. The ownership and family management of FPH was more diffuse, less dominated by the Liem family. Manuel Panglinan ushered in radical change in growth and diversification in the early 1990s. This change corresponded with increased activity in the Philippines, both in finance and property.

There were dramatic changes in the Salim group as a result of the currency crisis of 1997. FPH faced a US$3 billion debt. To reschedule this, it had to sell its most lucrative asset – Hagemeyer, the Dutch trading company, in January 1998 for US$1.7 billion. FPH also divested itself of its telecommunications units for US$2 billion and sold USB in California and First Pacific Bank in Hong Kong. These difficulties were closely linked to the crisis in the Salim Corporation in Indonesia, where government subsidies and finance were withdrawn in 1998. Indofood Sukses Makmur alone had debts in foreign currencies of US$ 1 billion. FPH's turnover fell from US$3,774 million in January–June

Table 10.1 First Pacific Holdings (FPH) Ltd Co., 1984–94 (US$ 000)

Year	1984	1985	1986	1987	1988	1989	1990	1991	1992	1993	1994
Net profit						33,400	38,500	34,500	63,100	101,200	135,300
Retained earnings	8,314	5,725	4,236	444		22,000	21,500	14,000	37,700	69,000	95,900
Proposed dividends	2,657	911	1,383	1,727		6,700	9,200	10,000	11,900	15,800	20,400
Total shareholders' fund	138,456	136,647	135,407	152,273		261,300	269,400	294,800	326,100	405,900	439,800
Reserves						248,000	230,700	217,900	210,600	287,700	336,800
Revenue	8,314	5,725	4,236	444		22,000	21,500	14,000	37,700	69,000	95,900
Total Assets	144,430	143,461	145,217	160,459							
Turnover						1,622,900	1,984,800	2,424,400	2,786,900	3,084,400	3,681,900

Source: FPH, 1984–95, Consolidated Profit and Loss Accounts, Balance Sheets and Financial Summaries.

1997 to US\$ 2,285 million in January–June 1998. Operating profits fell from US\$300 million to US\$190 million between January and June.[28] Salim lost control of BCA to the government, and sold his flourmills, cement factories, oil palm plantations and property. He had debts of US\$5 billion. The fall of Soeharto, the riots in Jakarta, and the massive debts of the corporation precipitated the sale of its lucrative food interests to an Australian firm. The decline of Liem Soei Leong and sons had already been anticipated by the rise of Manuel Panglinan and the shift to the Philippines and a new patron in Estrada.

Changes in performance were reflected in changes in management. For example, in the early phase, family control was maintained, while part management was delegated to executive non-family members such as Sudwik Katmono (Soeharto's cousin) and Risjad, and to professional managers – Filipinos, American, British and Japanese. The Board of Directors remained with family and friends. With the rise of Manuel Panglinan there was a return to increased investment in the Philippines in property (Fort Bonifacio City), banking, telecommunications and marketing.[29] In 1998, FPH made US\$1.7 billion of investment in the Philippines.

The developments in the financial system outlined above contained the ingredients for a crisis. The dominance of state-owned banks and their relations with powerful capitalists – often guaranteeing credit as well as absorbing losses – made it inevitable that during the crisis, non-performing loans were concentrated in the state-owned banks. The lack of effective state regulation of domestic and offshore banking led the external debt owed to foreign banks to quadruple between 1990 and 1997. Short-term liabilities to foreign banks rose by 181 per cent in the same period.[30] The pegging of the rupiah to the US\$, with only limited movement of 5 per cent, encouraged over-borrowing. Between 1990 and 1997, the real exchange rate appreciated by 8 per cent in Indonesia.[31] The private corporate sector had absorbed much of the domestic credit, which rose by 160 per cent. The domestic corporate sector was therefore over-leveraged, creating a volatile situation. A large proportion of this credit leaked into the real estate sector, as well as into stock market speculation and investment in new industries such as telecommunications throughout Asia. By June 1997, bank lending to the property sector had grown by 40 per cent from 1995.

The deregulation of domestic financial markets, the liberalisation of international capital flows, the rapid innovation in financial instruments and the diffusion of information technology encouraged speculators in both the currency and equity markets. The inflow of short-term portfolio capital created bubbles in asset markets which, when combined with the dramatic expansion in domestic credit and weakness in accountancy mechanisms, fostered a volatile situation. In contrast to this volatility aided by an unregulated legal and economic environment in Indonesia, Singapore, with a more regulated and prudent financial system, still experienced instability as a result of its extended involvement in Indonesia and Thailand from the late 1980s.

Singapore banking – vulnerability despite prudence

Four main banks have dominated the commercial banking and finance sector in Singapore since the 1960s. The four are the DBS, the Overseas Union Bank (OUB), the Overseas Chinese Banking Corporation (OCBC), and the United Overseas Bank (UOB). Western banks, which had been active in international trade and finance until the mid 1960s, were threatened by the emergence of powerful Chinese banking cliques formed through the merger of smaller banks catering to the various Chinese dialect groups in Singapore. The OCBC, the only pre-war bank to survive, began operations in 1949. Chung Khiaw Bank of the Aw Boon Haw family was established in 1947, and absorbed by the UOB Group in 1971, one of the four major banking cliques in Singapore. The mergers and acquisitions of the 1970s and 1980s created further financial concentrations. OCBC, for example, acquired Four Seas Communications Bank and the Bank of Singapore.

UOB was the most active in its take-over strategy. Besides the take-over of Chung Khiaw Bank in 1971, Far Eastern Bank in 1984, and the Industrial and Commercial Bank in 1987, UOB possessed a joint-venture bank in Indonesia from 1990. UOB was the second largest banking group. DBS was the largest. OUB was the only Teochew banking group; the others were Hokkien. UOB absorbed Asia Commercial Bank in 1983 and International Bank of Singapore in 1984. The fourth group, the DBS, was formed in 1968, on absorbing the Economic Development Bank. Only Tat Lee Bank remained independent, concentrating on Singapore and Indonesia.

The concentration of financial activities in the four groups was intensified through the incorporation and assimilation of finance companies within them. The three main financial groups – OCBC, UOB, and Keppel – emerged through mergers between 1976 and 1988. The inclusion of finance companies into the large banking groups increased the oligopolistic pattern of finance in Singapore. In 1989, there were 13 bank-affiliated finance companies in a total of 28 finance firms.

Between 1965 and 1988, the number of finance companies had declined from 96 to 31.[32]

Finance companies grew in the 1950s and 1960s. Finance companies were permitted to accept only fixed and savings' deposits; they were active in housing mortgages, hire purchase loans, and other forms of consumer finance. Finance companies were also involved in lease finance, investment in real estate and property stocks and shares. There were more restraints on consumer finance than on business finance.

In the early phase, a majority of the merchant banks were of foreign origin, although increasingly domestic banks took over the functions of arranging large syndicated loans and capital from securities markets. Between 1972 and 1994, the merchant banks made the transition from commercial, industrial finance to consortium funds, new capital issues, discounting short-term money market business and other forms of innovative finance. From the 1970s there was a phase of accelerated growth in wholesale banking and corporate finance, as a result of the establishment of the Asian Dollar Market (ADM) (1968) and the Asian Bond Market (ABM)(1971). Merchant banks were not restrained by commercial banking regulations with respect to capital adequacy reserves and ceilings on interest rates.

The creation of an offshore capital market with offshore banking and currency trading was crucial for raising large funds for infrastructural as well as corporate growth. The ADM responded to the increased demand for syndicated loans, nominated in US dollars, and increased bond activity. In 1984 a futures and options exchange, SIMEX, was established, and was active in the derivatives market, trading in international currencies. Only in 1986, Hong Kong surpassed Singapore in terms of the size and volume of issues of currencies and bonds, as a consequence of the opening up of China.[33]

Singapore's advantages were in regional currencies and derivatives. The involvement of the state ensured efficiency and accountability. Further, the resurgence of the countries of the Indo chinese peninsula assisted Singapore's growth. The number of fund managers increased fivefold in the period 1989–93, while in 1993 managed funds amounted to S$61.8 billion. Japanese banks were active in the bond market from the mid-1980s. By 1992, 222 issues had been floated, valued at US$15.8 billion. Offshore banks increased from 72 in 1984 to 88 in 1989, attracted by tax advantages, exchange control relaxation and increased access to capital from the Middle East, Japan, the US and Europe.

In addition to this phenomenal growth in the short-term money market, the ADM, and in the medium- and long-term capital market, the ABM, there was increased activity on the stock exchange, following its separation in 1973 from the Kuala Lumpur exchange. This was an important source of long-term funds, both in new issues of shares and in the secondary market. The stock exchange faced a crisis in 1985 caused by the collapse of the Pan Electric Group of 13 companies because of fraud. The world stock market crash of 1987 caused shares to plunge further. This had important consequences for the banking groups. The big four were encouraged to create their own securities firms and introduce rigorous checks to create a stable financial environment. Singapore's economy was dominated by large state enterprises, which also curbed intense stock market interest. To facilitate growth of the capital market, a secondary market was created in 1990 for the listing of shares of foreign companies. This was called CLOB (Central Limit Order Book) and included companies from Malaysia, Hong Kong and the Philippines. Foreign listing accounted for 22 per cent of the total market capitalisation in 1992. Much of the region had capital markets that were immature and volatile, with inadequate transparency and disclosure of information. Singapore's stock exchange grew less than the others, especially Malaysia and Thailand, because of rigorous supervision.

The liberalisation in the 1990s of CPF (Central Provident Fund) funds so that they could be used for private investment, together with the privatisation of some companies in Singapore, unleashed increased trading in stocks. These developments in the increased flow of international funds and increased interaction between stock markets and between international investment houses and banks, meant a switching of funds from one centre to another, from one activity to another, creating a frenzied mobility that could prove risky because of difficult political relations with financial groups elsewhere in the region. Singapore banks, in spite of a highly regulated, efficient and transparent domestic environment suffered heavy losses during the financial crisis, as a consequence of their trading in Indonesian and Thai financial markets.

The discussion now focuses on the DBS, which is important because it suffered serious losses during the crisis as a consequence of its extensive financing of the activities of private Chinese corporations in Southeast Asia. DBS, a state bank, became seriously embroiled in private sector bankruptcies throughout Southeast Asia, in particular in

Indonesia and Thailand. However, the regional presence prior to the crisis had enabled it to participate in the restructuring of troubled banks in Thailand and Indonesia after 1997. DBS was able to take up majority stakes in Thai and Indonesian banks, assist in their recapitalisation, and introduce new managerial hierarchies with the power to alter credit and cost-management policies. The respective governments' abilities to direct credit via banks in Indonesia and Thailand are now limited with the increasing intervention of foreign banks, such as the DBS. Both before and after financial liberalisation, commercial banks were the main suppliers of funds to the corporate sector throughout Southeast Asia. The insider knowledge of these banks held by DBS assisted in screening and monitoring the banks' lending relationships. Thus DBS' role as a regional bank has been enhanced, even though it recorded substantial losses as a consequence of the bailing-out of troubled banks in the region during the 1997 financial crisis.

The DBS was incorporated in 1968 with more than 40 per cent equity held by the state. A real estate company was formed in 1969, followed by a merchant bank and finance subsidiary in 1970, and a securities firm in 1986. DBS had access to state and offshore funds, and its main aims were to finance manufacturing, undertake urban renewal programmes and promote tourism. From the early 1970s, DBS engaged in raising capital through the ADM and ABM, holding critical joint ventures with Japanese and American finance houses. Overall, in the early 1980s it was responsible for a third of the issues in the ADM and ABM.

Regional expansion was achieved through the creation of branches in Asia, as well as in the US and Europe, while the establishment of joint-venture banks through equity holdings and mergers with domestic banks in Indonesia, Thailand and the Philippines, gained pace in the 1990s. In 1977, DBS' first overseas branch was opened in Tokyo, and by 1986 there were 589 correspondent networks in 72 countries. The emphasis was on financing manufacturing. In Singapore, a third of DBS' loans in the 1970s and 1980s was for manufacturing. DBS engaged in offshore banking; in February 1985, negotiable certificates of deposits to the value of 3 billion yen were issued with Daiwa in Singapore. DBS was also active in Japan's financial markets by the middle of 1985, and in 1986 another 4.85 billion yen was raised.[34] DBS also established relations with American merchant banks operating in Tokyo. In absorbing the National Discount Company in 1986, DBS became a major dealer in underwriting issues of government bonds and treasury bills.

The involvement in the Asian market, dealing in debt securities, bonds and underwriting facilities in the 1980s, was crucial in establishing the bank as a major participant in the yen bloc.[35] This brisk trade accelerated in the 1990s. DBS had an 11-year link with Daiwa Securities, Sumitomo Bank and Nomura Merchant Bank from 1972, which was crucial for raising funds for industrial finance in Southeast Asia. This enabled DBS to become the first non-Japanese bank to issue yen certificates of deposits, leading, in the 1990s, to DBS involvement in fund management in northern Asia for Chinese manufacturing.[36] A third of DBS revenues in 1996 were derived from these regional activities in Asia.

From 1988, DBS acted as banker for the Singapore Government in China. The consortium of DBS with Keppel Corporation and Sembawang Corporation was critical in innovative financing of Chinese development. In 1993, DBS and Tat Lee Bank provided a loan of US$420 million for automobile production in China. This was a joint venture between Volkswagon and the First Automobile Works, a Chinese state-owned enterprise.[37] DBS fitted in with Singapore's ambition to construct a regional role in Asia that would ultimately neutralise Malaysian antagonism towards the island republic.

DBS' involvement in Indonesia and Thailand constituted its first moves into multinational banking. In 1990, DBS bought a 42 per cent equity stake with Tat Lee Bank in Bank Buana Indonesia. This secured entry into corporate and retail finance in Indonesia. DBS' interests remained in international trade financing for large corporations. In 1991, DBS Merchant Bank had revolving credit facilities to the value of US$40 million in Indonesia. P. T. Gadjah Tunggal was the major corporate debtor, and DBS issued substantial credit for its expansion. Gadjah Tunggal, a tyre manufacturer, saw a growth in sales revenue from 269,652 million rupiah in 1992 to 746,824 million in 1995, and to 986,880 million in 1996.[38] The 1997 crisis brought serious difficulties for Gadjah Tunggal and a take-over by Pirelli was launched. DBS faced serious defaults in Indonesia. In Thailand, DBS had purchased equity in Thai Dhanu, which led to a merger in 1997, following the crisis. In 1997, DBS injected US$137.5 million into Thai Dhanu, increasing its stake from 3.4 per cent to 50.27 per cent, although management control remained with Thai executives.[39]

The wish of DBS to emerge as a pre-eminent financier of hi-tech industries in Asia led to the creation of the Venture Capital Fund in August 1986 to finance investments in both domestic and foreign hi-tech industries.[40] In 1983, DBS expanded its stock-brokering activities from Singapore to Hong Kong, Sri Lanka, and other countries in Southeast Asia. In 1984–85, DBS was responsible for raising 30 per cent of the total funds raised on the Singapore Stock Exchange and in 1987 it was responsible for 83.6 per cent of the new share issues, amounting to S$670.8 million. DBS also became the lead manager for share issues on Singapore's second securities board, the SES DAQ, introduced in February 1987. With the creation of its own Asset Management Unit in 1990, DBS aggressively targeted the Asian stock market.

DBS formed joint ventures or acquired existing securities firms in Asia; it acquired its own securities firm in Singapore in 1987, while in 1993 it formed joint ventures in Sri Lanka, Thailand, Korea, India and the Philippines. The joint venture with Sri Dhana Finance and Securities was finalised in 1994 with a 30 per cent stake. In February 1995 DBS held a majority stake of 75 per cent with Capital Trust to form the largest Indian stock-broker firm. In Indonesia, DBS operated a joint venture arrangement with Tat Lee Bank and Bank Dagang Nasional Indonesia. P. T. DBS Securities Indonesia saw a growth of 30 per cent in 1995. DBS also expanded into Shanghai where it was permitted to trade in 'B' shares. In Malaysia, there were serious obstacles to its entry. However, close ties were established with Public Bank. In the Philippines securities sector, DBS was assisted by its acquisition of fully licensed banking facilities in June 1996.[41]

DBS achieved spectacular growth in two decades in its capacity as a state bank with a broad regional mission in Asia to participate in innovative financing of industry and corporate growth (see Tables 10.2 and 10.3). By 1994, it was the largest Southeast Asian bank with assets of US$39.3 billion. In comparison, Bangkok Bank, had assets of US$ 30.65 billion. Sumitomo, the largest Asian bank had assets of US$486.9 billion.[42] Changes in DBS' lending portfolio in Singapore are described in Table 10.4. DBS' business in Singapore recorded impressive profits (see Tables 10.2 and 10.3) and these profits and large reserves enabled DBS to compensate for its losses in Indonesia and Thailand incurred as a result of the currency crisis in 1997.

In 1999, the group's net profits were S$223 million, after providing S$1 billion to cover non-performing loans. Total non-performing loans leapt from S$1 billion to S$7 billion between December 1997 and December 1998.[43] Thai Danu Bank alone accounted for losses of S$2.9 billion, or 41 per cent of the total loss. About three-quarters of the total provision of US$752 million was for losses in Malaysia, Indonesia, Thailand, South Korea and the Philippines.

DBS had to face US$260 million in losses in 1998 over Thai Danu, together with another US$132 million in connection with revenue reserves and another US$137 million because of depreciating asset values. Tables 10.5 and 10.6 illustrate the difficulties faced by Singapore banks as a direct result of the economic crisis in 1997.

In March 1999, DBS undertook further recapitalisation of Thai Danu, having lost 8.1 billion baht in 1998. The recapitalisation involved raising up to 10 billion baht through a share issue. The Thai Danu debts had meant that DBS suffered the worst losses among the four big banks in Singapore – S$7 billion. DBS' links to large Chinese capitalists, such as Ng Teng Fong, also meant serious losses in financial and property markets. The bank's involvement in the international expansion of Singapore state enterprises, such as Singapore Technologies and Temasek Holdings, were lucrative compared to its joint ventures with private corporations, domestic and international, particularly in Indonesia and Thailand. The foregoing analysis illustrates the risks faced by even the most prudent of banks in Southeast Asia. Even DBS in the highly regulated banking environment ofSingapore could not escape the crisis.

Conclusion

This chapter has exposed the weaknesses of banks that were part of industrial conglomerates. With Chinese business, growth was finance driven. Consequently, the issue is not the informational advantages of banks that had close relationship with corporations but how Chinese corporate growth became reckless. The recklessness partly resulted from intimate relations with financial institutions and the culture of financial abundance and confidence created by state patronage and access to internal funds within large conglomerates. Risk appraisal was impaired or absent. Long-term relationships between banks and business groups assisted the growth and preservation of monopoly capital. The lack of a screening role for banks affected not only financial markets but also capital markets, where financial intermediaries would have vetted firms before approving listing. Uneasy coalitions of financial promoters and industrial caucuses flourished. Above all, the concentration of finance in the hands of large Chinese conglomerates eroded competition. Hostile take-overs and mergers were continuously undertaken as a result of these financial linkages. Thus the debate does not concern the German model – with banks sustaining long term stable lending to their associated firms – but the lack of competition

Table 10.2   The Development Bank of Singapore (DBS) Group, 1969–95 (S$ 000)

Year	Gross profit	Net profit	Operating profit	Unappropriated profits carried forward	Issued and fully paid-up capital	Rese
1969	5,558	1,196	6,373	612	100,000	1
1970	3,104	1,903	7,778	1,666	100,000	3
1971	5,511	2,866	8,375	3,305	100,000	7
1972	9,073	4,640	11,237	5,417	100,000	11
1973	11,305	6,509	14,680	4,414	100,000	14
1974	8,206	7,580	25,595	4,831	100,000	18
1975	14,700	11,598	24,271	5,218	100,000	2
1976	29,030	18,435	36,219	9,078	100,000	37
1977	34,415	20,575	42,495	14,753	100,000	53
1978	54,903	37,071	67,305	22,645	100,000	79
1979	81,911	48,455	91,622	41,039	130,739	196
1980	118,625	69,578	139,778	58,731	228,519	408
1981	188,358	112,736	219,923	93,421	228,519	497
1982	198,901	128,952	250,494	162,630	228,565	988
1983	231,916	132,143	325,438	239,414	230,710	1,111
1984	181,963	124,327	248,018	303,737	290,197	1,391
1985	129,668	91,267	239,262	342,244	290,556	1,437
1986	184,159	135,971	279,267	392,178	293,284	1,539
1987	249,314	165,699	333,919	401,592	346,019	1,966
1988	296,699	213,213	302,939	498,769	419,094	2,076
1989	359,716	250,338	378,805	654,882	431,093	2,318
1990	404,238	286,348	482,304	824,020	474,202	2,502
1991	421,654	315,308	451,832	1,010,004	522,082	3,191
1992	429,116	328,379	479,618	1,259,015	522,088	3,451
1993	618,778	465,159	528,084		905,812	3,69
1994	681,917	527,843	609,396		1,124,936	4,224
1995	760,585	588,107	659,229		1,279,703	4,835

Year	Current assets	Fixed assets	Total assets	Current liabilities
1969	139,249	8,351	261,180	72,008
1970	184,410	12,030	369,255	144,711
1971	240,211	17,799	647,499	206,518
1972	429,618	29,269	945,797	520,297
1973	680,203	41,417	1,532,753	671,271
1974	843,733	95,999	1,852,029	790,714
1975	964,442	100,899	2,345,552	926,593
1976	1,236,916	102,845	3,232,505	1,174,760
1977	1,441,533	105,070	3,446,267	1,539,844

Revenue	Share-holder funds	Long-term borrowings	Deposits	Industrial loans	Total loans & advances
563	101,563	62,284	140,021	64,269	91,178
1,666	103,866	77,509	170,998	105,067	156,775
3,305	107,325	144,744	171,734	169,890	232,951
5,417	111,965	198,187	480,170	3,104	548,807
4,414	114,507	464,088	576,493	449,465	679,405
4,831	118,487	609,726	634,960	549,562	822,330
5,218	125,885	647,384	767,312	630,773	974,391
9,078	137,850	743,500	990,766	663,764	1,068,714
14,753	153,025	632,752	1,239,130	699,877	1,051,331
22,645	179,585	648,974	1,731,637	613,066	1,549,467
41,039	326,739	846,801	2,055,928	936,111	1,972,115
58,731	637,190	1,252,064	3,039,928	1,379,309	3,219,584
93,412	725,563	2,097,353	4,621,876	2,377,083	4,754,394
162,630	1,216,612	2,598,068	5,246,152	2,730,668	5,833,609
239,414	1,341,877	2,482,789	6,615,651	2,968,099	6,536,476
303,737	1,681,423	2,575,796	7,135,319	2,946,827	6,629,803
342,244	1,728,553	2,095,603	8,862,639	2,789,066	6,298,536
392,178	1,832,305	1,807,347	9,366,861	2,594,376	5,816,164
401,592	2,312,523	1,433,124	12,323,197	2,398,818	6,530,628
498,769	2,495,289	1,246,502	15,016,938	2,293,231	6,999,797
654,882	2,746,322	1,100,905	25,860,417	3,036,346	9,048,046
824,020	2,977,074	937,561	27,085,755	3,914,413	12,002,410
1,010,004	3,713,214	770,469	27,060,822	4,104,081	13,190,290
1,259,014	3,973,535	323,777	31,378,674	5,124,720	15,902,949
2,220,201	4,599,640	792,930			
2,670,537	5,349,419	1,217,295			
3,179,118	6,115,261	1,279,148			

ash hand	Loan/deposit ratio	Fixed assets/total assets ratio	Dividends per share	Net EPS
7,418	0.4507	0.0320		
2,304	0.6309	0.0326		
9,147	0.7361	0.0275		
7,426	0.8090	0.0309		
0,174	0.6529	0.0270	0.0500	0.07
9,093	0.6607	0.0518	0.0600	0.08
1,952	0.6888	0.0430	0.0700	0.11
2,137	0.6162	0.0318	0.0800	0.17
8,635	0.5616	0.0305	0.0900	0.19

Table 10.2   The Development Bank of Singapore (DBS) Group, 1969–95 (S$ 000) – *c(*

Year	Current assets	Fixed assets	Total assets	Current liabilities
1978	2,235,008	103,777	4,318,806	2,342,012
1979	2,732,914	124,252	5,488,737	2,781,423
1980	3,796,218	127,942	7,182,511	3,797,300
1981	5,437,661	142,975	11,271,194	5,393,350
1982	6,675,234	555,502	13,413,150	6,510,572
1983	7,808,565	606,514	16,989,110	8,015,467
1984	8,208,173	631,311	17,754,649	8,224,707
1985	10,281,675	666,434	22,058,911	10,122,608
1986	10,812,289	698,041	23,215,373	10,653,035
1987	14,504,620	201,799	28,069,157	13,752,508
1988	18,085,044	248,618	32,157,593	17,279,866
1989	27,781,332	207,854	44,393,757	27,718,090
1990	28,758,128	267,712	55,018,965	29,629,948
1991	28,922,991	377,592	54,953,581	29,539,052
1992	31,846,203	454,747	62,928,620	33,853,252
1993				
1994				
1995				

Source: DBS, 1968–97, Balance Sheets and Annual Reports.

h and	Loan/deposit ratio	Fixed assets/ total assets ratio	Dividends per share	Net EPS
5,721	0.6509	0.0240	12.5000	0.28
9,898	0.6794	0.0226	12.5000	0.32
0,541	0.7501	0.0178	0.1400	0.31
9,233	0.7076	0.0127	0.1400	0.45
4,531	0.7437	0.0414	0.1400	0.51
5,754	0.7184	0.0357	0.1400	0.51
7,981	0.6827	0.0356	0.1600	0.46
1,140	0.5748	0.0302	0.1400	0.30
7,330	0.5205	0.0301	0.1500	0.34
1,399	0.4747	0.0072	0.1600	0.45
0,213	0.4304	0.0077	0.1600	0.48
4,906	0.3356	0.0047	0.1600	0.58
0,370	0.4283	0.0049	0.1600	0.6
8,156	0.4739	0.0069	0.1600	0.62
0,706	0.5016	0.0072	0.1600	0.63
3,494				
5,650				
8,133				

Table 10.3 Growth rates over previous year (%) for the Development Bank of Singapore (DBS) Group, 1970–95.

Year	Total assets	Total loans and advances	Deposits	Long-term borrowing	Operating profit	Net profit	Total capital and reserves
1970	41.38	71.94	22.12	24.44	22.05	59.11	2.27
1971	75.35	48.59	0.43	86.74	7.68	50.60	3.33
1972	46.07	135.59	179.60	36.92	34.17	61.90	4.32
1973	62.06	23.80	20.06	134.17	30.64	40.28	2.27
1974	20.83	21.04	10.14	31.38	74.35	16.45	3.48
1975	26.65	18.49	20.84	6.18	-5.17	53.01	6.24
1976	37.81	9.68	29.12	14.85	49.23	58.95	9.50
1977	6.61	-1.63	25.07	-14.90	17.33	11.61	11.01
1978	25.32	47.38	39.75	2.56	58.38	80.17	17.36
1979	27.09	27.28	18.73	30.48	36.13	30.71	81.94
1980	30.86	63.26	47.86	47.86	52.56	43.59	95.01
1981	56.93	47.67	52.04	67.51	57.34	62.03	13.87
1982	19.00	22.70	13.51	23.87	13.90	14.38	67.68
1983	26.66	12.05	26.10	-4.44	29.92	2.47	10.30
1984	4.51	1.43	7.86	3.75	-23.79	-5.91	25.30
1985	24.24	-5.00	24.21	-18.64	-3.53	-26.59	2.80
1986	5.24	-7.66	5.69	-13.76	16.72	48.98	6.00
1987	20.91	12.28	31.56	-20.71	19.57	21.86	26.21
1988	14.57	7.18	21.86	-13.02	-9.28	28.67	7.90
1989	38.05	29.26	72.21	-11.68	25.04	17.41	10.06
1990	23.93	32.65	4.74	-14.84	27.32	14.38	8.40

Table 10.3 Growth rates over previous year (%) for the Development Bank of Singapore (DBS) Group, 1970–95. – *continued*

Year	Total assets	Total loans and advances	Deposits	Long-term borrowing	Operating profit	Net profit	Total capital and reserves
1991	-0.12	9.90	-0.09	-17.82	-6.32	10.11	24.73
1992	14.51	20.57	15.96	-57.98	6.15	4.15	7.01
1993				144.90	10.11	41.65	15.76
1994				53.52	15.40	13.48	16.30
1995				5.08	8.18	11.42	14.32

Source: DBS, 1968–97, Balance Sheets and Annual Reports.

Table 10.4   Industrial distribution of loans and advances of Development Bank of Sin

Industry	1978 (%)	1979 (%)	1980 (%)	1981 (%)	1982 (%)	1983 (%)	1 (
Agriculture mining & quarrying	1.6	0.3	2.5	2.1	1.3	1.2	
Manufacturing	47.0	31.9	28.5	28.8	26.8	29.6	
Building & construction	8.8	8.1	6.5	8.9	10.8	14.7	
General commerce	7.3	9.3	9.7	7.9	8.5	9.0	
Transport, storage & communication	13.8	20.7	24.8	25.0	21.3	19.1	
Financial	8.6	13.7	14.8	12.0	14.4	12.4	
Others	13.0	15.9	13.2	15.4	16.9	14.0	
Total (S$million)	1,310.40	1,680.40	2,793.70	4,023.20	5,001.70	5,644.40	5,5

Source: DBS, 1968–1997, Balance Sheets and Annual Reports.

DBS), 1978–92

1985 (%)	1986 (%)	1987 (%)	1988 (%)	1989 (%)	1990 (%)	1991 (%)	1992 (%)
1.5	0.7	0.5	0.2	0.1	0.1	0.1	0.1
21.6	20.2	24.3	24.5	21.0	14.5	15.6	15.3
20.5	19.9	14.1	11.7	13.6	13.7	14.7	16.8
8.3	9.2	11.4	11.6	11.6	9.7	7.5	9.2
11.4	8.1	6.7	5.1	5.2	3.8	3.2	3.9
14.1	17.1	18.9	21.9	23.4	36.1	34.3	27.0
22.6	24.8	24.1	25.0	25.1	22.1	24.6	27.7
202.70	4,684.30	5,174.20	5,661.60	7,438.80	101,428.00	11,276.00	13,715.1

Table 10.5 Non-performing loans (NPLs) of the banks in Singapore (S$million)

	DBS		OCBC		OUB	
	1998	+/- %	1998	+/- %	1998	+/- %
Provisions ($m)	996.4	+101.1	938.0	+64.9	474.5	+49.7
Total NPLs ($m)	7,086.0	+537.2	4,059.0	+120.0	2,888.0	+371.1
Singapore NPLs ($m)	2,705.3	+316.7	2,607.0	+100.0	1,924.0	+749.8
Total NPLs/total loans (%)	8.2	+331.6	8.1	N/A	6.1	+238.9
Cumulative provisions ($m)	3,147.4	+221.1	2,266.0	+78.3	1,061.0	+76.5
Cumulative provisions NPLs (%)	44.0	-50.0	55.8	-19.0	36.7	-62.6

Notes:
NPL: non-performing loans;
DBS: Development Bank of Singapore;
OCBC: Overseas Chinese Banking Corporation;
OUB: Overseas Union Bank.
Sources: Reports on DBS, OCBC, OUB cited in *Straits Times*, 9 March 1999.

Table 10.6 Performance of the main banks in Singapore, 1997–98 (S$m)

		OCBC	UOB	DBS	OUB	KTB	Total
Net profit ($m)	1997	581	502	436	255	73	1,847
	1998	425	368	223	180	53	1,249
	% change	-27	-27	-49	-29	-28	-32
Provisions ($m)	1997	569	335	496	317	123	1,840
	1998	938	654	996	474	105	3,167
	% change	+65	+95	+101	+50	-14	+72
NPLs ($m) [Bank loans]	December 1997	1,850	991	1,112	613	840	5,406
	June 1998	2,600	1,488	3,908	1,534	1,492	11,022
	December 1998	4,059	2,191	7,086	2,888	2,213	18,437
NPLs ($m) [Non-bank loans]	December 1997	4.7	3.3	2.7	2.6	6.2	N/A
	June 1998	6.9	5.2	8.6	6.3	11.0	N/A
	December 1998	11.2	7.9	11.9	11.5	17.2	N/A
Cumulative Provisions	December 1997	1,271	872	980	601	N/A	3724
	December 1998	2,266	1,637	3,147	1,061	1,309	8111
ROE (Return on equity) (%)		6.5	6.7	2.7	4.3	2.9	N/A

Notes:
NPL: non-performing loan.
DBS: Development Bank of Singapore;
KTB: Keppel Tat Lee Bank;
OCBC: Overseas Chinese Banking Corporation;
OUB: Overseas Union Bank;
UOB: United Overseas Bank;
Source: Straits Times, 9 March 1999.

and rigour in the financing of corporate growth. Banks exploited economies of scale and scope, resulting in monopoly power, rather than in providing an efficient model of financial investment.

Instability was inherent in the financial development of the post-war decades, but it was intensified by the financial liberalisation of the late 1980s, making the crisis of 1997 more serious. Bank lending booms, arising from excessive domestic lending and inflows of private portfolio capital, led to bubbles in the property and stock markets. The private corporate sector soaked up credit, which rose to 150 per cent of GDP in Thailand and 160 per cent in Indonesia. Easy access to offshore capital markets led Chinese banks to indulge in risky operations in foreign currencies without restraint. The weaknesses of the accounting system, disclosure practices and legal frameworks meant that a serious mismatch could occur between banks' assets and liabilities, as well as the currencies in which they were nominated. Excessive political intervention distorted the banks' investment practices. The volatility of banks was increased with the rising levels of investment activity in Southeast Asia. In Malaysia, investment as a share of GDP rose from 35.2 per cent in 1987–92 to 42.6 per cent in 1993–96. In Thailand, the corresponding increase was from 37.9 per cent to 41.6 per cent between 1987 and 1996. This was more serious in view of the fact that by mid-1997, the share of bank lending to the property sector had reached 40 per cent in Malaysia and Thailand, 30 per cent in Indonesia, and 20 per cent in the Philippines.[44]

The debt owed to foreign banks quadrupled between 1990 and 1997. In Indonesia, short-term liabilities to foreign banks rose by 181 per cent of foreign reserves, and in Thailand by 169 per cent. Malaysia had a foreign debt ratio of only 47 per cent, and the Philippines, 77 per cent. Of Southeast Asia's foreign debt, 60 per cent came from Japanese banks, 20 per cent from European banks, and 10 per cent from American banks. Peak non-performing loans, by 1997, would reach 330 trillion rupiah in Indonesia, 3.5 trillion baht in Thailand, 114 billion ringgit in Malaysia and 173 billion peso in the Philippines. The total loan losses suffered by the banks wiped out 480 per cent of bank equity in Thailand, 571 per cent in Indonesia, 134 per cent in Malaysia, and 28 per cent in the Philippines.[45] These figures clearly establish the presence of distress borrowing in a booming economy, as financial institutions ran on without internal or external controls.

The pattern of high-risk, speculative activity was facilitated by financial abundance and the lack of genuine industrial competition. The crisis of 1997 exposed these weaknesses and paved the way for a new competitive regime through foreign entrepreneurs, in both the banking and non-banking sectors. Chinese conglomerates are now pursuing restructuring and specialisation to recover their economic position.

11
Conclusion: Old Problems, New Solutions

A common criticism of Chinese capitalism in Southeast Asia is that it is 'ersatz' or even 'crony' capitalism.[1] Undoubtedly, within Chinese business there are elements of dependency and subservience to dominant interests. However, simply to dismiss Chinese capitalism as ersatz, with a high level of state involvement that breeds cronyism, is to miss the fact that the Chinese have had a major role in determining the growth, pattern, and direction of Southeast Asian capitalism in recent decades. Indeed, the Chinese have been the agents of economic change in Southeast Asia at least from the early nineteenth century: they have created phases of rapid growth although, it must be said, they have still to create the institutions that would secure *stable* rapid growth. These Kirzner-type entrepreneurs need institutions and 'learning' to become Schumpeterian. The ability to drive economic change and to sustain growth is dependent on corporate organisation and governance, and on innovation in core technological competencies.[2] The Chinese capitalist substitutes relationships for all these.

I will begin with an historical analysis of Chinese capitalism and its complexities. 'History' provides an understanding of continuity and change in Chinese capitalism, the legacies of the past casting a shadow over modern developments. In tracing the antecedents of the growth of Chinese capitalism it also becomes possible to see that Chinese growth coincided almost precisely with business cycles. In the pre-modern period – prior to the nineteenth century – state building in Southeast Asia was firmly tied to the monopolisation of the conduct of trade and the extraction of resources. These were mercantilist states, in which the state commanded trade, production and labour in an enlargement of the earlier tribute system between the powerful and the weak. These structures needed effective intermediaries, often foreign

276

merchants, who were Chinese, Indians, and Arabs. The *syahbandar*, who collected the ruler's duties on trade, his levies on produce and services, and his tithes and labour obligations was succeeded in the nineteenth century by the revenue farmer. Almost invariably Chinese, the revenue farmer collected the duties on certain goods and services for the colonial state. This gave him considerable economic power, based on a monopolistic control of specified products and services, the accumulation of wealth through those activities, and a culture of co-operation with the state and foreign trading interests. The exploitation of labour extended to the provision of opium, gambling and prostitution. Chinese capitalists created multi-product, multinational enterprises through their relationship with the state; enterprises that largely escaped competitive pressures.

At the close of the nineteenth century, a number of revenue farmers moved into banking, a movement that involved innovation, risk-taking, speculation and a response to new commercial opportunities. The move was also a response to an upturn in the business cycle. The revenue farming élites, such as the Khaws (Penang), Zhang Bi Shih (Sumatra), Ng Boo Bee (Perak), Tang Seng Poh (Singapore), Loke Chow Kit (Selangor) and Be Tan (Java), who had formed powerful *gongsis* in the nineteenth century, were in decline in the early twentieth century, partly because of the transition from tin to rubber and the growing economic power of the colonial state, but principally because their inefficiencies had produced oligopolistic structures and rigidities, corruption and violence.

The inter-war decades saw the growth of a new group of Chinese capitalists, few of which (Oei Tiong Ham in Java is an exception) had family links with the earlier generation. Lee Kong Chian, Tan Kah Kee and Wang Lee built powerful multinational conglomerates in rice, rubber and other commodities. This was achieved through limited corporate restructuring and the creation of modern banks. However, the inherent flaws in Chinese business structures, corporate governance and financial and accounting procedures continued to threaten long-term survival. In addition, the 1930s saw increased competition and diversification into manufacturing, often in alliance with Japanese or Western capital.

The Pacific War years saw the arrival of the Chinese élites that were to dominate Southeast Asia's economic growth in the second half of the twentieth century. The Chinese capitalists who forged links with Japanese *zaibatsu* (including Mitsui) and with the indigenous political élites, emerged pre-eminent in the post-war economic boom. While

Wang Lee declined partly because of difficulties in the rice industry, it was his ambivalent relationship with the Japanese that really caused problems. Despite these setbacks, the Wang Lee group prospered, although it was overtaken by new entrepreneurs in Thailand including Sophonpanich and Chearavanont. Chin Sophonpanich's rise was in part a product of his liaisons with the Japanese and with the Thai army and bureaucracy in the early 1950s. Liem Soei Liong had vital links with the Japanese and with Soeharto. Robert Kuok and Quek (Hong Leong) also built on ties with the Japanese *sogo shoshas* and Southeast Asia's political élites. The *sogo shoshas* were vital in refocusing local production and trading networks towards the United States and Japan. Their role in drawing investment and dependence away from the former colonial rulers opened up opportunities for Kuok, Salim, Quek and Sophonpanich. This restructuring had begun in the 1930s but accelerated greatly in the 1940s and 1950s.

The relationships with the Japanese and with the Southeast Asian states were now more important than the Chinese networks. Chinese capitalism was now a comprador capitalism; facing a weak local bourgeoisie and a compliant state, Chinese capital was under no pressure to change. Links with Japanese, European and American capitalism allowed Chinese businesses to fail to absorb external economic philosophies or technologies. The indifference to 'learning' while responding to immediate economic opportunities was crucial in shaping the nature of Chinese capitalism.

The historical perspective also draws attention to the cycles of merchant activity, each cycle introducing new merchant groups with their own functional ambitions but each having the same attitude to risk and finance. McVey and Mackie refer to old and new Chinese business élites – capitalists in one cycle being susceptable to failure because they are unable to respond effectively to the mix of economic opportunities in the next.[3] Each product change brings with it new capitalist groups.

The turnover of business élites also arose from an inability to respond to the changing circumstances of the state, foreign economic interests and the global economy. Failure to establish a capacity in research and development and a dominance in any single industry meant that Chinese capitalism in Southeast Asia occupied a constantly changing territory. Karl Polanyi has argued that economic acts occur in socially constructed frameworks, interactions of capital, political power and social organisation.[4] Chinese business groups, however, emphasised power rather than product specialisation or learning. Size mattered more than efficiency; growth and diversification were more important than consolidation. Chinese capitalists were entrepreneurial in the Kirzner sense, they readily identified opportunities for exploitation, yet were unable to create the structures that internalise risks.

The Chinese attitude to risk and their apparently reckless behaviour may in part be explained by the observation that in Chinese society, economic roles were not enshrined in contracts that could be rigorously enforced. There existed a bargaining element between political and economic structures, fostering a climate that created an attitude towards risk that impacted on the family and the network. For example, if contracts were enforced through co-operative exchange relations between individuals with personal knowledge, an institution of reliability would be created, which Williamson has identified as having low transaction costs.[5] These same institutions could also be a source of inefficiency and corruption. They defined entrepreneurial attitudes as maximising profit and the opportunities for expansion rather than improving productivity and developing knowledge and skills. Socio-political institutions may in themselves have reduced uncertainty by making the actions of entrepreneurs more predictable and thus stabilising the expectations of others as to what they might do. This conformism is historical; there is continuity in such attitudes.

The evolutionary economics of Nelson and Winter and the path dependency theory of Arthur are useful in understanding Chinese business in Southeast Asia.[6] Hayek's work on 'group selection', in which some groups in any economy secure the greatest advantages, also fits well here.[7] The selection of specific groups is then reinforced, as outsiders identify them as suitable partners. One example is CP in Thailand; having secured control over Thailand's independent farmer-suppliers, with the assistance of the state, CP found itself courted by Japanese and American multinationals eager to invest in the kingdom. Indeed, they courted CP in other parts of Asia where, to be frank, CP had little reputation. This is historical path dependent growth, where later developments reflect the historical legacy.

The ability of Chinese capital to drive economic change was strongly influenced by corporate organisation and governance, and the ability to create and manage joint ventures and relations with the state. Chinese corporate institutions provided a 'gene coding' that reinforced the patterns of growth. In this context, the Southeast Asian economies had mimicked the trends that had earlier produced rapid growth and rapid industrialisation. Corporate structure was critical here in the selection of appropriate market strategies. Family domination and the absence of managerial hierarchies made the

Chinese corporation inherently unstable, which in turn destabilised economic growth as a whole.

The success of Chinese capital in creating conglomerates has been striking. While the basic objectives of diversification are clear, the forms in which it has been achieved have serious flaws. The Japanese model of diversification brings together clusters of competitive advantage in technology, capital accumulation and market strategies.[8] The Chinese practice is far more random because it is simply seeking risk aversion and market power. Diversification was not achieved through horizontal merger but through vertical integration. As the earlier chapters have shown, Chinese capitalism often operated in oligopolistic industries (with high barriers to entry) and involved alliances with the state and foreign multinationals. In this way, diversification in production and markets occurred through internal growth. For example, in telecommunications and electronics, the commercial rewards were considerable: yet the state restricted entry, with the result that a few companies that had strong links with the state dominated the sector. Firms that dominated one sector then sought entry into another, as CP did in entering the power and petroleum industries. There was insurance against failure because the state and joint-venture partners absorb the risk. In addition, the costs of research and development were absorbed by the state and foreign multinationals.

The absence of competitive pressures stood in contrast to the position of *kereitsu* firms, which diversify into related activities and continuously innovate in order to realise economies of scale in research and development. Chinese firms pursued unrelated diversification – reducing productivity – while the Japanese firm exploited complementarities in research and development and markets across industries. Although there were monopolies within Japanese industries, distinctive R&D strategies and constant innovation secured increases in productivity. The Chinese model of R&D – involving the state or foreign partners – resulted in 'short-run' initiatives and a duplication of activities, which ultimately eroded the original oligopolistic advantages. This was the case with telecommunications in Thailand, Malaysia and Indonesia. CP lost its advantage in Thailand to Shinawatra, Samart and Loxley, but instead of developing a new specialist advantage in local niche markets, CP went for expansion overseas.

The Chinese business strategy of conglomerate diversification was highly predatorial and uncooperative. In contrast, the Japanese strategy of complementary diversification, through networks of suppliers and contractors, created a culture of co-operative capitalism. This culture generates research, which enables the individual cluster to compete both domestically and overseas.

The response of Chinese firms was to form strategic joint ventures and to eliminate competition. The institutional and cultural differences behind diversification need to be emphasised. John T. Scott has drawn a distinction between purposive diversification and random diversification. Chinese firms clearly fit the latter model.[9]

Economies of scale, the rigorous allocation of capital, the effective exploitation of information, the sharing of research and development, the use of joint ventures to 'internalise the positive externalities' of individual firms – each seen in Japanese conglomerate creation – was absent from Chinese business. For the Chinese, diversification was undertaken to grow, reduce risk, and to acquire and pool the resources of the state, foreigners and ethnic networks. Ultimately this created instability, because risk was built into the financial liabilities of the firm.

In the process of diversification, the holding company was critical for organisational, institutional and economic reasons. Chinese corporations often have not one but several holding companies. The multiplicity of holding companies brought in external shareholders without threatening the position of the core family. This was an effective instrument for tapping into the resources of stock markets around the world. Through the holding company structure, Chinese capitalists could construct linkages with the state and with banks throughout Asia, and so share risk. However, risk was also heightened by the holding company structure. One feature of the financial crisis of 1997 was that conglomerates were unable to assess or internalise risk because ownership and control had been obscured by the maze of holding companies. The holding company structure secured family ownership and also encouraged opportunistic behaviour and the shirking of risk assessment. It reinforced centralising tendencies, which stifled flexibility and innovation. Innovation depended upon organisational structure and the creation of a skills base that had effective relations with both suppliers and research and development interests. Instead, the Chinese capitalists focused on finance; they accumulated, and their holding company structures reflected their multiple links in financing, not the urge for product innovation or marketing initiative. In Japan, the trading firm brought trade and finance interests together. The *sogo shosha*, acting with the core technology interests in the group, was at the heart of the Japanese conglomerate. Those who controlled the *sogo shosha* co-ordinated the wider structure and made the key decisions. In this framework it was possible to develop highly effective functional divisions in production, marketing, and R & D. This structure did not require the creation of holding companies.

The Chinese firm in Southeast Asia faced a further problem: that of structure versus sequence. The business structure at each stage was the product of the preceding sequence. Thus, unless the structure was effectively sequenced, collapse was likely. Effective sequencing was often lacking because of political–economic threats to the position of the Chinese. A key issue was, therefore, the political and economic environment. It is easy to accept that, despite the major changes in business structure and scope in recent decades, family control was still firmly maintained, not least because it served the underlying ambition of the Chinese entrepreneur to accumulate finance.

Family control and finance were at the heart of Chinese business impermanence. The two major features in the evolution of Chinese business – family control and a relentless search for finance – produced recurring instability. The diverse forms of financial accumulation, while family control was retained, led to the creation of highly risky conglomerates. Soft loans from state banks encouraged volatile growth; state support for cartels and oligopolistic practices encouraged a gambling culture. The rise of new financial institutions and mechanisms, together with the growth of stock markets, was used to mobilise capital and extend the geographical base. The risk preference of Chinese capitalists flooded with funds meant that enterprise was directed into short-term, risky ventures. The recipient of a huge influx of foreign direct investment, Chinese capitalism was both dynamic and complacent. Risk-taking capitalists, driven by abundant finance and *rentier* opportunities, produced a volatile situation that exploded in 1997.

The speculative attitude towards finance was again a product of history and environment, although it was also nurtured by the cyclical pattern of growth. Cycles of growth shake up and release inflexibilities in structure and practices and overcome inertia. They also introduce new portfolios of economic interests and financial opportunities within Chinese capitalism.[10] These sub-systems in politics and the economy ensure that Chinese capitalism operates in an environment of financial abundance, sustained by both domestic and external funds. The Chinese emerged as venture capitalists because of their risk-taking culture, accelerated economic growth in the region, and because of their family networks and relationships with the state.

It would be valuable at this point to reflect on the Italian firm, which has also been dominated by families, for example, Agnelli, Cini, Volpi,

Pirelli, Falck, Olivetti, Gardini and Berlusconi. This would help us understand the deficiencies of Chinese family firms. The growth of Italian big business was determined by trajectories or path dependencies that crystallised the firms' form and continuity. Italian firms passed from craftsmanship to modern manufacturing, creating niche specialisations. In capital-intensive industries, the Italians achieved prominence in tyres, chemicals, automobiles and light machinery. The state played a key role but the founding families were successful in integrating scientific advance with production practices. Dynamic product innovation was maintained with the help of this 'precocious state capitalism' and the craft culture.[11] The opening up of the Italian market by the creation of the European single market might well pose a serious threat, although the tradition of 'learning' and maintaining a craft culture may sustain Italian success. Here, possibly, is the 'missing link' for the Chinese family business.

The Chinese relationship to the state was highly complex; it was a changing relationship, particularly during the financial and economic liberalisation of the 1980s and 1990s. The privatisation of public utilities, the opening of China, and the growing importance of global capital drew the Chinese into a closer relationship with the state. The immaturity of the regulatory framework, in particular in Thailand and Indonesia, made it more difficult to control Chinese capital. The opening up of China, Cambodia and Vietnam enhanced their strategic position, in that the state needed the co-operation of Chinese capitalists to develop those overseas initiatives. The regional role and the adoption of a multinational identity were important, in that they were often used to disguise a weakening domestic performance. The Porter model – in which success at home is reproduced abroad – does not fit here.[12] For the Chinese capitalist, globalisation was driven as much by declining domestic profits as by foreign opportunities.

The long relationship of Chinese capital with the state and foreign capital encouraged factor accumulation rather than efficiency. Much of the investment was wasteful. The state and foreign interests provided capital funds but there were few incentives for them to be used efficiently. Innovation was made more difficult not simply by the oligopolistic structure of industry but by the absence of tight supervision of investment and more effective regulation of banks and capital markets. The state is a critical force in development, but it must promote competition, not provide a protective patronage, as it frequently did in Asia. Unlike Chinese firms, Japanese, European and American companies developed their human resources, productivity and market knowledge through economies of scale and innovation. The Chinese concentrated on pure and simple growth, funded by abundant capital.

Much of the literature on Chinese business has concentrated on culture and social norms, notably on the importance of the family and of lineage.[13] The overriding impression is that, because of these norms, the Chinese act in clusters, assisting each other to mutual benefit. A rather different picture has been painted in this study; here, Chinese businesses have been portrayed as predatorial, competing with each other rather than against outsiders. Chinese capital was often sub-servient towards outsiders, taking the less advantageous position in joint-venture initiatives. For example, in telecommunications, the foreign partner – BT or Nynex – retained control of the core technol-ogy, while exploiting the commercial connections of their Chinese partner. The Chinese were used for their ability to provide access to local political and commercial élites. In the long run they had far less commercial power than their foreign partners.

The argument has been made throughout this study that Chinese business and the rapid economic growth of the region were deeply intertwined. It has also been argued that the rapid growth achieved by the economies of Southeast Asia since the 1960s was essentially the product of Japan's economic ties with the region. This is the argument that intra-Asian trade and industrialisation since the nineteenth century has been driven by Japan, with the assistance of Chinese trading networks.[14] The argument goes on to say that Southeast Asia's growth has been driven by the high volume of foreign direct invest-ment and by Japan's industrial restructuring. There is some truth in this, but Japan's role can easily be exaggerated.

The broad significance of intra-Asian trade – the overall impact of Japanese investment in Southeast Asia – must be separated from the precise micro-level changes it produced, its impact on individual cor-porations and industrial sectors. The relationship between macro- and micro-economic change has to be understood if the role of Japan is to be assessed. For example, in Chapter 6 – on the textile industry – it was argued that the hypothesis of the 'flying geese' pattern of development was flawed.

Kaoru Sugihara, following other Japanese scholars, has advanced the concept of an intra-Asian trading system, in which the volume of trade conducted within Asia is greater than Asia's trade with the outside world. This view has considerable significance for patterns of industri-alisation and technology transfer. The concept of the intra-Asian system, however, is fraught with difficulties for Southeast Asia. In the interwar decades, Southeast Asia's trade with the West was greater than that with Asia. In 1913, exports to Asia accounted for 41 per cent, those to the West, 55 per cent. Imports from Asia were 38 per cent, those from the West, 58 per cent. In 1928, exports to, and imports from, Asia accounted for 34 per cent: those to and from the West were 53–56 per cent. In 1938, exports to Asia were 25 per cent, imports from Asia were 31 per cent: exports to the West were 51 per cent, imports from the West, 55 per cent. In the post-war decades, the share of ASEAN trade with East Asia was 54.9 per cent in 1981 and 50.6 per cent in 1992. ASEAN's trade with the United States rose from 18 per cent in 1981 to 21 per cent in 1992, while that of Europe rose from 11.6 per cent to 16.1 per cent.[15] Japanese capital goods made up a high proportion of imports – 46 per cent in 1981 to 53 per cent in 1990.[16] Japanese industrial materials also formed an important part of capital goods exports to Southeast Asia. Close scrutiny of the composition of the trade shows that a higher share of final consumer durables was traded with the West. In addition, after 1987, ASEAN exports of consumer durables to Japan, Korea and Taiwan rose, while the share of raw material exports from ASEAN fell – from 74 per cent in 1981 to 47 per cent in 1990.[17]

The 'flying geese' pattern of industrialisation and the concept of the intra-Asian system assume a dependence on Japan without an understanding of the complexities of the relationship and of the changing nature of the linkages. Perhaps they have greater relevance for Korea, with its heavy industrialisation; Southeast Asia had a more varied experience.

While accepting that Japan's influence was considerable, its impact on trade patterns, the regional division of labour and on technology transfer was complicated. The earlier study of the textile industry identified the relative contributions of different influences and institutions that attracted investment and promoted growth. Southeast Asia did not conform to a 'stages of growth' model; it did not simply move from labour-intensive to capital- intensive production. Both forms of industrial structure co-existed, not least in the textile sector where Chinese firms pursued both labour- and capital-intensive methods. Consequently, there were differing degrees of technological assimilation even within a single sector. Here, Japanese investors concentrated on the capital-intensive segments. In the electronics industry, which attracted the largest share of foreign direct investment, Japan was preeminent, investing 3,429,782 million yen in Indonesia, 1,027,901 million in Malaysia, 1,173,676 million in Thailand and 1,631,390 million yen in Singapore between 1987 and 1995.[18]

In brief, rather than focusing on the broad trade statistics and advancing generalised models of intra-Asian trade, scholars should examine specific firms and industrial sectors, looking in particular at local equity holdings, product sophistication, technology absorption and procurement strategies. The study of the Chinese firm can tell us a great deal about the impact of Japanese foreign direct investment and technology transfer, and ultimately a great deal about the intra-Asian system and the working of the yen bloc.

The concept of the intra-Asian system and the 'flying geese pattern' of development make assumptions about the maturation of products and technology that ignore the complexities of the hierarchy of production and technological diffusion.[19] In attempting to revise the 'flying geese pattern' of development, some important points need to be noted. First, despite the dramatic relocation of Japanese industrial production to Southeast Asia, there is no substantial trade in assembled goods from Southeast Asia to the rest of Asia. Southeast Asia's exports go to markets in Europe and North America. Second, subsidiaries of major Japanese corporations or *kereitsu*-linked firms follow the multinationals to Southeast Asia. For example, the *kereitsu* firms of Sony follow Sony into the region, to produce components. Consequently, when Japanese electronic firms in Southeast Asia increased their local procurement of components, they procured from associated, not local, interests. In 1981, only 1 per cent of the components for semi-conductor firms in Malaysia was provided by Malaysian firms and only low-grade components at that. In 1996, the figure was still only 10 per cent. The import content in the semi-conductor industry remained at 90 per cent.[20] In brief, location is not linked to an intensification of technology transfer.

Innovation is a product of competition, but in Southeast Asia, the state strengthened the cartel structures of business through the establishment of restricted entry to the market. Consequently, the state curtailed innovation. Attempts to force innovation through research and development failed through the absence of a local skills' base. In Taiwan, market liberalisation intensified competition and thus forced innovation in components industries.

In the Proton project, the Malaysian state attempted to secure transfer of technology but achieved little success. Buying technology does not build innovation from the bottom: and the competitiveness of the components sectors was further hampered by the *bumiputera* policy and cronyism. In 1986, only 36 per cent of the Proton components were locally produced: and only 56 per cent in 1993. The high technology components were all imported. In a protective, oligopolistic culture, competition is emasculated and innovation dies. The response of Proton was to expand overseas to the Philippines and Vietnam in partnership with Mitsubishi,[21] although this was expansion into small markets. In Europe, firms responded to difficulties by price-cutting in the domestic market; in Southeast Asia, escape was sought overseas.

Technological upgrading in Southeast Asia has also been hampered by the fact that the standardisation of global technology has resulted in imitation rather than innovation through learning. Learning by doing and innovation by discovery was left to the Westerners and the Japanese. Fundamental research was absent, even in Singapore. Southeast Asian firms proceeded by striking partnerships with foreign technological leaders; endogenous development was neglected both by the state and Chinese capitalists.[22] Japanese firms were able to exploit American research because Japan possessed its own skill base and research and development infrastructure.

What impact did the 1997 crisis have on Chinese business? The financial crisis saw a massive collapse of asset prices, which magnified the value of the debt burden of Chinese companies. As a result, many Chinese companies were permanently closed or they were induced to restructure and shed their non-profitable sectors. Secondly, governments had to intervene in both banking and non-banking sectors and allow foreign investors to take majority stakes in many of the Chinese business groups, which eroded family ownership, although it is difficult to say how far Chinese family control has diminished. There have been cases of foot-dragging by Chinese capitalists reluctant to lose control; they often exploited political turmoil to halt radical change. Gadjah Tunggal in Indonesia has resisted take-over by Pirelli, while Bangkok Bank and Thai Farmers Bank sold 49 per cent of their shares to foreign investors in a move towards recapitalisation. In Malaysia, the government undertook restructuring and recapitalisation of corporations and banks through government agencies, and with the assistance of equity capital supplied by foreign multinationals.

The implications of the crisis for the long-term prospects of Chinese business in Southeast Asia should now be considered. At the outset, it is useful to note that economic growth in Southeast Asia has long been subject to periodic trauma, as has Chinese business since the mid-nineteenth century. In spite of dramatic changes in economic structures and economic roles, Chinese business has remained centralised, family-dominated, and able to exploit the varying economic relationships with the states of Southeast Asia and China, and foreign capital throughout the region.

The future may be different. Chinese capitalists may have to face increasing and direct competition from foreign capital. Before 1997, foreign capital was a subservient partner to Chinese capital. The growing presence of foreign capital and management within Chinese firms would now provide serious competition. Secondly, the role of government (state) may also change. The state's ability to provide generous credit, contracts, and concessions may now be limited. This change, together with more rigorous regulations surrounding foreign capital inflows, may in the future asphyxiate one mode of Chinese capitalist growth through financial accumulation. Financial liberalisation throughout Southeast Asia from the 1980s only accentuated the disposition towards growth through finance and high capital gearing. The high debt to equity ratio has characterised Chinese entrepreneurs since the revenue farming era of the late nineteenth century. The financial constraints imposed by the crisis of 1997 may conceivably introduce a new psychology of 'cash flow vigilance'.

The financial crisis has brought attention to the need for Chinese business to specialise and the urgency for strict regimes to control debt and the responsibility of corporate management to manage growth. The monitoring of debt is possible only when transparency in accounting policies and adequate supervision by finance departments is maintained.

The extensive cross-ownership and inter-relationships between firms and banks have to be disentangled if rigorous, prudential financial foundations are to be instituted within Chinese corporations. Whether these changes will be implemented is uncertain. Southeast Asia has recovered, many of the countries are recording positive growth, dissipating the urgency for change. Chinese business in the past has bounced back without making serious concessions to change; this might well still be the case.

The final point to be made about Southeast Asian growth is that the agricultural sectors of these rapidly growing economies continued to grow despite the collapse of the late 1990s. Southeast Asian economic growth is affected by cycles and crises triggered by trade imbalances, changes in the prices of primary products and currency values, which provoke uncertainty but also provide opportunities. In this non-linear growth, there exist complex inter-dependencies. There are not simply macro-economic configurations feeding into company performance but chains of relationships woven by the state, Chinese capital and foreign funds. Consequently, cycles theory does help towards an understanding of structure and change in Chinese capitalism. There are cyclical waves or bunches in Chinese capitalist growth, located in specific sectors; but these are overtaken by a new wave of capitalists as the cycle comes to an end. Cycles are the result of growth spurts in certain sectors of the economy. The primary production boom of the late nineteenth century produced a generation of Chinese capitalists that was swept aside by the collapse of revenue farming in the first decade of the twentieth century and then the inter-war depression. The industrialisation generation of the 1930s faded by the late 1940s, to be succeeded by the present generation – the generation that built Southeast Asia's transformation from the 1960s, but built wealth insecurely, transforming the Pacific Rim to the Pacific Grim.

Appendix   Dramatis Personae

Dhanin and Sumet Chearavanont are owners of CP. The group has interests in agribusiness, chemicals, retailing, property, land and telecommunications and political connections with the New Aspiration Party and the Thai People's Party. The Group had a fortune of US$5.5 billion (1996).

The Darakanonda Family (Saha Union). Damri Darakanonda was born in 1922 and moved from retailing into textile manufacturing. They are also involved in electronics and finance. They possess joint venture connection with Sime Darby Malaysia, YKK (Japan), Daewoo (South Korea) and Far East Textiles of Taiwan. In Thailand they are connected to the Chokwatana family, owners of the Sahapathanapibul Group.

Sumitro Djojohadikusumo, economist and adviser to Soeharto. His son Hashim Djojohadikusumo is Chairman of Semen Cibinong with an estimated fortune of US$1 billion. The company is the third largest cement and concrete producer in Indonesia, behind Salim's Indocement and has a total production share of 25 per cent in Indonesia's cement industry. The Group has a stake in four small banks and has business interests with Soeharto's daughter, Titiek, in the power industry, real estate and coal mining. Hashim's brother, Major-General Prabowo Subianto, is married to Titiek.

John Gokongwei (Philippines) His family is from Fujian and are based in Cebu. The conglomerate J. G. Summit Holdings has interests in textiles, property, retailing, banking, aviation, petrochemicals, telecommunications and in infra-structural developments. He has an estimated fortune of US$1 billion. His son, Lance, is Vice-President of J. G. Summit Holdings.

Robert Kuok Hock Nien, is a Hokkien who traces his ancestry from Fujian province in China. He has had interests in sugar, rice, flour, palm oil and timber since 1948. In the 1960s, Kuok diversified into property, hotels, news and television media, retailing, shipping and financial services. Kuok's interests in food and drink led to investments in Philippine Tabacalera cigars, instant noodles, vegetable oil and flour mills in Southeast Asia and China. Kuok has had a 9 per cent stake in Coca Cola Amatil (Australia) since 1996. Kuok has used his Hokkien background to form close links with Soedano Salim of Indonesia, whose ancestors also originated from Fujian. Kuok's main interests are in Malaysia, although he has substantial investments in Singapore, Hong Kong, China and the Philippines. Between 1957 and 1974 his core business investments were in Malaysia. In 1974, with the establish-ment of Kerry Trading Co. in Hong Kong, he launched his expansion into Hong Kong. Kuok's ambitions to move into China involved the transfer of his sons and himself to Hong Kong and China, while his extended family managed Southeast Asia. Kuok's personal fortune is estimated at US$3.5 billion.

Kwek Leng Beng (Singapore). His estimated wealth in 1993 was US$4 billion. The family is descended from Kwek Hong Png who established Hong Leong in

Singapore. The group has interests in manufacturing, property and hotels. CDL is core to its interests.

Ng Teng Fong was born in China in 1928; he became a Singaporean property developer in the 1960s and expanded into Hong Kong in the 1970s. Ng Teng Fong remained active principally in property development and infrastructure projects such as the new airport and mass transit railway stations in Hong Kong and Singapore. Ng's purchase of Yeo Hiap Seng, the food and drink company, provided moderate diversification. His corporate wealth is estimated at US$3.5 billion. Ng Teng Fong's son, Robert Ng, is head of Sinoland in Hong Kong.

Sjamsul Nursalim (Liem Tek Siong) Indonesia. The Group's main company is Gadjah Tunggal, Indonesia's largest tyre manufacturer. The Group is also involved in chemicals, textiles, electronics, telecommunication, property and finance. Gadjah Tunggal had a market capitalisation of US$335 million in January 1997. By January 1998 it had collapsed. The main bank in the group is Bank Dagang National Indonesia which too faced collapse despite possessing shareholder funds of US$573 million in early 1997. It rejected a takeover by Pirelli.

Prajogo Pangestu (Indonesia) had an estimated fortune of US$2 billion in 1993. The company Barito Pacific is involved in timber, agribusiness, banking chemicals and property.

Sukree Photiratanankul founder and owner of the Thai Blanket Industry Group. They have close connections with the Choluijarn, Sombatsiri and Krailert families through marriage and business ties. Their political connections are with the New Aspiration Party. Sukree's son-in-law closely collaborated with General Chavalit Yongjaiyut of the New Aspiration Party. The Sukree family also maintained close connections with General Suchinda Krapayoon and the Thai army.

Quek Leng Chan (Malaysia) is head of the Malaysian Hong Leong Group. The Group has interests in infrastructural projects, land and finance.

Soedano Salim (Liem Soei Liong) is a Hokkien who was born in 1917 in Fujian Province in China. His interests include food, cement, construction, the motor industry, chemicals, property, textiles, financial services, media and telecommunications. His son, Anthony Salim, is the head of the corporation. Soedano Salim's personal wealth is estimated to be US$4.5 billion.

Thaksin Shinawatra was educated in the US. He has interests in silk, telecommunications, electronics and real estate. Shinawatra has strong political connections in Chiangmai as well as with the central government. Thaksin Shinawatra became Foreign Minister in 1994 in the Chuan government, but resigned over a technical detail of eligibility. He was later appointed Deputy Premier in the Banharn Silapa-racha government. Shinawatra has close links with AT&T and Singapore Telecoms. His close connections with the PAP (Peoples Action Party Singapore) arouse fears in Thailand.

William Soeryadjaya, founder of Astra. His sons, Edward and Edwin, were also active in the business, as were the extended family. The Soeryadjaya family lost control of the corporation in 1991 because of foreign exchange losses by one of the sons. Astra started off as a motor assembler and distributor, and commodity trader, and later moved into telecommunications. Estimated wealth is US$1 billion.

Chin Sophonpanich was comprador and founder of Bangkok Bank. He died in 1988. His son, Chatri Sophonpanich is now head of the group. His estimated fortune is US$3 billion. The Sophonpanich family has interests in banking, finance, securities, insurance, electronics, land and trade. The family had ties with Phin Choonhavan, an army general whose son Chatichai, was the Thai prime minister in the late 1980s.

Notes

1 Introduction

1. Derived from data provided by the stock exchanges in the region for 1994–8.
2. See Arif Dirlik, 'Critical Reflections on "Chinese Capitalism" as a Paradigm' in R. Ampalavanar Brown (ed.), *Chinese Business Enterprise*, London, Routledge, 1996, pp. 17–38.
3. R. H. Coase, 'The Nature of the Firm,' *Economica*, no. 4, 1937, pp. 386–405.
4. M. Casson, *Economics of Business Culture: Game Theory, Transaction Costs and Economic Performance*, Oxford, Clarendon Press, 1991.
5. Weng Eang Cheong, *Hong Kong Merchants in Sino-Western Trade, 1684–1798*, London, Curzon, 1997.
6. A.D. Chandler, *Strategy and Structure*, Cambridge, Mass., MIT Press, 1962.
7. K. Yoshihara, *The Rise of Ersatz Capitalism in South East Asia*, Singapore, Oxford University Press, 1988; R. Robison, *Indonesia: The Rise of Capital*, St Leonards, Allen and Unwin, 1986, and A. MacIntyre, *Business and Politics in Indonesia*, St Leonards, Allen and Unwin, 1990.
8. R. McVey (ed.), *South East Asian Capitalists*, Ithaca, Cornell South East Asia Program, 1992.
9. Wong Sui-Lun, 'The Chinese Family Firm: A Model, *British Journal of Sociology*, 36, 1, 1985 pp. 58–70.
10. Lillian Ng, 'Keeping the Family in Business', *Singapore Business*, December 1992, pp. 20–2.
11. Antony Reid, 'The Seventeenth Century Crisis in Southeast Asia', *Modern Asian studies*, 24, 1, 1990, pp. 639–59.
12. Ian Brown, *Economic Change in South-East Asia*, c. 1830–1980, Kuala Lumpur, Oxford University Press, 1997, p. 260.
13. A. Booth 'The Economic Development of South East Asia, 1870–1985,' *Australian Economic History Review*, XXXI, 1, March 1991, p. 24.
14. World Bank, *World Development Indicators, 1997*, Washington: World Bank.
15. Pasuk Phongpaichit and Chris Baker, *Thailand, Economy and Politics*, Kuala Lumpur, Oxford University Press, 1995, p. 137.
16. Akira Kohsaka, 'Interdependence through capital flows in Pacific Asia and the Role of Japan', in Takatoshi Ito and Anne O. Krueger, (eds), *Financial Deregulation and Integration in East Asia*, Chicago, Chicago University Press, 1996, pp. 127–8.
17. F. A. Hayek, *The Fatal Conceit*, London, Routledge, 1988.
18. I. M. Kirzner, *Competion and Entrepreneurship*, Chicago: University of Chicago Press, 1973; M. Kirzner, *Perception, Opportunity and Profit*, Chicago: University of Chicago Press, 1979. J. A. Schumpeter, *Capitalism, Socialism and Democracy*, London, Unwin University Books, 1943.

2   Chinese Business Organisation

1. R. Coase, 'The Nature of the Firm', *Economica*, N.S., 4, 1937, pp. 386–405.
2. O. E. Williamson, *Markets and Hierarchies: Analysis and Anti-Trust Implications*, New York: Free Press, 1975; O. E. Williamson, *The Economic Institutions of Capitalism: Firms, Markets, Relational Contracting*, New York, Free Press, 1985.
3. A. Alchian, 'Uncertainty, Evolution and Economic Theory', *Journal of Political Economy*, 58, 3, 1950, pp. 211–21.
4. D. North, *Institutions, Institutional Change and Economic Performance*, Cambridge, Cambridge University Press, 1990.
5. Alfred D. Chandler, *Scale and Scope: the Dynamics of Industrial Capitalism*, Cambridge, Mass., Harvard University Press, 1990.
6. M. E. Porter,*The Competitive Advantage of Nations*, London, Macmillan, 1990.
7. See John Butcher and Howard Dick (eds), *The Rise and Fall of Revenue Farming*, London, Macmillan, 1993, pp. 258–9.
8. Jennifer W. Cushman, *Family and State: the Formation of a Sino-Thai Tin Mining Dynasty 1797–1932*, Singapore, Oxford University Press, 1991.
9. Rajeswary Ampalavanar Brown, *Capital and Entrepreneurship in South East Asia*, London, Macmillan, 1994, p. 171.
10. *Aliran Monthly*, March 1993.
11. *The Star*, 28 November 1994.
12. *The Economist*, 27 April 1991.
13. Keiretsu are vertical groupings of small companies dominated by major firms at the top of an industry. Kigyo shudan are horizontal groupings of companies from a range of industrial specialism. The keiretsu and kigyo shudan were often linked by cross-share holdings and diverse economic transactions.
14. MUI Bank is Malayan United Industries Bank of Khoo Kay Peng.
15. Hong Leong Malaysia, Annual Report, 1994.
16. Hong Leong Malaysia, Annual Report, 1994.
17. *Far Eastern Economic Review*, 8 August 1994.
18. Under The New Economic Policy introduced after the race riots of 1969, there was a serious attempt at redistributing economic power to the indigenous Malays. This implied Malay participation in the private as well as the public sectors of the economy.
19. *Far Eastern Economic Review*, 22 February 1990.
20. For further details on Shinawatra, see Chapter 7 on telecommunications.
21. *Business Times*, 14 June 1994. For further details on Yeo Hiap Seng, see Chapter 5.
22. Barings Securities Report on P. T. Astra International, February 1994. For more on the financial scandal, see Chapter 4.
23. *Business Times*, 21 January 1995, 22 March 1995, 9 April 1996. *Straits Times*, 10 January 1996. See also *Companies Handbook 1994*, Singapore, 1995.
24. *The Economist*, 15 June 1996.
25. This estimate is based on the annual reports and consolidated balance sheets of Hong Leong (Malaysia and Singapore), Tan Kah-kee, Yeo Hiap

Seng and Bangkok Bank and the Hongkong and Shanghai Bank records for the period 1920–72.

3 Chinese Business and Outsiders

1. Brown, *Capital and Entrepreneurship in South-East Asia*, London, Macmillan, 1994, p. 130.
2. NHM Records, 1919, 1928, 1930, 1933, 1934, 1939.
3. Brown, 1994, p. 158.
4. Barbara Ingham, *Economics and Development*, London, McGraw-Hill 1995, p. 185.
5. *South China Morning Post*, 26 May 1990, 26 September 1990, 14 May 1992.
6. P. T. Astra International Annual Report, 1995.
7. Yoshihara Kunio, *The Rise of Ersatz Capitalism in South-East Asia*, Singapore, Oxford University Press, 1988, Richard Robison, *Indonesia: the Rise of Capital*, Sydney, Allen and Unwin, 1986, Chatthip Nartsupha and Suthy Prasartset, *The Political Economy of Siam, 1851–1910*, Bangkok, Social Science Association of Thailand, 1978.
8. R. McVey (ed.), *South East Asian Capitalists*, Ithaca, Cornell South East Asia Program, 1992.
9. Ross Garnaut and Peter Drysdale (eds), *Asia Pacific Regionalism*, Canberra, Harper Collins, 1994, p. 206.
10. P. T. Astra Annual Reports, 1990–1993.
11. *Malaysian Business*, 16 April 1992, 16 December 1993, 1 March 1994.

4 Socialising Capital in Indonesia

1. Indonesian Department of Information, 1993, XXII/73, as quoted in Anne Booth, 'Sources of Investment and Technological Change in Colonial and Post-Colonial Indonesia', Paper for First EUROSEAS Conference, Leiden, 1995, p. 20.
2. World Bank, *The East Asian Miracle: Economic Growth and Public Policy*, New York, Oxford University Press, 1993, p. 57.
3. See figure 4.3 for joint-venture arrangements.
4. Yuri Sato, 'The Astra Group: a Pioneer of Management Modernisation in Indonesia', *The Developing Economies*, 34, 3, 1996, p. 260.
5. P. T. Astra International, unpublished Annual Report, 1990, 1993. See also P. T. Toyota Astra Motor Company Report, enclosed in Astra International (Hong Kong) Annual Report, May 1994.
6. P. T. United Tractors, Annual Reports, 1986–95. See also *Asian Company Handbook 1997*, Tokyo, Toyo Keisai Inc., p. 396.
7. P. T. United Tractors, Annual Report, December 1989. See also Richard Robison, *Indonesia: the Rise of Capital*, St Leonards, Allen and Unwin, pp. 289–92.
8. P. T. United Tractors, Annual Report, December 1989.
9. William Soeryadjaya worked closely with Ibnoe Sutowo (Pertamina), Ir Soehartoyo (Department of Industry) and Probosutejo (Soeharto's brother).

10. Astra International, Annual Report, April 1993.
11. Ibid.
12. Astra International, Annual Report, April 1993.
13. Ibid.
14. P. T. Astra Graphia, Annual Reports, 1991, 1992, 1993.
15. For a discussion of the Summa Bank crisis, see Adam Schwartz, *A Nation in Waiting: Indonesia in the 1990s*, St Leonards, Allen and Unwin, 1994, pp. 150–1; David C. Cole and Betty F. Slade, *Building a Modern Financial System: the Indonesian Experience*, Cambridge, Cambridge University Press, 1996, pp. 95, 136–7, 182.
16. For an excellent discussion of P. T. Astra's management, see Yuri Sato, op. cit., and Philippe Lasserre, *The Coming of Age of Indonesian–Chinese Conglomerates*, Fontainebleau, INSEAD – Euro-Asia Research Paper, 1993.
17. Yuri Sato, op. cit., pp.258–59.
18. *Asian Company Handbook*, Tokyo, Toyo Keisai, Inc., 1998, pp. 452.
19. P. T. Astra International financial reports 1993,1994.
20. Astra International (Hong Kong) Statement of Finance, June 1993.
21. Indonesian Ministry of Finance, *Directorate of Banking and Non-deposit Financial Institutions, 1988–94* and reports of Asian Leasing Association and Ministry of Finance, cited in Cole and Slade, op. cit., p. 278.
22. P. T. Astra International, Annual Report, 1993; see also Baring Securities Report on P. T. Astra International, 1994.
23. Baring Securities Report on P. T. Astra International, 1994, Hong Kong.
24. Ibid.
25. Philippe Lasserre and Hellmut Schutte, *Strategies for Asia-Pacific*, London, Macmillan, 1995, pp. 107–8.
26. Cole and Slade, op. cit., pp. 114–5.
27. Bank Indonesia, *Indonesian Financial Statistics 1988, 1990, 1991*.
28. Bank Indonesia, *Indonesian Financial Statistics 1988–1994*.
29. Astra International (Hong Kong), Annual Reports, 1989–95.
30. Cole and Slade, op. cit., pp. 280–1.
31. P. T. Astra International, Annual Reports, 1989–93. See also Ministry of Finance, *Directorate of Banking and Non-Deposit Financial Institutions, 1988–94*, various issues.
32. Cole and Slade, op. cit., p. 136; Yuri Sato, op. cit., pp. 264–5.
33. Yuri Sato, op. cit., pp. 266–7; Astra International Hong Kong, Financial Statements, 1989–94 (Registrar of Companies, Hong Kong).
34. Astra International Hong Kong, Financial Statements, 1989–94 (Registrar of Companies, Hong Kong).
35. Astra International Hong Kong, Financial Statements, 1989–94 (Registrar of Companies, Hong Kong).
36. Astra International Hong Kong, Financial Statements, 1989–94 (Registrar of Companies, Hong Kong).
37. International Finance Corporation (IFC), *Emerging Markets*, 1995; IFC, *Fact Book*, 1995. See also *Badan Pengawas Pasar Modal* [Capital Market Supervisory Agency], *Annual Reports*, 1988–95; Jakarta Stock Exchange, *Fact Book, 1993*.
38. *Asian Company Handbook, 1998*, Tokyo, Toyo Keisai Inc., p. 452; Yuri Sato, op. cit., p. 251.

39. Cole and Slade, op. cit., p. 178.
40. *Far Eastern Economic Review*, 31 December 1998, 7 January 1999.
41. *Far Eastern Economic Review*, 17 December 1998.

5 The Food and Drink Industry

1. Robert Tollinson, David Kaplan and Richard Higgins, *Competition and Concentration: the Economics of the Carbonated Soft Drink Industry*, Lexington, Mass., Lexington Books, 1991.
2. Alan Yeo is the son of Yeo Thian In. He graduated in Chemistry from the UK and dominated the firm since 1975. His cousin Michael Yeo is the son of Yeo Thiam Kiew, the third son of Yeo Keng Lian the founder of YHS in Guangzhou in China in 1901. Michael Yeo obtained an MA from Dublin and worked for the firm upon his return, becoming deputy Chairman in the 1990s.
3. Yeo Hiap Seng, Annual Report, 1995; *Business Times*, 2 June 1978.
4. *Business Times*, 13 February 1984.
5. *Business Times*, 28 September 1994.
6. *Business Times*, 6 July 1994.
7. *Business Times*, 6, 7 August 1994; *Straits Times*, 29 August 1994. Yeo's main competitor in drinks, F&N, had Coca Cola as its partner in Singapore, Nepal, Sri Lanka, Vietnam and Cambodia. In Singapore, Coca Cola had 60 per cent of the cola drinks market in 1995: *Straits Times*, 9 April 1996.
8. *The Star*, 16 May 1995. Part of the loss is attributable to rising material costs, including aluminum, paper and plastics.
9. The founder-patriach was Yeo Keng Lian. He had five sons. The eldest Yeo Thian In and the third son Yeo Thian Kiew moved to Singapore in 1938, followed by their brother Yeo Thian Seng. Thian Kiew a teacher was involved with the firm in Sarawak and Sabah. The controlling shares in the Yeo group is held by the families of Thian In and Thian Kiew. Yeo Hiap Seng in Malaysia has four Yeo family members and has been managed by Yeo Chee Yan since the 1960s after graduating in commerce from Australia. Alan Yeo was chairman from 1985.
10. *Straits Times*, 18 May 1994.
11. Wing Tai is in the garment industry with interests in property.
12. *Straits Times*, 28 February 1995.
13. *Straits Times*, 28 March 1995.
14. *Listed Company Handbook 1996*, vol.2, Manager Information Services, Bangkok, pp. 42–43.
15. CPF Annual Report, 1994. Thailand's prawn exports in 1991 were largely farmed prawns. In that year, exports were US$1.35 billion, of which CP accounted for US$150 million of frozen prawns. Thailand produced 163,000 tons, out of a world total of 729,000 million tons, of tiger prawns; China produced 140,000 tons.
16. Securities One, *Handbook,* 21 March 1997.
17. Ruth McVey made this point in a paper, 'Greed and Violence in Thai Politics', Fifth International Conference on Thai Studies, London, 1993.
18. CPNE Annual Report, 1993–95; see also Moody's Global Company Data Reports, 1995–96.

19. *Far Eastern Economic Review*, 28 May 1998.
20. Ibid.
21. Ibid.
22. *Far Eastern Economic Review*, 7 February 1991.
23. *Straits Times*, 7 February 1991, 14 June 1994.
24. *Straits Times*, 7 February 1991.
25. *Straits Times*, 30 March 1972.
26. Cie Commerciale Sucres et Denrées = Sucden, the world's largest commodities trader in sugar, also with substantial interests in rice, cocoa, petroleum.
27. *Far Eastern Economic Review*, 7 February 1991.
28. *Far Eastern Economic Review*, 14 June 1994.
29. *Malaysian Business*, 16–31 October 1992.
30. MISC = Malaysian International Shipping Corporation, SCMP = South China Morning Post.
31. Kerry Securities, Annual Report, 16 May 1998. In October 1995, investment fund management with Kerry Financial Services, the holding Company of Kerry Securities, was involved in a joint venture with Temasek Holdings of Singapore and a Thai Finance Company to raise funds for Indochina and Myanmar.
32. PPB, Annual Report, May 1994.

6   The Textile Industry in Southeast Asia

1. Akamatsu Kaname, 'Shinkoku kogyokoku no Sangyo Hatten', *Ueda Teijiro Hakushi Kinen Ronbunshu*, 4, July 1937. For an English-language summary, see 'A Theory of Unbalanced Growth in the World Economy', *Weltwirtschaftliches Archiv*, 86, 1, 1961. See also Raymond Vernon, *Sovereignty at Bay*, New York, Basic Books, 1971.
2. Sukree Thai Blanket Industry (TBI), Annual Report 1992.
3. Akira Suehiro, 'Comparative Advantage of Manufacturing Industries in Asian Countries', Tokyo, Institute of Developing Economies, Economic Development Research Unit, Cam Series, 16, 1982, p. 83 (Unpublished report).
4. Suehiro, op. cit., pp. 83–5. In the U.K. in 1973 60 per cent of spinning and 35 per cent of weaving was in the hands of the largest 3 firms. John Singleton, *The World Textile Industry*, London, Routledge, 1997, pp. 129–30.
5. Singleton, op. cit., p. 138.
6. ASEAN countries included here are Malaysia, Singapore, Indonesia, Thailand and the Philippines. To identify trends Asian data is used because the information for individual countries is more diffuse and varied.
7. Singleton, op. cit., p.17. See also International Economic Data Bank (IEDB), Australian National University, Canberra, for trade and production data.
8. Suehiro, op. cit., p. 74.
9. Ibid., p. 97.
10. Ibid., p. 98.
11. *Report on Overseas Investment by Synthetic Textile Industry*, Tokyo, MITI, 1978; *Overseas Activities of Japanese Companies*, Tokyo, MITI, 1980; Suehiro, op. cit., p. 88. Between 1979 and 1991, textiles output in Thailand grew by

14 per cent, garments by 16 per cent per annum. Textile and garments increased from 14.7 billion baht in 1981 to 129.6 billion baht in 1993. There was a slowdown in 1991, and Thai companies began locating in China, Vietnam, Burma and Bangladesh (*Key Indicators of Developing Asian and Pacific Countries, 1997*, Manila, Asian Development Bank, 1997, pp. 330, 334).

12. See National Statistics of these countries for 1982–93

13. Biro Pusat Statistik, (Central Bureau of Statistics) *Indikator Ekonomi*, Jakarta, 1982–1993. See also Badan Kordinasi Penanaman Modal, Investment Co-ordination Board, Jakarta, 1993, 1994.

14. Varavidh Charoenloet, 'Shop House Ready Made Garment Manufacturing: a Case Study of the Informal Sector in Bangkok', in Pasuk Phongpaichit and Shigeru Itoga (eds), *The Informal Sector in Thai Economic Development*, ASEDP, 15, Tokyo 1992, pp. 35–57; Myrna S Austria, 'Textile and Garments Industries: Impact of Trade Policy Reforms on Performance, Competitiveness and Structure', Manila, Philippine Institute for Development Studies Research Paper Series, no. 94–06, 1994, pp. 1–90; Richard F Doner and Ansil Ramsay, 'Post Imperialism and Development in Thailand', *World Development*, 21, 5, 1993, pp. 691–704; Chuta Manusphaibool and Koji Taniguchi, 'Changing Pattern of Comparative Advantage and Its Impact on Firms' Behaviour: the Case of Thai Manufacturing Industry', Tokyo, Institute of Developing Economies, JRP series, 96, March 1992.

15. Thailand, Board of Investment, Annual Reports, 1969–92. These firms were encouraged by the relaxation of rules on foreign ownership. A 100 per cent foreign ownership was permitted if production was for export.

16. Suehiro, 1982, p. 85.

17. In 1950 Phibun banned textile imports and Sukree exploited this ban. Myrna S. Austria, op. cit., pp. 1–90; Suehiro, op. cit., p. 98

18. Suehiro, op. cit., pp. 92, 107.

19. In 1957 the US imposed a ceiling on the import of Japanese cotton textiles. In 1959 Britain imposed a ceiling on cotton cloth from Hong Kong, Pakistan and India. In 1961 and 1962, under General Agreement on Tariffs and Trade (GATT) regulations quotas were to be negotiated bilaterally. Japan shifted from cotton to man-made fibres to overcome this. In 1971 international restrictions were imposed on man-made textiles. In 1974 the Multi-Fibre Arrangement imposed controls by advanced economies on imports of cotton as well as other fibres. Tariff and non-tariff restrictions were applied. Such protection persisted from the early 1970s into the 1990s, restricting competition from Japan, Hong Kong and Taiwan. The effect for these developing countries was to upgrade or move production to countries which had unfilled quotas.

20. Suehiro, op. cit., pp. 85–6.

21. Akira Suehiro, *Capital Accumulation in Thailand, 1885–1985*, Tokyo, East Asian Cultural Studies, 1989, pp. 236–37.

22. A third of Thailand's manufacturing employment was in the textiles and garments industry. The latter accounted for 73 per cent of textile exports in 1987. Annual Reports of Sukree group 1987-92.

23. Suehiro, 1982, p. 107.

24. Singleton, op. cit., p. 181.
25. Japan Ministry of Finance, *International Finance Year Book*, 1987–92. This source provides a detailed breakdown of foreign direct investment by various industries in Asia.
26. Suehiro, 1989, p. 238.
27. Manusphaibool and Taniguchi, op. cit., p. 83.
28. Suehiro, 1989, p. 238. Eight firms in the Sukree Group had Japanese as joint venture partners, and another 2 firms had Western partners: Suehiro, 1982, p. 90.
29. Suehiro, 1989, p. 238.
30. Thailand moved into synthetic fibre in 1968 with Japanese assistance. Two Japanese firms in Thailand controlled 100 per cent of synthetic fibre production in 1976. Two years later this proportion had fallen to 53 per cent. Chinese and Sino-Thai textile firms used the Japanese multinationals and then pushed them out.

    Much of the Japanese activities in Southeast Asia between 1961 and 1971 was located in Thailand. In textiles, Japanese firms – Mitsui, Mitsubishi, Sumitomo, Kanebo, C. Itoh, Marubeni and Nomura Trading – were dominant between 1963 and 1972, both as independent firms and in joint ventures with Sukree and Saha Union. Where the Japanese provided majority equity they controlled production as well as financial decisions. However, where their equity contribution was partial, their role was essentially limited to providing finance and technology. The linkage often meant that Thai firms like Sukree were developing a close relationship with Japanese. The inventory adjustments between subsidiaries and the parent company could mean Thai firms were exporting components to Japan: Suehiro,1982, pp. 74 –5.
31. Masahiko Aoki and Hugh Patrick (eds), *The Japanese Main Bank System*, Oxford, Oxford University Press, 1994.
32. Doner and Ramsey, op. cit., p. 698.
33. MITI, *Survey on Cotton Yarn and Chemical Fibres, no. 20*, Tokyo 1989, p. 100. See also Japan Garment Association, 1979 report, cited in Suehiro, 1982, pp. 102–3.
34. Suehiro, 1982, pp. 102–3.
35. Ibid. p. 107.
36. The percentage growth in real average wage in Bangkok rose by 5 per cent per annum between 1991–96 and in some industries the rate of increase averaged 8 per cent per annum. Report of the Labour Force Survey in the whole Kingdom of Thailand 1983–97 (National statistical office, Bangkok.)
37. Hourly labour costs in the Textile Industry; US$, 1993:
    Japan=23.65; Thailand=1.04; Indonesia=0.49; Vietnam=0.37; China=0.36; S.Korea=3.66; Hong Kong=3.85; Taiwan=6.76; USA=11.61 (*Far Eastern Economic Review*, 28 July 1994).
38. *Far Eastern Economic Review*, 28 July 1994.
39. Akira Suehiro, 'Survey of Textile Firms in Thailand', unpublished report, kindly provided by the author; Ministry of Economic Affairs, Department of Commercial Intelligence, *Commercial Directory for Thailand 1961–62*; Thailand, Ministry of Commerce, 1979–89, Bangkok. In 1993 Thailand's garment exports were 89.6 billion baht (US$ 3.6 billion), rising from 15

billion baht in 1985. Garment exports achieved 20 per cent increase per annum between 1987 and 1991. Growth in textile products slowed to 3 per cent in 1993. The textile industry absorbed 20 per cent of the industrial work force in the same period: *Far Eastern Economic Review*, 28 July 1994.

40. Spinning machines in Thailand rose from 42,000 spindles in 1960 to 244,336 in 1972, and to 463,712 in 1986. In 1972, Sukree possessed 38 per cent of all domestic spinning machines in Thailand, though this fell to 25 per cent in 1986: Suehiro, 1989, p. 337.

41. Medhi Krongkaew (ed.), *Thailand's Industrialisation and its Consequences*, London, Macmillan, 1995, p. 91.

42. Aurora Sanchez, 'The textile industry in Thailand and Philippines: a comparison', *Journal of Philippine Development*, XVII, 1, 1990, p. 70; Myrna S. Austria, op. cit., pp. 1–90; Mitsuru Toida and Daisuke Hiratsuka (eds), *The 1994 Economic Forecasts for Asian Industrializing Region*, PAIR Economic Forecasting Report No 3 Tokyo 1994 (on Malaysian textiles); Hal Hill, 'Government Policy and Selection of Technology in the Indonesian Weaving Industry', in *The Developing Economies*, Vol. XXI, no. 2, June 1983. pp. 134–48.

43. Sanchez, op. cit., p. 70.

44. Ibid., p. 71.

45. Between 1975 and 1979 Thailand's growth in textiles was 14.24 per cent per annum; in the Philippines, it was 3.85 per cent. In the period 1980 to 1984, Thai growth was 5.33 per cent, but the Philippines had negative growth of –2.73 per cent: Sanchez, op. cit., p. 71.

46. Kunio Yoshihara, *The Nation and Economic Growth: the Philippines and Thailand*, Singapore, Oxford University Press, 1994, p. 49.

47. Philippine growth in spindles and looms achieved a growth of 3 per cent and 2 per cent between 1963 and 1984: in Thailand it was 15 per cent and 13 per cent respectively. See Sanchez, 1990, p. 70; Yoshihara, op. cit., p. 49.

48. Sanchez, op. cit., pp. 77–8.

49. Austria, op. cit., pp. 34, 65, 79.

50. See Temario C. Rivera, *The Chinese-Filipino Business Families under the Ramos Government*, Tokyo, Institute of Developing Economies, JRP Series 114, 1995.

51. Makarim Wibisono, 'The Political Economy of the Indonesian Textile Industry under the New Order Government', PhD dissertation, Ohio State University, 1987, p. 38.

52. Ibid., p. 38.

53. Hal Hill, 1996, p. 165

54. Singleton, op. cit., pp. 16–17.

55. Biro Pusat Statistik, *Indikator Ekonomi*, various issues.

56. Wibisono, op. cit., p. 92.

57. See Hill, op. cit.

58. Peter Van Diermen, *Small Business in Indonesia*, Aldershot, Ashgate, 1997, pp. 69–70.

59. See Mitsuru Toida and Daisuke Hiratsuka (eds), *The 1994 Economic Forecasts for Asian Industrialising Region*, PAIR Economic Forecasting Report no. 3, Tokyo, Institute of Developing Economies, 1994.

60. The Multi-Fibre Arrangement (1974) permits economically advanced countries to control imports of textiles.

61. Malaysia, Ministry of Finance, *Economic Report on Average Monthly Wages of Manufacturing Workers*, 1974–79, 1980–88. For Korea, Taiwan and Hong Kong, see Annual Reports of Japan's Chemical Fibre Association, 1970–85.
62. Rajah Rasiah, 'Free Trade Zones and Industrial Development in Malaysia', in K.S Jomo (ed.), *Industrialising Malaysia: Policy, Performance, Prospects*, London, Routledge, 1993, p. 128.
63. For an excellent critique of the 'flying geese' model, see Mitchell Bernard and John Ravenhill, 'Beyond Product Cycles and Flying Geese: Regionalism, Hierarchy and the Industrialization of East Asia', *World Politics*, 47, 1995, pp. 171–209; Wolfgang Hillebrand, *Shaping Competitive Advantages: Conceptual Framework and the Korean Approach*, London, Frank Cass, 1996.
64. Calculated from International Economic Data Bank, Australian National University, Canberra, cited in Myrna S. Austria, 1994, and Sanchez, 1990.
65. See T. Tanaka and others, 'Economic Development and the Structural Change of Trade in the Pacific Asian Region', *The Developing Economies*, vol. 21, no. 4, 1983, p. 348.
66. W. Lazonick, *Comparative Advantage on the Shop Floor*, Cambridge, Mass., Harvard University Press, 1990; and 'Industrial Organization and Technological Change: the Decline of the British Cotton Industry', *Business History Review*, 57, 2, 1983, pp. 195–236.

7 Chinese Attitudes to Technology and Innovation

1. *Asia Pacific Telecoms Analyst*, 9 October 1995. In Southeast Asia, the growth rate of fixed line networks in 1994 was 26 per cent in Thailand, and 50 per cent in Singapore. Thailand's rate in 1992 had been a mere 4 per cent, while that of Singapore had been 40 per cent. The penetration of cellular phones was 1.42 per cent in Thailand, 3.04 per cent in Malaysia, 3.11 per cent in Japan, 8.16 per cent in Singapore, 7.2 per cent in Hong Kong, and 9.2 per cent in the USA (Peregrine Report 1996, International Telecommunications Union Report 1996). The increase in intra-Asian foreign direct investment in telecommunications rose from US$2.7 billion in 1985 to US$34 billion in 1994 (Nynex Asia Communications, 9 October 1995).
2. *Asia Pacific Telecoms Analyst*, 9 October 1995. Cellular phone growth in Thailand between 1986 and 1992 was 61 per cent, and 81 per cent in 1994: Sakkarin Niyomsilpa, 'The Political Economy of Telecommunications Liberalization in Thailand', Ph.D thesis, Australian National University, Canberra, 1995 p. 235.
3. See also Sakkarin Niyomsilpa, op. cit., pp. 178–268.
4. Alfred D. Chandler, *The Visible Hand*, Cambridge, Mass., Harvard University Press, 1977, p. 373.
5. World Bank, *Thailand Telecommunications Mission – Aide-mémoire*, Bangkok, World Bank, 1991, p. 6. The anxieties of the World Bank revolved around CP's 25-year concession, which implied that the government would have little control over new assets or over revenues.
6. Consolidated Balance Sheets and Annual Reports of Telecom Asia (Bangkok), November 1991 to December 1994.

7. Securities One *Investment Guide*, Bangkok, March 1997, pp. 32–6, 44–6, 49–51; June 1997, pp. 53–61, 66–70.
8. *The Nation*, 18 March 1997. Telecom Holding was involved in Nepal's telephone expansion, and in telephone installation in the Philippines and Vietnam.
9. Report of Directors of Chia Tai, 31 March 1992 (Registrar of Companies Hong Kong).
10. Annual Report, OTTH, 5 April 1993, see table 7.3. OTTH was Chia Tai in the 1980s. Thus the table covers the period 1989–95.
11. Report of Dhanin Chearavanont, Chairman of OTTH, 22 March 1995 (Registrar of Companies, Hong Kong).
12. Annual Report, OTTH, 28 July 1995. OTTH had joint ventures in satellites and in fibre-optic cables, with the ambition of creating a link from Asia to the Middle East, with Thailand as the regional hub: 'Asia Pacific Telecoms', *Financial Times*, Business Report, 25 September 1995; *Institutional Investor*, 22 October 1996.
13. Annual Report, OTTH, 11 May 1996.
14. K. Ohkawa and H. Rosovsky, *Japanese Economic Growth*, Stanford, Stanford University Press, 1973.
15. M. Abramovitz and P. A. David, 'Convergence and Deferred Catch Up: Productivity Leadership and the Waning of American Exceptionalism', in R. Landau, T. Taylor and G. Wright (eds), *The Mosaic of Economic Growth*, Stanford, Stanford University Press, 1996.
16. UCOM began as an agency selling specialised communications equipment to the Thai armed forces. A fair range of their equipment came from Motorola.
17. D. J. Teece, 'Profiting from Technological Innovation: Implications for Integration, Collaboration, Licensing, and Public Policy', *Research Policy*, 15, 1986, pp. 285–305.
18. Annual Report, Telecom Asia (Bangkok), 18 March 1997.
19. Dow Jones Asian Equities Report, 16 May 1996.
20. *The Nation*, 19 February 1997, 18 March 1997; Telecom Asia, Annual Report, March 1997.
21. Chia Tai was the original family firm of the CP group registered in Hong Kong and China. Chia Tai was variously used as an investment company, as a holding company, and as a core family firm to form and spin off new companies in the new ventures of the group in Asia and the Middle East.
22. Chia Tai International Annual Report, 18 February 1992. Hong Kong Registrar of Companies. CP's most important investment company was CP Overseas Investment, established on 11 July 1975. By 1977 it had paid up capital of HK$1 million, which was increased to HK$125 million by 1993. It had financial, agricultural interests, as well as telecommunications in Indonesia and Malaysia. In June 1986, CP Luxembourg was established. The ultimate investment holding company was Carrington Ltd, incorporated in Liberia: Annual Report, CP, Hong Kong, 18 February 1992. The relations between these investment companies possessed a distinct institutional mix. The exchange of shares, lending practices, appointment of directors (both family and non-family members), and contractual details complicated intra-firm relations.

23. *Far Eastern Economic Review*, 11 February 1993.
24. CP Bangkok, 1993 Balance Sheet and Annual Report.
25. *South China Morning Post (SCMP)*, 23 October 1992.
26. *SCMP*, 21 February 1994.
27. The rate of interest on a floating rate note is linked to short-term investment rates. Some of these have no date of maturity and are more risky than certificates of deposit or commercial paper but appeal to investors because of their higher yield.
28. Securities One, *Investment Guide*, March 1997; *Thailand Equity Market*, Research Institute of Finance One, Bangkok, pp. 19–21, 44–47, and June 1997, pp. 57–9.
29. Arthur D Little International Inc., *Report on Telecommunications*, 1997; *SCMP*, 21 October 1993.
30. Telecom Asia, Bangkok, Report, March 1994; *SCMP*, 21 October 1993.
31. Telecom Asia, Bangkok, Annual Report, 8 September 1995.
32. Siam Fortune, Bangkok, Annual Reports, 1992–97.
33. Telecom Asia, Bangkok, Annual General Meeting, 26 April 1996.
34. *SCMP*, 29 April 1996, 10 June 1996.
35. Telecom Holding, Annual Report, 11 May 1996.
36. See chapter 9 for a discussion of CP's investments in China.
37. Associated Press, *Dow Jones News*, 27 February 1995.
38. Securities One, *Investment Guide*, March 1997, pp. 16–17; *Thailand Equity Market*, Research Institute of Finance One, Bangkok.
39. Ajva Taulanada, with a PhD in engineering, joined Telecom Asia in 1993 from C P Bangkok. He had been in the Thai government in 1991–92, as a senior bureaucrat in the Ministry of Agriculture. CP had 26 professional managers, three of them from Nynex. The divisional structure in Telecom Asia included planning, construction, marketing, and technology support sections.

8 Land and Property Development

1. Ministry of National Development, Singapore, *Monthly Digest of Statistics*, 1991.
2. Construction Industry Development Board, Singapore, *International Survey of Building Construction Costs*, 1988, p. 211.
3. Ibid. See also 'Asian Property not to be tarred with Western brush', Saloman Bros Hong Kong, *Equity Research on Property*, October 1991.
4. Construction Industry Development Board, Singapore, op. cit., fig. 4.13, p. 211.
5. Land Bureau, National Land Agency, and the Japanese Association of Real Estate Agents, 'Values of Land, Homes, and Rentals', *The World Land Survey*, Tokyo, 1995, p. 8.
6. Ibid. See also reports on property in the *Financial Times*, 13 September 1990, 9 September 1995.
7. Construction Industry Development Board, Singapore, op. cit., fig. 4.13, p. 211. See also Ministry of National Development, Singapore, *Yearbook of Statistics 1989*.

8. *Straits Times*, 31 March 1993, 4 February 1995, 20 August 1996, and 11 April 1997. In the 1990s, CDL's expansion in the United States and China was with Temasek Holdings, a Singapore government corporation.

9. *Straits Times*, 29 June 1971.

10. *Straits Times*, 28 June 1972.

11. Report of CDL Chairman H. K. Franklin, 23 March 1973.

12. *Straits Times*, 31 October 1976; Annual Reports of CDL, 1977, 1978.

13. *Straits Times*, 28 July 1979.

14. *Straits Times*, 18 August 1980, 30 April 1980.

15. *Business Times*, 31 January 1981.

16. *Business Times*, 11 February 1981.

17. *Straits Times*, 31 March 1993, 2 April 1993.

18. *Straits Times*, 4 February 1995.

19. *Business Times*, 7 May 1981.

20. *Business Times*, 7 May 1981, 2 December 1981.

21. *Business Times*, 9 December 1986, 10 December 1986.

22. *Business Times*, 31 July 1986.

23. *Straits Times*, 30 March 1994.

24. Despite the opposition of the Monetary Authority of Singapore to financial firms retaining non-financial interests, HLF had maintained non-financial units within its group. In 1984 HLF had assets of S$1,169 million and share capital and reserves of S$284 million. Its subsidiary, Singapore Finance, had total assets of S$734 million and share capital and reserves of S$95 million: *Straits Times*, 24 July 1985.

25. *Malaysian Business*, 1 March 1994; *Far Eastern Economic Review*, 8 September 1994.

26. Securitisation is the practice by which borrowers reduced their dependence on bank loans and instead request merchant or investment banks to raise money through the issue of shares and bonds. This reduced costs to borrowers and lenders and the practice grew since the 1980s with improved technology and financial sophistication.

27. Barras suggests that property booms occur in every second long cycle of development, and in every fourth short cycle of business activity. R. Barras 'Property and Economic Cycle: Building Cycles Revisited', *Journal of Property Research*, 11, 3, 1994, pp. 183–97.

28. SHK Properties, established in 1963, had residential and office properties in the New Territories. Henderson Land Development emerged in 1976 after Lee's separation from SHK.

29. *Business Times*, 27 April 1994.

30. *Straits Times*, 8 January 1993, 6 July 1996, 20 August 1996.

31. *Business Times*, 16 January 1997.

32. *Straits Times*, 17 September 1993, 16 October 1993, 13 April 1993.

33. *Business Times*, 31 December 1993.

34. Ibid.

35. *Straits Times*, 27 April 1993, 2 February 1994.

36. *Straits Times*, 29 January 1996.

37. *Straits Times*, 26 March 1997.

38. Ng's difficulties in Hong Kong affected his companies in Singapore – FEO and OPH. Only the Singapore Government's easing of legal penalties for

non-completion of building projects by the contractual dates provided some relief to Ng Teng Fong in 1997. Kwek faced fewer difficulties because of greater financial prudence and partly because his investments in Europe and USA, were unaffected by the crisis.

39. *Euroweek*, 16 July 1997, 11 April 1997.
40. *Straits Times*, 3 November 1998.

9 Pokphand in China

1. *Key Indicators of Developing Asian and Pacific Countries*, Oxford, Oxford University Press/Asian Development Bank, 27, 1996, pp. 88–97.
2. Ibid., pp. 88–97.
3. Ibid., p. 41. UNCTAD, Division of Transnational Corporations and Investment, *World Investment Report: Transnational Corporations Employment and the Workplace*, New York and Geneva, United Nations, 1994, p. 69.
4. Charoen Pokphand Hong Kong, Annual Report 1996, p. 5.
5. Robert Ash and Y. Y. Kueh, 'Economic Integration within Greater China: Trade and Investment Flows between China, Hong Kong, and Taiwan', *The China Quarterly*, 136, 1993, 711–45; Qi Luo and Christopher Howe, 'Direct Investment and Economic Integration in the Asia Pacific: the Case of Taiwanese Investment in Xiamen', *The China Quarterly*, 136, 1993, 746–69.
6. JETRO, Report, 119, November–December 1995, p. 15.
7. *China Foreign Economic Statistical Yearbook, 1994*, Beijing, China Statistical Publishing House, pp. 315–24.
8. Unpublished Government Report from Center for Market and Trade Development, Beijing, 1990–1995.
9. *Almanac of China's Foreign Economic Relations and Trade 1995/96*, Hong Kong, China Resources Advertising, 1996, pp. 977–8.
10. Ibid., pp. 977–8; *Business Times*, 6 November 1995.
11. Hongkong and Shanghai Bank Briefing, July 1993.
12. 'Statement of Sino-Foreign Joint Ventures 1995', *China Statistical Yearbook 1996*, Beijing, China Statistical Publishing House, 1991, pp. 791–899.
13. Ibid., pp. 791–899; *Straits Times*, 22 March 1996.
14. *China Foreign Economic Statistical Yearbook, 1994*, Beijing, China Statistical Publishing House, 1995, pp. 315–24.
15. *Almanac of China's Foreign Economic Relations and Trade, 1995–96*, Hong Kong China Resources Advertising, 1996, pp. 792–s3.
16. Y. Y. Kueh and Robert F Ash, 'The Fifth Dragon: Economic Development', in Brian Hook (ed.), *Guangdong: China's Promised Land*, Hong Kong, Oxford University Press, 1996, pp. 150–92.
17. Charoen Pokphand Hong Kong, Annual Report 1990; Chia Tai International, Annual Report 1990; Hong Kong Fortune, Annual Report 1990.
18. *China Foreign Economic Statistics 1979–91*, Beijing, China Statistical Information and Consultancy Service Center, 1992, pp. 424–5.
19. Unpublished Report on CP by the Center for Market and Trade Development Beijing, 1990–95.
20. Ibid.

21. *China – Britain Trade Review*, September 1996, p. 23.
22. *Asian Wall Street Journal*, 23 June 1995; *Dow Jones Asian Equities Report 197*, 1995.
23. *Time International*, 14 October 1996.
24. Center for Market Trade and Development, op. cit.
25. Dow Jones, *Emerging Markets*, 21 July 1995.
26. Jean C. Oi, 'The Role of the Local State in China's Transitional Economy', *The China Quarterly*, 144, 1995, pp. 1132–49.
27. Unpublished report on Charoen Pokphand by the Center for Market Trade and Development, Beijing, 1990–1995.
28. *Far Eastern Economic Review*, 21 October 1993, *Asian Wall Street Journal*, 23 June 1995.
29. Ibid.
30. Center for Market Trade and Development, op. cit.
31. Hong Kong Development Council, *Retail and Wholesale Distribution of Consumer Goods in China*, Hong Kong, 1994; *China Statistical Yearbook*, various years 1979 to 1995/96.
32. CP (Hong Kong), Annual Report 1996.
33. *Beijing Review*, 12 August 1996.
34. Report of Shanghai Finance and Trade Office, 1995.
35. Asian *Wall Street Journal*, 10 January 1996.
36. Charoen Pokphand Hong Kong, Annual Report 1995.
37. *Far Eastern Economic Review*, 5 August 1993.
38. Charoen Pokphand Hong Kong, Directors' Report, 13 August 1994.
39. Ibid., 24 July 1995.
40. *Dow Jones International News 1995*.
41. Hong Kong Fortune, Annual Reports, 10 August 1993, 24 July 1995.
42. Hong Kong Fortune, Annual Report, 2 July 1992.
43. Hong Kong Fortune, Annual Report, 13 August 1994, 24 July 1995. Siam Fortune was partly owned by CP.
44. Ibid.; *South China Morning Post*, 31 December 1993.
45. *Jetro China Newsletter No. 115*, March–April 1995.
46. *South China Morning Post*, 5 December 1995.
47. Bangkok Bank (Overseas), Annual Reports, 1994–96.
48. *Far Eastern Economic Review*, 8 April 1999.

10   Financial Development

1. David George McKendrick, 'Acquiring Technological Capabilities: Aircraft and Commercial Banking in Indonesia', PhD thesis, University of California at Berkeley, 1989, p. 192.
2. State commercial banks contributed 44 per cent of total bank credit in 1968, reduced to 43 per cent in 1994. Private commercial banks accounted for 6 per cent in 1968 rising to 47 per cent in 1994. Foreign banks accounted for 1 per cent in 1968 rising to 10 per cent in 1994, often in joint venture relations with domestic banks. Bank of Indonesia contributed 49 per cent of credit in 1968, falling to 1 per cent in 1994 (Bank Indonesia, *Lapuran Tahunan* [Annual Reports]; *Indonesian Financial Statistics*, Jakarta, various years).

3. Andrew J. MacIntyre, 'The Politics of Finance in Indonesia: Command, Confusion, and Competition', in Stephan Haggard, Chung H. Lee and Sylvia Maxfield (eds.), *The Politics of Finance in Developing Countries*, Ithaca, Cornell University Press, 1993, p. 138.

4. K. S., Jomo, *Tigers in Trouble: Financial Governance, Liberalization, and Crisis in East Asia*, London, Zed Books, 1998, p. 170. See also *Far Eastern Economic Review*, 26 March 1998.

5. *Far Eastern Economic Review*, 25 September 1997.

6. Ibid., 6 October 1994, 31 March 1994.

7. Ibid., 6 October 1994. See also Hank Lim, 'Chinese Banking and Indonesian Economic Development', in Ngaw Mee-Kau and Chang Chak-yan (eds), *Chinese Banking in Asia's Market Economies*. Hong Kong, Chinese University of Hong Kong, 1989, pp. 183–206.

8. Hank Lim, op. cit., p. 191; *Far Eastern Economic Review*, 6 October, 1994.

9. Moody Investors Service, Global Credit Research, 24 October 1997, teleconference proceedings, 'The impact of market turmoil in S.E. Asia and Korea on Japanese banks and other Asian financial institutions', October 1997; Bank Indonesia, *Indonesian Financial Statistics* and Central Bureau of Statistics, *Monthly Statistical Bulletin*; Lapuran Bank Indonesia, *Tahun Pembukaan, 1979–83*. Yayasan Management Informasi, *Indonesian Financial Profile*, 1981, 1983, Jakarta, Indonesia; Hank Lim, 'Chinese Banking and Indonesian Economic Development', in Ngaw Mee-Kau and Chang Chak-yan (eds), op. cit., pp. 183–206.

10. Moody Investors Service, op. cit.

11. McKendrick, op. cit., p. 174.

12. Philippe F. Delhaise, *Asia in Crisis: the Implosion of the Banking and Finance Systems*, Singapore, John Wiley Asia, 1998, p. 130.

13. Infobank 1995, p. 26, cited in Ross H. McLeod and Ross Garnaut (eds), *East Asia in Crisis: from Being a Miracle to Needing One*, London, Routledge, 1998, p. 295.

14. Ross H. McLeod and Ross Garnaut, op. cit., p. 295.

15. *Far Eastern Economic Review*, 6 October 1994.

16. *Far Eastern Economic Review*, 24 April 1999.

17. *Asian Company Handbook, 1998*, Tokyo, Toyo Keizai, Inc., p. 460.

18. See Delhaise, op. cit., p. 130, and *Far Eastern Economic Review*, 22 April 1999.

19. *Far Eastern Economic Review*, 19 October 1995, 28 September 1995, 29 February 1996, 3 October 1996, 5 September 1996, 30 January 1997, 22 May 1997, 24 July 1997, 16 October 1997, 25 September 1997, 13 November 1997, 22 January 1998, 9 April 1998, 16 April 1998.

20. Ibid., 22 April 99, 25 September 97. See also *Panji Utama*, 11, 30 June 1997.

21. Lawrence J. White, 'Structure of Finance in Selected Asian Economies', in Shahed N. Zahed (ed.), *Financial Sector Development in Asia*, Hong Kong, Oxford University Press and Asian Development Bank, 1995, p. 106. See also Cole and Slade, op. cit., p. 185.

22. Cole and Slade, op. cit., p. 185.

23. *Far Eastern Economic Review*, 22 May 1997.

24. Cole and Slade, op. cit., pp. 278–81.

25. McKendrick, op. cit., p. 394; Yuri Sato, 'The Salim Group in Indonesia: the Development and Behaviour of the Largest Conglomerate in SE Asia', *The Developing Economies*, 31, 4, 1993, p. 417.
26. Sato, op. cit., pp. 408–41.
27. Salim Group Accounts, contained in First Pacific Holdings, Annual Report, 15 May 1995.
28. *International Herald Tribune*, 17 May 1999.
29. *Far Eastern Economic Review*, 12 March 1998.
30. *Indonesian Financial Statistics*, Jakarta, Bank Indonesia, monthly and annual reports, 1990–98.
31. *Key Indicators of Developing Asian and Pacific Countries*, 18, 1997, pp. 136–37; K.S. Jomo (ed.), 1998, pp. 176–7.
32. Lee Sheng-yi, *The Monetary and Banking Development of Singapore and Malaysia*, Singapore, Singapore University Press, 1990, p. 242.
33. Ngiam Kee Jin, 'Singapore as a Financial Centre: New Developments, Challenges and Prospects,' in Takatoshi Ito and Anne O Krueger (eds), *Financial Deregulation and Integration in East Asia*, Chicago, University of Chicago Press, 1996, p. 378
34. *Business Times*, 27 April 1985, 15 August 1986.
35. Ibid., 27 February 1985, 20 March 1987.
36. *Straits Times*, 27 June 1996, 6 May 1993, 20 March 1987.
37. *Business Times*, 18 January 1993.
38. *Asian Company Handbook, 1998*, Tokyo, Toyo Keizai Inc., 1998, p. 484.
39. DBS, Annual Report, May 1998.
40. *Business Times*, 22 September 1986.
41. *Straits Times*, 25 November 1996.
42. *Business Times*, 16 September 1994.
43. *Straits Times*, 9 March 1999.
44. J. P. Morgan, Report, May 1998.
45. Moody Investors Service, op. cit., 24 October 1997.

11 Conclusion

1. Yoshihara Kunio, *The Rise of Ersatz Capitalism in South-East Asia*, Singapore, Oxford University Press, 1988.
2. I. M. Kirzner, *Competition and Entrepreneurship*, Chicago, University of Chicago Press, 1973; I. M. Kirzner, 'Uncertainty, Discovery and Human Action: a Study of the Entrepreneurial Profile in the Misesian System' in I. M. Kirzner (ed.), *Method, Process and Austrian Economics: Essays in Honor of Ludwig von Mises*, Lexington, Mass., D.C. Heath, 1982, pp.139–59.
3. Ruth T. McVey (ed.), *South-East Asian Capitalists*, Ithaca, Cornell University, South-East Asia Program, 1992; J. C. Mackie, 'Changing Patterns of Chinese Big Business', in McVey (ed.), op. cit., pp. 161–90.
4. Karl Polanyi, *The Great Transformation*, Boston, Beacon Press, 1957.
5. O. E. Williamson, 'The Transaction Cost Economics: the Comparative Contracting Perspective', *Journal of Economic Behaviour and Organization*, 8, 1987, pp. 617–25.

6. R. Nelson and S. Winter, *An Evolutionary Theory of Economic Change*. Cambridge, Mass., Harvard University Press, 1982; W. B. Arthur, 'Self Reinforcing Mechanism in Economics', in P. W. Andersen, K. J. Arrow and D. Pines (eds), *The Economy as a Complex Evolving System*, Reading, Mass., Addison Wesley, 1988, pp.9–32.
7. F. A. Hayek (ed.), *New Studies in Philosophy, Politics, Economics, and the History of Ideas*, London, Routledge and Kegan Paul, 1978; F. A. Hayek, *The Fatal Conceit*, London: Routledge, 1988.
8. Since the 1970s Japanese corporations have become more streamlined and more specialised. This was in response to global economic pressures.
9. John T. Scott, *Purposive Diversification and Economic Performance*, Cambridge, Cambridge University Press, 1993.
10. J. Schumpeter, *Business Cycles*, New York, McGraw-Hill, 1939, 2 vols.
11. Franco Amatori, 'Italy: the Tormented Rise of Organizational Capabilities between Government and Families', in Alfred D. Chandler (ed.), *Big Business and the Wealth of Nations*, Cambridge, Cambridge University Press, 1997, pp. 246–76.
12. M. E. Porter, *The Comparative Advantage of Nations*, New York, Free Press, 1990.
13. S. Gordon Redding, *The Spirit of Chinese Capitalism*, New York, Walter de Gruyter, 1993; Joel Kotkin Tribes, *How Race, Religion, and Identity Determine Success in the Global Economy*, New York, Random House, 1992.
14. Kaoru Sugihara, *Patterns and Development of Intra-Asian Trade*, Kyoto, Minerva Shoba, 1996, ch. 4 [in Japanese].
15. *Direction of Trade Statistics Yearbook*, AUDXT System, table 3.8, p.42, Tokyo, Institute of Developing Economies, 1993.
16. Ibid.
17. Koichi Ohno and Yumiko Okamoto, *Regional Integration and FDI: Implications for Developing Countries*, Tokyo, IDE, 1994, pp. 37–52.
18. Motoshige Itoh, 'Foreign Direct Investment, International Trade, and Transfer of Technology', in John Piggott and Alan Woodland (eds), *International Trade Policy and the Pacific Rim*, London, Macmillan, 1999, p. 373.
19. Sue Mitchell Bernard and John Ravenhill, 'Beyond Product Cycles and Flying Geese: Regionalization, Hierarchy, and the Industrailization of East Asia', *World Politics*, 47, 1995, pp. 171–209.
20. Goh Pek Chen, 'The Semi-conductor Industry in Malaysia', in K. S. Jomo, Greg Felker, and Rajah Rasiah (eds), *Industrial Technology Development in Malaysia*, London, Routledge, 1999, p. 133.
21. Shigeki Higashi, 'The Automotive Industry in Thailand: from Protective Promotion to Liberalization', in Institute of Developing Economies, Spot Survey, *The Automotive Industry in Asia: The Great Leap Forward*, Tokyo, Institute of Developing Economies, 1995.
22. Alwyn Young, 'A Tale of Two Cities: Factor Accumulation and Technical Change in Hong Kong and Singapore', in O. J. Blanchard and S. Fischer (eds), *NBER Macro-Economics Annual*, Cambridge, Mass., MIT Press, 1992, pp. 13–54; Alwyn Young, 'Invention and Bounded Learning by Doing', *Journal of Political Economy*, 101, 3, 1993, pp. 443–72; Alwyn Young, 'The Tyranny of Numbers: Confronting the Statistical Realities of the East Asian Growth Experience', *Quarterly Journal of Economics*, 110, 1995, pp. 641–80.

Select Bibliography

Primary sources

This book has drawn extensively on the records of Chinese companies. In all, some 40 companies were studied in detail, all from the ASEAN region. It was unfortunate that I was unable to carry out research in the Philippines, partly because I could not locate a good research assistant but also because of the lack of research data. The gap is evident throughout this book.

Most of the research was carried out in the Registrars of Companies in Kuala Lumpur, Singapore and Hong Kong; the Ministry of Commerce in Bangkok; and the Ministry of Finance and Bank Indonesia in Jakarta. I also carried out research in the archives of the Hongkong and Shanghai Bank and the Mercantile Bank, both now in the Midland Bank Archives in London. In addition I undertook research in Asian securities firms and Western merchant banks and stock brokering firms throughout Asia. Much of this primary research in Asia included extensive examination of minutes of meetings of directors, correspondence, balance sheets, annual reports, profit and loss accounts, as well as company publications. Bank archives contain important confidential correspondence, invaluable for research on Asian firms. I have maintained discretion where necessary.

I did not interview businessmen, partly because, as an historian, I am more at home with the documents but also because I was never convinced that that would yield much insight. I was not interested in producing hagiography: I kept my distance. I sincerely hope that my conclusions have not been seriously affected by this single lacuna.

Secondary sources

Abramovitz, M. and P. A. David, 'Convergence and Deferred Catch Up: Productivity Leadership and the Waning of American Exceptionalism', in R. Landau, T. Taylor and G. Wright (ed.), *The Mosaic of Economic Growth*. Stanford, Stanford University Press, 1996.

Akamatsu Kaname, 'Shinkoku kogyokoku no Sangyo Hatten', *Ueda Teijiro Hakushi Kinen Ronbunshu*, 4 July 1937.

Akamatsu Kaname, 'A Theory of Unbalanced Growth in the World Economy', *Weltwirtschaftliches Archiv*, 86, 1, 1961.

Alchian, A., 'Uncertainty, Evolution and Economic Theory', *Journal of Political Economy*, 58, 3, 1950, pp. 211–21.

Almanac of China's Foreign Economic Relations and Trade 1995/96. Hong Kong, China Resources Advertising, 1996.

Amatori, Franco, 'Italy: the Tormented Rise of Organizational Capabilities between Government and Families', in A. D. Chandler (ed.), *Big Business and the Wealth of Nations*. Cambridge, Cambridge University Press, 1997, pp. 246–76.

Arthur D Little International, *Report on Telecommunications*. 1997.

Arthur, W. B., 'Self Reinforcing Mechanism in Economics', in P. W. Andersen, K. J. Arrow and D. Pines (ed.), *The Economy as a Complex Evolving System*. Reading, Mass., Addison Wesley, 1988, pp. 9–32.

Ash, Robert and Y. Y. Kueh, 'Economic Integration within Greater China: Trade and Investment Flows between China, Hong Kong and Taiwan', *The China Quarterly*, 136, 1993, pp. 711–45.

Asian Company Handbook 1997. Tokyo, Toyo Keizai, 1997.

Asian Development Bank, *Key Indicators of Developing Asian and Pacific Countries, 1997*. Manila, 1997.

Austria, Myrna S., *Textile and Garments Industries: Impact of Trade Policy Reforms on Performance, Competitiveness and Structure*. Manila, Philippine Institute for Development Studies, Research paper Series 94–06, 1994.

Badan Pengawas Pasar Modal, *Annual Reports*, various years.

Bank Indonesia, *Indonesian Financial Statistics*, 1979–97.

Bank Indonesia, *Lapuran Tahunan*, 1975–97.

Bank Indonesia, *Tahun Pembukaan*.

Barras, R., 'Property and Economic Cycles: Building Cycles Revisited', *Journal of Property Research*, 11, 3, 1994, pp. 183–97.

Bernard, Sue Mitchell and John Ravenhill, 'Beyond Product Cycles and Flying Geese: Regionalism, Hierarchy and the Industrialization of East Asia', *World Politics*, 47, 1995, pp. 171–209.

Biro Pusat Statistik, *Indikator Ekonomi*.

Board of Investment, Thailand, *Annual Reports*.

Booth, A., 'The Economic Development of South-East Asia, 1870–1985', *Australian Economic History Review*, 31, 1, 1991.

Booth, A., 'Sources of Investment and Technological Change in Colonial and Post-Colonial Indonesia'. Unpublished paper for the First EUROSEAS Conference, Leiden, 1995.

Brown, Ian, *Economic Change in South-East Asia, c.1830–1980*. Kuala Lumpur, Oxford University Press, 1997.

Brown, Rajeswary Ampalavanar, *Capital and Entrepreneurship in South-East Asia*. London, Macmillan, 1994.

Brown, Rajeswary Ampalavanar (ed.), *Chinese Business Enterprise in Asia*. London, Routledge,1995.

Brown, Rajeswary Ampalavanar (ed.), *Chinese Business Enterprise: Critical Perspectives on Business and Management*. London, Routledge, 1996, 4 vols.

Butcher, John and Howard Dick (ed.), *The Rise and Fall of Revenue Farming*. London, Macmillan, 1993.

Casson, M. *Economics of Business Culture: Game Theory, Transaction Costs and Economic Performance*. Oxford, Clarendon Press, 1991.

Central Bureau of Statistics, Indonesia, *Monthly Statistical Bulletin*.

Chandler, A. D., *Strategy and Structure*. Cambridge, Mass., MIT Press, 1962.

Chandler, A. D., *The Visible Hand*. Cambridge, Mass., Harvard University Press, 1977.

Chandler, A. D., *Scale and Scope: the Dynamics of Industrial Capitalism*. Cambridge, Mass., Harvard University Press, 1990.

Chatthip Nartsupha and Suthy Prasartset, *The Political Economy of Siam, 1851–1910*. Bangkok, Social Science Association of Thailand, 1978.

Cheong Weng Eang, *Hong Kong Merchants in Sino-Western Trade, 1684–1798*. London, Curzon, 1997.

China Foreign Economic Statistical Yearbook, 1994. Beijing, China Statistical Publishing House, 1994.

China Foreign Economic Statistics, 1979–91. Beijing, China Statistical Information and Consultancy Service Center, 1992.

China Statistical Yearbook 1996. Beijing, China Statistical Publishing House, 1996.

Chuta Manusphaibool and Koji Taniguchi, *Changing Pattern of Comparative Advantage and its Impact on Firm's Behaviour: the Case of Thai Manufacturing Industry*. Tokyo, Institute of Developing Economies, JRP series 96, 1992.

Coase, R. H., 'The Nature of the Firm', *Economica*, no. 4, 1937, pp. 386–405.

Cole, David C. and Betty F. Slade, *Building a Modern Financial System: the Indonesian Experience*. Cambridge, Cambridge University Press, 1996.

Companies Handbook 1994. Singapore, 1995.

Construction Industry Development Board, Singapore, *International Survey of Building Construction Costs*. 1988.

Cushman, Jennifer W., *Family and State: the Formation of a Sino-Thai Tin Mining Dynasty, 1797–1932*. Singapore, Oxford University Press, 1991.

Delhaise, Philippe F., *Asia in Crisis: the Implosion of the Banking and Finance Systems*. Singapore, John Wiley Asia, 1998.

Diermen, Peter van, *Small Business in Indonesia*. Aldershot, Ashgate, 1997.

Dirlik, Arif, 'Critical Reflections on "Chinese Capitalism" as a Paradigm', in Rajeswary Ampalavanar Brown (ed.), *Chinese Business Enterprise*. London, Routledge, 1996, pp. 17–38.

Doner, Richard F. and Ansil Ramsey, 'Post Imperialism and Development in Thailand', *World Development*, 21, 5, 1993, pp. 691–704.

Garnaut, Ross and Peter Drysdale (ed.), *Asia Pacific Regionalism*. Canberra, Harper Collins, 1994.

Goh Pek Chen, 'The Semi-Conductor Industry in Malaysia', in Jomo, K. S., Greg Felker and Rajah Rasiah (ed.), *Industrial Technology Development in Malaysia*. London, Routledge, 1999.

Hayek, F. A. (ed.), *New Studies in Philosophy, Politics, Economics and the History of Ideas*. London, Routledge and Kegan Paul, 1978.

Hayek, F. A., *The Fatal Conceit*. London, Routledge, 1988.

Hill, Hal, 'Government Policy and Selection of Technology in the Indonesian Weaving Industry', *The Developing Economies*, 21, 2, 1983.

Hill, Hal, *The Indonesian Economy since 1966*. Cambridge, Cambridge University Press, 1996.

Hillebrand, Wolfgang, *Shaping Competitive Advantages: Conceptual Framework and the Korean Approach*. London, Frank Cass, 1996.

Hong Kong Development Council, *Retail and Wholesale Distribution of Consumer Goods in China*. Hong Kong, 1994.

Ingham, Barbara, *Economics and Development*. London, McGraw-Hill, 1995.

Institute of Developing Economies, Tokyo, *Direction of Trade Statistics Yearbook*, 1993.

International Finance Corporation, *Emerging Markets* Washington D.C., 1997.

International Finance Corporation, *Fact Book* Washington D.C., 1996.

International Monetary Fund, *International Financial Statistics Yearbook*.
Jakarta Stock Exchange, *Fact Book*.
Jomo, K. S. (ed.), *Tigers in Trouble: Financial Governance, Liberalization and Crisis in East Asia*. London, Zed Books, 1998.
Kirzner, I. M., *Competition and Entrepreneurship*. Chicago, University of Chicago Press, 1973.
Kirzner, I. M., *Perception, Opportunity and Profit*. Chicago, University of Chicago Press, 1979.
Kirzner, I. M., 'Uncertainty, Discovery and Human Action: a Study of the Entrepreneurial Profile in the Misesian System', in I. M. Kirzner (ed.), *Method, Process and Austrian Economics: Essays in Honor of Ludwig von Mises*. Lexington, Mass., D. C. Heath, 1982, pp. 139–59.
Kohsaka Akira, 'Interdependence through Capital Flows in Pacific Asia and the Role of Japan, ' in Takatoshi Ito and Anne O. Krueger (ed.), *Financial Deregulation and Integration in East Asia*. Chicago, Chicago University Press, 1996.
Koichi Ohno and Yumiko Okamoto, *Regional Integration and FDI: Implications for Developing Countries*. Tokyo, Institute of Developing Economies, 1994.
Kueh, Y. Y. and Robert F. Ash, 'The Fifth Dragon: Economic Development', in Brian Hook (ed.), *Guangdong: China's Promised Land*. Hong Kong, Oxford University Press, 1996, pp. 150–92.
Lasserre, Philippe, *The Coming of Age of Indonesian–Chinese Conglomerates*. Fontainebleau, INSEAD, Euro-Asia Research Paper, 1993.
Lasserre, Philippe and Hellmut Schutte, *Strategies for Asia-Pacific*. London, Macmillan, 1995.
Lazonick, W., 'Industrial Organization and Technological Change: the Decline of the British Cotton Industry', *Business History Review*, 57, 2, 1983, pp. 195–236.
Lazonick, W., *Comparative Advantage on the Shop Floor*. Cambridge, Mass., Harvard University Press, 1990.
Lee Sheng-yi, *The Monetary and Banking Development of Singapore and Malaysia*. Singapore, Singapore University Press, 1990.
Lim, Hank, 'Chinese Banking and Indonesian Economic Development', in Ngaw Mee-Kau and Chang Chak-yan (ed.), *Chinese Banking in Asia's Market Economies*. Hong Kong, Chinese University of Hong Kong, 1989, pp. 183–206.
MacIntyre, A., *Business and Politics in Indonesia*. St Leonards, Allen and Unwin, 1990.
MacIntyre, A., 'The Politics of Finance in Indonesia: Command, Confusion and Competition', in Stephan Haggard, Chung H. Lee and Sylvia Maxfield (ed.), *The Politics of Finance in Developing Countries*. Ithaca, N.Y., Cornell University Press, 1993.
McKendrick, David George, 'Acquiring Technological Capabilities: Aircraft and Commercial Banking in Indonesia', PhD dissertation, University of California at Berkeley, 1989.
Mackie, J. C., 'Changing Patterns of Chinese Big Business', in Ruth T. McVey (ed.), *South-East Asian Capitalists*. Ithaca, N.Y., Cornell South-East Asia Program, 1992, pp. 161–90.
McLeod, Ross H. and Ross Garnaut (eds), *East Asia in Crisis: from Being a Miracle to Needing One?* London, Routledge, 1998.

McVey, R. (ed.), *South-East Asian Capitalists*. Ithaca N.Y., Cornell South-East Asia Program, 1992.

McVey, R., 'Greed and Violence in Thai Politics'. Unpublished paper presented to Fifth International Conference on Thai Studies, London, 1993.

Manager Information Services, Bangkok, *Listed Company Handbook, 1996*.

Masahiko Aoki and Hugh Patrick (ed.), *The Japanese Main Bank System*. Oxford, Oxford University Press, 1994.

Medhi Krongkaew (ed.), *Thailand's Industrialisation and its Consequences*. London, Macmillan, 1995.

Ministry of Economic Affairs, Department of Commercial Intelligence, Thailand, *Commercial Directory for Thailand, 1961–62*.

Ministry of Finance, Indonesia, *Directorate of Banking and Non-Deposit Financial Institutions, 1988–94*.

Ministry of Finance, Japan, *International Finance Yearbook*, various years.

Ministry of Finance, Malaysia, *Economic Report on Average Monthly Wages of Manufacturing Workers* 1974–79, 1980–88, Kuala Lumpur.

Ministry of National Development, Singapore, *Monthly Digest of Statistics*.

Ministry of National Development, Singapore, *Yearbook of Statistics, 1987–97*.

MITI, *Overseas Activities of Japanese Companies*. Tokyo, MITI, 1980.

MITI, *Report on Overseas Investment by Synthetic Textile Industry*. Tokyo, MITI, 1978.

MITI, *Survey on Cotton Yarn and Chemical Fibres no. 20*. Tokyo, MITI, 1989.

Motoshige Itoh, 'Foreign Direct Investment, International Trade and Transfer of Technology', in John Piggott and Alan Woodland (ed.), *International Trade Policy and the Pacific Rim*. London, Macmillan, 1999.

National Statistical Office, Thailand, *Report of the Labour Force Survey in the Whole Kingdom of Thailand, 1983–97*. Bangkok, 1997.

Nelson, R. and S. Winter, *An Evolutionary Theory of Economic Change*. Cambridge, Mass., Harvard University Press, 1982.

Ngiam Kee Jin, 'Singapore as a Financial Centre: New Developments, Challenges and Prospects', in Takatoshi Ito and Anne O. Krueger (ed.), *Financial Deregulation and Integration in East Asia*. Chicago, University of Chicago Press, 1996.

North, D., *Institutions, Institutional Change and Economic Performance*. Cambridge, Cambridge University Press, 1990.

Ohkawa, K. and H. Rosovsky, *Japanese Economic Growth*. Stanford, Stanford University Press, 1972.

Oi, Jean C., 'The Role of the Local State in China's Transitional Economy', *The China Quarterly*, 144, 1995, pp. 1132–49.

Pasuk Phongpaichit and Chris Baker, *Thailand: Economy and Politics*. Kuala Lumpur, Oxford University Press, 1995.

Polanyi, Karl, *The Great Transformation*. Boston, Beacon Press, 1957.

Porter, M. E., *The Competitive Advantage of Nations*. London, Macmillan, 1990.

Qi Luo and Christopher Howe, 'Direct Investment and Economic Integration in the Asia Pacific: the Case of Taiwanese Investment in Xiamen', *The China Quarterly*, 136, 1993, pp. 746–69.

Rasiah, Rajah, 'Free Trade Zones and Industrial Development in Malaysia', in Jomo, K. S. (ed.), *Industrialising Malaysia: Policy, Performance, Prospects*. London, Routledge, 1993.

Redding, S. Gordon, *The Spirit of Chinese Capitalism*. New York, Walter de Gruyter, 1993.

Reid, Anthony, 'The Seventeenth-Century Crisis in Southeast Asia', *Modern Asian Studies*, 24, 1, 1990, pp. 639–59.

Rivera, Temario C., *The Chinese–Filipino Business Families under the Ramos Government*. Tokyo, Institute of Developing Economies, JRP Series 114, 1995.

Robison, R., *Indonesia: the Rise of Capital*. St Leonards, Allen and Unwin, 1986.

Sakkarin Niyomsilpa, 'The Political Economy of Telecommunications Liberalization in Thailand', PhD dissertation, Australian National University, 1995.

Saloman Bros, Hong Kong, *Equity Research on Property*, Hong Kong, 1991.

Sanchez, Aurora, 'The Textile Industry in Thailand and the Philippines: a Comparison', *Journal of Philippine Development*, 17, 1, 1990, pp. 67–87.

Sato Yuri, 'The Astra Group: a Pioneer of Management Modernization in Indonesia', *The Developing Economies*, 34, 3, 1996.

Sato Yuri, 'The Salim Group in Indonesia: the Development and Behaviour of the Largest Conglomerate in SE Asia', *The Developing Economies*, 31, 4, 1993, pp. 408–41.

Schumpeter, J. A., *Business Cycles*. New York, McGraw-Hill, 1939, 2 vols.

Schumpeter, J. A., *Capitalism, Socialism and Democracy*. London, Unwin University Books, 1943.

Schwartz, Adam, *A Nation in Waiting: Indonesia in the 1990s*. St Leonards, Allen and Unwin, 1994.

Scott, John T., *Purposive Diversification and Economic Performance*. Cambridge, Cambridge University Press, 1993.

Securities One, Bangkok, *Handbook*. Bangkok, March 1997.

Securities One, Bangkok, *Investment Guide*. Bangkok, 1997.

Shigeki Higashi, 'The Automotive Industry in Thailand: from Protective Promotion to Liberalization', in Institute of Developing Economies, Spot Survey, *The Automotive Industry in Asia: the Great Leap Forward*. Tokyo, 1995.

Singleton, John, *The World Textile Industry*. London, Routledge, 1997.

Suehiro Akira, 'Comparative Advantage of Manufacturing Industries in Asian Countries'. Unpublished report: Tokyo, Institute of Developing Economies, Economic Development Research Unit, Cam Series 16, 1982.

Suehiro Akira, 'Survey of Textile Firms in Thailand'. Unpublished paper 1982.

Suehiro Akira, *Capital Accumulation in Thailand, 1885–1985*. Tokyo, East Asian Cultural Studies, 1989.

Suehiro Akira, 'The Shinawatra Group: Thailand's Telecommunications Industry and the Newly Rising Zaibatsu', *Asia Economies*, 36, 2, 1995. [In Japanese]

Sugihara Kaoru, *Patterns and Development of Intra-Asian Trade*. Kyoto, Minerva Shoba, 1996. [In Japanese]

Tanaka, T. and others, 'Economic Development and the Structural Change of Trade in the Pacific Asian Region', *The Developing Economies*, 21, 4, 1983.

Tara Siam Business Information, *Thai Telecommunications Industry, 1993/94*. Bangkok, 1995.

Teece, D. J., 'Profiting from Technological Innovation: Implications for Integration, Collaboration, Licensing and Public Policy', *Research Policy*, 15, 1986, pp. 285–305.

Toida Mitsuru and Hiratsuka Daisuke (eds), *The 1994 Economic Forecasts for Asian Industrializing Region*. Tokyo, PAIR Economic Forecasting Report 3, 1994.

Tollinson, Robert, David Kaplan and Richard Higgins, *Competition and Concentration: the Economics of the Carbonated Soft Drink Industry*. Lexington, Mass., Lexington Books, 1991.

Tribes, Joel Kotkin, *How Race, Religion and Identity Determine Success in the Global Economy*. New York, Random House, 1992.

UNCTAD, Division of Transnational Corporations and Investment, *World Investment Report: Transnational Corporations Employment and Workplace*. New York and Geneva, United Nations, 1994.

Varavidh Chareonloet, 'Shop House Ready Made Garment Manufacturing: a Case Study of the Informal Sector in Bangkok', in Pasuk Phongpaichit and Shigeru Itoga (eds), *The Informal Sector in Thai Economic Development*. Tokyo, ASEDP, 1992.

Vernon, Raymond, *Sovereignty at Bay*. New York, Basic Books, 1971.

White, Lawrence J., 'Structure of Finance in Selected Asian Economies', in Shahed N. Zahed (ed.), *Financial Sector Development in Asia*. Hong Kong, Oxford University Press and the Asian Development Bank, 1995.

Wibisono, Makarim, 'The Political Economy of the Indonesian Textile Industry under the New Order Government', PhD dissertation, Ohio State University, 1987.

Williamson, O. E., *Markets and Hierarchies: Analysis and Anti-Trust Implications*. New York, Free Press, 1975.

Williamson, O. E., *The Economic Institutions of Capitalism: Firms, Markets, Relational Contracting*. New York, Free Press, 1985

Williamson, O. E., 'The Transaction Cost Economics: the Comparative Contracting Perspective', *Journal of Economic Behaviour and Organization*, 8, 1987, pp. 617–25.

Wong Sui-Lun, 'The Chinese Family Firm: a Model', *British Journal of Sociology*, 36, 1, 1985, pp. 58–70.

World Bank, *Thailand Telecommunications Mission: Aide Mémoir*. Bangkok, 1991.

World Bank, *The East Asian Miracle: Economic Growth and Public Policy*. New York, Oxford University Press, 1993.

World Bank, *World Development Indicators, 1997*. Washington D C, World Bank, 1997.

World Land Survey. Tokyo, 1995.

Yayasan Management Informasi, *Indonesian Financial Profile*. Jakarta, 1981, 1983.

Yoshihara, K., *The Rise of Ersatz Capitalism in South-East Asia*. Singapore, Oxford University Press, 1988.

Yoshihara, K., *The Nation and Economic Growth: the Philippines and Thailand*. Singapore, Oxford University Press, 1994.

Young, Alwyn, 'A Tale of Two Cities: Factor Accumulation and Technical Change in Hong Kong and Singapore', in O. J. Blanchard and S. Fischer (eds), *NBER Macro-Economics Annual*. Cambridge, Mass., MIT Press, 1992, pp. 13–54.

Young, Alwyn, 'Invention and Bounded Learning by Doing', *Journal of Political Economy*, 101, 3, 1993, pp. 443–72.

Young, Alwyn, 'The Tyranny of Numbers: Confronting the Statistical Realities of the East Asian Growth Experience', *Quarterly Journal of Economics*, 110, 1995, pp. 641–80.

Newspapers and magazines

Aliran Monthly
Asia Pacific Telecoms Analyst
Asian Wall Street Journal
Beijing Review
Business Times (Singapore)
China–Britain Trade Review
China Newsletter
Dow Jones Emerging Markets
Dow Jones Asian Equities Report
Dow Jones International News
Dow Jones News
The Economist
Euroweek
Far Eastern Economic Review
Financial Times
Institutional Investor
International Herald Tribune
Malaysian Business
The Nation (Bangkok)
Phujadkarn (Thai)
Singapore Business
South China Morning Post
The Star
Straits Times
Time International
Warta Ekonomi (Malay).

Company reports and accounts

Bangkok Bank
Chareon Pokphand
Charoen Pokphand Hong Kong
Chia Tai International
City Developments
Development Bank of Singapore
Federal Flour Mills Berhad
First Pacific Holdings
Hong Kong Fortune
Hong Leong Group
Hong Leong Malaysia
Keppel Tat Lee Bank
Kerry Securities
Kuok Group
Malaysian Sugar Manufacturing Company Berhad
Orchard Parade Holdings
Orient Telecom and Technology Holdings

Overseas Chinese Banking Corporation
Overseas Union Bank
Perak Plantations Berhad
Perlis Plantations Berhad
P. T. Astra
P. T. Astra Graphia
P. T. Astra International
P. T. Astra International (Hong Kong)
P. T. Toyota Astra Motor Company
P. T. United Tractors
Saha Union
Shinawatra Computer and Communications
Siam Fortune
Sinoland
Sukree
Sukree-Thai Blanket Industry
Telecom Asia
Telecom Holding
Thai Iryo
Thai Melon Polyester
United Overseas Bank
Yeo Hiap Seng
Yeo Hiap Seng (Malaysia)

Company records

Hongkong and Shanghai Banking Corporation
Nederlandsche Handel Maatschappij

Index